For Mo, Happy Birthday. With love from Wendy

Early 20th Century
Opera Singers

Early 20th Century Opera Singers

Their Voices and Recordings from 1900–1949

Nicholas E. Limansky

YBK Publishers, Inc.
New York

This book is dedicated
In memory of William Ashbrook (1922–2009)
*Who actively supported this book when it was
called something different a long time ago.*

And in memory of Anne-Lynn Gross (1947–2014)
a great friend and fellow traveler with historical singers.

Early 20th Centruy Opera Singers: Their Voices and Recordings from 1900–1949

Copyright © 2016 by Nicholas E. Limansky

YBK Publishers, Inc.
39 Crosby Street
New York, NY 10013
www.ybkpublishers.com

ISBN: 978-1-936411-43-6

Library of Congress Cataloging-in-Publication Data
Names: Limansky, Nicholas E.
Title: Early 20th century opera singers : their voices and recordings from
    1900-1949 / Nicholas E. Limansky.
Description: New York : YBK Publishers, [2016]
Identifiers: LCCN 2016011323 | ISBN 9781936411436 (pbk. : alk. paper)
Subjects: LCSH: Singers--Biography. | Opera--20th century. |
    Singers--Discography.
Classification: LCC ML400 .L717 2016 | DDC 782.1092/2--dc23
LC record available at http://lccn.loc.gov/2016011323

Manufactured in the United States of America for distribution in
North and South America or in the United Kingdom or Australia
when distributed elsewhere.

For more information, visit
www.ybkpublishers.com

CONTENTS

PREFACE
by Davyd Booth

The world of historical vocal recordings was first opened up to me at the age of eleven when I found a group of 45 rpm records in an abandoned car close to where I lived in a small town in West Virginia. This mini treasure trove of about thirty small disks contained recordings of Mary Garden, Feodor Chaliapin, Jussi Bjoerling, Franco Tagliavini, Enrico Caruso, and several other legendary singers. I was already a serious music student at the time, but this was a totally new world and one with which I was immediately enthralled. As a violin student, I was suddenly confronted with the glorious sound of what would become one of my biggest inspirations and also an ideal to emulate on a mechanical instrument. This has continued to this day and very rarely does a day pass that I don't listen to or make new discoveries about the seemingly endless world of vocal records.

In reading Nick Limansky's words I had a strong sense of déjà vu in his similar vivid discovery of the vocal world and the lengths we both went to in acquiring and finding new recordings—skipping school lunches and using the lunch money to acquire new treasures, and such. I perhaps most relish passions such as these that become an obsession that really rules over a substantial portion of our lives. These are the moments that give our lives meaning and color our lives with beauty and, even, ecstasy.

We are often confronted with the Golden Age of this and the Golden Age of that. I certainly do admit that golden ages did indeed exist in both the instrumental and vocal categories and am forever thankful that vast amounts of material was captured on even the earliest and most primitive recording devices. I feel that we are in another Golden Age, that of the Golden Age of Listening. Never before have we had at our fingertips access to such an amazing amount of recorded material, and also in such inexpensive formats. Even thirty years ago the ability to hear some of the very rarest vocal recordings was limited to those very few collectors who had them and could afford them. Now, thanks to a number of specialized labels and fantastic sound engineers, the fabled recordings of singers such as Angelica Pandolfini, Amalia Pinto, and myriad others, whose recordings exist as sometimes only one or two copies, can be in everyone's collection. Even more important is the technology that has been an incredible boon to the historical record enthusiast. Digital technology has been incredibly good to the information contained in those old grooves, giving us unimagined improvement in sonic realization. With labels such as Preiser, Marston, Symposium, Pearl, and True Sound Transfers, the rarest of the rare have become easily available in frequently startlingly clear and vivid sound.

There have been, throughout history, many wonderful writers who studied and recorded in words these great vocal performances, but to me one stands head and shoulders above all others, the Englishman, J. B. Steane. His pivotal work *The Grand Tradition* is literally my bible for vocal information and historical recordings. His taste, his ear, and above all an ability to describe a voice so vividly and accurately in mere words, puts him in a class quite literally by himself. This volume is on the nightstand by my bed and is by far my favorite and most frequently turned-to reading material, always stimulating and inspiring. This work has educated me, piqued my interest in new and otherwise unheard-of singers, and causes me to listen in an ever-expanding and appreciating manner.

One of J. B. Steane's most unique abilities is to hear both the good and the bad and point out the bad without being nasty or bitchy—something I find many vocal writers to be guilty of. He can give a very detailed and sharp critique of a singer while never destroying a reputation; an extremely rare and wonderful ability.

Since Steane's great work was published, even more advances in sonic restoration have occurred, and even greater numbers of rarities have become available. The mantle is now passed to Nicholas Limansky, who, in this new work, proves himself to be a rare and worthy successor to Steane. I have been for many years impressed with his writings on singers: they are infused with great intellect, musical training, and, yes, the important passion one must have for one's subject. That he was a very fine singer and had a lengthy career gives him an almost unique perspective for the ability to judge a voice. I was struck by the incredible thoroughness of his vast listening and his research of the individual recordings and the many labels, thereby enabling him to define their strengths and weaknesses. This volume takes up where Steane leaves off. Limansky realizes the many advances and new availabilities that have occurred during the thirty years since *The Grand Tradition* appeared. The careful manner in which he has put forth the research on the various labels on which singers first appeared and have since been re-released is of the utmost importance and usefulness. A hallowed place has been cleared on my bedstand. I am sure I will value and cherish this book as much as I do the Steane volume.

Davyd Booth
Philadelphia Orchestra
Temple University
PBS Great Singers Remembered

INTRODUCTION

I remember listening to a Metropolitan Opera broadcast a number of years ago. During an intermission discussion, three rising young opera singers proudly stated that they did not listen to "historical" recordings of their arias or roles; they preferred to "learn" and do it on their own.

At first I thought they were joking. Then I realized that they weren't.

Operatic recordings have been made since 1896, when Ferruccio Giannini first recorded an operatic solo. They provide a wealth of information about tradition, stylistic proprieties, and voices that is absolutely amazing. To intentionally ignore that heritage is foolish.

This book is about singers who recorded from 1900 to about 1950. Its purpose is to give the reader a taste of the vastness of this heritage.

It is also about record collecting—at least in New York City—and my growth as a musician and record collector. My story is similar to that of many other collectors of early vocal recordings, just having my own unique shadings and twists.

At one time the number of resources available to the collector of historical vocal recordings was remarkable. There were many mail order lists as well as brick and mortar stores; these have all but disappeared. They have been replaced by a single, perhaps even more powerful, resource, the Internet. While my own story deals with those stores and resources known in New York City at the time (the 1960s to the 1980s) all major cities offered similar facilities.

Although heavily slanted to the soprano voice—because that is my specialty—I have tried to include representative singers from all voice ranges. Unfortunately, because of the tremendous amount of material available, many singers that I had hoped to include had to be cut.

The vocal heritage is enormous. The payback one obtains from time spent combing through the many recordings from different eras is equally huge and important. Most people have heard of Enrico Caruso, but what of the lesser-known singers? How about Bernardo de Muro, Francisco Viñas, or Giuseppi Taccani? There are many artists who remained on the outskirts of the circle of the most famous. Many, who for the most part performed in the Italian, German, or French provinces, made recordings during the infancy of the process. It is not only the most famous, but the more obscure artists as well who provide us with the traditions and heritage of their countries as it shines through their singing.

Sixty years ago one could never mistake an Italian singer for a German singer. Now they sound alike. This is good and bad. Good is that the level of training today is more consistent and, overall, the art of singing is higher in quality. Bad are the missing idiosyncratic touches that come out of the individual heritages and traditions of each country. This is why these early recordings are so important. They preserve a country's singing traditions.

Today's listeners are remarkably fortunate. Because of the expiration of copyright on early recordings and changes in international politics during the last decades, the amount of material available to us is staggering.

Because of this (and the relatively low cost of recordings) we have become gluttons of quantity. We are collectors of time as well as of artists. This is proven by the recent obsession with "complete" editions—the collecting of a singer's (or a pianist's, or a violinist's, or a conductor's) complete recorded legacy—including alternate takes, unpublished, and/or test recordings.

I will be the first to admit to my own guilt in this obsession and its undeniable allure. In the case of singers, complete editions are invaluable because they give important insight into how the artist worked—how they made their recordings and how they felt about them. Complete editions offer the luxury of sampling a singer's discography at our leisure, as often as we wish. That one can hold Claudia Muzio's entire legacy of over one hundred and twenty recordings in the palm of one's hand is a remarkable achievement in recording technology. Even more amazing, is that you can listen to the same selection a hundred times in a row without worrying that you are destroying the precious grooves that hold the music. One could not have done this fifty years ago.

In previous eras few people had the ability even to locate all the recordings of a given singer much less choose to expend the financial resources to buy them; or the space in their homes to house these heavy records. This new situation is becoming so commonplace, however, that we are in danger of taking these remarkable circumstances for granted. There is great truth in the adage that there can be "too much of a good thing." As mentioned, it is wonderful to possess an artist's entire legacy, but there also needs to be an amount of discretion applied.

Many singers are now represented by complete editions. Some of them can be found on a single CD label while others are broken up among various labels. To give you an idea of their availability, here is a partial list (in no particular order): Mario Ancona, Geraldine Farrar, Enrico Caruso, Luisa Tetrazzini, Claudia Muzio, Beniamino Gigli, Aureliano Pertile, Emmy Destinn, Ivan Ershov, Olympia Boronat, Amelita Galli-Curci, Rosa Ponselle, Lucrezia Bori, Elisabeth Rethberg, Marcella Sembrich, Bernardo De Muro, Giovanni Zenatello, Mattia Battistini, Francesco Tamagno, Nellie Melba, Eugenia Mantelli, and many others.

There have been many fine books written about singers and the art of singing. I am especially fond of a few of them. If you are spurred on by curiosity, I suggest you buy these:

Herman Klein (1856–1934) *Herman Klein and The Gramophone* edited by William Moran. (Amadeus Press, Portland, Oregon, 1990)

W. J. Henderson (1855–1937) *The Art of Singing*, Books for Libraries Press, Freeport, New York, 1938

Henry Pleasants (1910–2000) *The Great Singers* (Simon and Schuster, 1966)

Kurt Pahlen (1907–2003) *Great Singers: From the 17th Century to the Present Day*, (Stein and Day Publishers, 1974, in a wonderful and rich translation by Oliver Coburn)

J.B. Steane (1928–2011) *The Grand Tradition* (Charles Scribner's Sons, 1974)

Michael Scott *The Record of Singing* (two volumes) Charles Scribner's Sons, 1977, Holmes & Meier Publishers, 1980)

Each can be found at Internet booksellers and are invaluable references. They make for stimulating and thought-provoking reading. Some will seriously challenge your notions about many singers.

Herman Klein's book is a collection of his Gramophone magazine essays and record reviews from about 1925 to 1931. Klein was a noted authority on the music of Gilbert and Sullivan and he wrote six books about singers and singing as well as many translations for song and operas. He knew many of the singers who premiered operas of Verdi and other composers, and his collection makes for fascinating reading.

W. J. Henderson was a revered music critic in New York who wrote extremely articulate reviews for *The New York Times* and *The New York Sun* during his career. He was born in Newark and graduated from Princeton University. Henderson wrote a number of books, but his *The Art of Singing* was published posthumously (in 1938). It contains some of the most fascinating reviews (and singer analyses) that one can read. He knew intimately the work of such singers as Luisa Tetrazzini, Emma Calvé, Adelina Patti, Enrico Caruso, Geraldine Farrar, Victor Maurel, Lilli Lehmann, Rosa Ponselle, Kirsten Flagstad, Nellie Melba and many, many others. And, most importantly, he knew and understood singing. This remarkable book was reprinted in 1968. Copies can still be found online. His writings span fifty years and this 500-page book should be mandatory reading for any music journalist. Henderson reminds us that a review of an operatic performance should primarily be about musical matters—the conductor and singers and their art—not the surrounding production.

Henry Pleasants' book was one of the first books of its kind that I had ever read. He instilled a curiosity in me about the people he wrote about. He covers a tremendous amount of information, all within a manageable book.

I came across Kurt Pahlen's book while doing research on Yma Sumac many years ago. Around 1980 I had checked it out of the library, but a number of years later I managed to win a copy in one of Larry Holdridge's wonderful auctions. Pahlen's book is most comprehensive, presented in a very good translation. He covers a huge number of singers with a minimum of words within its 259 pages to give you a fine taste for a singer's merits and reason for fame.

I very much remember buying J. B. Steane, *The Grand Tradition*, a tome, in the late 1970s. I bought it on September 28, 1977 at Patelson's Music House (behind Carnegie Hall) right after my first professional audition in New York City (in the Steinway building). At more than 600 pages, it is quite hefty. It became my constant companion. Over the decades I have done much underlining and made many notes in the text. Despite its size, I would lug it on the New York subways and took it to rehearsals to read during breaks. When I sang appearances outside of Manhattan, the Steane was always packed in my suitcase. Quite battered now, it has a place of honor on my shelves.

After absorbing what Steane had to say, I would look for recordings of the singers I found intriguing. That meant creating voluminous lists (that constantly had to be updated) to aid in trips to any record store I thought might carry an LP featuring that singer's work. It was often a long and frustrating process.

Michael Scott's immense volumes are amazing accomplishments and, like the Steane, I keep them ever at hand. Although I often disagree with his criticisms, one realizes after reflection that they are always informed. His comments have often caused me to re-examine my conclusions. More often than not, he is correct in his judgements. It is mostly the manner in which he frames them that annoys. He also wrote a remarkable book on the art of Enrico Caruso and a superb one on the art of Maria Callas. He is an accomplished and erudite author.

Never before has there been such easy access to so many historical singers. My hope is that this book will help to guide you and other interested readers on their own journeys with historical singers. It is a glorious adventure!

In compiling this book, I took some singers from my previous writings, creating new appreciations for additional singers whom I felt would be appropriate to include. When completed, there were more than 500 pages!

A book that large is simply not easily marketed. In order to make the book as inclusive as I had originally planned, and in order to keep printing costs down, the book comes in two parts. You hold part one in your hands; part two is to come.

Singers such as Selma Kurz, Lily Pons, Marguerite Siems, and many others are planned to appear as a printed supplement or a CD Rom. I am equally proud of these appreciations and analyses, but there simply was no room for them in this printed book. Go to the publisher's website, www.ybkpublishers.com for more information.

Nicholas E. Limansky
May, 2016

My warmest and most heartfelt thanks to Joe Pearce for his invaluable contributions in the proofing of this text. His gracious giving of time and energy helped to make this book better than I could have hoped.

THE EARLY RECORDING INDUSTRY

To understand the recordings of today, it is necessary to be aware of the changes that have taken place in the recording industry since wax cylinders were made in 1900. There was the era of the 78 rpm (1899–1950), the LP (1950–1980), and the CD (1980 on). I will give only the most cursory descriptions of these changes, but I urge that anyone who is curious about the subject surf the net for more information.

In 1974, long before the advent of the CD, J.B. Steane wrote:

> Very soon the output of long-playing records will be unmanageable and so enormous in relation to the first fifty years, that the period of 78s may seem a kind of pre-history. It will be unfortunate, I think, if this happens. An artist who has left no more than a dozen records on 78 may have as much to teach about singing as another who has recorded several miles of track on LP. (*The Grand Tradition*, Charles Scribner's Sons, New York 1974, pg 1)

The 78 rpm Era

Before we get into specifics of this era let me make a general observation about singers and the early recording process. I cannot stress enough that, from a technical standpoint, this discussion is only a most basic overview. For more detailed explanations I encourage the reader to check an article by Roger Beardsley and Daniel Leech-Wilkinson: *A Brief History of Recording to ca. 1950*, Center for the History and Analysis of Recorded Music (2009) (http://www.charm.rhul.ac.uk/history/p20_4_1.html)

Making acoustic recordings (1896–1925) was not pleasant, at least for the singer. Many artists found the experience a nightmare and never warmed up to the process. Stuck in a cramped, claustrophobic little room crowded by either a piano, or

1

orchestral instruments he or she was forced to sing into a horn sticking out from a wall (which hid the recording apparatus). Depending on whether the singing was to be soft or loud, the singer was guided (moved) back and forth (toward or away) from the horn.

The singer had to remember cuts that would be made to their music to accommodate the four-minute time span of the discs, while also being sure to not make any mistakes lest the entire recording would have to be redone. Considering the circumstances, it is a wonder that decent recordings were made at all.

The recordings we hear today, more than one hundred years later, are truly live performances—accurate demonstrations of what these singers could do at that moment in which they made the recording. There was no editing or splicing back then. For that reason, some of these early recordings are marvels.

By 1925, and the advent of electrical recording, the experience was somewhat better for the singer, though still not ideal.

The electrical process has certainly made things easier for today's restorer of historical recordings because it was then that the recording speed was standardized at the 78 revolutions per minute that gives these records their common name. Before 1925, there was no set speed; recordings ranged from about 64 to 80 rpm. The recording and playback speed was supposed to be (but seldom was) listed on the label. When it *was* listed, it was often incorrect. Complicating matters further, singers occasionally transposed their music to another key. Some recording companies showed on the label the key in which the selection was sung as a guide to its playing speed.

Although the best way to listen to these old disks is to use the now-antique machines for which they were originally made, CD restorations created by Keith Hardwick, Ward Marston, Mark Obert-Thorn, Seth Winner (and others), parrot the original recordings extremely well. They show a loving care in their work and often extract outstanding results.

Thomas Edison invented the phonographic device in 1877. However, this was a very primitive version of what later commonly became known as a "phonograph." The first had a sheet of tinfoil wrapped around a cylindrical drum that rotated as well as moved laterally.

> As it moved it passed under a touching metal stylus, attached to one side of a diaphragm. On the other side of the diaphragm was a small mouthpiece into which the operator spoke. The sound- waves focused onto the diaphragm caused it to vibrate, which in turn caused the stylus to vary the pressure on the tinfoil. (Roger Beardsley and Daniel Leech-Wilkinson: *A Brief History of Recording to ca. 1950*, Center for the History and Analysis of Recorded Music (2009) http://www.charm.rhul.ac.uk/history/p20_4_1.html; accessed October 24, 2014)

The first sound that came from this device was barely audible and were the words "Mary had a little lamb" spoken by Thomas Edison himself. Having taken it that far, Edison moved on to other projects. The idea of recording music did not enter into his thoughts. During the next decade a number of other inventors worked on the idea including Alexander Graham Bell and Charles Tainter, who created the wax cylinder phonograph. At that point, the recording of music began to take place. Hearing of their success, Edison found a renewed interest in the process and made improvements on his original invention. Emile Berliner created the flat disk that was easier to play and also, most importantly, for commercial reasons, found that it was very cheap to reproduce for mass distribution. Berliner developed this version of the phonograph between 1887 and 1893.

Over the ensuing years many alterations and improvements were made to the recording apparatus and the discs used for recording. Soon an industry evolved, and by 1901 such people as Fred Gaisberg and his brother, Will, undertook a series of worldwide tours to advertise and promote the merits of a new recording company: the Gramophone and Typewriter Company (G&T), which eventually evolved into HMV and then, EMI. Gaisberg was originally an agent for Berliner but he became most successful when he moved to G&T—especially after securing the services of a certain tenor, Enrico Caruso. Gaisberg traveled in Europe, Russia and India. As is true even today, it was popular music that brought in the most money and helped to support (finance) the more classical efforts of singers such as Caruso, Feodor Chaliapin, and Francesco Tamagno.

It is interesting that the first "celebrity" records originated in Russia in 1901 and featured singers from the Russian Imperial Opera—such as legendary soprano Medea Mei-Figner, her husband, tenor Nikolai Figner, and Feodor Chaliapin.

Although celebrity records in Russia had some impact in that country, they held little importance elsewhere in the Western world. It wasn't until the 1902 release of the Enrico Caruso recordings that were made in a Milan hotel room that things began to change.

"Caruso...was," as Gaisberg later said, "the answer to the recording man's dream." Some of his first records, made in April, 1902, were so popular that the original masters wore out and he had to re-record them (in November of 1902).

While G&T were promoting their own records, other companies were quickly getting into the game—Columbia was such a name—although, when it came to big classical recordings, Columbia never fully involved themselves in either Europe or the United States until the introduction of the electrical process in 1925. In France, Pathé became a name to be reckoned with—especially given the fine artists they hired—but their mechanical process involved dubbing from master cylinders, the result of which was exceedingly poor. In Italy, Fonotipia became one of the reigning forces for Italian operatic voices while Germany's Odeon became known for its superb stable of vocal artists. As one would expect, many other labels began to appear throughout the world.

With the popular emergence of radio in the 1920s, it became obvious that the quality of sound using a microphone and a loudspeaker was considerably better than the acoustic recording process used for the gramophone and its large horn. Naturally, companies began to experiment with ways to record using a microphone. This became known as the electrical era of recording. It was a break-through in sound and changed the recording landscape forever. Very soon Victor and Columbia, in the U.S., adopted the process. As would be expected, the first electrical recordings were mostly of popular music, but classical music eventually followed.

By the end of 1925, virtually all recording studios were using this method of recording and singers who had recorded their arias acoustically, re-recorded them using the electrical process.

The machine that played 78 rpm recordings was called a phonograph, and that term generally referred to machines made by Edison. Sometimes the term was used generically to include cylinder machines made by others, but it was considered incorrect to apply it to the Gramophone, a very different machine that played discs. "Talking machine" was the comprehensive generic term, but in the early twentieth century, the public increasingly used the word "phonograph" to refer to both cylinder and disk machines and to the recordings they played.

Because of Victor's preeminence in America, it soon became common here to refer to any machine that played these recordings as a "Victrola." Eventually, by 1930, the term "record player" was used to refer to any record-playing machine.

Although "Gramophone" was initially used, after 1901 it was no longer used in the United States. It survived, however, as a nickname—*Grammy*—as in the Grammy Awards. Fittingly, the Grammy trophy resembles a "Victrola" with a playing arm.

The Long Playing Record

The vinyl-based disk that became known as the "LP" was introduced commercially in the United Sates by Columbia records in 1948. By 1949, the LP had become the preferred format for commercial sale and remained that until the advent of the CD in the early 1980s. (That does not mean that the 78 format let go its grasp on the consumer without a fight!)

Although the LP took off like wildfire, in 1952 the "old" 78 rpm format still accounted for a bit more than half of the records sold in the United States, and was just under half of total sales.

In 1949, RCA Victor (Victor became RCA Victor during the late 1920s) introduced the 45 rpm disk that was meant to compete with the larger LP; instead, it eventually became the preferred format for single-release popular songs. For a few years, popular albums were released simultaneously as 78 rpm collections, as well as on 33, and 45 extended-play formats.

Generally the LP was either 10 or 12 inches, was finely grooved, and made of vinyl. Although time often varies, generally each side of a 10" could hold about 12–15 minutes of music while the side of the slightly larger 12" could handle between 20–24. The format was quite suited to the longer compositions of classical music but was also found to be an excellent showcase for a "collection" of popular music selections. Ironically, the term "album" originally referred to the heavy (and bulky) record albums comprised of 78 recordings, but it soon became the general term for a single LP album as well.

Early Live Recordings

Paralleling the growth of the 78 disk there began the recording of live performances. The first were made by Lionel Mapleson, (1865—1937). Mapleson was the librarian at the Metropolitan Opera House in New York City. These hundred or so recordings were his hobby and were made between 1900 and 1903. They are three-minute records recorded with a Bettini cylinder recorder and reproducer. Primitive amateur recordings, they were mainly recorded from the prompter's box on the stage, or forty feet up in the flies of the Met. Although difficult to listen to, some are quite informative about the size of voices and tempi taken during performances in that era. So why were these unusual recordings made only between 1900 and 1903?

In his introduction to the original 1985 LP release of the 100 Mapleson cylinders as a six-LP set produced by the Rodgers and Hammerstein Archives of Recorded Sound at the Performing Arts Research Center of the New York Public Library at Lincoln Center, David Hall wrote:

> A number of reasons have been suggested for this, including the hypothesis that things dropping from the catwalk, whether cylinders or bits of apparatus, were menacing the lives and limbs of the expensive talent below. In March 1903, the commercial disc recording industry, as represented by Columbia, announced its Grand Opera recording series with major Metropolitan Opera stars (the Victor Talking Machine Company would soon follow and achieve dominance, thanks to the success of Enrico Caruso), and this may have suggested to Mapleson—or encouraged the opera management to suggest to him—that his amateur activities could become problematic. Alternatively, Heinrich Conried, the new general manager in the 1903–04 season, may have restricted Mapleson's activities, either directly or as a result of his extensive rebuilding of the stage area in the summer of 1903 to accommodate the planned production of Wagner's *Parsifal,* which may have abolished Mapleson's vantage point.

The making of the Mapelson cylinders was very casual. Mapleson would install his recording mechanism in the prompter's box and during a performance would insert a blank cylinder and make recordings while the performance took place. It may seem incredible to us today, given all our orchestral, vocal, and stage-worker unions, that this was permitted, but at that time there was no objection to his doing this. No one anticipated the commercial possibilities that could arise from the result. Luckily for us today, many of the singers that Mapleson caught mid-song are singers that recorded little or not at all—Jean and Edouard De Reszke, Milka Ternina, Lillian Nordica, Albert Alvarez, as well as such popular singers as Nellie Melba, Emma Calvé, Johanna Gadski, Emma Eames, Louise Homer, Marcel Journet, Pol Plançon, and many others. All were recorded mid performance. Of course, because the discs last only 2–3 minutes they would often cut off before the end of an aria or scene. They are but fragments.

By the mid-1920s and the improving electrical process, other companies undertook recording live. Most important, at the time, was the joint venture of HMV and the Covent Garden Opera House in London. They recorded a number of important performances during the 1926 and 1928 seasons beginning with excerpts from a May 31, 1926 performance of Boito's *Mefistofele* with Feodor Chaliapin. Nine sides were recorded; four were published. Another important event captured was the formal *Farewell Concert of Dame Nellie Melba* on June 9, 1926. Eleven sides were recorded. Next were ten sides from an *Otello* with the famous tenor Giovanni Zenatello. Two years later Covent Garden also recorded major excerpts from Gounod's *Faust* and *Boris Godunov* both with the bass, Feodor Chaliapin. These remain, arguably, the most famous of live recordings.

By the mid-1930s the famous matinee radio broadcasts from the Metropolitan Opera in New York City were being recorded—though mostly for the edification of the artists or producers as "study" copies. The earliest complete performance that exists from that time (and is now on CD) is the February 10, 1934 broadcast of Howard Hanson's *Merry Mount* (its world premiere) with Lawrence Tibbett, Göta Ljungberg, Edward Johnson and Gladys Swarthout, conducted by Tullio Serafin. Before this particular broadcast, brief excerpts from earlier broadcasts were preserved—including Frida Leider and Lauritz Melchior in *Tristan und Isolde* (3/3/33 and 3/11/33); excerpts from *Elektra* (12/3/32) with Gertrude Kappel, and Göta Ljungberg; and *Manon* excerpts from March 5, 1932 with Grace Moore and Beniamino Gigli. Today, recording Metropolitan Opera broadcasts continues as an active hobby for many; although, for the most part, they are now recorded as wave or mp3 files. Thankfully, many of the "special" performances during the 1950s and 1960s have been preserved on CD. Although for many years the Metropolitan Opera frowned on the recording, buying, and collecting of their broadcasts, in 2013, in conjunction with Sony, they released two large boxed sets of their broadcasts: Verdi Operas (twenty discs) and Wagner Operas (twenty-five discs), all professionally refurbished.

Similar to the Mapleson cylinders, but better in sound quality, are the disks recorded by Hermann May at the Vienna Staatsoper from 1933 to 1943. But, like the Mapleson disks, most of May's disks end mid-phrase and before climaxes. Such recordings are only suitable as reference material because, for the most part, they are so frustratingly short.

In the 1990s, Koch Schwann released twenty-four two-CD volumes of the Vienna Staatsoper discs that remain important references, although disappointingly truncated. There are some surprises—such as performances conducted by Richard Strauss and other conductors in repertoire one might not expect. Koch Schwann presented the volumes attactively, with photographs of the participants and good biographical information.

Compared to the much larger number of singers who have performed since the inception of recordings, those covered in this book are an admittedly small number. Some of the articles are taken (and were updated) from my website (divalegacy. com); some were written for other publications (again, each has been updated);

and many are newly written for this book. Some are what I call a "quick appreciation" in that they are brief; others are highly detailed. The reasons for each choice is purely subjective. No matter—they are meant to be starting points for your own research and journey of discovery. There is nothing more exciting than discovering a new voice—or one that is new to you. No matter what, this is a *wonderful* pursuit.

The Art of Listening, Part I

All record collectors and opera lovers can tell you their story about how they came to love the art of singing. Mine is like many of those, but has some interesting twists.

I grew up in the middle of the era of the LP. At that time—around 1965— there were so many record stores that you could go to a different one every day of the week. Even the department store chain, E. J. Korvette (now defunct), off of the beltway in Baltimore (where I was raised) had an excellent selection of operatic recordings. Only major labels, of course—Angel, London, Deutsche Grammophone and Philips—but, for a beginner like me, it was paradise. There were also specialty shops that carried the more obscure import labels and even illegal "pirate" recordings. (Some were literally sold under the counter.)

Although bulky, LPs had a definite allure. When you slit open the protective plastic, oh, the smell of vinyl—there was nothing like it. I still recall the smell of vinyl on opening a DGG Rita Streich recital—it wafted over me like a rare drug. Removing the protective sleeve was equally involving—the black, shiny surface of the LP was beautiful to behold.

There was the cleansing ritual before and after playing an LP. For me this was not only to protect the record, but a form of homage. There were all sorts of cloths and solutions one bought to help with this task. As my record collection grew this became a sacred ceremony. I remember many rainy Saturday afternoons when I reverently (and tirelessly) cleaned my records while listening to the Metropolitan Opera broadcast from New York. What a sense of pleasure it gave me to maintain those records! They held precious information and beloved sounds. For me this was not a chore; it was a privilege.

This was, of course, long before the Internet—before CDs, MP3s, or any form of digital music. Back then, if you wanted a record you made a special trip on foot (if you were too young to drive), or, if it was a more obscure, or a smaller, independent label, you bought it through mail order. This was part of the allure—the hunt. In most cases you paid by check or by cash. This was long before children were given credit cards (often *only-for-emergency* credit cards) by their parents. One had to be a bit more savvy at finding ways to get or save money for records. In any case, one looked at mail-order lists or went from store to store to see what records were newly released and, in the search, try to find bargains.

One could handle the records in the store, read the liner notes on the back, and decide whether it was affordable. Sometimes it was the cast; sometimes the liner notes that would tip the scales, and sometimes it was the look of the cover.

I remember buying the Angel (EMI) recording of the highlights of Massenet's *Herodiade* with Régine Crespin, Rita Gorr, Albert Lance, and Michel Dens at Korvette's in 1965. I knew nothing about the opera and there were no liner notes on the back. I bought it because of the colorfully elegant cover. At that time I knew only of the mezzo-soprano Rita Gorr (from her Amneris in *Aïda* with Solti), but I was intrigued by the cover and I knew the opera had something to do with Salome. I knew of the composer, Massenet, and I knew about *Thaïs* (which I loved) so I calculated that I would like *Herodiade*. Listening to the recording I was enthralled. Little did I know that I had chosen one of *the* classic operatic recordings. I still have that LP!

Holiday trips home from college always included a trip to Silver Spring, Maryland to go to the "Record Hunter" to check out the imports or pirate recordings available. This was not simple. It took about an hour and two busses to get there. I spent at least another hour looking things over and agonizing about what I could and could not afford; then it was another hour home—I would leave in the early morning and not get back until mid-afternoon. But, oh my, what treasures I brought home!—and what fun I had!

I discovered Ingeborg Hallstein's beautiful, high voice on a Eurodisc recording I bought at that store in the early 1970s. I had not heard of her before, but her image on the jacket showed that she was very pretty and she sang the Bell Song and Zerbinetta's aria; I similarly discovered Sylvia Gestzy on another Eurodisc LP.

The first pirated recording I ever bought was in 1971 from the Record Hunter: *I Vespri Siciliani* from Florence 1951, with Maria Callas (Penzance). In time, that was followed by Callas's *Armida* and *Macbeth* (BJR), and then Christina Deutekom's *Armida* from 1970 (MRF). Of course, these purchases were over a period of years. For a student, recordings were way too expensive to buy indiscriminately. I had to carefully plan what I was going to buy and why. Each pirate recording was about $20 per disk and sets contained two LPs or more. In 1970, $20.00 was a lot of money for a single record—especially when LPs were regularly $5.98. Luckily, most of the pirated opera sets I was interested in were two discs rather than three.

I remember agonizing over whether to buy Callas's 1957 *La sonnambula* from Edinburgh or the *Armida* from 1952. I knew *La sonnambula*, but *Armida*? I had heard that it was a "special" Callas opera but I wasn't sure. I took a chance on the unknown and put down all the money I had that day to buy the *Armida*. I never regretted that purchase. It still is one of my all-time favorite live recordings.

Collecting records can become an obsession. When still in high school I would often go without lunch so I could save that money and go to a record store. Sometimes I would talk friends into taking me to Korvette's (I didn't drive). I would simply tell my parents that I was going out for a while. When I got back home I would sneak into the house through the basement because I knew they would not approve of my buying more records. I would hide the packages in the basement until I could get them later, when no one was around. My parents eventually figured out what I was doing. I didn't understand all the fuss! For me, buying records was a greater necessity (and more interesting) than a boring lunch.

I was raised in a household having very eclectic musical tastes. I grew up hearing music from Bizet's *Les pêcheurs de perles* (the first Angel set with Henri Legay and Martha Angelici), *Boris Godunov* (excerpts with Feodor Chaliapin on an Angel COLH LP) *Carmen*, *Die Fledermaus*, and numerous Broadway musicals and pop singers. My parents even had a Mercury LP of the German high-note specialist, Erna Sack. She particularly intrigued me—although I wasn't sure I liked her music or her voice. That said, there was something about the height and purity of her extreme high notes that intrigued my uninformed tastes.

My parents also had a copy of the *Victor Book of the Opera* which I read many times. There were some 78 rpm disks—most of them housed in big, heavy binders having brown kraft paper sleeves inside. I don't recall where those records came from but I remember two particular double-sided 78s that caught my attention. The singer's name was Miliza Korjus. On one record (a small 10") there were two arias ("Warum?" and "Es zogen zwei spielleut" from Mackeben's *Der Student von Prag*. The other record (a 12") had the "Voices of Spring" waltz coupled with Proch's "Theme and Variations." I didn't know anything about the Proch or the singer, but I knew I liked the bravura music and her cool and dazzling delivery with all those glittering high notes.

When I was fourteen, while singing as a boy soprano soloist at the Cathedral of the Incarnation in Baltimore, I became friends with another boy soprano, Landon, who had a passion for opera and sopranos. Although he was two years younger than I, he had a voracious appetite for opera with a matching knowledge, which I learned during rehearsals as we got to talking about things we were interested in. He was into opera and I was into anything about Ancient Egypt. He said he had music from an opera that took place in Ancient Egypt—*Aïda*. Thinking I might enjoy that, he suggested trading records.

That was in October of 1965. I traded him an LP of music from the movie *Cleopatra* for highlights from *Aïda* with Zinka Milanov and Jussi Bjoerling on an RCA Victor LP. I loved the cover, but the music didn't sound to me like it was from ancient Egypt, Even so, I loved every minute of it—especially Bjoerling.

Although I still knew very little about opera, about a month later I got my mother to take me to Korvette's (still no car) to search for opera recordings.

After looking through the bins for a while, it came down between highlights from *Tosca* with Renata Tebaldi or highlights from *Lucia di Lammermoor* with Joan Sutherland (from her first complete recording). I knew that Tosca jumped from a parapet at the end of the opera and in my naivité, I thought it would be really cool to hear her scream when she jumped, so I was opting for *Tosca*. My mother, however, said that she thought I would prefer *Lucia* as I would probably recognize some of the music (like the sextet, which I would have heard in cartoons). Big mistake on her part!

My mother bought the *Lucia* highlights for me. Before long she regretted this as her home soon became an auditorium for one high soprano after another.

Another thing happened almost simultaneously—a perfect example of strange coincidence—or fate: I was sick one day and had to stay home from school. It happened to be that day of the week when I usually visited the neighborhood "bookmobile" after school. When the woman who ran the bookmobile discovered that I was sick and that I was just coming to appreciate opera, she sent my mother home with a recording she thought I might like. It was *Maria Callas: Coloratura/Lyric Arias*

That kind gesture rocked my fourteen-year-old world. It would be the first time I heard the "Bell Song" from *Lakmé,* the "Shadow Song" from *Dinorah*, the "Bolero" from *I Vespri Siciliani*, and all the verismo arias. I knew nothing about the music, but I knew that I liked those arias because of all their high notes and that I was fascinated by Callas's dark, smoky voice and "wiry" top. I remember playing the final refrain of the "Bell Song" over and over again. Although I have heard that recording for fifty years, it remains one of my "desert island must-haves."

That Christmas (1965) my parents gave me the RCA Victor pressing of *Aïda* with Leontyne Price, Rita Gorr, and Jon Vickers, and the Westminster Recording of *Thaïs* with Renee Doria and Robert Massard. This was soon supplemented in February with birthday gifts of *Suor Angelica* with Renata Tebaldi on Decca and *Der Rosenkavalier* on Angel with Elisabeth Schwarzkopf and Christa Ludwig.

Another important thing happened on Wednesday, March 16, 1966, at 10:00 p.m. The Baltimore classical radio station, WCAO, played the Decca recording of *Lakmé* with Mado Robin. At the time I knew only the Bell Song, but when I heard the whole opera, I knew I had to own it. I went without lunch so I could save up the money secretly. On April 14, 1966 (the reason I know the actual date is because I wrote it onto the record sleeves), I went to the General Radio and Record Shop in downtown Baltimore and bought my first complete opera recordings: Robin's *Lakmé* (on London) and Milanov's *Tosca* with Bjoerling (on RCA Victrola).

Beginning to realize that I was becoming obsessive, I bought my first solo aria albums—a two-LP set of Luisa Tetrazzini on ASCO (singing thirty-two arias). I bought it mainly because she sang the bell song, shadow song, and mad scene from *Lucia*. I then bought *Twenty Coloratura Sopranos* on TAP Records that contained only historical recordings. It was from those two albums that I began to learn about the florid repertoire. They also taught me to love coloratura singers even going back to the dawn of recording. Completely preoccupied with my new obsession, everything else became unimportant.

A story my father often told with humor was taking me to my first baseball game at Oriole Park, at that time Oriole Stadium. While I was not that keen on the idea, I asked whether Landon could come with us. Well, I had a great time at the game! And so did Landon. We ate hot dogs, drank sodas, and talked about opera and singers for the entire time, never once paying attention to the game. Afterward, my father, somewhat irritated, asked why I had bothered to go. I looked at him blankly. I couldn't understand the question. I had had a GREAT time!

Contributing greatly to my knowledge and hunger to hear opera singers was a telecast on January 1, 1967, a Bell Telephone Hour program called "First Ladies of Opera." Now a cult classic on DVD, it was a wonderful, dignified, hour-long program that featured brief interviews with each of the four singers, suitable introductions to the arias that were sung with full costuming. Birgit Nilsson sang arias from *Tannhäuser* and *Turandot*, Leontyne Price sang from *Adriana Lecouvreur* and *La forza del destino*, Renata Tebaldi offered music from *Cavalleria rusticana* and *La Gioconda* and Joan Sutherland sparkled in *Lakmé* and Ricci's *Crispino e la Commare.*

At the end of the school year in 1967, my parents decided that I was spending entirely too much money on records. They had caught on to the fact that I was not eating lunch at school and was spending that money on records and (worse) that I was sneaking them into the house.

When told that I couldn't use my lunch money in that manner, I said, "Fine! I will just get myself a job." And, as my father used to laughingly remember, I marched my sixteen-year-old, smart-ass-self downtown and got a job at the General Radio and Record Shop.

I don't remember how I managed to convince the guy to give me a job, nor how much money I made, but I was given a job stocking record shelves and advising interested customers about which operatic records they should buy. I learned a lot that summer about what was in or out of print and how very extensive the operatic repertoire is. Of course I spent almost all my pay on recordings.

I remember it as being very crowded with shelves and bins, having very narrow aisles, and a lot of dust—especially in the basement where I had to store the overflow and out-of-print recordings. Even so, it was a very big deal for me to be there.

I remember buying recordings of Anna Moffo (her Angel coloratura album with Colin Davis); also a beautifully engineered Electrola LP called *Die Goldene Stimme* of Frieda Hempel with an elegant red cover. It had eleven selections—including not only operatic fireworks but some lieder. I also bought a Rita Streich recital on DGG containing the *Dinorah* shadow song. I bought many more of the "*20 Great*" TAP recordings and all of the recordings of Yma Sumac (except *Mambo!,* which was out of print).

Every recording I discovered inspired me to collect more recordings of other singers, composers, or collections. Early on were Roberta Peters, more Joan Sutherland, and Maria Callas (*lots* of Callas). Landon introduced me to recordings by Maria Ivogün (he gave me a ten-inch RCA Victor LP, "Critic's Choice," that had her classic recording of Zerbinetta's aria from *Ariadne auf Naxos*; as well as Leonard Warren in an aria from *Falstaff*; and the mezzo soprano Sigrid Onegin in an arrangement of a Chopin piano piece); as well as LPs of Mattiwilda Dobbs; and Jeanette Scovotti (one of my favorites—her Scope LP operatic recital has never made it on to CD, but it should have).

Then I discovered Leonie Rysanek, Elisabeth Schwarzkopf, the wonderful soprano Nancy Tatum, more Leontyne Price, Birgit Nilsson, and many, many more. Each new recording led to other music and other artists. I was awash with new information and new sounds! Despite his youth, Landon's knowledge was amazing to me and far ranging; together we fed each other's desire for operatic knowledge. Although I did not realize it then, he helped temper my vocal obsessions. My craving to hear coloratura singers was strong and constant. He took care that I learned about other fachs and voices as well. My operatic "education" during that period ended up being surprisingly evenly balanced.

Later, as I did, Landon went on to sing professionally. In 1973, Landon even made the long trip from Baltimore to Western Pennsylvania to attend my wedding to Gale—a fine singer whom I met and fell in love with at West Virginia University. The last time I saw Landon, he sang in an Eve Queler Carnegie Hall concert during the 1990s.

Gale was a student of Frances Yeend and I was a student of Rose Crain (wife of the tenor, Jon Crain) whose vocal studios were just next door to each other. Gale was a mezzo-soprano and the most sought-after singer for productions at West Virginia's music school. While studying there she sang various concerts and operas that included Dorabella in *Cosi fan tutte,* Carmen, Madame Flora in *The Medium*, Lucretia in *The Rape of Lucretia* and she performed Copland's "In the Beginning" with the composer.

After coming to New York, Gale made the transition to soprano and was chosen by Maxim Shostakovich to sing in the 1984 American premiere of the original version of his father's opera, *Lady Macbeth of Mtsensk*, at Juilliard's American Opera Center. In 1995 she was chosen by Tim Robbins to sing in his movie, *Dead Man Walking*.

Because of my early history, my operatic tastes are eclectic. The "Bell Song" from *Lakmé* continues as my favorite aria, but I have a passion for the music of Richard Strauss (*Elektra* is my favorite opera, with *Salome* a close second). I also love good old-fashioned, gutsy verismo (*Francesca da Rimini* by Zandonai my favorite). I like almost all Wagner and when I came to New York I even attended a performance of Lulu at the Met to explore my dark side. I loved it.

And then *came college*!

During my freshman year in Applied Voice at West Virginia University I would periodically go to Pittsburgh with friends (a violinist, a pianist, and an English major) to give blood. We were only allowed to give blood once a month, but each month that I could, I would skip classes to go to Pittsburgh to give blood so that I could buy more opera records.

We would crowd into the violinist's little Volvo, make the hour-long trip, patiently give blood, and then go down the block to a record store. If I remember correctly, one got about twenty dollars for a pint of blood. This meant that I could buy two double-LP opera sets or similar combinations. I did that a number of times during that year gaining me some of my favorite Joan Sutherland albums.

Anne-Lynn Gross and I first traded records in front of my locker in the Creative Arts Center. She was a masters-level voice student who studied with my teacher, Rose Crain (the wife of New York City Opera and Metropolitan Opera tenor, Jon Crain). Anne-Lynn had an exceptionally high register, which went up to at least A above high C, a real trill, and a remarkably fleet coloratura technique. Naturally, we became fast friends. I introduced her to my beloved Yma Sumac and she gave me an RCA Camden LP of Miliza Korjus singing Strauss Waltzes. That was forty-five years ago, and even though I now have that album on CD (Preiser), I have always kept that original LP.

After Gale and I moved to New York (right after graduation) we remained in contact with Anne-Lynn, who, over the years, became like a sister to me. She became the first woman auctioneer in the state of Maryland and for thirty-six years was known fondly as "The Singing Auctioneer." She was also the first woman in the nation to serve on the National Auctioneers Foundation Board. In 2001, Anne Lynne worked with the Women's Center at Frederick Community College and the Frederick Community College Foundation to establish the Anne-Lynn Gross Breast Cancer Resource Center, an information center where anyone, patients, families, or friends, can go to read and do research on such topics as prevention, early detection, alternative treatment options, after care, emotional impact and nutrition, all to better understand the disease. Despite the fact that we lived in different states, every year or so Anne-Lynn and I would get together for a sporadic listening session, recalling the times we spent in college.

We each have our guilty, secret pleasures and I confess that the Miliza Korjus album of Strauss waltzes is one of mine. I love the silly coloratura arrangements of roulades and staccati that she and the conductor, Giuseppe Bamboschek, inflict on those waltzes, and I appreciate her obvious enjoyment in what she is doing.

It is the quest, the hunt, for recordings that provides much of the thrill of new discoveries as well as the memories produced. Nowadays, most brick and mortar stores in cities have disappeared and CDs are ordered on-line from Amazon, Norbeck Peters and Ford, or other on-line stores—including eBay.com. Although I miss the excitement of browsing through record bins at a store, the Internet has opened up record collecting to an unprecedented degree, offering tremendous opportunity to collectors to find the elusive recordings they have always sought.

LP Reissues of 78 rpm Records (1950–1980)

The period between the 1950s and the 1970s was a fertile time for the appearance of re-pressings of historical singers; LPs that dubbed 78 rpm disks and presented them as recitals. Often produced by small, independent labels, they were offered as a "Limited Edition." While I can't discuss every label produced, I would like to review some of the more important ones. These were record labels that played a crucial part in collecting circles in New York City during the 1960s and 1970s.

For today's listener/collector of CDs and mp3 files it is hard to understand the impact that the long playing record had, particularly on the collector in the 1950s. Before the LP, if you had a recording or two, or, maybe, four, of a singer, you had a "collection." It was a costly business to increase that collection.

When LPs arrived—especially recital-style compilations—this changed. Instead of having but two selections of a given singer, you could buy a recording having 12, or even 16, selections. One's personal collection of historical singers could be increased greatly. For $3.98 (or $5.98) each, one could build a serious library of historical recordings. In a single purchase one might double or triple a collection.

During this period, record-listening was an isolated activity. Therefore, in the summer of 1956, in order to gather together people having a similar interest, the New York Vocal Record Collector's Society (VRCS) was formed. This society still meets every first Friday of the month at Christ's Church on Park Avenue and 60th Street in New York City. (see their website at http://www.collup.com/vrcs/vrcs.html)

One of the features of their meetings (that included lectures by learned members, famous singers, accompanists, and critics) was a record auction. The auction originally featured 78 rpm recordings, but as time passed, and that format was replaced, the auction switched its emphasis to LP recordings. The recordings were contributed by members and the money was used to help defray operating costs. When the LP format was replaced by the CD, the auction, over time, was discontinued.

The meetings and the group became so popular that in 1959 the VRCS issued its own "Christmas Record," a ten-inch LP that paid for itself by providing incentive to members to remain in the society and attract new members to join. The 10" LP was soon issued as a standard 12" LP. In all but one of the ensuing fifty-five years a Christmas record (in two cases, double-LP sets) has been issued and some of the earlier records are now prized as collectors items.

Beginning in 1993, the VRCS Christmas recording assumed CD format; since then there have been two double-CD issues, in 2006 and 2009. There are presently more than 200 members, making VRCS the largest group of voice enthusiasts in the United States. I am a lecturer for the society and, in 2004, I was elected to its board of directors. For the past eight years I have written the liner notes for the Christmas recording.

Around the time that the VRCS first began to meet in 1956, a number of LP labels began to appear that produced reissues of historical vocal recordings. Before long, some of these labels became recognized within collecting circles: the Austrian-based Lebendige Vergangenheit (with their beautiful purple-hued covers), and Court Opera Classics (an off-shoot of Lebendige Vergangenheit that dealt with even earlier artists), Rococo (with their elegant light blue covers and note leaflets), and OASI, produced by Bill Violi in New York, offered some fascinating programs and singers. Two other labels that originated in New York were Club "99" and Top Artists Platters (TAP)

Top Artists Platters (TAP) and Eddie J. Smith

A most important series of LP reissues were Top Artists Platters, an Eddie Smith label that debuted in late 1959 with thirty-two disks. The records were in the compilation format having twenty selections per disk, each side averaging a long thirty minutes. At that time, a reissue of a historical singer on other labels had six or seven bands per side, depending on the length of the selection, and most sides lasted eighteen to twenty minutes.

TAP records offered many fascinating dubbings of historical vocal recordings. In total, the series contained about 640 sides of 78 rpm recordings—some quite rare.

The cover of a TAP record had a list of its contents while the back had introductory information and a descriptive paragraph about each singer that was written by Eddie Smith (who is discussed later). This represented a great deal of work and research. Generally, this biographical information was accurate and, although brief, it gave one a flavor of who one was listening to. As an example, here is what appears for Maria Galvany on *Twenty Coloratura Sopranos*:

> Maria Galvany, Spanish born coloratura, never sang at the Metropolitan, but her imported records caused a furor in this country as well as at La Scala where she starred for many years. [This is not true, as she never actually sang at La Scala. A.N.] The rapidity, accuracy and bell-like top of her coloratura has perhaps never been equaled in the memory of the living.

In the first set in the series, 18 titles included:

Mattia Battistini	Twenty Tenors
Twenty Baritones	Golden Age of Singers at the Metropolitan Opera Company (1883-1903)
Twenty Great Sopranos	Enrico Caruso
Foremost Puccini Singers	Titta Ruffo and Feodor Chaliapin
Twenty Coloratura Sopranos	Twenty Great Contraltos
Twenty Great Bassos	Richard Tauber in Opera, Lieder and Song
Twenty Verdi Operas	Twenty Great Italian Singers of the 20th Century
Twenty Great Spanish Singers	Twenty Great French Singers
Twenty Great German Singers	Twenty Great American Singers

Not long after this another set appeared:

Twenty Great Russian Singers	Twenty Great Duets of the Twentieth Century
Twenty Great Wagnerian Singers of the Twentieth Century	Twenty Great Mozartian Singers of the Twentieth Century
Twenty Great Meyerbeer Singers	Singers of Oscar Hammerstein, The First
Stars of La Scala 1890-1900	Three and a Half Centuries of Italian Opera
The Three Melodists of Opera	

Although not all of the 78 rpm pressings used were the best to be found, TAP's generosity with the number of bands was very impressive.

In December 1959, W.R. Moran reviewed the first 18 TAP releases for *The Record Collector*. He noted that:

> The records are attractively packaged, some with photographs on their covers; all contain notes....Space limitation have generally restricted biographical comments to a few brief lines. Technically the transfers range from adequate to excellent.

Moran noted that there were many different types of recordings represented and that "there will hardly be a record in this series which will not contain some new material for even the advanced collector."

In a later issue of *The Record Collector*, Moran reviewed the rest of the series noting:

> Tucked away here and there are some really rare records...note for example inclusion of Anton van Rooy's bit from Der Fliegende Holländer in Album 322...the original of this is an almost unknown Columbia cylinder.

Also available was the occasional test pressing or alternate take—such as Lillian Nordica's alternate take of Verdi's "Tacea la notte placida" from *Il trovatore,* originally recorded for Columbia. This rarity appeared on "Twenty Great Sopranos." (On some covers twenty is spelled out while on others it appears in numerals.) Some of the singers were well known enough to recognize, while others were lesser known. The educational importance of those LPs cannot be denied. The amount of knowledge they imparted to the novice listener or student was valuable.

Because of these Eddie Smith Top Artists Platter LPs I was familiar not only with arias from the "traditional" operas even before I went to college in 1969, but I also became familiar with arias from such obscure operas as Smetana's *Dalibor,* Donizetti's *Maria di Rohan, Poliuto, Linda di Chamonix, Don Sebastiano, Belisario,* and *Duca d'Alba,* Bizet's *Jolie Fille de Perth,* Leoncavallo's *Zazà,* Thomas' *Le Caïd,* Alfano's *Risurrezione,* Massenet's *Roi de Lahore,* Gomez's *Il Guarany,* Saccinni's *Oedipus Rex,* Wolf-Ferrari's *Sly,* Catalani's *Loreley,* Giordano's *Siberia* and *Madame Sans-Gene,* and Peri's *Euridice.*

An early-purchase recording I mentioned earlier, TAP # 310—"Twenty Coloratura Sopranos" was a treasure trove of knowledge; new singers and new music. There were many surprises. Here is a listing of the performers and the music for that recording:

Frieda Hempel-Adam—Variations on "Ah vous dirais je maman" (*Toreador*)
Gabriella Ritter-Ciampi—Mozart: "L'Amero sara costante" (*Il re pastore*)
Elvira De Hidalgo—Chapi: "Carcelaras" (*Las Hijas de Zebedeo*)
Selma Kurz—Thomas: "Styrienne" (*Mignon*)
Maria Ivogün—Mozart: "Der hölle rache" (*Die Zauberflöte*)
Maria Galvany—Gounod: "Waltz Song" (*Mireille*)
Nellie Melba—Verdi: "Ah fors e lui" (*La traviata*)
Bernice De Pasquale—Donizetti: "O luce di quest anima" (*Linda di Chamonix*)

Maria Barrientos—Bellini: "Sovra il sen" (*La sonnambula*)
Elisa Elizza—Goldmark: "Sulamith's Cavatina" (*Die Königin von Saba*)
Luisa Tetrazzini—Verdi: "Saper vorreste" (*Un ballo in maschera*)
Lilli Lehmann—Verdi: "Sempre libera" (*La traviata*)
Adelina Patti—Bellini: "Ah non credea" (*La sonnambula*)
Olympia Boronat—Bellini: "Qui la voce" (*I puritani*)
Suzanne Adams—Goundo: "Waltz Song" (*Romeo et Juliette*)
Maria Michailova—Delibes: "Bell Song" (*Lakmé*)
Marcella Sembrich—Verdi: "Ernani involami" (*Ernani*)
Rosalia Chalia—Meyerbeer: "Barcarolle" (*L'étoile du nord*)
Blanche Arral—Audran: "Allons Petite Serpent" (*Grand Mogol*)
Eugenia Bronskaya—Meyerbeer: "Shadow Song" (*Dinorah*)

As you can see, there is a good mix of the familiar and the unusual both in music and singers.

To say I was enamored of this disk would be a gross understatement. I spent hours listening to it, learning many new favorites. I became fascinated by an ancient recording of the florid "Barcarolle" from Meyerbeer's *L'étoile du nord* as sung by Rosalia Chalia. It wasn't until 2009 when Ward Marston released a full CD devoted to this wonderful soprano's work that I learned that this recording was quite a rarity—a seven-inch Zonophone record made in 1900.

I soon bought *20 Great Sopranos, 20 Great Spanish Singers*, and *20 Great German Singers*.

Many years later, living in New York City (on April 6, 1992, to be exact—I dated the record sleeves), I was offered a cache of the TAP series in a storage basement of now-defunct Dayton Records on 12th Street and Broadway. The records must have been in that storage area for many years as they had, even then, been out of print for at least twenty years. Realizing I would never again have such an opportunity, I bought all that I could at $1.00 each! I was ecstatic!!

Even though I now have most of the TAP LP selections on CDs, I still treasure the original vinyl. It would never occur to me to get rid of them.

There was criticism of the TAP records. Some of their standards were slipshod—W. R. Moran questioned Eddie Smith's rationale, "if a selection from a French opera is sung in German, why give the title of the opera in English and the first words of the aria in Italian?"

Another concern was a general inconsistency in presentation, especially an inconsistency in dubbing speeds which is, of course, of extreme importance. In his review, Moran commented that it was obvious that in some instances great care had been taken to find the accurate dubbing speed; in other instances, not so much. He also bemoaned the "hit-or-miss" way the albums were organized which "is a perfect anathema to the collector with an orderly mind." This inconsistency puzzled him, but, all in all, he felt that these and other criticisms did not detract from the importance of these odd collections:

> This series presents a very attractive package for most collectors. The scope is so wide and varied there will be few collections indeed which include the originals of all these recordings, and for the exceptionally reasonable price which the series commands, one can afford to purchase the records for one or two titles which they contain which one may want.

He concluded: "All in all, collectors should welcome this new series."

Edward J. Smith, who produced the TAP LPs (and many other recordings) was quite a character. He was one of the most important people involved in the preservation of the historical vocal legacy during the 1950s–70s. From 1956 until his retirement in 1982, he transferred, produced, and issued approximately 900 long-playing recordings devoted mostly to live operatic material, although he did offer some commercial releases that were dubbed from 78s; the TAP releases earlier mentioned, and the American Stereophonic Corporation (ASCO) which released only monaural material. (I recall fondly listening to the Lauritz Melchior, Rosa Ponselle, Giovanni Martinelli and Luisa Tetrazzini double LP albums.)

His "private" releases were usually available only by subscription mail order, although there was limited circulation in some retail stores. His first "private" label was Golden Age of Opera (GAO), a series that, by the time it ended in 1971, included 479 numbered releases.

Around 1972, Smith created the Unique Opera Records Corporation label (UORC), offering 280 releases over the next five years; his last record label, the A.N.N.A. Record Company, was launched in 1978. A total of 73 recordings were issued on that label when cancer forced Smith to retire four years later. Despite the sonic and pitch inaccuracies of some of his releases, and the tendency today to roll one's eyes when his name is mentioned in historical vocal circles, Eddie Smith provided an invaluable service to opera collectors, historians, and students by making such a great amount of material available.

Unfortunately, most of his commercial releases are not considered to be of great importance today:

> Smith's commercial labels offered relatively little of interest, outside of the occasional rarity (the Florence Wickham "O Promise Me" on TAP T-311 "20 Contraltos—20 Arias") the slightly grotesque novelty (the Trovatore "Di quella pira" compilation, "40 tenors—80 high C's" issued as TAP T-333) and in the case of ASCO A-125 ("Rosa Ponselle—Soprano Assoluto"), a few otherwise unpublished items of real stature." (from *More EJS: Discography of the Edward J. Smith Recordings*—William Shaman, William J. Collins, and Calvin M Goodwin. Greenwood Publishing Group, 1999, pg xiii)

Even my beloved Top Artists platter releases come under great criticism:

> Smith's commercial LPs were often haphazardly pitched, poorly transferred, and pressed on noisy vinyl, with grooves so narrow that skipping and riding atop the groove was commonplace. (ibid)

Although this may have been generally true, I never ran into any of the "groove" problems on the recordings I bought. I did, however run into problems with the grooves on many of the UORC LPs (such as an Opera Rara Gala; London, 1977).

After a few years the records became quite dim-sounding and the grooves extremely worn, suggesting that poor-grade vinyl had been used in the pressing. The *Opera Rara Gala* was a spectacular two-LP set of Opera Rara's Silver Jubilee Concert—*Kings and Queens of England*—a performace given in London on August 7, 1977, and released by Eddie Smith on UORC 356 in November. It is a release I had never seen before or since. It featured obscure works by Donizetti and others sung by many wonderful singers such as Yvonne Kenny, John Brecknock, Della Jones, Milla Andrew and the incomparable soprano, Janet Price. Fortunately, a number of years ago I dubbed a CD version of my favorite selections from that Gala set as the LPs are now completely unplayable. One of those selections was a rarity: the rondo from Donizetti's *Alfredo Il Grande* sung by mezzo-soprano Della Jones, which is the stuff of legends.

Joe Pearce, the current president of the Vocal Record Collector's Society of New York, has a fascinating and touching story about the eccentricities of Eddie Smith. With his permission I quote from his email to me in June of 2014:

> Around 1960/1961 I was a young collector just starting to get to know other, more veteran collectors (in some cases, veteran enough to go back to the de Reszkes!), having previously been operating pretty much by myself with no real knowledge that other such people of like interests existed. It was through them that I first found The New York Gramophone Society (the NYGS, the first two programs I ever attended, both in 1960, being devoted to Margaret Matzenauer, who was there to enjoy the tribute, and then to a remembrance of Lawrence Tibbett, who had just died; my dim recollection is that Francis Robinson presented both programs, but he certainly presented the Tibbett one because I recall that he had broken one of his Tibbett records in making up the program and was hoping that someone in the audience could replace it!). Around this time, they also made me aware of the series that Edward J. Smith had been issuing for several years on his Golden Age of Opera (GAO) label. (I knew of Smith before, thanks to his notes on so many of his LPs issued on the Allegro, Allegro-Royale, Asco, Rondolette, etc. labels, all of which were more or less his public commercial labels, whereas GAO was certainly one of the very first, and still probably the most wide-ranging of "pirate" labels. I requested a catalog of his issues from him, and also to be placed on his mailing list, as he usually announced about six to eight issues per month, at what was even then a very bargainish price of $2.50 or $2.75 per LP.
>
> Well, when I got the catalog, I really wanted to cry. Here were myriad issues devoted to the great singers of the past, Metropolitan Opera and other broadcasts, loads of bel canto and verismo opera performances of recent vintage (many just coming back into the repertoire after very long absences; some not heard for a hundred years at that time). Especially where the singers of the past and the Met Opera broadcasts were concerned, I had absolutely no idea that such things were available or, indeed, had even been maintained in the "vaults" of singers, conductors, radio stations, etc. for all the intervening years. In 1960, for a guy who had been collecting opera recordings since he was 12, it was like hitting an unsuspected Mother Lode. Ah, but there was a problem. Most of the issues in his catalog, which ran single-line entries on about four sides of regular 8" x 10" pages, had asterisks next to them indicating that the supply had run out and that they were no longer available. Making do as best I could, I determined to collect all the new ones of interest and hope that occasionally I'd find one of the old issues through a friend or just plain luck

(I had absolutely no idea that there were a few specialist stores, like Discophile and Music Masters, that sold the GAO LPs under the table, but at the prices I later learned they were charging, I couldn't have afforded to buy them anyway.)

When I would order from Eddie Smith, he at first mailed the recordings to me, but then suggested that I might want to pick them up from Ben Lebow (at that time, the fellow who had founded Scala, and was about to embark on his Club "99" label) at meetings of the Vocal Record Collectors Society. Although a bit shrouded in clouds at this point, I think this is how I first learned of the VRCS, which I joined in April of 1962. Anyway, from that point on, until I went into the army on April 30, 1963, I was in heaven, because I was attending meetings of both the NYGS and VRCS every month, also attending a third group's meetings (The New York Society for Recorded Music), getting Eddie Smith's heretofore-unsuspected issues, and making fast and longtime friendships with a couple of dozen collectors, some of whom were among the most famous collectors of their time— Bill Violi, Albert Wolf, and Geoffrey Lyon were three of them. Geoffrey's mother, Flora Lyon, at that time in her early 90s and still going strong, had been at the opening of the Met in 1883 and so had heard Christine Nilsson, Italo Campanini et al, had been exposed to the Lehmann-Fischer-Robinson-Materna German seasons, the de Reszke, Melba, Nordica Golden Age (which, of course, included seasons with de Lucia and Tamagno!) etc., and I never knew enough back then to ask the right questions of her (she died in 1963).

When I went into the army, I had to drop all of the various 78rpm record lists I was receiving, as $78.11 per month didn't go very far even in 1963, but I did continue to receive two lists—Bill Violi's (because most of his 78 listings were priced at about 25% of what others were asking) and the Eddie Smith GAO list (because I did not want to experience a second instance of his issues going completely out of print and then never being able to obtain them).

Two years later, when I was about a month from being separated from the army, I had written resumes to a number of banks as I did not want to go back to my previous company, and had arranged for interviews with them at the beginning of April 1965 while on my last furlough.

Then, returning to my post in Maryland, I received the latest supplement of new issues from Eddie Smith and almost fainted upon opening it. Eddie said (later, we all knew that what Eddie said wasn't necessarily what really happened in the world, but I was still young) that he had suddenly discovered (in an out-of-the- way spot in his basement), hundreds of copies of those LPs and complete operas he had previously reported as being out of print and no longer available, and that he would make the small supply available to his subscribers on a first-come-first-served basis at his usual price, which by then was $3.00 per disc. I had about $12 to my name and no expectations of having much more until I had gotten out of the army and worked for a while at the bank I had decided to go with. So, plucking up my chutzpah, I wrote him a letter, explaining my situation, and asking if it might be at all possible for him to segregate at least some of the issues I wanted from the rediscovered treasure trove, hold onto them, and that I would devote all of my efforts upon leaving the army to saving up enough dough to be able to pay him for them, even making periodic payments toward the total if he desired.

The thing was, the records I wanted came to over 200 LPs or a bit over $600, which was a lot of money in 1965. I did not hear from Eddie, assumed the worst, and finally arrived home on May 1, 1965 (after being assured that the country could now remain safe without my personal contribution to its defense). Almost as soon as I got in the door, my mom's first words to me were something like,

"What the hell did you get? There are two boxes waiting for you in the living room. They weigh a ton!"

Mystified, I opened the boxes, and there were all 200-plus LPs I had asked Eddie to segregate for me—not some of them, but every single one. On the top of one of the piles of LPs was a handwritten note:

Thanks for your service. Just pay me when you can!

It took me four or five months to pay him and I never heard another word from him in all that time, except for his monthly flyers.

To this day, that is about the single most generous act I have ever experienced from any collector, and every time anybody has a bad word to say about Eddie's somewhat questionable relationship with the truth where label attributions or made-up performance data may be concerned (although he promised it to us, his cylinder of Wagner conducting PARSIFAL at Bayreuth has yet to turn up, possibly because Wagner didn't conduct PARSIFAL at Bayreuth, but that's a minor point in the Eddie Smith Pantheon of Tall Stories), I am the first person in the room or in print to rise to his defense, and I will continue to do so until that cylinder of Wagner conducting PARSIFAL shows up, which surely means forever."

Rococo

Rococo Records, with their light blue covers and centered, white labels, were very distinctive. Rococo concentrated on rare 78s and cylinders. It was introduced in the mid-1950s by Ross, Court & Co, a firm established in 1951 in Toronto by André Ross and Leonard and Peter Court as a retail outlet for historic and European recordings. In 1972, after the sudden death of his younger brother, the older Court moved to England, opening a store, The Old Record, in Twickenham. André Ross assumed sole direction of the Rococo label, moving to Coral Gables, Florida, but maintaining a stockpile in Canada and continuing to market Rococo records from Toronto.

The first Rococo record (R-1, a ten-inch LP) was released in April of 1955 and featured singers Sir Charles Santley, Francesco Marconi, Selma Kurz, Emilie Herzog, Felia Litvinne, and Feodor Chaliapin (a rare 1901 recording).

By 1977, some 400 LPs of vocal and instrumental music had been released. Among Canadian artists represented were Emma Albani, Thérèse Deniset, Pauline Donalda, Louise Edvina, Jeanne Gordon, and Edward Johnson. Rococo also distributed Cantilena Records, a label established in 1966 on similar principles by John Stratton. Rococo and Cantilena were praised for the faithful, vivid sonics of their pressings, and for the simple elegance of their presentation. In most cases a leaflet was included offering biographical and sometime discographic information.

By this time (1966), the work of certain singers very often could only be found on a specific label. For instance on Rococo you could find sopranos Gitta Alpar, Marcella Sembrich, Tiana Lemnitz, Alma Gluck, Lina Pagliughi, and tenor Léon Escalaïs. Each label, Rococo, Club "99", Preiser, etc. had its own merits and specialties. Because of this they all were able to function and thrive together since they rarely trod on each other's toes when it came to the rosters of their singers. That does not mean that the people running these labels got along.

Scala and Club "99"

The Scala label appeared in the mid-1950s and reputedly was produced by Bernard Lebow in New York. (He later created Club "99", and was a member of the New York VRCS.) Supporting this, many of the Scala LP releases had liner notes written by Lebow. For some of the releases it was noted that the original recordings were from the collection of William Violi (who founded the label OASI) suggesting that, at that time in New York, the "historical singer re-issue world" was rather incestuous.

Scala had some wonderful titles and some very important issues. It was through the Scala releases that I was able to learn about and delve into the work of such singers as Maria Ivogün, Jose Mardones, Nellie Melba, Sigrid Onegin, Frieda Hempel, Rosa Raisa, Selma Kurz, Leo Slezak, Rosa Ponselle, Giuseppe Anselmi, Emmy Destinn, Alessandro Bonci, Claudia Muzio, Rosa Raisa, Giannina Russ, Antonio Cortis, Frida Leider, Geraldine Farrar, and Hermann Jadlowker.

As with most of the LP labels discussed here, Scala covers had a particular look (often there was an odd satyr in the top left hand corner playing pan pipes). The back covers provided pertinent biographical notes about the featured singer or singers; again, many written by Bernard Lebow.

Whenever I went into a record store, the Scala releases were on my list to check. Despite minor flaws I found them very interesting and easy to listen to, either straight through—as a recital program—or in segments of three and four selections. Both methods worked, mainly due to the excellent sequencing of the arias on the recordings. The programming showed thought and preparation. I also found the transfers to be very good (at least the original Scala releases.).

In the late 1960s Scala was taken over by the Everest Group and became "Everest/Scala Great Voices of the Century." The covers changed to a uniform format of pink and white, and the liner notes on the back were replaced by a listing of the releases available along with a "Statement of Purpose."

This Statement of Purpose made much of the fact that:

> Everest engineers spent literally hundreds of hours tediously splicing, editing and adjusting. A microscope had to be used to select the proper stylus for playback. As many as 500 splices may be made in one recording to eliminate the 'pops' and distortions without impairing the performance.

As far as I can tell from careful examination, all they did was copy the original recordings produced by Scala, adding artificial reverberation! The selections and their order of appearance remained the same.

Although this did present the voices in a slightly different ambiance, what the Everest Group did to the Scala recordings cannot be compared to the savvy of Nimbus and their "Ambisonic technique" (discussed later) in the Prima Voce series. Everest/ Scala had simply provided a phony stereo impression to the recordings. I must admit that in a few (a very few) cases, it did improve on the original—as in the Selma Kurz release. But that is a special case and hers is a special voice. Mostly it did nothing to help and in many cases ruined what Scala originally took so much time to prepare and release. Other changes included the labels—from the original bright yellow to a burnt orange. At the bottom of the back cover of each LP there was information that Everest Records was located on Wilshire Boulevard in Los Angeles, California.

No matter the changes that Scala releases underwent, for decades their library was very important. There were at least seventy-two issues which included not only volumes devoted to single singers, but such unusual compilations as "Fabulous Vienna" (two volumes), and "Cantorial Gems" (three volumes). There were also LPs of highlights from *La Juive* and *Les Huguenots* featuring historical singers, and "*Carmen*—A Connnoisseur's Cast," "Echoes of Naples" and "Coloratura Gems." Where else on an LP could one find the recordings of Lina Cavalieri, Alessandro Bonci, Alfred Piccaver, Miguel Fleta, Edmond Clement, and Antonio Cortis?

Another label of importance that originated in New York was Club "99" founded in the early 1960s by Bernard Lebow and his wife, Ellen (real name Helen), using their home in Elmhurst, Queens, New York. (As mentioned before, Lebow was reputedly the originator of the Scala issues.) Club "99" was one of the most important historical labels in America. The Lebows had a huge library of recordings. In its original concept, Club "99" created limited editions made for a specific purpose: the Lebows issued LPs of historical singers in a quantity of ninety-nine copies meant for fellow collectors; these included members of the New York Vocal Record Collector's Society. By 1965, these LPs were so popular that they began to issue them commercially. When Bernard died in 1968, Ellen took over production of the records. In addition to sprucing up newer releases she began to include excellent liner and biographical notes.

> Much work is spent preparing a new album. After choosing the 78s that were to make up the record, Mrs. Lebow must spend between 5 days and 3 weeks 'declicking'—the lengthy process of editing out pops, hisses and various other surface noises that are found on all 78 recordings of this vintage, Mrs. Lebow first tapes the 78s and then makes tiny splices where there is any imperfection in the sonic quality. It is an exhausting process; one recent reissue involved make over 6,000 little spices. But the care taken in the making of a Club "99" reissue really shows. Club "99" remains a unique institution: a record label where quality is the first and foremost factor in the choice of what gets reissued. (Tim Page, *Columbia Spectator* April 3, 1978)

More than one hundred and twenty LPs were released by Club "99" and some were of utmost importance to collectors. In many cases, and for many years, these well-produced LPs, with their solid black cover having red, white, or yellow wraparound labels, were the only recordings available of such singers as Marie Delna, David Devries, Paul Franz, Sofia Del Campo, Charles Dalmores, Maria Galvany, Evelyn Scotney, Ellen Beach Yaw, Johanna Gadski, Bernardo de Muro, Mabel

Garrison, Frances Alda, Agustarello Affre, Emma Carelli, Eugenia Burzio, Gabriella Ritter-Ciampi, Lotte Schöne, Regina Pacini, Maria Nemeth, and many others. Transferred with great care, and pressed on good vinyl, these American LPs were along the same line of excellence as the Austrian label, Preiser. Later, labels such as OASI would issue additional LPs of some of these artists, but as far as I can tell, Club "99" was there first.

When Ellen Lebow died in 2001, Andy Karzas, a much-loved radio broadcaster and opera lecturer in Chicago wrote of Club "99":

> Many of us learned dozens of singers through their joint efforts. Ellen continued the company after her husband's passing, concentrating more and more on French artists. There were wonderful issues devoted to Vanni Marcoux, Rosa Raisa, Xenia Belmas, Hina Spani.... many others... and Collector's Showcase LPs loaded with unimaginable rarities. She was meticulous in pitching the records correctly for the transfers, and declicking them for the best possible sound reproduction. The Lebow record collection was the basis of many interesting gatherings at their home during those years. Ellen sold her interest in Club "99" many years ago, and LPs originally issued by Ben and Ellen continue to be transfered to CD, some still labeled CLUB "99", others simply pirated from those LPs. (Opera L; 3-3-01. Listserv 15.5, Opera L, list at listserv. BCCLS.org)

Like the Scala LPs, many Club "99" releases can be found for purchase on eBay. They represent a notable piece of vocal nostalgia in the history of releases of historical singers.

OASI

Also prominent in New York collecting circles were the OASI LPs produced from his home in Brooklyn by William Violi. He began his business as a hobby while working for a construction company during the early 1960s.

His obituary in *The New York Times* (January 28, 1989) noted that "His concern for sonic purity was well-known among collectors, and his recordings, which he sold through mail-order and from a small store in Brooklyn, were sought after by vocal enthusiasts."

OASI recordings were always popular with collectors; however, from my experience, they did not seem to have been as carefully produced as the Club "99" releases. In almost every instance, the quality of the vinyl used in Club "99" releases was much better than that used by Violi for OASI. Also, OASI was a barebones production. By that I mean that although there was a listing of the contents and matrix number on the cover, there were no liner notes or information about the singer/singers. Violi did, however, release some wonderful and rare material. His compilations were always interesting and showed much thought. Some of the unusual singers that he promoted included Miliza Korjus (at least 3 volumes), Ada Sari, additional recordings of Maria Galvany, Emmy Destinn, Eugenia Burzio and many others, including a number of releases from the library of a famous collector at that time, Aida Favia-Artsay.

Bill Drake of Chicago summed it up nicely when he wrote on Opera-L (9-20-95)

> In ages past, fellow collectors and I would nickname the OASI label "Old and Scratchy Incisions" purely out of affection and not out of any dissatisfaction with the product, which at the time was of a high level….we collectors really owe a great debt of gratitude to these entrepreneurs who made available enormous quantities of rare recordings taken from the libraries of generous collectors who were willing to share their treasures with the rest of us. In most cases profits were small and the whole operation was a labor of love."

Lebendige Vergangenheit and Court Opera Classics

There were also some important labels that were imported from Europe.

Syd Gray's Rubini Records was the Preiser of England—wonderful, well-produced collections of unusual artists—Josefina Huguet, Alice Verlet, Giuseppe Borgatti, Lydia Lipkowska, Elena Katulskaya, Maria Barrientos, Francesco Navarini, Vanni Marcoux; and in 1979, a critically acclaimed four-LP set of Fernando De Lucia's G&T discs. Many of their collections caught favor with not only European, but American collectors as well. Rubini disappeared with the emergence of the CD, but during the LP era it was an important and revered reissue label—one that stood for excellence in programming and its choice of releases. The original records often came from private libraries. There was also a budget label, Oympus. From Germany there was Discophilia

The main European rival of American re-issuers was Preiser records. Their Lebendige Vergangenheit LP series in the mid-1960s quickly began to have an impact on collectors of historical voices. Preiser offered recordings of originals that ranged from the late teens until the 1940s. They were unique in that they were pressed using excellent vinyl and had gentle, purple-hued covers with a photograph of the singer in the center.

Court Opera Classics (an off-shoot of the Lebendige Vergangenheit series) had uniformly white covers that also had a photograph of the singer in the center. The Court Opera series concentrated on singers who had made recordings between 1900 and 1915. As one might expect, there were occasionally crossovers between the two series. Both labels quickly became the new standard of excellence for presenting historical singers on LP; clean, unfussy transfers that highlighted the voice, but did not distort, being well-pressed and made on good, durable vinyl. I still have many of the originals that I bought in the mid-1970s; they still play well. Each release showed imaginative programming, had adequate biographical notes and were especially clean, robust pressings with elegant graphic presentation.

Preiser Records was founded by Otto Preiser (1920–1996) in 1952. In December, 1966 he and his producer and partner, Jürgen Schmidt (1937–2010), launched a new series of recordings of historic singers. The first record in the Legendary Voices series was dedicated to the Viennese bass, Richard Mayr. Its enthusiastic reception established the reputation of this new series. Together with "Court Opera," Lebendige Vergangenheit provided collectors with unimaginable treasures that were lovingly transferred and documented. In 1987, the series began to be transferred to CD. Until the death of Jürgen Schmidt, the CD releases maintained the excellence of the original LP issues. At the time of this writing (October, 2014) about 334 titles have been transferred to CD. Every issue is worth owning!

Writing about the Lebendige Vergangenheit series, Dr. Charles Ritterbrand noted:

> Preiser has set new, high technical standards in the field of re-mastering and processing. The credo of the expert Jürgen Schmidt is to create an authentic sound that is far more satisfying than that of recordings that have been clinically "enhanced". What you will not find in this collection are singers who owe their fame more to their lurid private lives than to the quality of their singing or those whose voices have been preserved countless times on other labels. The catalogue series directed by Schmidt and called Lebendige Vergangenheit, (Legendary Voices) now features more than 400 titles and has become a reference collection for opera connoisseurs."—*Dr. Charles Ritterbrand, Neue Zürcher Zeitung*

For many collectors, the Preiser LPs (and later CD releases) are considered among the cream of the crop in dubbings. Their roster of singers is impressive and varied (some singers represented by two or three volumes): Aureliano Pertile, Lauritz Melchior, Frida Leider, Alexander Kipnis, Hans Reinmar, Tino Pattiera, Alfred Piccaver, Marta Fuchs, Charles Kullmann, Miguel Fleta, Maria Galvany, Lina Pagliughi, Miliza Korjus, Lotte Schöne, Apollo Granforte, Julius Patzak, Lea Piltti, Erna Berger, Graziela Pareto, Fritzi Jokl, Maria Gentile, Maria Gerhart, Torsten Ralf, Meta Seinemeyer, and many others. Not only is this group large, but their LP collections have been translated faithfully to CD. The death of Jürgen Schmidt in 2010 leaves the future of the historical singer section of the Preiser listings undecided. One hopes that it will not disappear.

Court Opera Classics ended with the emergence of the CD, but in many instances, when appropriate, the original recordings were incorporated into the Lebendige Vergangenheit CD series. Like Lebendige Vergangenheit, the Court Opera Classics LP pressings were superb and although the liner notes were in German, the generous programs and interesting singers made up for the effort American listeners made to translate the German text. Many later Preiser CDs have notes in English.

New York City Retail Record Stores

In the mid-1970s many of the recordings mentioned, and various other live and second-hand recordings were available at the following stores that I visited regularly. The list is in no special order:

Discophile 26 West 8th St. (near Sixth Avenue) in Greenwich Village. In 1975, the heyday of pirate recordings was in full swing. There were two shops in Manhattan where you mostly found them. One was Music Masters—which I found to be over-priced and not friendly. The other was Discophile, a tiny store hidden down dark stairs on crowded 8th Street in the West Village. My friend Anna Schumate—a coloratura soprano with whom I went to West Virginia University, and who studied with my teacher, Rose Crain—lived in the Village. Learning that I was looking for a record store that carried live recordings, she suggested Discophile; I almost missed finding it the first time I went.

> "Discophile occupied a small semi-basement space a few steps below street level, and entering the store, with its vinyl-laden bins, was like stepping into a secret temple of music. Presiding as high priest was Mr. Jolowicz, whom former customers described variously last week as urbane, opinionated and, frankly, terrifying...
>
> "Shopping there was a very involving experience; you just didn't stand in line with your bundle," the playwright Terrence McNally, a regular Discophile patron, said in a telephone interview on Thursday. "If you wanted a new recording of 'Parsifal,' you'd have to ask, and that started a conversation: 'Which version do you want? The Solti? That's terrible!' " (*The New York Times*, Margalit Fox—Obituary for Franz Jolowicz, 12/4/2005)

The shop was opened in 1958 by Joseph Greenspan; when I went in the mid-1970s, it was run by Franz Jolowicz. Franz had worked in the shop for many years. When Greenspan died in 1975, he bought the shop from the estate. *The New York Times* called the Discophile "a Greenwich Village institution that was for decades a mecca for classical record collectors..." (ibid)

Discophile was an eclectic shop in which "browsers could find albums from Poland, Sweden and China, rare French show music, swooshing electronic compositions from the international avant-garde, countless reissues devoted to great artists of the past, and, on private and commercial recordings, what seemed to be every note sung in public by Maria Callas." (Tim Page, "Record Store a Victim of Economics", *The New York Times*, July 15, 1984)

Going there was an adventure. In addition to traditionally-released and niche LP recordings you could find the entire known catalogue of pirate labels. Franz impressed me as an affable, erudite guide who seemed able to lead a seasoned collector as well as a novice (which I was) to the most interesting live recordings. I remember quizzing him on the merits of such recordings as *Robert le Diable* with Renata Scotto and Boris Christoff and the various Callas Medeas. One could buy mouthwatering revivals with Leyla Gencer, Joan Sutherland, Boris Christoff, Franco Corelli, Nicolai Gedda, Renata Scotto, Alfredo Kraus, and many others. A victim of its time, unable to compete against conglomerates such as Tower Records (which was nearby) the Discophile closed in July of 1984. "Writing in *The New York Times* shortly before Discophile closed, Tim Page called it 'possibly the finest record store in the world.'" (Obituary for Franz Jolowicz, Margalit Fox, *The New York Times*, December 4, 2005)

Darton Records (at the back of Patelson's Music House) 160 West 56th St. Patelson's was a venerable institution for classical musicians that, after six decades, closed in May, 2009. They primarily sold printed music and books about music. Due to its location (across from the stage-door of Carnegie Hall), many famous artists went there to buy music or to look for new music for repertoire. In an article about Patelson's, the list of artists who went there reads like a "Who's Who" of the classical music scene in New York City:

> Artur Rubinstein, David Oistrakh, Isaac Stern, Aaron Copland, Samuel Barber, Ned Rorem, Erich Leinsdorf, Maurice Abravanel, James Levine, Kurt Masur, Beverly Sills, Placido Domingo, Robert Merrill, Eileen Farrell, Maureen Forrester, Patricia Brooks, Vladimir Horowitz, Jorge Bolet, Andre Watts, Van Cliburn, Earl Wild, Richard Goode, Mitsuko Uchida, (as well as such celebrities as) Frank Sinatra, Judy Collins, Michael Jackson, Paul McCartney, Jaco Pastorius, Werner Klemperer, Claudette Colbert, Lee Remick and Kevin Kline." (http://slippedisc.com/2013/10/end-of-history-patelsons-has-been-demolished/)

When I first went to Patelson's in the mid-1970s, there was a store within the store set up in the back, Darton Records. Overseen by Joseph Darton, Joseph Patelson's brother-in-law, they sold LPs. Darton had a superb, eclectic selection of opera recital recordings as well as many small record labels of quality that larger stores ignored. In the stacks in the back, Darton carried Eddie Smith's infamous live UORC records, BJR records, and MRF records. BJR specialized in live Callas material. Some collectors continue to feel that the sound of BJR LPs has never been equaled, especially the sonically challenged Mexico City performances. MRF preserved many important European revivals, as well as broadcasts of London-based Opera Rara. Both of the last-named record labels were small, but they produced first-rate products. Not only did they often include complete librettos, but photographs and articles about the performances as well. Darton's large selection left newcomers like myself yearning for the many things we wanted, but couldn't afford all at once. I went there regularly until the record department was closed when Darton retired in 1991. Before then I purchased many Club "99", Lebendige Vergangenheit, Court Opera Classics, Rococo, OASI, Pearl, and even some Scala recordings. I also bought a number of Eddie Smith's UORC live opera recordings (in plain white sleeves with blue labels).

Ludus Tonalis at 24 8th Ave. near 12th Street mainly sold out-of-print LPs. This was one of few record shops that would happily play a record for you before purchasing it. You could find anything from an obscure recording of Blomdahl's opera, *Aniara* with Margherita Hallin to a 10-inch LP of Lily Pon's first recordings for Odeon in 1929.

In 1977, I wanted to find a copy of Roberta Peters' 1956 RCA Victor album "Famous Operatic Arias." It had been out of print for many years and featured the soprano in arias from *Il barbiere di Siviglia, Fra Diavolo, Lucia di Lammermoor, Lakmé, Rigoletto* and *Don Pasquale.* (It has yet to be released on CD.) Hearing that Music Masters was the place to go for this kind of second-hand record, I did find a copy for $40.00, but that was beyond my budget. In 1977, monthly rent was about $240 and the average income was $15,000.00. In today's terms, the price of that record would be more than $150.00!

My friend, Anna Schumate, once again came to the rescue. She suggested I try Ludus Tonalis on Eighth Avenue. I found a pristine copy of the Peters album there for $20.00.

To be sure, after that I revisited regularly! Ludus was a dignified, open-spaced, one-room store with a beautiful wood floor. "The walls of the store display a fascinating collection of letters and photographs signed by famous musicians, mostly of the past." ("Where to find Hard-To-Find LP's," *New York Magazine*, March 12, 1979, pg. 96)

Four Continents Book Store 196 Fifth Ave. at 20th St. This was a small store that specialized in Russian art and imported Soviet recordings that were unavailable anywhere else in the United States. It was an excellent source for Melodyia LPs of historical and then-current opera singers. I bought my first recordings of Eugenia Miroshinchenko, and the eight-record Feodor Chaliapin set—at the time quite a collector's item. I discovered the fabulous tenor Ivan Ershov, coloratura Goar Gasparyan, Lamara Chonkia, and many other Russian singers from purchases made there. Generally Melodyia LPs were not pressed onto as good vinyl as their American counterparts, but the singers Melodyia featured were often well worth the investment.

Dayton Records 824 Broadway at 12th St. Dayton carried reviewer copies of records just as the Strand (a bookstore across the street) carried reviewer's copies of books. Dayton also carried used "rock and jazz records, as well as classical discs... but the store's major focus is movie soundtracks and original–cast show albums of which there are thousands." ("Where to find Hard-To-Find LP's," *New York Magazine*, March 12, 1979, pg. 96)

Store (name unknown) 14th St. between 7th and 8th Avenues. This store specialized in Zarzuela and Peruvian recordings. They didn't have a large stock, but I found some wonderful LPs of Peruvian flute-singers at this shop when I was doing research for my book on Yma Sumac. Like many stores of this type, they carried other items as well—food, religious objects, and knick-knacks.

Second Hand Rose 525 Sixth Ave. near 14th St.. This store looked quite a mess on the outside and certainly not like a record store, but inside were many treasures. This shop sold knick-nacks, furniture, china and paperbacks, and a very large selection of LPs as well. For reasonable prices, I found some very rare 10-inch Capitol LPs of Yma Sumac during a visit in 1980.

Music Masters 25 West 43rd St. During its heyday, this shop was considered *the* shop for opera buffs. Its only major competition was a strong one, Discophile

Music Masters specialized in private label recordings of operas and musical shows. A number of people early in my "hunting days" in New York City advised going there—that I would find whatever I wanted there. Greatly overpriced, as I mentioned earlier, my one visit there was not a good one. Where LPs in most other specialty stores would be about $20.00 per LP, Music Masters charged $40.

Bremen House 220 East 86th St. at Third Ave. At the time, Bremen House was mainly known as a German food and department store. Downstairs, however, there was a section of imported LP records. They mostly carried Eurodisc and other imported labels from Germany and Europe. Interestingly, in October of 1985, after the close of Discophile, Franz Jolowicz did a stint at Bremen House. In an article for *The New York Times* on January 11, 1986, Susan Heller Anderson and David Bird noted that "Little by little, his old customers are finding him. 'This place is not well known enough for classical records,' he said. 'Aside from the German junk, they have a fine collection.'" Ironically, Jolowicz confessed that he "does not collect records....nor does he listen to them much."

And then there was Tower Records!

Tower Records Broadway and 4th St. Tower opened its flagship store in New York City in the old Silk building on 4th Street and Broadway in 1984. By mid-year it had pushed such small, neighborhood stores as Discophile out of business. Tower spearheaded a new kind of mega consumer store that became very popular in the 1990s in New York (Virgin was another, as was HMV).

Records, cassettes, CDs, and videos could be all found in the 25,000 square feet of its three floors and mezzanine. There was a Classical LP annex (down the block) that sold out of print and "over-produced" albums. (I bought many Club "99" and OASI albums there in the early 1990s.) Reportedly, it cost two million dollars to ready the store and more than two million more to set up the inventory. Before long, a somewhat smaller store was added near Lincoln Center. For about twenty years these two stores were the place to go to to find the record (or CD) you wanted. Not only was their inventory huge and comprehensive, but they staffed the stores with knowledgeable and helpful sales personnel and employed purchasing agents who knew their business. They offered activities such as celebrity signings and small "concerts."

> On an average day, Tower Records attracts some 6,000 customers, the company says— businessmen and punkettes, students and music critics and pop stars. Some come to purchase specific records. Others flip at random through 425,000 LP's and tapes, 30,000 45's and 7,000 video disks—all in easy reach in bins and stacks." (Merida Wells, "Tower's Costly Gamble to Sell records", *The New York Times*, August 5, 1984)

During the 1980s, the main store was famous for "selling albums of European new wave bands not yet popular in the U.S. and was a noted hangout for teenagers from the wider metropolitan area. (The) location near Lincoln Center was a magnet for those working in the field of Musical Theater. The company

published a music magazine, *Pulse!*, which was distributed free in its stores."
(Wikipedia)

For opera lovers, the Lincoln Center site was nirvana because one could stop at
Tower for a record or CD "fix" when attending the Metropolitan Opera. Their spec-
tacularly large inventory was regularly updated with new imports and releases. The
classical area was organized in a sensible manner with the opera section separate
from the others. Unfortunately, by 2004 they had serious financial problems.

> Tower Records entered bankruptcy for the first time in 2004. Factors cited were the heavy
> debt incurred during its aggressive expansion in the 1990s, growing competition from
> mass discounters, and internet piracy. Mismanagement, managerial incompetence, and
> crippling restrictions from the first bankruptcy deal also contributed to Tower's demise.
>
> Some observers took a pragmatic view. As Robert Moog, inventor of the Moog syn-
> thesizer, has stated: 'I'm sorry if Tower Records' and Blockbuster's sales plummet. On
> the other hand, it wasn't that long ago that those megastore chains drove a lot of neighbor-
> hood record stores out of business.'"
>
> The debt was estimated to be between $80 million and $100 million; assets totaled
> just over $100 million in February 2004. (Merida Wells, "Tower's Costly Gamble to Sell
> records", *The New York Times*, August 5, 1984)

Things did not improve.

> On August 20, 2006, Tower Records filed Chapter 11 bankruptcy for the second time in
> order to facilitate a purchase of the company prior to the holiday shopping season.
>
> On October 6, 2006, Great American Group won an auction of the company's assets
> and commenced liquidation proceedings the following day, which included going-out-of-
> business sales at all U.S. Tower Records locations, the last of which closed on December
> 22, 2006. The Tower Records website was sold separately. (*The New York Times*, August
> 5, 1984)

On Friday, December 22, 2006

> . . . the last Tower Records store in New York City closed down. It had been located at
> 1961 Broadway, one block north of Lincoln Center on Manhattan's West Side. It closed
> permanently along with all of the other remaining Tower Records stores in the United
> States." (*The New York Times*, August 5, 1984)

Within a few years Tower records was nothing but a memory.

Record Collecting in New York City
from the 1950s to the 1970s
(An essay contributed by Joe Pearce, President
of the New York Vocal Record Collector's Society)

From the introduction of the long playing record in 1950, the face of record collecting changed in big cities like New York. Joe Pearce, president of the New York
Vocal Record Collectors Society, grew up during the beginning of the change from
78 rpm recordings to LPs. His is a fascinating story and reflects what it was like to

collect operatic records in that early period. While I have some familiarity with that period, Joe is able to take it much further because of his deep involvement.

With his permission, quotes from an email to me in June, 2014 follow:

Joe Pearce:

When I first found classical music and opera I was very young and confined pretty much to the Elite Record Shop in Greenpoint, Brooklyn, but it is amazing what a small record store (I would say 10 feet wide and 25 feet deep) could carry in those days (say, 1950—1955), including hundreds of mostly current Victor Red Seals (78, 45 and LP), loads of symphonic albums (I got my Mitropoulos/Minneapolis version of Tchaikovsky's 4th Symphony on five Columbia 78s there), M-G-M and other soundtracks, etc., all of this peripheral to the pop records of the time by Como, Fisher, Clooney, Day, Monroe, Ray, Bennett, Laine, Page, Stafford, etc., etc.

Then, when I was about 12 years old, I began to go to Manhattan, where, before all else, I found three record stores along 6th Avenue, all of them called "Record Haven," the first, between 43rd and 44th Streets, was the big one that carried just about everything in LPs (but no 45s or 78s), and usually offered a direct 33% discount on every LP they had (except for Cetras, which were price-fixed—when that was legal—at $5.95). Most 12" LPs had a $5.95 list price, and most 10" ones a $4.95 list, but interestingly, Victor's list for 12" and 10" LPs was $5.72 and $4.72 respectively. Anyway, other than the Cetras, just about every 12" LP in the store (and they had thousands of titles) was $3.99. (Sam Goody was the "big" dealer at that time, but he almost never had discounts that good; those came later, after E. J. Korvette's went into the record business.) When my friend Joe Krajchy and I went to see various TV and radio programs, we would almost always first stop at Record Haven to see what they had, even though we rarely had even fifty cents on us in hard cash!

Amazingly, by the time I began working in 1956, at 17, I probably had at least 1,500 records (including dozens of complete operas which I learned intimately by listening to each of them dozens of times—and these were not all run of the mill works, but things like *Tiefland*, *Boris Godunov* (the Rimsky, of course) and *Salome*. In addition to what I saved up to buy, my mom and dad, starting in 1951, each gave me a complete opera for Christmas, and either another one each for my birthday, or else the money to purchase them. Greater love had no parents, because neither had the slightest interest in, or liking of opera, and since we had straight railroad flat rooms, they must surely have had years taken off their lives by my never-ending playing of such things.

Things changed somewhat when I began working as it happened, right down the block from the flagship E.J. Korvette's store on Fulton Street in Brooklyn. It was right around this time that Korvette's went into discounting records, and suddenly Goody, Macy's, Gimbel's and all the smaller record stores had real competition. You could often get $5.95 list price LPs at Korvette's for $2.19! But, except for a very occasional drop-in, I still wasn't frequenting stores other than the ones already mentioned, and Korvette's.

Everything began to change when I received in the mail, and quite out of the blue, a 78 auction list from the Connoisseur's Record Club, this run by an older collector, Geoffrey Lyon, who was simply trying to dispose of his very large 78 collection via a quarterly series of auctions. How he got my name, I cannot imagine, but in the long run it was probably the single best thing that ever happened to me in my collecting life. Although I was familiar with older singers, thanks to the 78s I owned, but especially thanks to the Eterna and Scala record labels, I saw things on that small list (maybe 800 items in all) that I had no idea had ever existed—including the IRCC issues of Mapleson Cylinders, which I had never heard of before.

Anyway, I bid on a group of these records from a standpoint of absolute imbecility where bidding experience was concerned—my highest bid probably no more than $3.51 or something like that—and won almost 20 recordings. Mr. Lyon found my phone number and called me up, suggesting that I might want to drop over to his place and pick up my winnings, as this would get them to me faster and he would be saved the trouble of packing and mailing them, so I did so. This was in mid- or late-1957. Well, that visit began one of the nicest and most memorable friendships of my life, remaining so until Mr. Lyon passed in 1974. He was fascinated by (and this is exactly what he called it) "the mental calisthenics that had gone into my bidding," since I'd won so many records at such low prices, and he found it hard to believe that my bidding was done in complete ignorance of record values; I just saw stuff that fascinated me, often by singers I'd never heard of, and bid what I could afford, which wasn't much.

Mr. Lyon's mother was alive and in her early 90s at the time, and she had been present as a teenager with her family at the opening night of the Met in 1883, also witnessing the German seasons and then the de Reszke era, although some of the latter and what followed only through periodic visits to NYC, as the family had relocated to Chicago in the mid-1890s and she had married there and had three sons to bring up. They had moved back to NYC in the late 1920s and had been in a large, beautiful 86th Street apartment ever since (there was a grand piano in the living room that was hardly even noticeable, so large was that living room!). Geoffrey had kind of lost touch with the opera-going world by then, but not with other collectors who remained steadfast friends, and, over the course of the next year or two, I was introduced to many of them—like Albert Wolf, Ely Winer, Walter Jaeck, Dick Porter, Barbara Stone, Morton Sodden, etc., etc., several of whom became lifelong personal friends. And through them, I learned of all the specialist dealers, the priced and auction 78 lists that were absolutely rampant at the time, the clubs that catered to collectors of early vocal recordings—the New York Gramophone Society (NYGS) and Vocal Record Collectors Society (VRCS) in particular. It really was like a dream world opening up as I had grown up with this intense love of opera and classical music and had known in all those years exactly one other person who shared any interest in it, and his not nearly as intense as my own, and here I now was with dozens and dozens of acquaintances and (in the best instances) friends, who not only shared that interest but could very often act as guides to my neophyte self.

From Geoffrey I learned so many things about (especially) American recordings and singers, and from Albert Wolf (who, after George F. Keating and before Laurence Witten came onto the scene may have had the premier collection of vocal recordings in the country), even more about German, Austrian and Russian 78s and singers, and the others also contributed much to my education in similar ways. Anyway, I was like a sponge at the time, and at least 30 years younger than any of the people I just mentioned, so it was like they were imparting specialized knowledge they'd acquired over 40 or 50 years in many cases, to the newest jerk on the block (me!). I wish I'd written down everything they ever told me or said about anything having to do with opera, because much of it is in a general haze now and, in a way, I have probably betrayed their trust by not being more of a "serious" collector (you know, discographies, matrix numbers, recording dates, that kind of thing). So now, here I am, at what was then their age (actually, older) and all I can now impart is a general feeling of what it was like back then, and a more detailed description of what it became like later on, say when I hit my 30s and my life was just full or records—in stores, 78 and LP auction lists, etc.

So, after gaining a lot of knowledge from these folks, increasing my collection to about 5,000 records by the time I went into the army in 1963, getting my post-army life in some kind of order and finally moving to Manhattan for about 15 years (about mid-1966 to the end of 1981), where I was certain the entire record-collecting world was just waiting for me to make an appearance and take everything in hand (ha!), we are arriving at the impetus for writing this diatribe at all—the general record scene in NYC from approximately the very late 1960s to around 1980. And I have to say by way of further introduction that I was never a collector of 'rarities'; I was totally happy at any time in my life to just have great 78s and singers of the 78 era on LP (or, now, CD) and collect 78s only of singers I loved whose output had not made it to LP or CD or of just about *any* singer I didn't know and whose records I could pick up for a couple of bucks. So, my record collection ended up having very few rarities in it (I can't imagine I have 3 records in my 18,000 78s that are worth a hundred dollars!), but was quite immense in its scope of the singers included in it (I stopped cataloguing in any specific way almost 20 years back, and never catalogued comprimario singers from complete opera recordings unless I also had some solo work by them, and when I stopped cataloguing I had something like 14,000 singers listed!).

So, a very polyglot collection, and the way to achieve that was to get every 78 list possible (and up to the early 1980s, the vast majority of those were priced lists rather than auction ones, so that I might get home at 2am, have to get up for work at 6:30am, but would still take an hour before bedtime to peruse a just-received priced list so that I could make the necessary phone call in the morning and get that—or those—priced 78s before anybody else!; you have to suffer for your manias!), and hit every record store—both current and second-hand varieties—as often as possible to make sure nothing escaped me (Ed Wolfe, long-time treasurer of the VRCS, was practically my other self in this respect!). To this day, about 66 years after I bought my first classical record, I still hit at least once a week, sometimes 3 times in 2 weeks, Academy Records, the only store left in NYC that really harkens back to the old style of collecting records via total immersion. Yes, you (and your bank account) suffer for your manias.

You can't imagine the number and scope of the 78 lists (classical vocal only) that were available from about 1960 to around 1980. Here are only a few:

Ross, Court and Co. (Toronto)—about twenty pages 78 rpm records—a monthly priced list, which also included Rococo and, later on, Cantilena LPs (of which they were the issuers).

Bill Violi (Brooklyn)—Monthly—oversized mimeographed priced list—at its zenith in the 1960s, probably about 50 pages of 78s; later, still 50 pages, but including a lot of 'pirate' LPs and the like. THE record list for New Yorkers!

Syd Gray (England)—Approximately monthly—maybe 10 or 12 pages and 600 or so 78 recordings, a priced list (he would also, for $15, convert a shell that you sent him that would fit your own tone arm to one that would play Edisons and Pathes).

Rubini Records (also Syd Gray, but after he had discontinued offering 78s, and was specializing in LPs, both of his own issue and anything else he could find)—monthly, maybe 10 or 12 pages.

Roland Teuchtler (Vienna)—this was the priced list that everybody waited for who had an interest in Central European 78 recordings; issued about once a year, it ran about 80 oversized mimeographed pages of tightly listed records (it probably had 5,000 or more records in it). Often had very hard to find or rare recordings for a few dollars each (but you had to pay attention to the condition).

Lawrence F. Holdridge (Long Island, New York)—Larry started this as a priced 78 list (and very low prices at that) in, I think, the very late 1960s or early 1970s, but within a few years switched it to an auction list. Originally, I seem to recall that it was about 20 pages of 78s, but without the photos and biographies that he includes in its 250 or so pages now. So, maybe 600 or so 78s listed back then.

A note from Nick: Larry was a well-respected high school music teacher in Massapequa. For many years he was on the board of the VRCS and president for a few years beginning in 2004. Larry is now considered "president emeritus" and remains actively involved in the Society and the making of its annual Christmas record. Although he never pursued it as a profession, during the 1960s he was widely known for the quality of the 78 transfers he created. In many ways he was the Ward Marston or Seth Winner of that period and many labels featured his work. It was around that time that he began issuing a sales list featuring records that were very reasonably priced. As Larry told me, "These were originally…purple ditto machine affairs of a few pages. It just grew from there, particularly after I retired from teaching." Over time the lists evolved into an auction listing that today is considered one of the premiere auctions of historical recordings in the United States. The drab, mimeograph printed sheets of before have been replaced by an elegant, reference-like annual for each auction that is a true work of art, running to hundreds of pages with biographies and pictures of artists (some quite rare), as well as color photographs of many of the more beautiful record labels. Held each January, Larry's website for the auction is as beautiful and as informative as his auction books (http://www.holdridgerecords.com). As Joe Pearce commented to me in an email, "In the entire world of 78 rpm record dealing there is no one who enjoys so sterling a reputation for knowledge, fairness and honesty as does he."

James Crawley (England)—probably the best-known English 78 list, on about 40 oversized mimeographed pages, issued more or less monthly. Any issue would easily have had 1,500 or so records listed on it.

NIPPER (later "Norbeck, Peters & Ford") (Woodstock, NY, now Vermont)—started as a quarterly 78 list back in the 1970s and is still around, but I never received it as a 78 list, only later when it specialized in LPs and listed thousands of them (as it still does with CDs).

P. V. (Ray) Winston (England)—monthly 78 list, about 12 pages oversized mimeograph paper, maybe 600 records per month. (Had great correspondence with Ray and also with Syd Gray for many years.)

Milt Weiss—(N.Y., later Florida)—this was probably the oldest 78 auction list in the world, certainly in the U.S. Milt, who died less than 2 years back, started it all the way back in 1951 and kept it going right up to 2012 (it has now been taken over by VRCS ex-board member, Mike Russell, who hopes to get it going again this year). Until the Holdridge list achieved the status it has had for the past 15 or 20 years, Milt's was almost certainly the premier 78 auction list in the country, maybe in the world. It was issued annually, ran about 100 pages, and probably had about 3,500 records listed.

There were many others, some of which came and went, some around for years. I recall terrific lists of Scandinavian 78s which came every so often from Denmark, a periodic list from Michigan that included hundreds of radio broadcast acetates at both 78 and LP speeds in between all the commercial 78s and LPs, etc. Today, we have the annual Holdridge and (soon to recommence) Weiss auctions, a twice-a-year auction from Axel Weggen, three-times-a-year auctions from Kurt Nauck and David Reiss, an annual auction from Phonopassion, and quarterly auctions from Tom Hawthorne. The Reiss and Hawthorne are primarily popular but include some classical; all of the earlier lists were strictly classical in nature. Anyway, the current auctions total fifteen per year.

Okay, so now we've arrived at my fifteen-year sojourn at the Ansonia, from which I sallied forth on Saturdays to hit those record stores I had not hit at lunch time or on the way home from work during the rest of the week (although sometimes I'd hit one or two again on Saturday as well). All were in Manhattan.

When I compiled (from memory) the list of stores that I visited, I was amazed that there were at least fifty-five in Manhattan alone! They included such stores as King Karol, Sam Goody, E. J. Korvette, Barnes and Noble, Rizzoli, The Record Hunter, and Colony Records—as well as those stores already mentioned by Nick Limansky.

I cannot stress enough that the most important difference between now and then is that in the 1960s and 1970s—up to maybe 1979—many Manhattan subway stations had lockers in them where you could store bags, packages, etc. You would deposit a quarter, turn the dial and take the locker key with you. The lockers were good for twenty-four hours from when you deposited the quarter. This was really convenient—you could unload a lot of the packages (and weight that you had accumulated) and start all over again at the next store you were going to hit.

When you were finished shopping, you could either go home with what you had at the time or go back to the train stations and pick up what you'd left in the locker and get a cab home. If you didn't want to go back to the locker (or lockers) that you had used that was OK. You had twenty-four hours to go back and get the stuff.

I especially did this at Christmastime, in the days when I really did a lot of Christmas shopping. It was great to just leave them in the subway on a cold December day for a few hours and then pick them up later.

The subway lockers were removed after various terrorist groups (long before the Middle East was an issue) started bombing buildings, or threatening to bomb buildings, and it became obvious that these lockers would be perfect for their purposes.)

Much as I hated the new inconvenience, it made a lot of sense to me. Anyway, originally there were lockers by the hundreds at Grand Central and Penn Stations, as well as at 59th Street, 50th Street, the various 42nd Street stations, 34th Street, 23rd Street, 14th Street—you can see that I particularly remember those on the Seventh Avenue Line, but that's because they were the most easily accessible for me, and I used them most often. But they were all over the city—at least, all over Manhattan.

—Joe Pearce

The Art of Listening, Part II

In 1907, when you bought a recording of Enrico Caruso you did just that—you bought one song, one aria, unless it was a double-sided record. Playing and collecting records was an expensive hobby. The ability to buy ten or twenty records at one time by a given singer was unheard of unless you were extremely wealthy. Each record (which played between two and four minutes) cost about the same as a pair of shoes. Records were sold individually. It might be a movement of a symphony, a piano sonata, or an aria. There was no such thing as buying a "complete" anything. One might be able to piece together a complete work if all of the movements had been recorded. Records were sold in paper (only sometimes, cardboard) sleeves, usually with the center cut out so that the record label was visible. They were extremely fragile and you could easily break one by dropping it or banging into something on the way home.

According to the 1913 edition of the *Victrola Book of the Opera*, the cost of a single-sided 78 rpm recording of a first-string singer (Caruso, Melba, Tetrazzini etc) was $3.00, the cost of a pair of shoes. In 1912, $1.00 was equal to $23.28 of 2015 money; therefore, a single-sided recording cost $69.84 for about four minutes of music.

At the time of this writing, the typical price for a CD of Enrico Caruso is $17.99 or less. There being twenty or more tracks on a CD, that breaks down to little more than $.90 per track, quite a bit less than $69.84 in 1912.

For another reality comparison, in 1907 a Victor Phonograph cost $60.00, translating into $1,300.00 today. To keep this in perspective, in 1912 an average house cost $5,935.00.

There were recordings listed in the *Victrola Book of the Opera* of lesser singers (Josefina Huguet, for example) that cost as little as $1.25, but, no matter what, we are talking about a *very* expensive hobby.

More important than simple cost, where does today's new listener start? And how does one listen?

How To Listen

When listening to modern recordings made from 78s, it is important to understand that acoustic and electrical 78 rpm recordings (1900–1948) were meant to be savored individually, not listened to in seventy-minute sessions, one selection after another. The recital format that we are all familiar with is a modern concept that dates from the beginning of the LP era (around 1949). It was a rather contrived (but very successful) effort to maximize the use of the new recording medium and the expansion of time restrictions.

To get the most from antique recordings one must approach them with patience and discretion. That is the secret in listening to pre-1950 recordings. They should be listened to in the way they were originally meant to be heard. That does not mean, however, that you can't listen to a couple at a time—or even more.

In June of 1990, the English critic of vocal traditions, John (J.B.) Steane (1928-2011), wrote a superb article for the magazine *Opera Now* about this very concept. Steane, a much-respected music critic wrote a number of books and reviews about singers—his criticisms were fair and honest yet supportive of both the singer and the complexity of the singing art. His most famous and rightly revered work, *The Grand Tradition* (1974), should be mandatory reading for all lovers and lovers-to-be of classical singing.

Steane gives logical, but priceless advice on how to listen to them:
"Intently and briefly."

To test his advice—to see if it really worked—I conducted a little experiment of my own (that you should try too).

I put myself in the false frame of mind that I had just bought a new record, that I only had a very few discs in my library, and that I would now listen to this one, brand new record. As I am a soprano aficionado, I decided to really put the idea to a test by choosing a tenor.

It was a 1903, single-sided recording of the tenor Francesco Marconi singing the "Ingemisco" from the Verdi *Requiem* (with a clunky piano accompaniment). (The Harold Wayne Collection, Volume 2, Symposium 1069).

I picked Marconi for a number of reasons. I wanted to stack the deck against myself as much as I could. Marconi did not make his first recording until he was fifty years old. He had been in vocal decline for ten years and had a well-documented history of vocal problems. Even so, he was considered one of the most important tenors of the early days of recordings and his records were highly prized. I reckoned that would make him a good candidate for this experiment.

I listened to the recording once, very carefully. I then immediately played it again. I stopped to take a couple of hours break, did something else non-operatic, and returned to replay the recording twice again.

During the second session I came to recognize Marconi's timbre and his manner of singing, slowly his good and bad points came to be filed away in my mind. By this time, too, his singing was becoming familiar.

When I returned to the recording the next day I had already listened to it four times—each time without distraction—and felt that I knew it inside out. I knew when, where, and why Marconi breathed; I came to understand and appreciate his technique, his diction, phrasing, and his particular interpretation compared to other artists. I had begun to form definite opinions on both the good and bad aspects of his performance that were based on this new, comfortable familiarity with the recording. Marconi was becoming a musical "friend."

A fascinating thing occurred during this experiment. I was no longer bothered by the scratchy and muffled sound quality of the 1903 recording. Because I had been listening so intently, by the fourth listening or so, my mind had come to filter out the extraneous interference and concentrate on the core of Marconi's sound. It was a wonderfully exhilarating and very satisfying experience.

I urge that you try this, but I warn you that it must be done without distraction; you can't do this while reading a book, watching TV, texting, or surfing the net. It does take that real, but small commitment of time. The ability to listen beyond the primitive recording process and hear the center of a singer's voice should not be a difficult feat for today's multi-tasking society. It does, however, require some patience. The rewards will repay the effort.

Granted, this kind of listening goes completely against the norm today. When one buys a 2-CD set of 32 selections sung by Rosa Ponselle, the idea of choosing only one or two selections to listen to seems ridiculous. You just want to put the disc on and let it run. But that is not how a singer thought they would be listened to when they originally made the recording. There can be serious drawbacks and aural consequences to this kind of "straight-through" listening. J. B. Steane provides a realistic scenario:

> (A record of Enrico Caruso) has been bought out of curiosity more than anything else. It opens with *Pagliacci*, 'Veste la giubba': yes, that's a voice alright, and it's coming through, from 1907 or whatever, better than expected. On to more *Pagliacci*, the outburst from Act II. Yes, it's magnificent, the intensity of emotion as well as the sheer voice. On to 'Celeste Aida': hmm. On to 'Di quella pira': ah yes, now that's really something. On to...But no: the records weren't *meant* to played like this, and the ears are already beginning to tire of so much voice and such intensity. Two or three more and our listener will think he (or she) now knows all about Caruso: and yes of course he was magnificent, but the record now placed upon the shelf will repose there for some considerable time to come. And in the mind something not unlike a caricature of Caruso will have taken hold—and only when, eventually, the purchaser chances to return to that record in order to hear a particular aria will the harm be undone, for properly reproduced, that voice (of all of them, past or present) almost always startles with its surpassing beauty. ("A Little Listening," *Opera Now*, June, 1990, p. 50)

Of course, this does not mean that you can't or shouldn't listen to an historical singer's CD straight through. But do try my little exercise. It may alter your perception of listening and add an appreciation of a singer you didn't have before. Always listen intently and briefly.

A General Overview of Reissues of Historical Singers on CD during the 1990s and 2000s

Early on, when I gave talks at the VRCS, a question that I was often asked was, "Where can I find that recording?" That had been a question I, too, had often asked of lecturers, so I made sure to put information into my handouts about where one could find the recordings that were played.

In this section I will discuss CD labels of historical voices and the artists that appear on them. A most frustrating thing about historical re-issue labels is that they regularly go out of print. In some cases, like Romophone, this is most unfortunate, as Romophone produced many important releases of historical singers. Fortunately, one can obtain many of their out-of-print recordings on Amazon.com, from private sellers, and on eBay without too much trouble. It is important for you to know about the availability of these and other, smaller labels (whether they are in print or not) rather than think they are wholly unavailable because the company has gone out of business.

There are a number of companies that are indispensable to the student of vocal art—Marston (still in print), Nimbus (somewhat still in print), Pearl (in print), Preiser (somewhat still in print), Romophone (out of print), Symposium (in print), IRCC (out of print). These labels can often be found on-line in such stores as Amazon.com,

Norbeck Peters and Ford and others. Unfortunately, each such label is a specialty enterprise and may go out of business at any time depending on demand and the economy.

At the time of this writing probably the most important site at which to find many of these labels is Norbeck Peters and Ford (http://www.norpete.com/). They have a huge inventory and access to the releases of many of the smaller companies. They are among the nicest people one can order from. Although it is possible to order online, I always prefer to call so that I can talk with someone. They are extremely knowledgeable and organized (and quick to ship) and very nice to chat with.

Romophone

Romophone was a U. K. label dedicated to restoring and transferring historic recordings of opera singers to CD. It was founded in 1993 by two sisters, Louise and Virginia Barder. Romophone issued its first release in 1993, and ceased operation in 2003 with their final release, *Geraldine Farrar: the Complete Victor recordings 1907–1909*. For a decade, however, they reigned supreme.

Romophone often presented the complete output of a singer on a particular label, and in chronological order—such as the complete Victor recordings of Emmy Destinn. Romophone produced a first-rate disc and were critically praised for their accuracy, faithfulness and presentation of the original material, both discographically and musically. The transfers were done by top restorers in Europe and the U.S. (many by Ward Marston). Texts were not translated, but that was something not expected from such a small organization. The booklet they included, however, was always excellent and comprehensive. Romophone's catalogue included some of the finest singers who ever recorded.

Their policy of releasing complete editions of artists—including un-issued and alternate takes— offers the listener/student/collector unprecedented opportunity to make valuable comparisons among versions of recordings.

Greatly valued are their volumes devoted to the recordings of Claudia Muzio (3), Elisabeth Rethberg (2), Beniamino Gigli (5), Amelita Galli-Curci (4), Rosa Ponselle (3), Pol Plançon, Marcella Sembrich (2), Nellie Melba, Luisa Tetrazzini, Edith Mason, Lucrezia Bori (2), Mattia Battistini, Emmy Destinn, Ernestine Schuman-Heink (2), Giovanni Martinelli, John McCormack (2) Tito Schipa, Leonard Warren, Edmond Clement, Emma Eames, Kirsten Flagstad, Emma Calvé, Léon David, Mario Ancona and many more.

Two complete opera recordings from La Scala, *Il Trovatore* (1930) and *Madama Butterfly* (1929/30), were also in its catalogue, including clever collections such as *Wagner en Français, America the Beautiful, The Century's Greatest Singers in Puccini*, and *Christmas From a Golden Age*. Romophone issues are items highly valued by collectors.

Romophone won a Gramophone Award (Grammy) for Best Historical Recording in 1996, for a set of recordings of Lucrezia Bori, remastered by Ward Marston.

It was in the following year that Marston founded Marston Records.

Marston Records

As the Marston Records website explains,

> In the past, Mr. Marston has produced records for BMG, EMI, CBS, Biddulph, and Romophone. Now, he is bringing his distinctive sonic vision to bear on works released by his own label. Ultimately, his goal is to make the music he re-masters sound "as natural as possible" and "true to life" by "lifting the voices" off his old 78s. Superior liner notes and performances are also part of the plan for Marston, which aims to "promote the importance of preserving old recordings" and make available the works of "great musicians who need to be heard. (http://www.marstonrecords.com/)

Ward Marston started his own label while working for Romophone. Not to be missed are his volumes dedicated to single artists such as the dramatic soprano Johanna Gadski (2 volumes), sopranos Mary Lewis and Rosalia Chalia, mezzo-sopranos Eugenia Mantelli and Conchita Supervia (4), Felia Litvinne, John McCormack, Marcel Journet, Fernando De Lucia, Rosa Ponselle (American Radio Broadcasts, 2), the complete recordings of Vanni-Marcoux, Arthur Endréze, Francisco Viñas, Solomea Krushelnytska, César Vezzanni (2), Rosa Raisa (the first Turandot) and Olympia Boronat.

There is an invaluable series (two volumes as of this writing) of the unpublished Treasures of the Edison Archive, which offers recordings that are often astounding in their rarity and their aural presence. There are also the two wonderful volumes of "Meyerbeer on Record" (both three discs). Marston also specializes in recordings of legendary pianists such as Josef Hofmann, Vladimir de Pachmann, Leopold Godowsky and Jorge Bolet. There is also the entire Enrico Caruso legacy (first for Pearl records and then for Naxos). Altogether, at the time of this writing, Marston has released 88 issues. Most are invaluable.

Pearl and Symposium

Pearl (released by Pavillion Records in the U.K.) and Symposium (also in the U.K.) claim fidelity to the original recording without having done any "cleaning-up" of the sound using equalizers or filters. This is an admirable policy and one that often produces startling results, but it is much dependent on the quality of the original recording. In some instances this method can be grating and hard on the ears. Generally, Pearl concentrates on more famous singers.

Since the LP era, Pearl has released more than 250 albums as well as a number of very important collections. These include the collected recordings of Dame Eva Turner (considered by many to be one of the greatest singers of *Turandot*), the complete recordings of tenor Giovanni Zenatello (8), the complete (at that time) Luisa Tetrazzini (5), the complete Titta Ruffo (6), the early Columbia disks of Rosa Ponselle, as well as discs devoted to Leo Slezak, Ellen Beach Yaw, Emmy Destinn, Herman Jadlowker, and many others.

Pearl produced an absolutely indispensable five-volume (fifteen well-packed CDs) *Singers of Imperial Russia* that offers recordings that are not only extremely rare, but have remarkable presence in their sound quality. These transfers are the aural magic of Keith Hardwick. It is hard to believe that some of these recordings were made more than one hundred years ago. The number of artists represented is huge. I cannot stress enough the importance of this release.

Symposium was founded in 1985, and has always been an issuer of CDs only. Because of their connection with Dr. Harold Wayne, a renowned English collector, Symposium offers some of the rarest 78 rpm disks to be found—many of them unfamiliar even to the most seasoned collectors. As the notes for one of their volumes reads:

> "Dr. Harold Wayne began collecting vocal records in the 1960s, when many collectors considered that it was already too late to assemble a substantial and representative collection of what P.G. Hurst has termed 'the pinnacles of the collector's ambition'. The Wayne collection is the result of an enthusiasm which developed into determination and—as he himself puts it—ultimately into an obsession with records. By correspondence and by telephone, personally and by proxy, by means systematic or serendipitous, but always relentlessly, he scoured Europe, the Americas, and the Antipodes. It is a collection which, for its scope, its completeness, its state of preservation, and for the importance of some of the singers of whom it holds specimens which are thought to be unique, is probably unparalleled."

Wayne amassed a huge collection that included many one-only copies. We can be thankful and pay tribute to his willingness to share such rarities with the rest of the world.

Since 1989, Symposium has released about forty volumes on CD. These include the generally unknown work of Giovanni Gravina, Guerrina Fabbri, Elena Teodorini, Giuseppe Kaschmann and Fanny Toresella. Much of the tradition that we now take for granted stems from the artistic struggle and work of such singers as these. Dr. Wayne's collection and Symposium's preservation of that collection in order to provide it to the world is a blessing.

Nimbus (Prima Voce Series)

The Prima Voce series of Nimbus is another British series that seems to have gone out of print. Over the years it amassed 154 releases. It was the brainchild of former Scottish Opera bass, Norman Wright, in 1988. Although the series produces no new releases, selections from their catalogue can be bought easily at their website and from Internet stores. Nimbus is an important label in preserving the historical voice. Their unconventional method of recording early acoustical and electrical singers (played back acoustically, through a horn, and then recorded via micro-phone thereby picking up natural room ambiance) is controversial.

> Prima Voce puts the performance first. Our aim in transferring 78s to compact disc is simple: to allow the full musical enjoyment of these recordings without the distraction of intrusive surface noise between the performer and the listener. This is achieved by a process which re-records rather than re-masters the original sound, a combination of the best of the latest and earliest technologies in sound reproduction. (http://www.wyastone. co.uk/prima-voce-series)

How this was done:

> They constructed a small, acoustically ideal "hall", where they placed a specially con-structed horn gramophone equivalent to the best models made in the early 20th Century. Thorn needles were used, as they produced the best sound. Digital microphones were placed in the tiny hall and a mint copy of the 78 played on the gramophone while the sound engineers recorded the playback digitally from outside the hall. Thus the voices were finally allowed to resonate in ideal playback circumstances in acoustically perfect surroundings. The results are much more satisfying than before, as the resonance of the little hall frees the voices from the acoustically dry recording rooms where the originals were made. Originally, only people with the highest quality gramophone placed in a room with fine acoustics (obviously a rare combination in a home) could have heard similar results. Nimbus has now made these wonderful old singers palatable to the ears of a more general modern audience than only the collectors and specialists, always a small minor-ity, who cannot help but be delighted as well. (January 16, 2015, Greg Stanford, http:// anotheramerica.org/category/the-operatic-ear/

Many purists take exception to the validity of the Nimbus process, but J.B. Ste-ane defends it:

> Nimbus are what is hedgingly called "controversial'. That is, for every youngster who suddenly sits up and says "I never knew these old records could sound like that", there is an expert who can scarcely conceal the pity and incredulity provoked when someone such as myself admits to frequently playing them with pleasure. Three purely subjective facts arise out of this present listening: on two occasions, like the newcomer instanced above, I sat up during the long session, with surprise at a sud-den vividness—this was once when switching to Nimbus to compare the first of the (Galli-Curci) Trovatore arias, and then at the start of the same disc with the sound of Lakmé's Bell Song—and the other fact is that I have never enjoyed the (Galli-Curci) Hamlet record so much as now on Nimbus, or thought it so fine a performance, the sound having previously seemed boxy and over-bright with the hardness of those ear-ly electricals. (John B. Steane, *Gramophone)*

As Steane mentions, many greatly dislike the sound of Nimbus CDs. I am not among them. I am very fond of Nimbus CDs. Not only for their admittedly quirky sound, but for the excellent program sequencing they offer. One tends to forget that historical singer releases need to be programmed— in some cases very carefully. Some companies prefer to program chronologically by matrix number, while others prefer to create listening programs. This is because the recordings were not originally made as a series or sequence and are therefore not meant to be listened to in one continuing sitting of twenty. Creating a collection of an individual singer can be tricky. There must be a logical (or inventive) playing order that provides the best "portrait" of that singer, as well as to enhance the listener's enjoyment.

I tend to prefer the Prima Voce series from Nimbus as appendices to the more "up-front," occasionally dry, but present sound of most other labels. Nimbus provides the listener with an alternate aural picture of a singer's voice, a hint of how they might have sounded when singing in a concert hall. Each listener will have to decide the kind of restoration they prefer.

Budget-priced and having a large catalogue, the Nimbus Prima Voce series offers such singers as Enrico Caruso, Frieda Hempel, Maria Ivogün, Luisa Tetrazzini (2), Lilli Lehmann, Lotte Lehmann, Antonio Cortis, Giovanni Martinelli (2), Feodor Chaliapin, Nellie Melba, Amelita Galli-Curci (2), Marcella Sembrich, Igor Gorin (2), Lev Sibiryakov, Vladimir Kastorsky, John Charles Thomas (2) and many more who are often eye-opening when first heard. Prima Voce also has some inventive collections—"Singers" of Covent Garden, Berlin, La Scala, New York Metropolitan Opera, the Liceo, the Mariinsky Theatre, Moscow, and *The Era of Adelina Patti,* as well as collections that serve to introduce new listeners to historical singers: "Great Singers" (2), "Great Divas" (2), "Legendary Tenors," and "Legendary Baritones."

Mention must be made of two special Prima Voce Collections, *The Golden Age of Singing* and *Treasury of Opera, Volumes I and II.* The first, *Golden Age,* is a remarkable four-volume release that appeared in 2001. Each volume has two CDs. The eight CDs together have a total of 149 selections. With excellent liner notes by J.B. Steane, this is a perfect way to begin a journey with historical singers. But there is another option as well. The second massive collection, *Treasury of Opera, Volumes I and II* consists of eleven CDs (Volume I, six CDs; Volume II, five CDs). The many, many selections date from 1906 to 1943. For an overall view of early operatic recordings, this is an excellent choice. These are 181 selections culled from the Prima Voce catalogue. For the novice, it is a perfect introduction to the glories of the 78 rpm era. Each volume costs between $21.00 and $28.00. Thus, if you spent $50.00 for both sets, each selection costs about twenty-eight cents.

Lebendige Vergangenheit (CD)

The aural priorities of the German firm, Preiser, are somewhere between Pearl and Romophone. The company's origins were as a labor of love, as noted on their website:

> "Over a period of decades, under the direction of Prof. Schmidt, thousands of unique recordings were transferred from original shellac records to master tapes. They provided the basis for the series "Legendary Voices "—which is probably the last and

only "catalogue" of this size in the world to present the great singers of the past century in a sound quality that is extremely close to the original...

As this series began on LPs, their catalogue is vast, making it one of the most important resources for a serious collector, student, or vocal historian. Attributable to the move to CD, the reproduction quality of the original recordings is often quite stunning. There are many gems in the Preiser catalogue. Just as the collections from Romophone, Marston, Pearl, Symposium, and Nimbus, almost all are worth owning.

IRCC

Although their recordings are now available only second hand, one of the more interesting companies was the now defunct International Record Collector's Society (IRCC). Special mention needs to be made of their four-volume CD series, "Souvenirs from Verismo Operas." It is a treasure trove of rare music rendered by often obscure singers. Little heard today are such verismo operas as Virgilio's *Jana*, Franchetti's *Germania, Figilia di Iorio,* or Pacchierotti's *L'Albatro*. These volumes included translations, photographs and biographies of the singers, and historical comment. They are extremely valuable for their interesting information and rare recordings, as well as the vivid glimpse they give into the heyday of the verismo movement and the fascinating stylistic priorities displayed by the singers during these premier performances. To become familiar with these early discs is to come to understand the verismo movement, its vocal style, and the good and bad traditions that it has bequeathed to us. These recordings can often be found on eBay. Notably, IRCC, having begun during the era of the LP, released more than twenty CDs.

Others

The Tima Club in Italy (http://www.timaclub.it/FRAMEPHL.htm) has released the complete recordings of such singers as soprano Rosetta Pampanini (born in 1900) and tenor Aureliano Pertile (a wonderful eight-CD set that is unfortunately out of print).

There is also Aria Recording, a Barcelona-based enterprise that specializes in preserving the historical recordings of Spanish artists, including sopranos Maria Barrientos, Mercedes Capsir, Josefina Huguet, Graziella Pareto, tenors Miguel Fleta and Jose Palet, and bass Jose Mardones. These CD sets, like the Tima Club volumes, are wonderful documents of singers who are undeservedly almost forgotten (http://www.ariarecording.com/cast/home.htm).

You will also find Hungarian, German, Russian, and Polish companies selling their recordings online that specialize in the historical recordings of their country's artists.

AN INTRODUCTION
TO THE SINGERS

One of the comments I hear most often about today's operatic singing and recordings is that the "great old deads" (artists who pre-date the Long Playing record and the CD) were better singers.

Is that really the case?

As with any art form, there are no hard and fast rules concerning interpretation. A number of factors should be brought into the equation for the result to be as accurate as possible. Singing has to co-exist with a number of outside influences that include audience and political taste in artistic matters of the time, training emphasis in vocal studios, and the predominant modes of accepted artistic expression at the time. One must then take into consideration the recording techniques employed when the recordings were made. I find it interesting that one can recognize strong parallels between earlier singers and more recent singers that are not necessarily detrimental to those of today. All voices are unique, but consider the similarities among the singers below:

- · Luisa Tetrazzini/Joan Sutherland
- · Miliza Korjus/Luciana Serra
- · Frida Leider/Hildegard Behrens
- · Pol Plançon/Samuel Ramey
- · Conchita Supervia/Cecilia Bartoli
- · Marcella Sembrich/Beverly Sills
- · Enrico Caruso/Placido Domingo
- · Beniamino Gigli/Luciano Pavarotti
- · Emmy Destinn/Gwyneth Jones

I don't mean to suggest that these voices are identical, but there are similarities. Those similarities have to do with timbre, technique, or the manner of singing. What this demonstrates is, that during the course of vocal history, a certain type of excellence re-appears with some frequency, subject to variation brought about by changes in the teaching of vocal studios, artistic preferences, and the world situation.

The state of recording today is, of course, markedly different from 1910. Aside from sound quality, the most important difference (and one that concerns us here) is recording time restrictions. In the earliest years (1900–1950) artists were hampered by there being a more or less presumed maximum of four minutes per side in which to record their interpretation of an aria when fitting that aria onto one side of a 78 rpm disk. This often resulted in brutally cut versions of music that would have been performed in twice the amount of time on stage. To judge an early artist without taking such things into consideration is unfair and unrealistic. How can it be established, for instance, whether Emmy Destinn sang "D'amor sull'ali rosee" from *Il trovatore* more slowly on stage than in the studio? Technically, we can't.

However, by listening carefully to her recording, noting her reserves of breath, the ease of her production, and the feel and phrasing she exhibits during the recording, you can almost (and I stress *almost*) reconstruct the slower, more relaxed, interpretive tempo that she probably used on stage. This is, of course, conjecture. However, there is definitely a difference between how a singer recorded an aria and its stage rendition. Lily Pons, for instance, made a recording of the bell song from *Lakmé* for RCA Victor in 1930. It is a two-sided 10-inch record that takes a total of 6 minutes and 27 seconds. On stage, when Lily Pons sang this aria, it took a full minute longer.

In matters of technique we are on more solid ground. 78 rpm recordings are quite like a live performance. Although an artist or producer could reject a take of an aria after it was recorded, a new one had to be immediately made to replace it if they intended to release a recording of that music. This is why recordings of such technicians as Lilli Lehmann, Luisa Tetrazzini, Maria Galvany and Marcella Sembrich are such remarkable documents. Without splicing, editing, or any other methods, these recordings exhibit a technical accuracy that was often staggering.

Are these singers better than more recent singers; say Joan Sutherland, Beverly Sills, or Edita Gruberova? Not according to the great number of live performances available today of these contemporary singers. Their approach to music and their artistic priorities, however, are quite different.

You can find both good and bad singers in all eras of the art. One often comes across recordings from the 1900s and wonders why these singers were allowed to make recordings at all. It is a given that in the year 2095, listeners and collectors will find recordings made by some of today's operatic artists and wonder the same thing. This is a matter of taste—which tends to alter with some rapidity—and a unique layering of factors that combine to produce what is considered "the art of singing" during a specific period of time.

A recent example of such changing in taste is the bel canto movement of the 1950s and 60s. In the 1920s, singers who specialized in bel canto works were considered anachronistic. Thirty-five years later, with the arrival of Maria Callas, Joan Sutherland, and Marilyn Horne, the situation reversed.

In the 1920s, this change of vocal priorities in studios coincided with a surge in the popularity of the verismo movement and the autonomic power of the conductor.

In the 1920s (and, again, after 1975) one finds opera conductors pruning scores of extraneous notes, taking liberties away from singers, and presenting re-studied performances that are often antiseptically clean, but having little emotional impact.

There is a problem with this. Opera's existence depends on the singers who interpret their roles. A singer cannot interpret music with artistic individuality if they are not encouraged to use their imagination. Taking away a singer's ability to infuse personal interpretation—whether it is in the form of ornamentation or stylistic subtleties of rhythm and tempo, or vocal inflections, you rob the music of its ability to breath and live.

Anyone who doubts this can easily find proof by comparing recordings of Verdi's *Rigoletto* as conducted by Jonel Perlea in 1956 with Roberta Peters, Jussi Bjoerling, and Robert Merrill, to that conducted by Riccardo Muti in 1988 with Giorgio Zancanaro, Daniela Dessi, and Vincenzo LaScala. Muti brings out elements and colors in the orchestral fabric that one rarely hears, while offering a crisply accurate vision of the work that clings to the textbook. Perlea, a less-polished conductor than Muti, provides a taut, living drama. He does so by allowing the singers to contribute their own concepts, even while maintaining a careful rein over things. Whether one agrees with Perlea's (or the singer's) concepts, it remains that a theatrical whole is being presented, whereas with Chailly's scrupulous version, there is the cool aura of a recording studio. Further, there is an uncomfortable feeling of, "look how careful we are not to corrupt Verdi's music."

No matter what purists believe, the thing that keeps operatic music fresh is a singer's imagination. It is the single quality that makes one sit up and take notice; that makes a given phrase stay with you such that when you hear other artists sing that music, you listen in vain for that same illuminating touch. This is not genius, it is artistic creativity based upon a free use of imaginative coloration. The ideal situation is for such a singer to be paired with a like-minded conductor—*then* you will find true magic.

A great artist is often a different creature from a great singer. They do not necessarily come in the same package. The great singer will produce glorious sounds that can seem unconnected to interpretation. A great artist may make questionable sounds that, through the originality of gift and temperament provide a fully-rounded aural portrait of a character. Luciano Pavarotti was a great singer. He was not a great artist. Conversely, Marta Mödl was a great artist, but not a great singer. There are, of course, those who fit into both arenas. They would include Feodor Chaliapin, Alfredo Kraus, Placido Domingo, and Jonas Kaufmann.

There is to be considered, too, the factors that went into making recordings over the decades in comparison to the factors now involved in recording. These days, operatic love duets can be recorded without either singer ever setting eyes on the other; they can be in different cities or even different countries. Like skilled surgeons, editors know exactly how and where to make silent splices so that the listener hears only the most perfect rendition possible. The booklets that accompanied the recordings of Joan Sutherland's second *Lucia di Lammermoor* and Beverly

Sills' *Roberto Devereux* make a point of stating that both singers were so concerned about interpretive honesty and continuity that when it came to their final scenes during the recording, they sang them in one take. I found it ironic that a record company would emphasize such a statement, hoping to impress its listeners. After all, isn't that exactly what Sills and Sutherland would have done in an audienced operatic performance?

Another consideration is the preferred type of voice for a role. This changes not only from era to era, but from country to country as well. Today, in Germany, the singer of Donna Elivra in Mozart's *Don Giovanni* often has a heavier voice than the singer of Donna Anna—the exact opposite of what is preferred in America. It is not a matter of which country is correct, but a matter of aural preference. Because one usually hears a certain type of voice sing a role does not mean that it cannot be sung equally well by a voice of a completely different size and weight. Success depends entirely on the singer's technique and suitability to the music. Despite the differences in their voice and approach, it would be difficult to choose as "correct" between Maria Ivogün's "Martern aller Arten" and Joan Sutherland's. Although Ivogün is lighter in weight than Sutherland, there is a feisty quality to her singing that is as appealing as the heavy thrust of Sutherland's brilliant coloratura. They are completely different, yet each is immensely satisfying.

Every era of singing boasts its great singers and great technicians, just as it must admit its failures—ludicrous artists who somehow became popular, who, when reckoned with hindsight, are judged uninspired and completely forgettable.

The whole of this book is devoted to singers who have intrigued me in one way or another throughout the decades. There are so many fine singers on recordings, not only those who are famous, but many who were less renowned. There are a great many who are *not* listed here, but I will leave those discoveries to your own findings. I have always felt that record collectors and lovers of the human voice need to be reminded, prodded if you will, to remember some of these many singers. The rewards are many. We all know that Caruso and Gigli were wonderful, but how about Giuseppe Borgatti or Bernardo de Muro? I am myself guilty of this. For instance, I know intellectually that Eleanor Steber (1914–1990) was not only a fine artist, she was actually one of the great singers. But, until I put on one of her recordings—usually by mistake or at the prompting of someone else—I tend to forget just how wonderful she was. It is then that I begin to have a new appreciation for her talent.

I hope to promote this recognition by the reader with this series of appreciations. Perhaps in reading them you will discover a singer who is new to you. Or you might remember a singer you relegated to a far corner of your awareness. I hope to help you rediscover the good and the bad points about their singing—their humanity. If, after reading these words, you feel compelled to seek out a singer's recordings to re-listen or to discover them for yourself, then I have done my job.

A Special Note About Adelina Patti and Mattia Battistini

Before we move on to the main section of this book, it is important to say a word or two about two artists who are crucial to the history of recorded vocal art, soprano Adelina Patti and baritone Mattia Battistini. They are the mater prior and pater prior of all those singers who recorded after them. Both were vitally important and influential.

Adelina Patti was born in 1843 in Madrid, and died in 1919. She made her debut in 1859 as *Lucia di Lammermoor* with the New York Academy of Music. In 1861 she was invited to sing Amina in *La sonnambula* at Covent Garden in London. The following decades saw her become *the* prima donna of international operatic stages. Her final appearance was in October of 1914 when she sang for a Red Cross concert to aid the victims of World War I.

Patti did not make records until December of 1905, when she was 63. Of course, by that time her voice was not that of the youthful, coloratura dynamo that critics wrote rapturously of during her prime. There are, however, clear hints of her vocal allure and demeanor that help one to understand why she was so famous. Her ego was certainly a healthy one. After hearing her records, Landon Ronald, her accompanist, recalls her exclaiming in awe and, he believes, naïve excitement: "What a voice! What an artist! Oh, now I understand why I am Patti!"

In 1992 Pearl released an incomplete collection of twenty-two of her recordings which is still in print. In 1998, Marston Records released her complete recordings made for the Gramophone and Typewriter Company in 1905 (G&T), thirty-two sides, but that album is no longer in print. In 2005, the English label, Symposium, released an album with all but two of her sides that is presently available.

There are also six selections on a Nimbus disc called *The Era of Adelina Patti* that features Patti and contemporary singers of the soprano.

For one who, at first, turned her nose up at the process of recording, Patti certainly cranked out quite a few recordings in the little time she allotted to the project.

She recorded selections from *Le nozze di Figaro, Norma, Don Giovanni, Faust, Martha, Mignon* as well as a number of songs, and the "Il Bacio Waltz" by Arditi.

J. B. Steane makes an important observation in *The Grand Tradition*:

> At times one still veers between laughter and rage at Patti's records...It is not, as is often said, the condition of her voice that so often spoils these records, nor is it the primitive technique of recording. It is rather that certain features of Patti's style at this date simply were not musical. (*The Grand Tradition*, Scribners, 1974)

Despite this, there are some very important Patti records. Aside from a bit of vulgar phrasing, the clean, clear timbre of her voice is quite special. As one listens to her discs, one momentarily forgets that the soprano was sixty-three years old when she recorded, and had had a long and fulfilling career on the stage.

When I introduce Adelina Patti to new listeners, I usually choose two contrasting records. One is her recording of Amina's "Ah non credea" from Bellini's *La sonnambula*. Although the voice has obviously aged, the control and phrasing is still remarkable and the basic timbre of her middle voice quite haunting—also her trill is still intact, rolling with a freedom and beauty that is hard to describe.

The other selection that I play is the "Calesera" by Yrader that shows Patti in playful and flirty form, with remarkable energy and vocal verve, and high notes thrown into the room's acoustics. This was a typical salon song of the period that Patti often used to entertain guests. Patti's charm practically jumps out of the grooves. Oddly, the record was withdrawn from circulation a few weeks after its release. The reason rumored was attributable to Patti's overly flamboyant singing that was considered quite scandalous!

There are many records that Patti left that are worth more than an occasional hearing.

Mattia Battistini (1856–1928) was born thirteen years after Patti, but belongs to the same school of singing. He was known as "The King of Baritones" and made many wonderful records between 1902 (when he was 46) and 1924. His career lasted almost fifty years.

Battistini made his debut in 1878 at the Teatro Argentina in Rome, in Donizetti's *La favorita*. He never appeared at the Metropolitan Opera or at any other American opera house. This was due to his dislike for ocean travel. This mattered little, as his recordings established his reputation in the Americas while he traveled to London, Barcelona, Madrid, throughout Italy, Paris, Lisbon, Berlin, Vienna, Prague, and Budapest. Particular of his stage appearance, he traveled with his own costumes, thirty trunk-fulls! He was especially loved in Russia, where he became one of the aristocracy's most beloved singers. He first went to Russia in the early 1890s, and returned every season for twenty-three years. His repertoire was large (at least eighty roles), including roles in *Rigoletto, Il Guarany, La forza del destino, I puritani, Lucia di Lammermoor, Il trovatore, Aïda, Ernani, Werther, The Demon, Eugene Onegin, Gli Ugonotti, Dinorah, L'Africaine,* and *Il barbiere di Siviglia*.

His voice was a mellifluous high baritone with a strong, masculine timbre and a range to an easy high A.

Desmond Shawe-Taylor in *The New Grove Dictionary of Opera* writes:

His voice was an unusually high baritone, verging on the range of a tenor. The quality was noble: clear, strong, vibrant, capable also of a deliberately 'villainous' harshness when required; then suddenly melting into the extremes of tenderness and delicacy." (*New Grove Dictionary of Opera*, Oxford University Press, 1992)

Battistini's legato singing was exemplary, and his control of dynamics and shadings were beautifully sculpted. Because of his bel canto training, his sense of line and the inner workings of phrases make his recordings fascinating to listen to and to study. Due to the rapid emergence of the Italian verismo movement in the 1890s, Battistini began to be considered an "old fashioned singer." His training, and the emphases he uses, predates the verismo movement by a number of decades.

Edmund St. Austell notes on his website: http://greatoperasingers.blogspot.com:

Battistini did not sound like the baritones of today, who are, virtually without exception, verismo singers, with dark, powerful voices that are often not very flexible and tend to a rather monochromatic intensity of volume, well suited to the Verdi and Puccini roles, but perhaps less so to the kinds of romantic operas that were popular in the 19th century. Battistini can sound like a tenor on occasion, but it is simply the open sound and the lightened volume. Because he was a bel canto trained singer, his voice evidences great flexibility and range, and his pronunciation, like that of the bel canto tenors, is extremely clear. Battistini was an intelligent singer, extremely musical by nature, and he took the dramatic end of opera very seriously. He was by all accounts a superb actor, with innumerable costumes that were historically accurate. His Italian is very refined, and the open and closed e's and o's are everywhere observed, and are capable of creating the effect of cultured gentility (if the role is heroic) or explosive vulgarity, if demanded by the role. So great was the esteem in which he was held that Massenet actually re-wrote *Werther* so that the title role could be sung by Battistini.

Battistini was a singer who was loved by audiences, critics, and colleagues alike. Unlike Patti, he left a large legacy, one hundred-twenty published sides, all of them worth collecting. Battistini is one of those singers who made no bad record. There is something to enjoy and learn from each of them.

When asked why he did not teach, Battistini replied: 'My school is in my records.' During a period of twenty-two years he made a great many and they must be numbered among the best and most revealing of any singer of that era. (Michael Scott, *The Record of Singing Volume I*, p. 104, Charles Scribner's Sons, 1977)

His recordings were not perfect and some may question certain stylistic proprieties, but across them all, there is a voice securely based in his earlier bel canto vocal technique and an individual, instinctive sensitivity to the music that he sings.

J.B. Steane writes:

His singing is never pedestrian, but is always animated by the detailed care of the artist and the strong feeling of the man. His records are quite as remarkable for their expressiveness as they are for what we might designate as 'pure singing'."(Liner notes for 1986 *Mattia Battistini, King of Baritones*, EMI seven-LP set)

Throughout the decades, Battistini's work has always been popular on LP and, later, CD. During the LP era his recordings appeared on TAP, Olympus, Scala, and EMI—most notably, the beautifully presented seven-LP boxed set: *King of the Baritones*, released by EMI in 1986.

In July of 2015, a complete Battistini collection (a six-CD set) was released by Ward Marston on his label, Marston Records. The set is elegantly produced and restored. If one wants Battistini's entire output, this is the collection to own. Lovingly presented by Marston, the Battistini voice has astounding brilliance and presence. Detailed notes by both Ward Marston and critic Michael Aspinal round out a most important historical release of 2015.

If one is not interested in owning his entire legacy, there are some alternatives:

In 1997, Romophone released a two-disc set of forty-two selections (including two unpublished sides) that represent Battistini's complete early recordings (1902–1911). They were restored by Ward Marston. One can still find this set on eBay.

Preiser released a three-CD set of recordings covering 1911 to 1914 with fifty selections, and in 2009 issued a single CD of his final recordings in chronological order from 1921 to 1924. The five discs of these Romophone and Preiser releases contain 113 of his 120 sides.

In the late 1990s Pearl released three CDs of the baritone, and Symposium has released two single CDs.

Nimbus offers a single CD collection having a cross section of his repertoire and sessions.

Battistini's recorded repertoire includes arias from familiar works, as well as those that are rarely revived: *Le nozze di Figaro, I puritani, Paride e Elena, Maria di Rohan, Maria de Rudenz, Tannhäuser, Faust, Werther* (the baritone version, written for Battistini), *Thaïs, Quo Vadis, Rigoletto, Ruy Blas, Herodiade, Nero, Linda di Chamonix, Eugene Onegin, Il barbiere di Siviglia, La forza del destino, La Favorita, La Gioconda, Don Giovanni, La traviata, Otello, Macbeth, Ernani, Don Sebastiano, Zampa, Il Guarany. Hamlet, Lucia di Lammermoor, Un ballo in maschera, Roi de Lahore, Per la Patria, L'Africaine, Guglielmo Tell, I Pagliacci, Tosca, Don Carlo,* and many songs.

I heartily recommend his recordings. They belong in every vocal enthusiast's library.

Maria Barrientos (1883–1946)

This unusual artist and musical prodigy was born in Barcelona. She began her instrumental training at the age of six at the Barcelona Conservatory. At twelve, she received a diploma in piano, violin, and composition. At that time she conducted a performance of her symphony. Vocal studies with Francisco Bonet began two years later at fourteen.

She made her professional operatic debut as Amina in *La sonnambula* at the Teatro Lirico in Barcelona in 1898. She then appeared at the Teatro Novedades, again as Amina in *La sonnambula*, Inez in *L'Africaine* and Lucia in *Lucia di Lammermoor*. Returning to the Lirico she added *Dinorah*; she was Rosina in *Il barbiere di Siviglia*, and Gilda in *Rigoletto*. After that she went to Milan to continue her studies and make her debut as *Lakmé* in 1899 at the Teatro Lirico in Milan. In 1903 she performed at Covent Garden as Rosina. She made her La Scala debut in March 1904 as *Dinorah*. She quickly began to reap tremendous success in Italy, France, Germany, and, especially, in Buenos Aires.

In 1907, she married Jorge Keen, an Argentinian, had a son, and decided to leave the stage. By 1911, the marriage had dissolved and she returned to the stage. Barrientos debuted at the Metropolitan Opera on January 31, 1916 as *Lucia di Lammermoor* with Giovanni Martinelli as Edgardo and Pasquale Amato as Enrico. She was quite loyal to the Metropolitan Opera for the next four years, singing such roles as *Lakmé*, *Mireille*, Amina in *La sonnambula*, Elvira in *I puritani,* Gilda in *Rigoletto*, Rosina in *Il barbiere di Siviglia*, Philine in *Mignon*, and the U.S. premiere of Rimsky-Korsakov's *Le Coq D'Or* in March of 1918. While she was popular in the United States, she was immensely popular in South America and Spain. Her repertoire consisted of 22 operas. She continued to sing in opera after she left the Met, notably in France, and by 1924 had retired from the operatic stage. During the following years she concentrated on giving recitals. From 1939 to 1945 she was a professor at the Buenos Aires Conservatory. She died the next year at the age of 63.

The Voice

Maria Barrientos proves to be a satisfying performer on recordings—if with some qualifications. During her career she recorded for two companies: Italian Fonotipia (1905–1906) and then Columbia (1916–1928). She began to record with Columbia just two months after her debut at the Metropolitan Opera; those recordings present the soprano in her artistic prime.

In his book, *The Grand Opera Singers of Today,* Henry Lahee wrote of Maria Barrientos at the time of her Metropolitan debut in January of 1916:

> (Her) voice is amazingly small but possesses resonance and carrying power, and she can emit ppp [pianissimi] tones that float like feathers down to the furthermost reaches of the house. A typical coloratura voice, flexible to a degree and in quality of tone often flute-like with all this quality implies. Nothing in her work affords greater pleasure than the infallible certainty of her intonation, attaining high E flat without effort. (Auger Down Books, Brattleboro, VT, 1912)

Her recordings certainly bear this out. They show her obvious delight in climbing not only to the high E flat but also high E and (at least on the Fonotipias) high F. But, it is true, her voice was of Dresden-like delicacy having a finely-spun vibrato. On none of her recordings does she exhibit the spontaneous outbursts of a Tetrazzini or a Sembrich. From all accounts, this is in keeping with the rather shy, introverted woman she was described as, who never made comments about her colleagues and who remained somewhat aloof socially. She was never known for being temperamental, but was calm and focused. Lauri Volpi claimed, however, that she could be "vibrant and willful." (*Voci parallele* Milan, Aldo Garzanti, 1955, from unpublished translation by George Nyklieck)

Photographs of the soprano generally do not give any hint of this. Indeed, in most she seems sadly withdrawn. Along with her lovely face, there is a calm, pensiveness to her expression much of the time which is quite haunting. Giacomo Lauri-Volpi noted:

> Barrientos was an artist of exceptional distinction on stage where the naturalness, spontaneity, and intelligence of her acting were best revealed in those roles that lie midway between romantic and modern operatic works…Her voice had an extensive range and was of virtuoso caliber, although it did not possess a distinctive timbre…Her technique was founded upon an exemplary method of breath control and modulation, producing unforgettable effects in the extreme upper range – slender, silvery notes as light as a feather, issuing from a mouth opened to its maximum. Audiences held their breath at hearing these tones, magically suspended in midair like tiny crystalline bubbles liable to burst at any moment into a thousand glittering fragments. (ibid)

From her recordings it seems that Maria Barrientos' voice was narrow in focus and could take on a nasal tinge that is colorful. She was a clever singer and knew how to make her merits work best for her. While her intonation was impeccable, her agility considerable, and her tonal sheen on high exquisite, there was one serious idiosyncratic drawback to her technique—a tendency to change vowel placement during complex scale passages—singing "Ahhh-oooo-ahh" in such arias as Zerlina's bravura "Or son sola" (*Fra Diavolo*), Dinorah's "Shadow Song," or Philine's "Polonaise" from *Mignon*. This creates some odd sounds that can be unintentionally comic. I have never found any reference to the reason that this peculiar quirk appeared in her singing method, but it was definitely caused by an unnecessary changing of facial position during scale passages.

Frances Alda, the New Zealand soprano, once bluntly remarked that "…[Maria Barrientos] was not at all pretty and made tremendous grimaces when she sang; but she was a very chic little person." (*Men Women and Tenors,* Boston 1937, page 74) I suspect Alda was carrying a bit of personal baggage—she married the man that Barrientos had once been engaged to. Barreintos had been engaged to Giulio Gatti-Casazza, the manager of La Scala Opera in Milan (1898 to 1908). In 1906 Barrientos broke their engagement, although to their credit, they remained friends. He was head of the Metropolitan Opera from 1908 to 1935. In 1910, he married Frances Alda (they divorced in 1928). Barrientos came to the Met in 1916, and the two sopranos were colleagues, not rivals, for roles, although I suspect they were not the best of friends. One of the main rivals for Barrientos' roles was Frieda Hempel.

Another idiosyncratic fault with Barrientos' technique was a curious hesitancy in her vocal production—almost a delayed phonation—especially during high staccato work. At times her staccati would sound as if they were stuck in her throat.

Selected Recordings

Maria Barrientos recorded fifty-seven selections for two companies: twenty-three sides for Italian Fonotipia (1905–1906) and thirty-four sides for American Columbia (1917–1928).

During the era of the LP in America, OASI offered three and 1/2 LP volumes devoted to Barrientos, that included thirty-nine selections, most taken from her Columbia recordings. Imports from such companies as Odeon offered her Fonotipias. The only important recording missing from the CD collections available today is the 1918 Columbia, "Ah fors e lui—Sempre libera" from Verdi's *La traviata*. This was an important role in her repertoire. The old OASI LP volumes included that wonderful recording.

At the time of this writing there are two single CDs of her work; an Opal CD (produced by Pearl) which offers thirteen of her twenty-three published Fonotipia sides (1905–06) and the artistically priceless 1928 Columbia creator discs of Manuel de Falla's "Seven Popular Spanish Songs" accompanied by the composer. There is also a CD in Nimbus' Prima Voce series devoted to eighteen of Barrientos' Columbia disks.

Better, though more difficult to find, is a two-CD set on Aria Recordings (released in 1996), a small label based in Barcelona (www.ariarecording.com). Their catalogue consists only of thirty-one releases, but they include some of the most important historical Spanish singers: Miguel Fleta, Josefina Huguet, Regina

Pacini, Graziella Pareto, Antonio Cortis, José Palet, and others. The program on the Barrientos' Aria release is excellent, (although some of the masters they used are not) including nineteen of the twenty-three Fonotipia sides, and fourteen of the Columbia sides (an additional nine can be found on the Nimbus release.)

If you are interested in this soprano and want to collect her recordings, the Aria Recordings release is the one to get. If you are a completist you should get the Aria Recordings set and the Nimbus. That way you will have nineteen of the twenty-three Fonotipias and twenty-three of the thirty-four Columbias, in addition to the Columbia De Falla "Seven Popular Spanish Songs" recorded in France in 1928.

Auber – Or son sola (*Fra Diavolo*) – Fonotipia, 1906

Although accompanied only with piano, this is a splendid performance full of color and imagination. "Or son sola" boasts some ravishing high notes, smooth legato, and an elegant octave jump to high D. The concluding, florid "Gia per la danza" is a remarkable tour de force of coloratura singing with an unaccompanied cadenza notable for its surety of intonation and the ease with which Barrientos emits high E naturals. The florid work in this aria does, however, underscore her idiosyncratic modification of vowels when singing complex coloratura. The staccato work is truly feather-like and all of the scales, trills, and arpeggios are spun out with great control and brilliance. All in all, this is a remarkable performance. The final unaccompanied cadenza (more than thirty seconds) highlights her excellent pitch and easy access to high E. The only performance of this aria that comes close to Barrientos' classic rendition is one recorded for RCA Victor by Roberta Peters in 1956.

Bellini – Polonaise (*I puritani*) – Fonotipia, 1904

Maria Barrientos sang *I puritani* seven times with the Metropolitan Opera Company. This piano-accompanied version was recorded a number of years before Barrientos arrived at the Met. She sings Bellini's florid lines and trills with grace and an inherent understanding of the correct style. Although heavy with cuts, they are reasoned and the piece is treated with seriousness by Barrientos. Especially fine is the return to the main melody. It is here that Barrientos pulls out an array of ornamental stops offering fine flights of staccati and finely-rolled trills. Her command of pitch is excellent and she brings the aria to a rousing finish with a cadenza which passes over a pointed, staccato high E; then a fine D.

Bellini: Mad Scene (*I puritani*) – Columbia, 1918

This is one of this soprano's best efforts. She obviously feels a true affinity with this music as its phrasing emerges not only masterfully, but also deeply felt. Because of this, I am surprised that she did not record this aria for Fonotipia earlier in her career. The break into chest voice on the phrase "Qui giurava esser fedele" is obviously intentional and works surprisingly well as an expressive device. It was an "effect" used during that era of Italian and Spanish sopranos with varying success. Because of Barrientos' handling of this effect it comes off as an added tinge of pathos. Her legato is sweet and firm and not once (despite the tempo) does one get the impression that the soprano is simply going through the motions. There is a definite interpretation at work here. The end of the aria is quite beautifully done.

"Vien diletto" is presented as a florid delight, although in the first verse she sings the music as written and adds little if any ornamentation. It is in the second verse that things get interesting. Here Barrientos' use of *rallentandi* is excellent. Although her version is less ornamented than that of her Met rival, Freida Hempel, her ornaments are well chosen and the short cadenza before the interpolated high E-flat works very well. The E-flat is sung as a beautiful, long note of exquisite color.

Bellini – Come per me sereno (*La sonnambula*) – Fonotipia, 1906

Even though Maria Barrientos first sang Amina in *La sonnambula* at the Metropolitan Opera on March 3, 1916, the role had been in her repertoire since her 1898 debut. She went on to sing Amina four more times in the house and two times on tour. At the time of her first performance of the role, an unsigned review in the *Herald* noted:

> ...chief honors were awarded the top notes of Mme. Barrientos...All the sensational qualities of singing previously revealed by Mme. Barrientos were employed with unusual effect—the beauty of her voice, the unimpeachable accuracy of her attack, the daring of her skyscraping staccato, and the swelling on a tone until the climax seemed thrilling—were all in evidence. Yet her singing of the "Ah, non giunge" left something to be desired, for the limited volume of her extraordinary voice in the big spaces at the opera house was more noticeable that at any earlier time...(Metropolitan Opera Archives, accessed November, 2014)

Bellini's music suited Barrientos' temperament and she is especially fine in this aria with its contemplative serenity. It should be noted that she recorded the aria and its cabaletta a half step lower. One wonders at the necessity for this as her voice was of great height. There are some wonderful interpolations here including a fine high D in the middle of "Come per me" that is not intrusive due to the way Barrientos approaches and delivers the note. She offers another cadenza of staccati before concluding the aria. The cabaletta "Sovra il sen" is taken at a gracious tempo, but even so one notices her tendency to mutilate certain vowel sounds. Her ornaments are primarily of the staccati variety but they are nicely done. The florid challenges of the ending are met well and Barrientos phrases better than most sopranos during the intricate coloratura. She offers a small cadenza that leads to a fine, penultimate high D.

Bellini – Ah non giunge (*La sonnambula*) – Fonotipia, 1904, Columbia, 1920

The 1904 Fonotipia record begins rather stately but then quickly increases tempo once Barrientos enters. She is obviously very comfortable with this music and has put thought into her delivery, using much *rallentando* to accent the loveliness of her upper register and to finesse phrases. The reprise has some fine ornamentation, most of it staccato (some being quite brilliant), and the pianist has no trouble following her pulling back and forth of the music (rubato). To top it all, she adds a short, interesting, unaccompanied cadenza that leads to a penultimate high F, perfectly struck and beautifully sustained.

The 1920 Columbia recording is also successful in delivery and similar to the earlier Fonotipia disk (minus the high F). The tempo begins stately and remains that way rather than becoming frenetic while Barrientos lovingly caresses her vocal line. The coloratura is clean and even and the second verse features nice ornamentation with an unaccompanied cadenza at the finish that is in keeping with the mood Barrientos has set, allowing her some nicely pointed high staccati and lovely *morendi* effects.

David: Charmant Oiseau (*La perle du Brésil*) – Columbia, 1917
This opera premiered in Paris in 1851, and Zora's Act III aria was very popular with high sopranos during the early 20th century. Historically, it seems to be the first French opera aria for soprano to incorporate a voice/flute cadenza. Although the opera disappeared from the world stages and has not been revived in many decades, the aria has always remained somewhat popular. Barrientos' recording was up against such fine renditions as those by Luisa Tetrazzini, Antonida Neshdanova, Maria Michailowa, Selma Kurz, Regina Pinkert, Lucette Korsoff, Ellen Beach Yaw, Emma Calvé and Frieda Hempel. Indeed, artists of almost all nationalities have made recordings of this aria. Its popularity is not difficult to understand. It offers the singer an elegant vocal line and some fine opportunities to display their agility. After the 1950s and Mado Robin, who made a couple of recordings of the aria, it fell out of favor.

The venerable critic, Herman Klein commented on Barrientos' singing of this aria (*Gramophone*, September, 1926):

> So again it is with…Charmant oiseau – you get the same marvelous Barrientos agility and ease combined with the same superlative breath-control and impeccable intonation. Her attack of high notes I consider a model for any singer, whether artist or student, to strive to imitate; it is altogether exceptional.

Klein certainly knew this recording well. The music suited Barrientos and she takes her time with the lovely main melody. Overall, it is one of her loveliest records and one of the best versions of the aria up to that time. The final duet with flute is the traditional one used by most singers and becomes the highlight of this recording. What sets Barrientos' version apart from others is her delicate and exquisite blending with the flute, her spiky, yet gentle, high staccato, the beautifully sculpted phrases, and a truly beautiful trill on high A followed by a sweetly-spun penultimate high D.

Defalla – *Seven Popular Spanish Songs* – Columbia, 1928
Recorded electrically in Paris, these historic creator discs give a fine aural portrait of this soprano's voice. Her authority with this music is unquestionable. DeFalla's accompaniment is supportive and yet quite brilliant on its own.

In the liner notes for the Opal release, Alan Blyth comments: "These (records) disclose a voice surprisingly well-preserved and confirm those special overtones found in the acoustics."

Especially evocative is the lovely "Asturiana" which Barrientos spins with great feeling. This is bettered by a truly haunting performance of the lullaby, "Nana." Both show the lovely quality of Barrientos' upper-middle register; full and easy flowing. A wonderful touch in "Cancion" is her singing of the word "Madre" with its descending 3rd into her round and full chest register—very colorful. The dramatic "Polo" brings the seven songs to a brilliant and very satisfying conclusion. Barrientos gives a wonderfully nuanced reading of these pieces. Valuable creator records, they belong in every home library whether an aficionado of Spanish music, sopranos, or creator recordings.

Delibes – Bell Song (*Lakmé*) – Fonotipia, 1904, Columbia, 1917

Maria Barrientos was born in the year following *Lakmé*'s premiere; she made two recordings of the aria. She first sang Lakmé in 1898, at the age of fifteen. In October of 1904 she recorded a heavily cut, Italian version with piano, for Fonotipia in Milan (Opal CD). As was typical of recordings during that era, only one bell strophe was included. Barrientos had a light, finely-spun voice, but the 1904 disk emphasizes a tart nasality in her singing as well as her idiosyncratic changing of vowels mid-scale. There is also a disconcerting hesitation of attack in the staccato as if the voice will not phonate correctly. Interestingly, after a grand flourish, she eschews the traditional ending to use a chromatic ascent (beginning on high C-sharp) to high E. Although a bit odd, it works.

In March, 1917, just weeks before her final performances of *Lakmé* with the Metropolitan Opera, (March 24, April 4) Barrientos recorded a French version with orchestra for Columbia. Having sung the role many times, this disk finds Barrientos providing a more appropriate somber mood and her singing is more reflective. One of the interesting things about this record is that it demonstrates that although her voice has matured, the peculiar hesitation in staccato attack still appears, proving it was not a condition of youth, but an inherent flaw in her production. She finishes the aria as on the Fonotipia disc. To her credit and the excellence of her technique, the final high E is as just as good as it had been thirteen years earlier.

Donizetti – Regnava nel silenzio (*Lucia di Lammermoor*) – Columbia, 1916
Donizetti – Mad Scene (*Lucia di Lammermoor*) – Columbia, 1916

These two arias from *Lucia di Lammermoor* were the first recordings Maria Barrientos made for Columbia Records on March 14, 1916. This was fitting as Lucia was her Metropolitan Opera debut on January 31, 1916, less than two months earlier. Barrientos sang Lucia at the Met (or on tour) 16 times between 1916 and 1920.

The famous critic of the day, W. J. Henderson, wrote an excellent review of her Met debut for the *New York Sun*. Henderson was one of the few critics at the time who understood the mechanics of singing and his review is a detailed study of Barrientos' voice; its faults and its merits.

Here is a portion of his review:

> Her intonation was almost flawless and her phrasing showed not only command of breath, but musical intelligence. Her mastery of the "messa di voce"—the art of taking a tone pianissimo and making a crescendo and a diminuendo on it—was extraordinarily fine and was used to make some beautiful effects. Her colorature in the first act showed a tendency toward staccato and her runs were not in perfect legato style. She sang "Quando rapito" with excellence in the general plan and with some beautiful touches, but the number was marred by some of the defects mentioned. In the sextet she lacked the tonal power necessary to give that number its proper balance. (Metropolitan Opera Archives, accessed November, 2014)

I find that I like her "Regnava" a great deal. From the outset, Barrientos sets a somber tone and her voice speaks very well in the lower reaches of the aria. There are slight rhythmical shifts that add a frisson of excitement and her manner of breaking into the low register helps emphasize Lucia's fragile mental state. The second verse has some unusual ornaments and her handling of Donizetti's music shows that she is completely familiar with both the style and the content of the music. She adds a rather silly-sounding unaccompanied cadenza and finishes with an absolutely beautiful decrescendo on high A.

Unfortunately, her recording of the cabaletta that follows, "Quando rapito in estasi" went unpublished.

The celebrated Mad Scene is one of Barrientos's great recordings. What Henderson wrote concerning her first *Lucia di Lammermoor* at the Metropolitan Opera holds true for her recording as well:

> In the mad scene she gave a display of her best qualities. Her singing of "Ardon gl'incenci" was marked by taste as well as by much elegance of style and musical intelligence. The cadenza was sung with great care. Perhaps hereafter she will show more abandon in it, but it was delivered with accuracy of style rather than brilliance. Her trill was particularly good and her staccati very clean and musical. It must be added that the soprano seemed to be very nervous and furthermore the house was very warm. Under better conditions she will doubtless sing even better. Her debut was on the whole successful. (Metropolitan Opera Archives, accessed November, 2014)

Her first phrase and the security she exhibits in the lower register tells the listener that this is going to be a special rendition. Throughout, her legato is strong and flows evenly, even when the voice cracks into the chest register (intentional). High phrases are beautifully sculpted and the text is interpreted, not merely vocalized. I especially like the way she set up "Del ciel clemente," which is not only extremely musical but thoughtful and highlights the passage. The famous, customary cadenza with flute is about a minute and a half long and is Barrientos' own composition, which is refreshing. That it is so well thought out and interpreted by Barrientos leaves no doubt where each phrase is going. The accent (as it was with the later soprano, Roberta Peters) is on the elegance of emission rather than dashing bravura.

This is lovely singing with nice trills and high staccato, all interpreted with musical poise. The ending finds Barrientos landing first on a soft high D which rises gently to an easy high E-flat; this performance is not easily forgotten.

Gounod – Waltz Song (*Mireille*) – Columbia, 1916

This is such a silly and wonderful piece, especially when evaluated along-side the rest of Mireille's music. This Act I waltz aria for Mireille, "O légère hirondelle" comes from a December 1864 addition to the original score (that premiered without success in March of that year). Barrientos sang Mireille (with Charles Hackett and Clarence Whitehill) at the Met Premiere of the work on February 18, 1919. The opera was given four performances and has not been revived at that house since. In this recording, Barrientos is obviously having a wonderful time, using her staccato whenever she can. Her singing is clean and clear and the staccati are sung without hesitation. Her use of rubato is excellent and her control over the dynamics is wonderful. In this aria, her vowel changes seem less obtrusive. She sets up the penultimate high D nicely with a brief cadenza and sustains it easily, gaining power and penetration as she goes. Excellent!

Mireille was the last performance Barrientos sang at the Met (on February 28, 1919). From her debut in January of 1916, to her departure from the Metropolitan Opera she sang a total of 116 performances of ten operas.

Handel: Lascia ch'io pianga (*Rinaldo*) – Fonotipia, 1906

One of the earliest recordingss of this aria, this is a rather surprising entry in Maria Barrientos' recorded legacy. Recorded with piano in 1906, she gives a musical and sensitive reading, though nowhere near as scrupulous in style as we are used to today. However, it is an attractive reading, full of emotion as Barrientos displays not only a fine legato, but a solid and attractive lower register.

Meyerbeer – Shadow Song (*Dinorah*) – Fonotipia (13 3/4-inch), 1904, Fonotipia, 1906, Columbia, 1919

The first record that Barrientos made was for the Italian firm Fonotipia and it was unusual: a 13 3/4-inch disk recorded in October of 1904. It can be found on a Symposium CD (The Harold Wayne Collection, Volume XIII, Symposium 1113). Recorded the year of her La Scala debut, this atypical record is a fascinating example of Barrientos's art. The 13 3/4-inch record was a "short-lived but enterprising invention of the Fonotipia company. The objective was to free artists from the tyranny of time: a very little extra would make a great deal of difference." (J.B. Steane, *Gramophone,* 12/93). While it was a good idea, it was not embraced by the recording community.

The recording allows Barrientos four minutes and forty seconds to sing Dinorah's Shadow Song. The added time permits exploiting more sensitivity in her singing, especially in the important echo effects. There is no shortness of bravura, but within the bravura she sounds more relaxed. Barrientos shows considerable charm in her descents into the lower register and certainly is fearless in accessing the top third of her range: high D-flats and E-flats. Unfortunately, the pianist makes a number of mistakes. The cadenza is unaccompanied and sprinkled with cascades of staccati and roulades. The finish has an excellent high E-flat left with a swoop to return to a final high D-flat.

Two years after her Milan debut in *Dinorah,* Maria Barrientos made a second version of this aria, also with piano accompaniment, and also for Fonotipia. The rapid tempi on the recording, and the echo effects highlight her odd, nasal vowel-mangling. A two-sided record, the second side begins at "Qui sola soletta" in the usually cut middle section. This was an unusual move on Fonotipia's part since recordings of that time rarely included that section of the music. There is some lovely singing—all musically sculpted and presented to the listener. Her return to the main melody of the waltz shows her adept ability to phrase coloratura logically. One notices that most of her staccati are immediate and some are actually flung out with true abandon. The final, unaccompanied cadenza is sung with much bravado, and yet with delicacy.

As in her earlier version, Barrientos uses a particular final cadential formula that springs to a fine, sustained high E-flat, into a descending portamento to A-flat, and then a clean leap to a final high D-flat. This was a particularly clever dramatic finish that was used by a number of the lighter sopranos to give the illusion of vocal power. It seems that Barrientos may have been the first to use it on a recording. After her, Amelita Galli-Curci (and other Italian sopranos), as well as Lily Pons, were fond of using it. In the late 1970s, Ruth Welting used this finish as a final flourish in performances of the Proch Variations which she interpolated into the Lesson Scene in *Il barbiere di Siviglia* when singing Rosina at the New York City Opera.

The 1920 Columbia recording of this aria is one of Barrientos' most famous recordings. It highlights her talents as well as her (at times) annoying vowel modifications. The astute listener will notice how well Barrientos "places" her voice so that no awkward or ugly notes emerge. Interestingly, the Nimbus CD, with its ambisonic method of transferring, de-emphasizes Maria Barrientos' vowel changes. This suggests that perhaps, in the opera house, this changing of vowels mid-scale was not as audible as it is on recordings. The final unaccompanied cadenza is one of the best of its kind, perfectly suiting Dinorah's wandering mind and allowing the soprano to show off her gifts. As in the earlier Fonotipias, Barrientos jumps to a beautiful high E-flat to descend (via *portamento*) to an A-flat and then a jump to a final D-flat.

Proch – Theme and Variations – Columbia 1920

These wonderful variations suited Barrientos very well. One of the surprises of her discography is that she only recorded this showpiece once—later in her career. This was her final Columbia recording before the De Falla songs eight years later. Barrientos offers a first statement of the theme that is emphatic with deep usage of her chest voice. The florid measures do not phase her at all, although one notices that she sweeps to some of the high E-flats instead of singing them staccato, as written. This does, however, provide textural coloration in the music. She occasionally changes the vocal line, and some of her ornamentation is a bit unusual. There is a real sense of bravura, although some of the staccati seem a bit troublesome. The final cadenza with flute is wonderful. Although a staccato or two fail to phonate, the final D-flat is triumphant.

Rimsky-Korsakov – Hymn to the Sun (*Le Coq D'Or*) – Columbia, 1918

Maria Barrientos sang in the U. S. premier of this work at the Metropolitan Opera on March 6, 1918, with Adamo Didur and Sophie Braslau. Today's readers may find it amusing that, at that time, this opera was coupled with *Cavalleria rusticana* (starring Florence Easton and Hipólito Lazaro). Barrientos sang in nine performances and two on tour (the rest were taken by the American soprano, Mabel Garrison). Barrientos recorded the famous aria of the Queen of Shemakha at the time of the Metropolitan Opera premier. It is a fascinating recording. She sings the aria in French with beautiful, sweeping legato and impeccable intonation during the many chromatic phrases. One suspects that she was quite wonderful in the complete role.

The conclusion, with its climb to an exposed high D, is wonderful, full of subtle dramaticism. The only regret is that she never recorded a version of the aria with the final cadenza that conductor Pierre Monteux wrote specifically for her voice. Unaccompanied, the cadenza rises to a number of high Ds before culminating on a sustained high E. When Lily Pons inherited the role at the Met, she used Barrientos' cadenza. Pons recorded the aria twice (RCA Victor and Columbia) singing the cadenza in both.

Rossini – Una voce poco fa (*Il barbiere di Siviglia*)—Fonotipia, 1906, Columbia, 1920

This was one of Maria Barrientos' most popular roles. She sang Rosina eighteen times at the Metropolitan opera and on tour.

The 1906 Fonotipia record highlights her concept of Rossini's humorous music with some colorful and intentional breaks into the chest register and with the raising of some melodic lines. Sung in the original key of E major with piano accompaniment, there is some fresh ornamentation; indeed, the music is at times quite ornate. A problem typical of recordings of this aria is that the ornamentation often selected is the same as is used by everyone, thus making recordings tiresome. "Io sono docile" is facile and although there is not a lot of "face" in her singing, the ornamentation is nicely done; the scales are clean, the staccato pings out nicely, and she interpolates a fine high E at the conclusion.

In an unsigned review for the *New York Bulletin*, the critic commented about the February 22, 1917 performance of the opera:

> ...The Spanish soprano gave a performance of the sprightly Rosina quite unlike that of any other singer locally associated with the part. She possesses a singular personal

charm: an appreciation of the amusing episodes that is altogether infectious; enthusiasm that goes hand in hand with youth, and refinement that dominates every act and gesture... Her coloratura could be delivered with a little more spontaneity to its improvement and to the increased enjoyment of her auditors. But spontaneity is not a part of Mme. Barrientos' equipment. However, she sang "Una voce poca fa" with rare taste and impeccable intonation. And in her aria in the lesson scene her bravura work was rewarded with a tremendous show of appreciation. (A.N. Barrientos sang the "Voices of Spring Waltz" by Johann Strauss) (Metropolitan Opera Archives, accessed, November, 2014)

The April, 1920 version (found on Volume II of Nimbus, *The Golden Age of Singers, 1910–1920*) is a wonderful rendition. Recorded over two sides, it shows her solid lower reigister and charming manner. Differently from many others, she plays with Rossini's rhythm and uses ornaments descriptively. Some may not care for her tendency to over-ornament as well as to prepare for some of the more difficult passages, but, to compensate, there is an exquisite decrescendo on the penultimate high B at the end of the first section. "Io sono dolcile" shows her absolute comfort with the music and although there is some vowel modification and staccati hesitation, it is quite successful. In this recording there is no final high E.

Strauss – Voices of Spring Waltz – Fonotipia, 1904, Columbia 1917

This piece was a recording favorite of coloratura sopranos in the early 20th century. Luisa Tetrazzini, Graziella Pareto, Marcella Sembrich, and many others recorded at least one version of the waltz. Barrientos recorded it twice, once for Fonotipia, and once for Columbia. The Fonotipia is one of her loveliest recordings and one of the best performances from those early sessions. She offers fine trills and much bravura, including the unexpected singing of a phrase up an octave that is as spectacular as it is beautiful. At the end, the final cadential flourish includes a brilliant passage of staccati that ascends to high E-flat that is repeated four times before spinning out a beautiful, penultimate high F.

Although the Fonotipia recording includes some extra high notes, Columbia's recording is just as good. One notices, however, a hesitancy in vocal production—once again, the odd feeling that she is having trouble phonating. Her feeling for Strauss' music is wonderful and there are nice ornaments that she throws into the music. On the Columbia record she retains the striking octave leap to high E-flat that she interpolates near to the reiteration of the main theme. The repeated volleys up to high E-flat in staccato are here and just as brilliant; each top note sparkles. Instead of a penultimate high F, Barrientos offers a stunning high E-flat which descends to the tonic.

Thomas – Polonaise (*Mignon*) – Fonotipia, 1906, Columbia, 1919

Philine was an important role in Barrientos' repertoire and her 1906 piano-accompanied disk highlights her knowledge of the aria and its pitfalls. There are nice rubati to demonstrate that Barrientos understands the Gallic style. She replaces Thomas's cadenza for one of her own that is surprisingly successful with a full high E-flat that brings the piece to a rousing finish.

The 1919 Columbia disk is as good a reading as the Fonotipia recording made thirteen years earlier. It is made even better because an orchestra is used. Grace notes are added to Thomas's original vocal line, the triplets are clean, and there is a good sense of fun throughout. Because of the increased tempo, there is remarkably rapid coloratura sung with great élan, and, as in the Fonotipia, she offers a fine top E-flat.

Verdi – Caro nome (*Rigoletto*) – Fonotipia, 1906, Columbia, 1916

Barrientos sang Gilda 29 times at the Met and on tour. It was her most-often sung role as Verdi's music and character suited Barrientos' voice and temperament. The 1906 Fonotipia disk (accompanied by piano) finds the soprano adding extra trills to Verdi's vocal line, which fit in nicely, and, surprisingly, do not offend. There is additional *fioriture* and the final cadenza is altered somewhat to highlight her high staccato. The high D-sharp at the peak of the cadenza is beautifully sustained.

The Columbia disk is a beautiful recording of Gilda's gentle thoughts about her new lover. Barrientos' legato is firm and her musical expression sensitive, although one is surprised at the sudden florid outburst in the middle of the aria. Some might question its need, but the way Barrientos presents the passage is almost as if Gilda had suddenly become excited and begun to have little heart palpitations. The end of the aria is a bit rushed in order to give the soprano time to add a bit to the cadenza that follows. Although one might question the necessity for the added notes, the repeated staccati could be interpreted as little laughs, and the penultimate high B is beautifully framed within a decrescendo.

Verdi – Tutte le feste (and scene) with Riccardo Stracciari (*Rigoletto*) – Columbia, 1919

Although heavily cut, (trimmed to just under seven minutes) this is a very successful pairing of two artists. Barrientos sounds delicate and feminine in her outpouring of shame and humiliation. Although the tempo tends to move along more rapidly than it seems it should, she keeps good control and fits her interpretation into that framework. Stracciari enters forcefully but becomes immediately consoling in nature. The interaction between the two plays out nicely. The "Vendetta" that follows is a whirlwind of fury and desperation having Barrientos leap to a perfectly placed, penultimate high E-flat. Stracciari takes over on the final high A-flat. Wonderful!

Although no longer held in the esteem they once had in decades past, Barrientos' recordings deserve to be heard and treasured.

Celestina Boninsegna
(1877–1947)

This Italian soprano was born in Reggio, Emilia and studied under Virginia Boc-cabadati. She made her professional operatic debut in 1897, in Bari as Marguerite in Gounod's *Faust*. By 1904 she had established herself as a front-line singer performing at Covent Garden, London, La Scala, Milan (1904–5), the Teatro Real, Madrid (1905–6), and the Metropolitan Opera, New York (1906–7). She also sang in Boston (in 1909–10), in Barcelona (1911–12), at the Mariinsky Theatre, St Petersburg (1914) and many other opera houses. One notices, that Boninsegna often sang just one season at each opera house, suggesting that despite her vocal allure, her primitive acting and emotional abilities may have worked against her vocal efforts in stage performances.

Her stage repertoire included such roles as Aïda, Elena in *I Vespri Siciliani*, Donna Anna in *Don Giovanni*, Elena and Margherita in *Mefistofele*, Elvira in *Ernani*, *La Gioconda*, Petrella's *Jone*, Elsa in *Lohengrin,* and the *Siegfried* Brünnhilde. Except for Santuzza in *Cavalleria rusticana* and *Tosca*, Boninsegna was never hired to sing verismo roles

The Metropolitan Opera website offers an interesting perspective on the soprano at the time of her debut:

> In her Met debut on December 21, 1906 she sang the title role of *Aida* opposite Caruso, Louise Kirkby-Lunn, and Riccardo Stracciari. The *New York American* praised her "fresh, supple, warm voice" but was alarmed by "the terrors of her make-up. She wore two mops of black wool, and her arms were apparently covered with dark cotton stockings. She drew the color line at her neck being almost white above. That she triumphed over these things is a tribute to her art." Most of her reviews were good but not outstanding. However, New York was used to Eames as Aida, proud and elegant of costume, with her own secret blend of flesh-colored make-up. Contracted for forty performances at $336 each, Boninsegna sang only five times in opera, plus two concerts. She left in February and may have been ill, since there was no contractual penalty involved. (Other salaries from this season: Eames, $1,500 per performance; Sembrich, $1,200; Johanna Gadski, $1,000; Geraldine Farrar, $700; Fremstad, $500.)

Years later, Boninsegna seemed to blame Eames for her lack of success. When the future critic Max de Schauensee visited her in 1937, almost her first words were "La Eames—è morta?" and she became reflective upon hearing she was still alive. On another visit to Italy, de Schauensee interviewed the baritone Stracciari. He declared, 'Only one woman sang the music of Aida the way I thought it should be sung, and that was la Boninsegna. Her voice was so big and beautiful, all silver and velvet. But she had no charm or elegance of person...the public would not forgive her, despite a voice that was unique in this role. Besides, the Metropolitan had Emma Eames—*una bellissima donna*!'" (Metropolitan Opera Archives, accessed January, 2015)

Boninsegna retired in 1921 and taught singing for twenty years in Pesaro and Milan. Her most famous pupil was the dramatic soprano Margherita Grandi. She died in Milan in 1947.

From all reports, Boninsegna was a dull actress and photos of the time support that observation. Although much is made of her bland stage presence, I sense that there may have been more behind the seeming lack of dramatic temperament. She simply may not have been comfortable as an opera stage actress; too conscious of how she appeared to others, which may have made her self-conscious.

In a 1958 article on Celestina Boninsegna in *The Record Collector* (Vol 12 #112) Clifford Williams and John B Richards write:

> Even though she did not sing oftener at La Scala and the Metropolitan (she hated intrigues and embarrassment, and admitted to some friends that she had neglected the largest theatres because in others there was less intrigue) her popularity remains at a high level...

I suspect that Boninsegna might have been better suited to the concert platform than the opera stage. She may have been a person of a retiring nature more so than one of flamboyant or overt dramaticism. She may have preferred a calmer balance in her dealings with people, situations, and acting. She also may have been a bit sensitive and defensive about her art (as witness the comment about Emma Eames above). There seems to have been an unspoken vein of insecurity or jealousy toward colleagues who sang the same repertoire. No matter what, in most operatic photos she looks almost frumpy and definitely uncomfortable in costume. Contrastingly, more casual photographs find her bearing to be quite noble and elegant.

None of this matters to recordings. At a time when verismo (and excessive dramaticism) reigned at so many opera houses, Boninsegna stuck steadfastly to what she did best. For the twenty-year period from 1900 to 1920, she was considered one of the most important Verdi singers on international stages. She certainly was not uncomfortable in front of the recording horn. She mastered the technique of making records, leaving posterity some amazing recordings. Her voice was extremely phonogenic and, because of this, she was a quite prolific recording artist. Between 1904 and 1918 she made one hundred and six 78 rpm sides for Gramophone & Typewriter Company (G&T), Pathé, Columbia, HMV, and Edison. Her Columbia sides, made between 1909 and 1910, are probably her most famous, and have been re-issued on both LP and CD.

Her recorded repertoire was nicely varied and includes arias and/or scenes from *Norma, I Vespri Siciliani, La bohème, Semiramide, Isabeau, Faust, Ernani, Tosca, Loreley, La forza del destino, Le maschere* (creator recording), *Il Guarany, L'Africaine, Ruy Blas, Lucrezia Borgia, Il trovatore, Aïda, Cavalleria rusticana* and others.

What we hear on these records is a well-produced voice that speaks very well through the primitive recording process of the time. One understands immediately why her records have been so prized through the decades. The lower register was strong, clean, and clear, and her use of it could be quite abandoned. The upper register was warm, roundly produced, and extended to a vibrant high C. The low A held no problems and she had a very good trill. Ironically, although photographs suggest that she was a dramatic cipher, her recordings are differently received. Her "Ritorna vincitor" from *Aïda*, is a wonderful recording, full of emotion and colorful singing. In her 1908 orchestrally accompanied "Madre, pietosa Vergine" from *La forza del destino*, she is forceful in her chest register up to F-sharp in the staff. Although a bit unorthodox pedagogically, it provides a fine emphasis to the text and music. By 1910, and the orchestrally accompanied Columbia discs made in the United States, Boninsegna's voice had settled into a full, vibrant column of sound; all high notes were admirably integrated into the musical line so that they emerge as part of a composer's phrase rather than isolated, virtuostic high notes.

Bellini's *Norma* was one of Boninsegna's favorite roles although the music did not suit her technique—at least not for the artistic priorities that we hold today. In her 1910 Columbia discs, the legato is aspirated using a seeming verismatic approach that is today considered incongruous to Bellini's gentle and elegant music. Boninsegna could handle the lengthy lines and the notes of the aria, it is just that her manner of delivery is not attractive. She interpolates a fine high C in the cadenza concluding "Casta diva,"but such deep chest register use on "va" of "Casta diva" does not work. The cabaletta has great energy and Boninsegna is obviously familiar with this music, knowing how to negotiate its hurdles. Some of the coloratura is quite impressive, and all the high Cs are sung with great abandon, especially the excellent penultimate high C. As a portrait of a performance from an earlier time period that supported different stylistic proprieties, this is an excellent recording. It is certainly an individual statement.

In Leonora's Act I aria, "Tacea la notte placida" from *Il trovatore,* there is little subtlety, but plenty of temperament as Boninsegna alters Verdi's triplet figures and rhythms while emphasizing her chest register. (Boninsegna's accentuation of her chest register was typical of most dramatic Italian singers of that era. While now considered to be in bad taste, as it disrupts the flow of legato, taken as an interpretive or highlighting device, it provides dramatic, rhythmic, and coloristic emphasis to the music.) It becomes apparent, however, that the foundation of her legato was unsound, based on a disruptive use of aspirates when moving from note to note. She avoids the extreme top, but, like many early recording artists, ends "Tacea" up the octave. After a successful cabaletta, Boninsegna interpolates an excellent B-flat, before the final A-flat.

Celestina Boninsegna first recorded an abbreviated "D'amor sull ali rosee" from act IV with piano, five years after her professional debut. This 1904 disk shows aspirated legato, little personality, and highlights her curious decision to alter the text underlay so that the final syllables are crudely accented, vitiating any artistic intentions. To avoid Verdi's difficult high D-flat she uses a (now traditional) variant to high B-flat, taking the final A-flat up the octave (also now traditional).

By 1909, and the orchestrally accompanied Columbia discs, "D'amor sull ali rosee" is permeated with nuance peculiar to this era of Italian singing. There is better characterization accompanied by some desperate lunges into the chest register, phrase tapering, and rubato not apparent in 1904, and capped with an excellent top C. This is a remarkably attractive performance, arresting for its strong individuality. It is dramatic–overtly intense and worrying–rather than nostalgic or soothing, but it is honestly sung.

I have come across a number of critics who mention Boninsegna's erratic or inconsistent work on stage. That matters little today, having been left her recordings; there is no inconsistency there. Taken as a whole her legacy is one of constant surprise and pleasure. She certainly deserves a complete collection. No matter what artistic failings are imposed on Celestina Boninsegna based on today's artistic expectations, as relics of a long-gone manner of singing, her recordings are fascinating and important documents.

Pearl has released two volumes of her material containing forty-five of her one hundred and six sides. The first volume, re-mastered by Ward Marston, was released in 1993; the second volume was remastered by Keith Hardwick and released in 1996. Both collect primarily the Columbia and G&T sides.

Symposium's 2004 release offers twenty sides and includes some of the wonderful 1910 Columbia sides. Preiser's issue, also in 2004, has twenty-one selections, most from the 1904–1905 G&T sessions. All are recommended. As an aside, if you are a completist, you might also want to get Ward Marston's, *The Edison Legacy, Volume II,* a two-disc set that includes some unpublished 1911 Edisons: three arias from *Il trovatore, Aïda* and *La forza del destino.*

In this chapter, and in many others throughout this book, the reader may notice that I often mention the British magazine, *The Record Collector.* In existence since 1946, and now edited by Larry Lustig, it continues as one of the most important and revered publications that deals with 78 rpm recordings of historical singers. Published quarterly, *The Record Collector* is essential reading for record collectors, historians, and vocal enthusiasts. It is subscribed to and collected not only by those interested in the singing voice, but also by major libraries, colleges and universities, and schools of music. I urge the reader to visit their website (www.therecordcollector.org). Like the New York-based The Vocal Record Collector's Society, *The Record Collector* releases an annual CD.

Giuseppe Borgati (1871–1950)

This tenor was born in the province of Ferrara, northern Italy. He is of great importance among historical singers because he created the title role in Giordano's *Andrea Chenier* at La Scala in 1896; he also was Italy's first great Wagnerian tenor. He was the first Italian tenor to appear at Bayreuth (1904), and he appeared regularly at La Scala (1896–1914). Unfortunately, deteriorating eyesight (caused by glaucoma) forced Borgatti to end his stage career prematurely. After leaving the stage, he became a successful teacher.

Borgatti grew up illiterate. While working as a mason, a wealthy patron, the Marchese Plattis (a music enthusiast) heard him singing and arranged for him to take singing lessons and acquire a basic education. His voice teachers included Alessandro Busi in Bologna and, later, Carlo d'Ormeville. He made his operatic debut in 1892, at Castelfranco Veneto, as *Faust*. After singing in the Italian provinces for a few years, he sang in *Manon Lescaut* in 1894, in Venice, and then sang his first Wagnerian role, *Lohengrin,* at at the Teatro Dal Verme in Milan. By 1896 he was at La Scala creating *Andrea Chenier*. After that, he appeared regularly in Verdi and Puccini and various verismo as well as Wagner roles, including Lohengrin, Tannhäuser, Walther, Tristan, Siegmund, Siegfried. and Parsifal.

Borgatti was a favorite performer of Toscanini's. In 1898 he toured South America with an excellent group of Italian singers, tenor Francesco Tamagno, coloratura soprano Luisa Tetrazzini, and baritones Mario Sammarco and Eugenio Giraldoni. During this time he visited Spain and Russia. In 1904 he was invited to perform at the famous Bayreuth festival and it seems that Cosima Wagner (Wagner's widow and the festival's director), and the important Wagnerian conductor, Hans Richter, were impressed not only with Borgatti's voice, but his artistry as well. Borgatti must have enjoyed challenges, as he sang Herod in the La Scala premier of Richard Strauss' *Salome* in 1906.

Wikipedia notes that:

> …good-looking and solidly built—as photographs attest—Borgatti is described in contemporary reviews of his performances as having possessed abundant reserves of stamina

and strong histrionic ability in addition to a smooth, well-schooled voice of robust size. Modern-day critics, including Scott, J.B. Steane and John Freestone, have praised him, too, for the clarity of his diction, the limpidity of his tone and the fineness of his phrasing. He took pride in the fact that even after he took on the heavy Wagnerian repertoire, he was still able to put across a bel canto aria like "Una furtiva lagrima" (from Gaetano Donizetti's *L'elisir d'amore*) with lyrical ease. Oddly enough, despite his exceptional attainments as a singer and interpretive artist, he never performed in London or New York City."

Around 1907, at the height of his career, Borgatti developed glaucoma. Within seven years he was forced to give up his stage career. Still in his vocal prime, he continued to give concerts for a while. His last public performance was in Bologna in 1928. After this, he taught singing in Milan, his most famous students being Heddle Nash (1894–1961) and Willi Domgraf-Fassbaender (1897–1978).

Borgatti married one of his singing teachers, Elena Cuccoli. They had a daughter, Renata Borgatti (1894–1964), who became a concert pianist. Borgatti published his autobiography, *La mia vita d'artista,* in 1927. He died in 1950, at age seventy-nine.

Borgatti recorded from 1905 to 1929 for Fonotipia, Pathé, and Columbia, with huge gaps between sessions. There are only fifteen published sides. Oddly, Borgatti did not record any of the arias from *Andrea Chénier*, or from some of the other operas with which he had become especially associated: *Mefistofele, Aïda, La traviata, La Gioconda, Pagliacci, Manon Lescaut* and *Fedora*. He did, however, record arias from *Lohengrin, Meistersinger, Tosca, Tannhäuser, Die Walküre,* and *Otello.*

During the LP period, his work was released on Rubini. For years, only a few of Borgatti's recordings were available on CD anthologies; these include Symposium, EMI's *La Scala Edition, Volume One* and Nuova Era Records.

In 2011, Preiser released a CD of all of the known Borgatti recordings supplemented by seven selections by Isidoro Fagoaga (1895–1976) the Spanish-born dramatic tenor. The Preiser CD was released in memory of Professor Jürgen E. Schmidt (1937–2010) who, for more than five decades, worked for Preiser as a producer and recording manager.

Although not known generally, Borgatti is one of those singers who should be studied and appreciated by students, collectors, and lovers of voice.

Michael Scott in *The Record of Singing, Volume I* writes of Borgatti:

> Borgatti's Wagner recordings, though all of them are in Italian, are among the finest ever made. (Charles Scribner's Sons, New York, 1977, p. 134)

Eugenia Burzio (1872[9]–1922)

This soprano began her musical studies as a violinist, but, in her teens, decided to concentrate on singing. She studied at the Milan Conservatory with Carolina Ferni, a student of Giuditta Pasta. Burzio made her debut as Santuzza in *Cavaleria rusticana* at the Teatro Vittorio Emmanuel in Turin in 1899. Her impassioned singing was immensely popular in South America, Italy, Egypt, and Russia. According to Wikipedia:

> Burzio was a magnetic actress and she became particularly associated with the music of the verismo school of composers, exemplified by Mascagni, Catalani, Leoncavallo, Umberto Giordano and, to a certain extent, Puccini. She was a star performer with a fanatical following at Italy's pre-eminent opera house, La Scala, Milan, during the first two decades of the 20th century. There Burzio appeared in a wide repertoire, often under the baton of Toscanini, her roles included Gluck's *Armide*, Bellini's *Norma, Alfano's Risurrezione, Franchetti's La Figlio di Jorio, Pacini's Saffo, Catalani's La Wally and Loreley, Aida, La Gioconda and Cavalleria Rusticana.*

A noted verismo specialist, some listeners may find Burzio's acoustic recordings of arias from *Norma, Saffo, L'Africaine, Zulma, Loreley, Aïda* and *Il trovatore* shocking for their individuality and intensity. For Burzio, every word is of the utmost importance, and the results she achieves are sometimes bewildering, sometimes revelatory. As with many sopranos impacted by the verismo era, Burzio could be everything from irritating to divine.

In 1906, Burzio was at La Scala singing Katarina in the world premiere of Alfano's *Risurezzione*. Although she sang all over Europe, she never appeared in London nor the United States. She was greatly popular with Italian audiences, but not so much with its "new" conductor, Arturo Toscanini.

Burzio suffered from nervousness and from insomnia, causing her to seek help from various medications. By 1911, she was becoming completely dependent upon them. Ultimately, the situation caused kidney failure and Burzio died before she was fifty years old. For the last three years of her life, she was cared for by her lifelong friend, soprano Rosina Storchio (the first Madama Butterfly).

Burzio had a full-bodied, verismatic voice of sufficient agility, but no trill and an individual manner of singing. Her diction was always clear and clean. Like Luisa Tetrazzini, and many other Italian- and Spanish-born singers of the time, Burzio indulges in quite a bit of the *bamboleggiante* (doll-like) timbre to portray youth and to lend a cutting edge to her vowels in the middle register. As William Ashbrook put it, "It seems as though she is always singing in italics."

She was a popular recording artist for Fonotipia, Columbia, Pathè, and Phonodisc Mondial, making sixty-six published sides. Because there are multiple record labels, there are nine duplicated titles, and four in triplicate. She is a unique and fascinating singer.

Since the LP era, Eugenia Burzio has been something of a mythological figure among record collectors. Burzio's art, in twenty-nine selections, is preserved on a two-LP set from Club "99".

In 1990, Club "99" re-released this Burzio collection on CD. In 1997, Pearl released a single CD collection of twenty-one selections that proved to be an excellent representation of this histrionic soprano's art (more than seventy-eight minutes). Then, in 1999, Marston Records released a two-CD set of forty-three sides, including a rare test disc of an aria from Catalani's *Loreley*. Marston offers sixteen of her Fonotipias from 1905–1910, and twenty-one of her Columbias, Pathés and Phonodisc Mondials from 1912–1916.

In the liner notes for the Marston release, William Ashbrook comments:

> The odds and ends of musicians recruited into a recording studio were there to accompany a vocal star, not necessarily to serve a composer scrupulously. It is this resulting sense of untrammeled interpretative freedom that makes Burzio's records such a particularly engrossing experience because she involved herself so intensely in the emotions of the characters she was representing. She was not a perfect singer with her lack of a trill and her occasional glottal bump or some attenuated *portamenti*, but such blemishes can easily be forgiven in a singer who, in my estimation, never made an uninteresting recording and also bequeathed us some unforgettable ones.

In 2000, Symposium released a CD with Burzio, Emma Carelli, and Ester Mazzoleni. Burzio's ten selections are duplicated among the earlier labels.

In 2009 Preiser added their CD release to the mix, containing twenty-four selections from her Fonotipia and Columbia sides between 1907 and 1913.

Burzio's method and manner of singing were not perfect. As J.B.Steane writes in *The Grand Tradition*:

> Burzio *means* everything she sings: there is a great fervour and dramatic intensity. But it is achieved at the expense of the vocal line, and often by such means as a little preliminary cry or gulp...before the note. (Scribner's Sons, NY, 1974)

Burzio's recordings are fascinating and I have always felt that one cannot have too many of them. Burzio approached the recording medium with utmost seriousness—in each and every one of her recordings, she presents a complete performance. Some are overwhelming, such as the *La favorita* selections, especially "Pietoso al par," portraying frantic desperation (on the Marston release). These selections underline her vigorous use of the chest voice, a common trait among dramatic sopranos of the time:

> Her emphatic use of the open chest voice—ugly to some ears, exciting to others—harkens back to the nineteenth century, when large-voiced Italian sopranos emphasized the *voce di petto* register for dramatic and emotional effect, and were expected to do so. Celestina Boninsegna, who belonged to this tradition, referred to her chest voice straightforwardly: *'Era la mia gloria'* she declared. (William Ashbrook, Liner Notes, Burzio release on Marston)

A Burzio disk easy to become fond of is the aria from Puccini's *La fanciulla del West* – "Laggiù nel Soledad," one of the first recordings of this aria. Burzio sang the Italian premier of the opera in Rome in the summer of 1911. Recorded in 1913 for Columbia, Burzio gives a wonderful, passionate performance full of novel shadings, including unusual, whispered pitches. There is an interesting, but not offensive, lowering transposition at "S'amavan tanto!" so that the sustained note is a high B rather than C. It is a good one; the finish is most vigorous.

I also like "Spunta l'aurora pallida" from Boito's *Mefistofele*. It was recorded in January of 1910 and is a remarkable piece of music (almost Bellinian in its gentle, floating vocal lines). Burzio, like the later verismo specialist, Magda Olivero (1910–2014), makes the most of its passionate, chromatic twists. (In this true to life recording, you can hear Burzio clearing her throat before she begins to sing.) Accompanied by piano, she gives a personable, extreme performance with a superb high B at its climax. Helping her interpretation is her inclusion of occasional illuminating gasps and demented intensity.

Similar to the over-the-top vocal histrionics found in the *Mefistofele* aria, is the difficult "Deh non volermi vittime" from the last act of *Norma*. Burzio's recording must be heard, to be believed. Although some will find her dramaticism amusing, I find it riveting. Technically, it is not sung in a bel canto style, but the textual accents, gasps, and various colorations are fascinating to hear, and certainly illuminate her perception of the music.

The "Casta diva" from act I of *Norma* is another spellbinding recording. Again, not bel canto, but something in between that and verismo. Burzio takes Bellini's music and shakes it like a dog with a bone to squeeze everything she can from his music. There is questionable taste and style, but it is truly intriguing to hear.

The two arias from Romani's now forgotten opera *Zulma*, recorded in 1911, make for interesting listening. Romani was Puccini's protégé, and *Zulma* premiered in 1909. Although the music is not particularly memorable, Burzio's completely committed and passionate dramaticism is unforgettable.

There is the unusual recording of Saffo's final scene (abridged) by Pacini. This was recorded in 1912 on Columbia, and, even back in Burzio's day, it was an unusual choice for recording. Burzio handles the fioritura with grace, if also with a gasping declamation more appropriate to verismo outbursts.

Burzio is an artist whose recordings, despite the primitive recording process, have amazing "face." They are absorbing and always attention-grabbing and, in many cases, truly out of the ordinary. Although one is tempted to listen to a number of Burzio's records in a row (because they are so engrossing) I find that two or three (maybe four) at a time are plenty for a listening session. She can be emotionally exhausting.

She is an engrossing singer with a palpable, almost tangible presence on the recordings she left us. One might question her manner of projecting her interpretations, but one could never question her commitment to providing the listener with the most gripping of listening experiences. I found it interesting that not once while listening to her recordings, did I feel that Burzio was being insincere in her overt emotions. Throughout the eras, Eugenia Burzio has remained an artist who refuses to be dismissed.

The choice among the various Burzio CDs is a matter of preference of the program offered, although one can never go wrong with Marston. If you are not interested in a two-disc set, Preiser is an excellent choice. I find their program (as is typical of that firm) logical, entertaining, and extremely well put together, not to mention excellently transferred.

Enrico Caruso (1873–1921)

This Italian tenor grew up modestly in Naples. When he was eleven years old he was apprenticed to a mechanical engineer who manufactured public water fountains. He sang in the church choir and, after his mother's death in 1888, he became a street singer, singing in cafes and for soirees. He began vocal studies with Guglielmo Vergine at the age of sixteen. After completing forty-five days of compulsory military service, he continued his vocal studies with Vergine.

He made his professional debut in 1895 at the Teatro Novo in Naples in *L'Amico Francesco* by Domenico Morelli. Caruso sang throughout the Italian provinces gaining experience. In 1900 he made his debut at La Scala as Rodolfo in *La bohème* with Toscanini conducting.

In April of 1902 he signed a contract with the Gramophone & Typewriter Company to make a series of recordings—done in a Milan hotel room. The ten sides that resulted quickly became best sellers throughout England and the United States. Caruso was one of the first singers to take advantage of (or to realize) the importance of making recordings. It was after the young Caruso began to earn large amounts of royalties that other, more famous singers of the time, like Francesco Tamango (the first *Otello*) and Dame Nellie Melba decided that, they too, should make records.

During the early years of his career Caruso created a number of roles that are now considered part of the repertoire: Loris in Giordano's *Fedora* (1898), Maruizio in Cilea's *Adriana Lecouvreur* (1902) and Federico in Alberto Franchetti's *Germania*.

In May, 1902 he made his debut at Covent Garden as the Duke in *Rigoletto*, paired with Nellie Melba. In November, 1903 he made his Metropolitan Opera debut in the same role. In February, 1904, he had signed a recording contract with the Victor Talking-Machine Company (RCA Victor, now BMG) remaining with them until his death in 1921.

Although he considered the Met to be his operatic home he appeared in various American cities and in Canada as well as in Belgium, Austria, Vienna, France, Germany, Argentina, and Brazil, as well as Mexico City and Cuba. Caruso was also an avid recitalist and had over 500 songs in his performing repertoire, both classical and popular. In 1910 he sang Dick Johnson in the world premiere of Puccini's *La fanciulla del West* alongside Emmy Destin and Pasquale Amato with Toscanini conducting. By this time he had begun to undertake roles that were more heroic—like Radames and Samson.

During the First World War Caruso did extensive charity work, and also proved during this time that he was a shrewd business man. He continued to record sporadically until September, 1920. Amazingly, Enrico Caruso was a smoker.

There is a wonderful book on Caruso written by Michael Scott: *The Great Caruso* (Alfred A. Knopf, New York, 1988)

The Voice and Recordings

From April of 1902 until 1920, Caruso made 245 recordings (which includes the unpublished items known to exist). Today, that equals twelve compact discs. Although he began recording with Gramphone in 1902, by 1904 he had moved to Victor and remained with them until 1920. Caruso's first recordings for Victor in 1904 were made in Room 826 at Carnegie Hall in New York.

To analyze each recording would need its own book. Suffice it to say that, like Feodor Chaliapin, there is no such thing as a boring Caruso record. Any and all are worth hearing many times over. Naturally with such a large legacy there are some selections that one will prefer over others. I have always preferred to listen to Caruso in operatic arias and scenes; others prefer to hear him in song. While I do not listen to his songs regularly, there are, of course, some that I cannot do without, like Cardillo's "Core 'ngrato," with its emotional vibrancy and the huge B-flat at the end, and Mascheroni's "Eternamente" (with its beautiful decrescendo on the top F). Both of these were recorded on the same day in 1911. I also confess an irrational fondness for Gartner's "Love is Mine," a typically tacky parlor song of that time sung in English with utter conviction and a triumphant high B-flat at the end.

Caruso's vast legacy is a perfect candidate for the "listen to just two or three at a time" experiment discussed earlier in this book. With the possibility of being able to buy his entire legacy for about fifty dollars, it is easy to gorge oneself on his voice and art, but hold back.

With that easy ability to buy his entire recorded legacy and play them in any sequence you prefer, the best purchase is the Naxos series lovingly transferred by the magician of restorers, Ward Marston (released between 2000 and 2004). At the time of this writing, the twelve-CD series is available for a few dollars each from various sellers on Amazon.com. The transfers are first rate and Marston does a fantastic job promoting the Caruso voice. Before this (in 1993), Marston had done the restoration for the complete Caruso set issued by Pearl Records. If cost is not an issue, another set worth obtaining is the Nimbus series.

The Nimbus recordings sound as if Caruso were singing in a recital hall with wood-paneled walls, beautifully resonant, and quite live. I find myself returning to them quite often for comparison listening. One might not want to have them as one's only version of the Caruso legacy, but the Nimbus issues provide fascinating and important contrasts to the more closely recorded editions on Naxos, BMG, and Pearl. Different from the chronological presentation of other releases, Nimbus offers its selections thematically grouped. This can make for interesting listening. There are three volumes of songs, three volumes of operatic arias, one volume of early recordings, Caruso in ensemble, and highlights from French opera (with Geraldine Farrar and Marcel Jounet). Writing in *Gramophone* of his impression of the Nimbus pressings, J.B. Steane writes:

> ...the (Nimbus) method brings me face to face, far more consistently than other transfers have done, with Caruso as I like to hear him and as I believe he sounded.

The RCA (BMG) complete boxed set appears to be out of print. I find it sadly ironic that the company that originally recorded Caruso has never come up with a decent sounding collection. Perhaps they will someday dispense with the grossly inadequate Stockham "Soundstream" processing they have used since the 1970s, and go back to the original discs. For the foreseeable future, however, one is much better off with either the Naxos or Nimbus recordings.

So why bother with the recordings of a singer of 112 years ago? It has to do with the burnished sound of his voice, a voice well-captured by the primitive recording process of that time, and the sincerity and devotion he put into those recordings. There is something very satisfying about listening to an Enrico Caruso recording.

There are a number of Caruso recordings that you should not be without. These would include his 1902 creator recordings of the two arias from Franchetti's verismo opera, *Germania* (re-recorded in 1910), as well as the arias and ensembles from *Faust*, *Il trovatore*, *Un ballo in maschera*, *La bohème*, *Andrea Chenier*, *Rigoletto*, *La forza del destino* (especially the duet with Amato from act IV, recorded in 1911), *Aïda*, and the indespensible aria from *La Juive* from 1920. For me, that is one of the greatest recordings of all time.

> Caruso last appeared at the Met in Halévy's *La Juive*. The opera had been revived with a new production in 1919. Caruso appeared in it 13 times. The unlucky 13th performance was on Christmas Eve 1920. Immediately following that performance he became seriously ill. He died the following August. At his penultimate recording session in September 1920 he recorded Eléazar's great aria Rachel, quand du Seigneur. The voice is dark and rich. The interpretation is noble, but there is the barest hint of strain in his high notes. After 25 years of singing and more of two pack a day cigarette smoking it's not surprising. Someone once described him as the world's most spectacular case of emphysema. (http://medicine-opera.com/2009/05/the-recordings-of-enrico-caruso-1919-1920-the-end/#sthash.eoUwKM3K.dpuf)

There are many more. Caruso's is a huge legacy and one that repays close attention. An aspect of the Caruso legacy that I enjoy is that largish chunks of the operas that he performed in were recorded from such operas as *Madama Butterfly* (with Geradine Farrar and Antonio Scotti), *Martha* with Alda and Journet, and *Faust* with Farrar and Marcel Journet. Other operas, like *Aïda*, *Rigoletto*, and *La forza del destino* merited a few scenes, although not as many as one might like. The consensus of opinion is that the sides he made between 1908 and 1914 are the most representative..

Wikipedia notes:

> Caruso possessed a phonogenic voice which was 'manly and powerful, yet sweet and lyrical'…Not surprisingly, he became one of the first major classical vocalists to make numerous recordings. He and the disc phonograph, known in the United Kingdom as the gramophone, did much to promote each other in the first two decades of the 20th century. Many of Caruso's recordings have remained continuously available since their original issue around a century ago, and every one of his surviving discs (including unissued takes) has been re-mastered and re-released in recent years…Caruso died before the introduction of higher fidelity, electrical recording technology in 1925. All of his recordings were made using the acoustic process, which required the recording artist to sing into a metal horn or funnel which relayed sound directly to a master disc via a stylus. This process captured only a limited range of the overtones and nuances present in the singing voice. Caruso's 12-inch acoustic recordings were limited to a maximum duration of about 4:30 minutes. Consequently, the selections that he recorded were limited to those that could be edited to fit this time constraint.

Essentially live performances, one marvels that there are so many fine recordings and such consistency in his legacy. It is true that early recordings often exhibit cracked notes, false entries, and other imperfections, but one notices that, by 1904, Caruso's voice and technique had settled and he had begun to master the difficult art of recording. There seems to have been a reason for this consistency. Many may not realize that Caruso worked closely with Calvin Child, the manager of the Victor recording library. Over the years, Child became Caruso's personal company representative.

> It is said that every record from 1905 on, was a cooperative effort between the two. Not only did Child work with repertory to be recorded, but after musical arrangements had been worked out and a piece rehearsed, Caruso always cut one or more experimental waxes which were immediately played back and discussed by the two men in detail. Only after full agreement by both Child and the singer with respect to all details would the final recordings be made. (William R. Moran, *Caruso and the Victor Talking Machine*, liner notes, BMG, *The Complete Caruso*, 1990 BMG Music, p. 107)

Caruso's belief in Child's judgement was so strong that no recording was released without Child's approval.

For more detailed discussion of his recordings, please visit the Musicweb International website at these links:

http://www.musicweb-international.com/classrev/2004/Dec04/Caruso_complete.htm

http://www.musicweb-international.com/classrev/2005/Jan05/Caruso_complete.htm

Feodor Chaliapin (1873–1938)

Feodor Chaliapin was born on February 13, 1873 in the Russian town of Kazan, into a poor household. His formative education consisted of four years of parochial school, after which he was apprenticed by his father to a shoemaker, then to a carpenter, and for a few kopecs, he helped his father copy documents in his office. Chaliapin learned to read from a neighbor across the street, the famous author, Maxim Gorky.

His young life seems to have been an unhappy one spent with a domineering and drunken father. He first began to sing at the age of nine in the local church choir as an alto. By age 16, he had left home to sing with traveling opera companies. In 1892, while in Tiflis, the teacher, Dimitri Usatov, heard him sing and became his first, and only, voice teacher. Usatov taught Chaliapin the art of *cantabile* singing while instilling in the young singer the importance of blending vocalism with acting. He also introduced Chaliapin to the music of Mussorgsky.

During the late 1890s Chaliapin gained experience from his touring performances and by 1899, at the age of twenty-six, he was singing at the Imperial Opera in Moscow, acknowledged by critics and audiences alike as an important artist of the Russian stages. He frequently sang throughout Europe, including Milan (1901, 1904), London in 1913, and New York in 1907 and 1921. Moscow was his home until 1921 and the creation of the Union of Soviet Socialist Republic (USSR). By that time, it seems that Chaliapin had become rather difficult and was considered by many to be a *monstre sacré*.

> The men of the revolution watched him go with mixed feelings; by then he had become an unmanageable embarrassment, for such was his prestige that there was no way in which they could discipline him. (Michael Scott, *The Record of Singing, Volume II* – Holmes & Meier Publishers, New York, 1979)

Artistically, he had developed rapidly, and quickly became known for his searingly dramatic, realistic portrayals and an almost tyrannical demand for control over productions. (He even presented opera companies with a contract *they* were to sign which granted him control of artistic decisions.)

Not surprisingly, having such a forceful character, he possessed a large ego. As Kurt Pahlen notes:

> Connoisseurs had the highest admiration for him. Directors, producers and, above all, conductors feared him. He was accustomed to having his own way in everything, including the tempi he took when singing. If the conductor was wise, he fell in with Chaliapin's wishes. When an incident occurred in a rehearsal, it could be kept to some extent *en famille*, although even here violent scenes might result when the conductor with a different opinion was as prominent or as stubborn as the singer. Once when Toscanini was rehearsing *Boris Godunov* with Chaliapin, the argument ended with the conductor breaking his baton into bits and leaving his stand with a classic oath…. A less famous and inferior conductor was brought in, and in the future Toscanini always chose other basses for *Boris Godunov*. It was worse if the difference of opinion occurred during a performance, for even then Chaliapin was by no means inclined to abandon his own ideas. Once at the Vienna State Opera, in Gounod's *Faust*, he did not agree with the tempo set by conductor Carl Alwin for the Rondo of the Golden Calf. So he came forward to the footlights to enforce his own view by huge conducting arm-movements and even stamping his feet. (Kurt Pahlen, *Great Singers from the 17th century to the present day*, Stein and Day Publishers, New York, 1974)

The Metropolitan Opera

Chaliapin first appeared at the Metropolitan Opera in 1907, making his debut in Boito's *Mefistofele* on November 20, 1907 (which was also the debut appearance of tenor Ricardo Martin).

An unsigned review in the *New York Press* noted:

> Chaliapin, who appeared for the first time in America last night in the Metropolitan Opera House, won a triumph. … allowing for the natural disadvantages in the popular ear of a low voice, the Russian singer accomplished wonders. One was reminded of Caruso nights, so boisterous were the demonstrations of approval in the standing room down stairs and the spaces near the dome…"

> A pity that the great Russian basso should have come forward in a work so tiring to the average listener, though full of interest to the student of operatic history. True, the character of Boito's spirit of evil, a big, heavy brutish creature, forceful and mighty, but without the subtleties we are wont to associate with Mephisto, gave to Chaliapin an excellent opportunity for displaying his gigantic frame, his magnetic temperament, his dramatic power in big effects and his remarkably robust voice…. (Metropolitan Opera Archives, accessed, November 2014)

Richard Aldrich of *The New York Times* wrote:

> Mr. Chaliapin was a striking and singular Mefistofele, seeking apparently to emphasize all the disagreeable traits that could be attributed to the Prince of the Powers of Darkness. He is of herculean size and an actor of resource and skill. His voice is a ponderous bass, but it was plainly not in good condition last evening. There were evidences of his hoarseness, and, indeed, it was at one time doubtful whether he would be able to make

his appearance at all last night. He made a deep impression, nevertheless, if not always a wholly agreeable one, and gave promise of doing much that will prove interesting in the course of the season. (Metropolitan Opera Archives, accessed, November 2014)

Despite the reported hoarseness, his debut performance was so applauded that he repeated a portion of "Son lo Spirito."

During this period he also sang in a Sunday night concert (February 16, 1908) performing two songs, with a third as an encore: Sokolov: "Chanson russe;" Glazunov: "L'appel à la vie;" Schumann: "Die beiden Grenadiere" (sung as the encore).

His last performance for the Met during that period was as Leporello in *Don Giovanni*, a Metropolitan Opera performance in Philadelphia, on February 18, 1908. It was conducted by Gustav Mahler.

Chaliapin did not return to the Metropolitan Opera until December 14, 1921 when he appeared as *Boris Godunov*. Chaliapin sang in Russian, everyone else in the production sang in Italian.

Writing for *The New York World*, Deems Taylor wrote:

He sang Boris at the Metropolitan last night for the first time here. One says "sang" because it is the conventional word and the most easily comprehended. It is not adequate. He lived Boris; he was Boris. When he strode upon the stage in the first act towering above his lords and nobles, his gold crown flashing in the sun, his kaftan heavy with embroidery, and swept his arm over his people in a great gesture of benediction, all sense of artifice, of the theatre, vanished....

Chaliapin must be the most stupendous stage personality in the world. There is no question of his creating an illusion. The thing he inspires is belief, instant, absolute, unquestioning. Even as he gazed, terrified, across the palace chamber at the ghost of the murdered Dimitri, the audience turned started eyes toward the spot at which he has gazing. And when they saw nothing there they turned again to the Czar, groveling on his knees by his chair, a tortured Rodin figure come to life, so huge, so pitiful—and wrung their hands and suffered his torment with him.... (Metropolitan Opera Archives, accessed November, 2014)

By this time he had begun to exile himself from Russia, being not in agreement with the emerging Communist party. His final performance with the Metropolitan Opera was on March 20, 1929 as Méphistophélès in *Faust* with Giacomo Lauri-Volpi and the lovely soprano, Mary Lewis as Marguerite. Between 1907 and 1929 he sang a total of 108 performances; seventy-eight in house and thirty while on tour.

Although his most famous roles at the Metropolitan Opera were in *Faust, Mefistofele* and *Boris Godunov*, he also sang in *Il barbiere di Siviglia, Don Carlo,* and *Don Quichotte*. He sang all over the world, touring Australia in recital during 1926, and by 1927 had settled in Paris. He married twice and had eight children. Chaliapin's last stage performance took place at the Monte Carlo Opera in 1937, as *Boris Godunov*. He died the following year, in Paris, of leukemia, at the age of sixty-five. He was initially interred in Paris but in 1984, his remains were transferred from Paris to Moscow in an elaborate ceremony and they were re-buried in Novodevichy Cemetery.

Interpretive Strengths

Not only was Chaliapin an accomplished singer he was a superb make-up artist and costumer. He would let no one do his makeup, doing it himself, and he brought his own costumes. To recognize his skill in this one need only look at the many photographs of him as Mefistofeles, Don Quichotte, Nilankantha, Boris, and Don Basilio. His portrayal of Don Basilio scandalized audiences and offended the clergy; all in the name of honesty in his operatic portrayals.

> At the Met he sang the role of Basilio in Rossini's *The Barber of Seville* as a vulgar, unctuous, greasy priest, constantly picking his nose and wiping his fingers onto his cassock. Audiences were appalled. Defending himself, Chaliapin said in an interview that Basilio 'is a Spanish priest. It is a type I know well. He is not the modern American priest, clean and well-groomed; he is dirty and unkempt, he is a beast, and this is what I make him, a comic beast.' (Harold C. Schonberg, *Virtuosi*, Vintage, books, New York, 1985, p. 340)

As one can imagine, this pushing of character extremes was admired by some and considered perverse by others.

Tall, athletic, and attractive, with smooth, large, peasant features ("free from any sharply distinctive features," Victor Borovsky) his face could be amazingly supple and adapted well to assuming other personalities. Chaliapin was also an accomplished painter and sculptor and published two biographical books during his life. Kutsch and Riemens accurately assessed him as follows: "On the stage he was characterized by a self-willed, but always artistic performance and by eminent acting skill."

> Met diva Geraldine Farrar said Chaliapin had a voice like "melodious thunder" but warned of his unannounced antics to hog the limelight onstage. 'Chaliapin was a wonderful opera partner, but one had to be watchful for sudden departures from the rehearsal plan, and the touches of originality favorable only for the aggrandizement of Chaliapin.' (Harold C. Schonberg, *Virtuosi*, Vintage, books, New York, 1985, p. 336)

Chaliapin's egocentric manner of dealing with artistic situations and his demand for autonomous control seems to have been rarely at the expense of the work at hand. Like many artists, his moods were mercurial and he could be extremely temperamental. I suspect he was the kind of artist that one would readily go to see perform, but not someone with whom one would want to spend much private time.

Highly willful, he could appear callous to the point of being offensive. On one occasion he left the stage before his final exit at the end of a performance of *Faust* during a Met tour performance (in Rochester, New York, 1924) because he did not want to miss a train home. But, as are many other willful artists, he could be extremely generous. In 1914, after an exhausting schedule of performing in London:

> An exhausted Chaliapin planned to rest and get some medical treatment in Karlsbad, however his train was stopped just a couple of hours after it left Paris, and everyone was ordered to vacate it. Chaliapin later wrote in his book: 'We heard that war had been declared and the train was proceeding no further. Nor were there any trains for Paris. In addition, all horses had been requisitioned, and I was left with my suitcases at a little

station among crowds of anxious and excited Frenchmen. To make my return to Paris easier, I opened my cases and started giving away most of their contents to poor people, leaving myself with the barest essentials'.

Chaliapin's only goal at that time was to return home. Since there was no chance of doing so by the usual way – via train through Germany, he was forced to go back to England. After overcoming all obstacles (political, financial, administrative, etc.), he boarded a ship in Glasgow, and via Norway, Sweden, and Finland, he eventually came home. Immediately upon his return, Chaliapin organized two private hospitals (25 beds each), and covered all their expenses for more than three years; one in Moscow, the other in Petrograd (a name given to St.Petersburg at the beginning of the war). During those years, not only did he give many charity recitals for the wounded and refugees, but also donated large amounts of his own money to other needy war victims. (Allan Evans in liner notes, Feodor Chaliapin, Volume 4, Arbiter Recording, 2002)

To appreciate the degree of Chaliapin's acting ability, it should be noted that Constantin Stanislovsky stated that he patterned much of his acting method on Chaliapin's performances.

To create a character Chaliapin had to comprehend the logic of his mental world and in addition, to define his psychological relationships with the other operatic characters. It was Chaliapin's firm conviction that an actor's incarnation of a role was woven to a significant extent of relationships with the other characters and opinions about them. These interrelationships revealed contradictory traits out of which the image of a real person would emerge. This could be achieved, however, only by deep study of all the roles in a production. (*The Art of Chaliapin*, Victor Borovsky, Opera, 1/82)

Chaliapin did not interpret a role, he *was* the character. He explained the difference best himself when he wrote of watching the performance of a tenor in the role of Canio in *I Pagliacci*. The singer wept and suffered loudly on stage, but the audience found it amusing rather than moving. Backstage the singer continued in distress, explaining to Chaliapin, "I can't help myself, I cry. I was so sorry for the poor clown." Chaliapin wrote, "I saw where the problem lay. A not entirely untalented singer ruined his role by crying not the clown's tears but his own tears of sympathy. This produced a comic effect because the tenor's tears were of no interest to anyone." (*The Art of Chaliapin*, Victor Borovsky, Opera, 1/82)

The Voice and Recordings

When it comes to discussing the Chaliapin legacy, it is not so much a matter of selecting recordings or discussing "which are the best?" because all are worth listening to and collecting. Based on this, to do a worthy analysis of his recordings would (and should) require a book of its own. The amount of artistic and musical nuance that Chaliapin brought to the music is much too complicated to deal with in a cursory manner. Like Maria Callas, Chaliapin's art is a matter of colors and hues, accents and emphasis, and textual felicities.

So what was the voice like? It was a dark-hued, long-ranging bass instrument, more brilliant on top than at the bottom (similar to the 1980s Samuel Ramey), fastly spun and slightly dry in timbre. As with his physical appearance, this dryness, or lack of rich, distinctive timbre, allowed him to infuse his music with a kaleidoscopic array of colors, all of which promoted his characterizations.

> … (He) could sing of death and make one's flesh creep: he could sing comic songs in Russian and make English audiences laugh: he could sing love songs to make feminine hearts of all ages flutter. With his voice alone he could suggest the carefree gaiety of youth, the resignation of old age, modesty or arrogance, cringing or bullying – in fact every emotion from the cradle to the grave. (*Playing for Chaliapin*, Ivor Newton, 1964 – liner notes for Angel COLH 141)

His technique was not perfect. Anyone familiar with Donizetti, Bellini and Rossini recordings, knows that his manner of dealing with floridity was comically idiosyncratic and would never be tolerated from a singer today. Instead of using the typical flaw of an aspirate "h" for the delineation of multi-note patterns, Chaliapin used a "w."

As J.B. Steane notes:

> Chaliapin's odd "wubber' is no delight to the ear (it must be one of the few mannerisms of great singers not to have found its imitators), but it does not affect the tone production. And, though it is impossible to make a hard-and-fast distinction in this kind of thing, I would register it as a fault of style rather than of technique… (*The Grand Tradition*, Charles Scribner's Sons, New York, 1974)

He tampered with other music as well. His riveting recordings of the Clock Scene in *Boris Godunov*—really a mad scene— includes text and exclamations not in Mussorgsky's score. There has ever been criticism of his performance of Leporello's and Basilio's music, but this was not empty willfulness on Chaliapin's part. If one compares photographs of his Basilio in *Il barbiere di Siviglia* with his recordings of the aria, one realizes that they are just different "images" of the same thing; one visual, one aural. It is the striving for honesty of character that causes one to embrace the glory of his concepts.

There were a number of reasons for Chaliapin's vocal longevity. High on this list is his early training with Usatov. Then there is the preoccupation he had with his voice and technique and his desire to always improve:

In the liner notes for the 1961-released, eight-LP Melodyia set devoted to Chaliapin's recordings, J. Andronikov wrote:

> The well-known Soviet cellist Victor Kubatsky, professor of the Moscow conservatoire, recollects that at the Bolshoy stage rehearsals in 1920 Chaliapin would use every spare minute to step down to the proscenium and listen to the cello group playing, shielding his eyes from the dazzling light with his hand. Kubatsky, who was the first cello had an idea that Chaliapin was not content with the cello group and asked him the question. "No, it is not so," answered Chaliapin. "I learn to sing from cellos."

There is another, a physiological factor about Chaliapin that few take into account. He habitually sang on the topside of pitch rather than in the center or underneath. (Part of this was undoubtedly due to the natural oscillation of his vibrato.) This kept his tone and pitch high and, consequently, his voice was kept constantly "stretched". There are other singers who have instinctively sung in this manner: Leonie Rysanek, Leontyne Price, Placido Domingo, Birgit Nilsson, Boris Christoff, and Samuel Ramey among them. Each of these singers has had an unusually long performing career.

Just as this group did, Chaliapin had a tendency to sing a bit sharp. If you are not sure exactly what I mean, compare the vocal structure of the singers listed above with such singers as Jessye Norman, Deborah Voigt, James McCracken, and Cheryl Studer whose natural vibratos tend to oscillate on the lower side of a pitch and whose pitch errors veer toward the lower, rather than the upper, side of pitch. As he aged, Chaliapin's voice gained a throatiness and, occasionally, a coarse, guttural quality. Not surprisingly, he would sometimes successfully use this defect as an interpretive device.

Then there is Chaliapin's treatment of text; not the mere articulation of words, but something far deeper. It was an innate sensitivity he had to the physical peculiarities of the production of sounds within the mouth cavity. Callas had this instinct, as did Fischer-Dieskau, and Schwarzkopf. It is the understanding that not only the words and their timbre carry meaning, but also the manner in which you emit them. Not only could Chaliapin "bark" out dramatic recitative, but a moment later he would caress the vowels and consonants of words in a way that was almost erotic. (To hear an example of this, listen to the aria from Rachmaninov's *Aleko* that he recorded in 1929. It is one of the most emotionally wrenching examples of yearning ever recorded.) The ability to find and utilize those degrees of sensitivity and unite them with timbre variation and innate musicality is true interpretive genius. Some of his most fascinating recordings are unaccompanied folk songs in which, using his sound alone, he bewitches the listener. To Chaliapin, the music was of the utmost importance. Ivor Newton, who often accompanied the bass in recital and on tour, wrote:

> At his recitals, Chaliapin often sang the aria from Rachmaninov's *Aleko*, which ends with a very long postlude – and this he would never allow to be cut. As I played, Chaliapin would listen with such intensity that there would be no sound or movement in the audience until I finally lifted the pedal at the end of the last bar. (*Playing for Chaliapin*, Ivor Newton, 1964, liner notes for Angel COLH 141)

The Legacy

Chaliapin was a contemporary of Caruso and his recorded legacy is as vast. His first recordings were made in 1898 (six privately made wax cylinders that have survived) and continued until 1936, almost forty years later. His first flat disks were made sometime in early 1902 (accurate documentation was not a priority in the infancy of serious recording) at the Hotel Continental in Moscow.

Chaliapin recorded more than 450 sides during eighty-four recording sessions. As Alan Kelly notes:

> Altogether, 456 different recordings, including multiple takes, have been traced. 197 of these were issued on 78 rpm records and a further 7 have appeared on LP only. They cover some 132 separate titles of which many were recorded over and over again at different times. (*The Record Collector*, Vol XX, Nos. 8–10, August 1972, p. 181)

A striking thing about this huge legacy is the fact that not one of them is uninteresting. There is always something that one can obtain from his many, many recordings. As Keith Hardwick of EMI once noted, Chaliapin rarely, if ever, made a bad recording.

Since the days of the LP, Chaliapin has been well represented. First and foremost among these is a set from Russia, an eight-disk Melodyia set (*The Art of Feodor Chaliapin*, Melodyia 018101-018116) that was released in 1961 containing 108 selections.

Rubini had a volume (GV 10 with twelve selections). Rococo had a single volume (#5337 with fifteen selections). Scala records issued five volumes (Scala 801, 807, 852, 869, 870) that offered sixty-nine selections, and EMI released two LPs in the Great Recordings of the Century series. The Great Recordings releases were beautifully (and warmly) transferred and sumptuously presented. They came with two booklets, one containing the texts of the selections and one having biographical and discographic information. Many other labels offered what they considered to be representative collections of the bass's recordings. Even Eddie Smith TAP Records offered some Chaliapin selections paired with Titta Ruffo (TAP #309).

As Alan Kelly notes in his article on Chaliapin for *The Record Collector* (Vol XX, August, 1972) when it came to Chaliapin's discography and the many duplications of repertoire, one of the main problems for collectors during the LP era was that it often was "…very difficult to identify the contents of LP transfers, since companies were usually loth to disclose which originals were used…"

With better documentation, the era of the CD caused much of this inaccuracy to be corrected.

To learn more about this artist, I suggest you get as many of his recordings as you can. Unfortunately, at this time there is no complete edition. There are, however, a number of CD collections of his recordings:

Symposium—1105 – Harold Wayne Collection, Volume 10. This compilation includes six of Chaliapin's 1902 disks in remarkably fine condition showing to great advantage his unique voice at the age of 29, at the beginning of his international career.

Naxos—(8.110748-49)— an excellent two-CD set with thirty-two selections from *Prince Igor, Robert le Diable, Lucrezia Borgia, Boris Godunov, Ernani, Norma, La sonnambula*, and other operatic excerpts, as well as twelve songs.

EMI—Great Recordings of the Century (CDH 7610092) – Russian Opera Arias.

Pearl—Feodor Chaliapin Sings Russian Music – two volumes (GEMM 9920, 9921), three CDs of forty selections, with some previously unpublished material.

Pearl—Two additional compilations, including a two-disc set called *The Great Chaliapin* having thirty-three selections.

Nimbus—(7823/24) A 2-CD set of 36 selections from *Boris Godunov, The Demon, Faust, Sadko, Don Quichotte, Don Giovanni, Aleko, Price Igor*, as well as eight songs. These ambisonic recordings serve the Chaliapin voice well.

Preiser—three Lebendige Vergangenheit volumes (PR 89030, 89087, 89516) featuring fifty-one selections

Preiser—The Feodor Chaliapin Songbook (PR 89207) – two CDs of thirty-eight selections.

Preiser—Feodor Chaliapin on Stage (PR 89965) –Covent Garden 1920s live performances from *Mefistofele, Boris Godunov*, and *Faust*.

Guild—Feodor Chaliapin in *Boris Godunov (2006)* – London, July 4, 1928. A carefully restored, if rather unorthodox edition. On the Norbeck Peters and Ford website, R.E. B. reviews this disc:

> Richard Caniell, obviously a great fan of Chaliapin, produced the Guild CD which contains all of the previously issued excerpts from the live Covent Garden performance. In an attempt to include more of that performance, Canelli has 'cut and pasted' from the live performance—including several restored damaged sections—and Chaliapin commercial recordings. He also has interpolated two excerpts from a performance by another fine Boris, Nicola Moscona, to provide continuity. A 20-page booklet focuses on Chaliapin and details of performance restoration.....this is a valuable CD."

Arbiter—(http://www.arbiterrecords.com). This small, independent label deserves special mention. In conjunction with the wife of the late Chaliapin collector, Vladimir Gurvich, Arbiter had planned to release all of Chaliapin's recordings—a projected fourteen CDs. Unfortunately, the project was halted in 2005 with only five volumes released; nevertheless, they are very important. Volume I (1902–1908) Arbiter #125 was released late in 2001; Vol. 2 #126 (1908–1911); Vol. 3 #127 (1911–1914); Vol. 4 #132 (1913–1921) (song repertoire); and Volume 5 #142. Vol. 5 (1921–1923) appeared in 2004.

The Arbiter transfers are very well done and the original Russian texts and English translations are provided for all selections. Considering the great importance in which Chaliapin held texts, and his interpretive strength, even unfinished, this is an indispensable collection, especially as the recordings are presented chronologically. The booklets include costumed photographs of Chaliapin in various roles.

Among the five volumes of the Arbiter Chaliapin series there are 111 sides provided.

It is an impossible and subjective task to consider, but if I were to choose a single issue that was most important, it would be either the Naxos 2-CD set remastered by Ward Marston or the Nimbus 2-CD set. It boils down to which of his recordings you are interested in, the repertoire you prefer to hear, rather than recommendation. Of course, his *Boris Godunov* recordings (all of the versions) are recommended, but then so, too, are his many folk songs—some are un-accompanied and hauntingly beautiful. Many of the releases include a portion of the famous 1928 live performance of *Boris Godunov* in London.

With such a large discography some repertoire is duplicated. Over the years that he recorded, Chaliapin released:

eight versions of the Prologue of Boito's *Mefistofele.*
seven versions of Don Basilio's "La Calumnia," (*Il barbiere di Siviglia*).
seven versions of Schumann's *Two Grenadiers.*
seven versions of Strokin's "Now let us depart in peace" (Prayer).
seven versions of the Song of the Viking Guest from *Sadko.*
seven versions of the Death of Boris (*Boris Godunov*). (Between 1911 and 1931,
   Chaliapin attempted thirteen times during seven recording sessions to record
   this scene. Only six were released.)
five versions of the Coronation Scene from *Boris Godunov.*
five versions of the "Song of the Volga Boatman."
four versions of Mussorgsky's "Song of the Flea."
four versions of King Philip's "Dormiro sol" (*Don Carlo*)
four versions of Schubert's "Doppelgänger."

In Chaliapin's case, these are not the boring, identical repetitions made by other artists; each version offers different, often memorable, characteristics.

In addition to Russian, Italian and French arias, Chaliapin recorded (in Russian) songs of Schubert, Schumann, Brahms, Massenet, Grieg, and Ibert.

Were his song recitals replicated today, they would horrify audiences. At a Chaliapin recital, audience members were given the opportunity to purchase a small (5" x 7") booklet of approximately seventy-eight pages called *Book of Songs in the repertoire of Feodor Chaliapin.* The booklets were sold for twenty-five cents each. Inside were English translations from 101 songs. Chaliapin would announce from the stage the number of the song he would elect to sing, giving the audience a moment to find the appropriate text.

In his book, *Am I Too Loud,* Gerald Moore describes this rather bizarre Chaliapin behavior. (He also notes that he prepared a repertoire of 200 songs for Chaliapin's recitals in London.)

> Before each song Chaliapin boomed out, 'Numbaire 45 Numbaire 45' – then he would give the audience a moment to read the translation and this would give the accompanist time to find the music. All this gave the impression that the great man was obeying a whim. No indication was given to me in the artist's room as to his intentions and for my first two concerts I was on tenterhooks wondering what was coming next. But the realization soon dawned on me that he kept pretty much to the same programme on every occasion and always 'The Volga Boat Song.' Eighty-five per cent of the music I had sweated over was never performed. (Liner notes for *Feodor Chaliapin on Stage,* Presier 89965)

Those who have heard Chaliapin in the theater all agree that his recordings give only a dim representation of his tremendous interpretive power.

So, where does one begin about making recommendations? Anywhere! Any of his recordings are recommended, but there are some that are very special. One is the 1907 recording of Mussorgsky's "Song of the Flea." This version was orchestrated by none other than Igor Stravinsky and is one of his earliest works.

Although I do not always agree with Michael Scott's assessment of singers, I happen to agree wholeheartedly with his thoughts about Chaliapin:

> The gramophone cannot preserve a singer's physical presence, yet Chaliapin's art was so perfectly integrated, his singing so much an expression of the man himself, that his records almost achieve the impossible....The timbre of the voice is characteristic, the tone limpid and correctly placed on the breath, the registers smoothly blended and like Battistini, his mastery of the head voice is complete. All of Chaliapin's technical skill was deployed for expressive purposes. (Michael Scott, *The Record of Singing, Volume II* – Holmes & Meier Publishers, New York 1979)

Because Chaliapin made so many recordings, and a number of versions of some arias or songs, you might want to refer to a discography to guide you in your collecting. A wonderful online reference for 78 rpm vocal recordings is 78 Opera (www.78opera.com). Robert Johannesson of Kristianstad, Sweden creates discographies as a hobby. Even so, he has done a remarkably thorough job and provides the collector an invaluable service. His discographies are arranged alphabetically and are available as PDF downloads. The site offers photographs of singers as well as the sale of recordings. There is a section where you can listen to rare 78s. It is a valuable site to visit on a regular basis.

One of my favorite CDs is the EMI "References" (EMI CDH 7610092), a collection of Russian music that Chaliapin recorded in the 1920s . Transferred with care by Keith Hardwick, the selections offer an excellent portrait of this singer's strengths. Included is the not-to-be-missed aria from *Aleko,* as well as the must-have disks of *Boris Godunov* recorded live at Covent Garden in 1928. This includes one of the most remarkable death scenes ever captured on disk—and pianissimo singing, the production of which should be studied by all voice types. Chaliapin not only proves that a well-placed pianissimo will travel throughout the largest house, he also hints at how to accomplish that feat. (It is there for anyone to decipher.) It is remarkable to realize that in 1928 he was fifty-five years old and had been singing professionally for thirty-eight years.

When discussing this recording David Hamilton writes:

> The tonal colouring of the farewell really suggests a dying man, who only later summons up reserves of power to assert his tsardom one last time and the prayer is spun out on an incredibly suave, apparently endless *fil da voce*....

> From these discs, it is clear that Chaliapin liked to take his time playing before an audience, and most of the studio recordings have nothing like the same atmosphere. (*Opera on Record*, Hutchinson & Co, London, 1979)

Another fascinating aspect of the 1928 London performance is something that only J.B. Steane emphasizes:

...(The Death Scene) is a masterpiece of dramatic resource and command, but what impresses afresh with every hearing is the tonal beauty of the quiet passages, the Prayer being incomparably haunting in its warm and sustained pianissimo. Chaliapin must have put his voice through some considerable stresses during his long career...but in fact (his) records show hardly any evidence of ageing in the voice at all. His tone never spread; there was never even the hint of wobble, but always a perfectly defined sound, the vibrations regular, the sheer volume somewhat diminished but the resonance and sonority still warm and healthy as in his prime. (*The Grand Tradition*, Charles Scribner's Sons, New York, 1974)

Another indispensable CD is Preiser's "Feodor Chaliapin on Stage" (89965) which gathers all the live recordings from London including the *Boris Godunov* recordings of 1928, adding *Faust, Mefistofele*, and *Mozart and Salieri* (Rimsky-Korsakov) also from 1927–28. This is a well-transferred disc and an education in itself.

Nimbus (due to their ambisonic method of transferring) gives the listener an idea of what the Chaliapin voice would have sounded like in the recital hall; the voice bouncing off wooden walls. This two-disk set of thirty-six selections (NI 7823/24) offers indispensable recordings; included is the Death Scene from Massenet's *Don Quichotte* (written for and premiered by Chaliapin)—a moving and unforgettable experience. Chaliapin premiered this Massenet work in Monte Carlo on February 19, 1910.

One must include Beethoven's "In questa tomba" (one of my favorites) that is deemed by the famous critic, Irving Kolodin, as a "potent and imaginative" performance. There are arias from *La bohème, Prince Igor, Faust, Mefistofele, Rusalka* (Dargomyzhsky), *Sadko* and others. At a budget price this (or the more typically transferred Naxos double-CD set) may be an excellent starting point for new listeners.

Although Pearl has a number of releases, some listeners may find their undoctored method of transfer difficult to listen to, especially some of the more obscure, worn recordings.

Perhaps some enterprising label will one day release a complete issue of all of the Chaliapin recordings. Until that time, one must be content with the piecemeal collecting of Chaliapin recordings. Truly, it doesn't matter. Any of the CD releases mentioned in this appreciation are good starting points to become representative collections for a personal library. When it comes to Chaliapin, it is not how many of his recordings you have, but that you have any at all. I was fortunate to have been introduced to Chaliapin's recordings as a teenager when I was forming my artistic and musical tastes. His voice and art have been an important part of my life for more than fifty years and for that I am very grateful.

Chaliapin is one of those rare singers whose recordings will enrich your life and art. His striking individuality and his willingness to take chances and stand up for what he believed was the truth in his art remains an inspiration to all singers today, more than seventy-five years after his death.

(A shortened version of this article first appeared in *Classical Singer* magazine, April, 2001.)

Fernando De Lucia
(1860–1925)

De Lucia is probably among *the* most infuriating singers to deal with in a restoration project. He was notorious for using transpositions, making the selection of the correct playback speed a nightmare. Each restorer has their own idea about what speed is the one at which a recording should be played. They seem mostly to not agree, and in many cases, it is a subjective exercise as they each have valid reasons for their choices. Naturally, this will have tremendous impact on how de Lucia's voice comes across to the contemporary listener, especially because of his rapid vibrato. On one hand, the incorrect playing speed can make his voice sound comical. On the other hand, who could believe that he would transpose an aria down a fourth? And what are the artistic ramifications of doing that?

At first I thought only to touch briefly on De Lucia's work. His recordings are very controversial and he is a complicated performer. Before I completed my decision, however, I made the mistake of listening carefully to a few of his recordings—I was hooked! Before I knew what was happening, I became addicted to De Lucia's very personable manner of singing.

He was born in Naples and studied at the Naples Music Conservatory with Vincenzo Lombardi and Beniamino Carelli. He made his debut in Naples in 1885 as *Faust* and then sang in the Italian and South American provinces for a number of years, gathering stage experience. In 1887, he was hired to sing Alfredo in *La traviata* at Drury Lane in London, but was overshadowed at the time by tenor Jean de Reszke. English audiences did not appreciate his manner of singing or his rapid vibrato. In 1891 he created the role of Fritz in Mascagni's *L'Amico Fritz* at the Teatro Costanzi in Rome and everything changed. The next year he created the tenor lead in Mascagni's *I Rantzau* in Florence. In the 1893–94 season at the Metropolitan Opera in New York, he appeared as Canio in *Pagliacci*, Don Ottavio in *Don Giovanni* and the Duke in *Rigoletto*.

Despite his bel canto training, De Lucia quickly became known as a specialist in the new verismo works. And, despite the fact that his voice was rather short on top, many verismo composers wanted him to sing the premieres of their works. De Lucia sang at La Scala in 1895, in the world premiere of Mascagni's *Silvano*, and also appeared in the first Milan performances of Puccini's *La bohème* and Massenet's *La Navarraise*. In November, 1898, he created the role of Osaka in Mascagni's *Iris* and, at Covent Garden in July 1900, he played Cavaradossi in the first performance of *Tosca* in England. In 1916, De Lucia gave a farewell performance at La Scala as Rodolfo in *La bohème*. His final public appearance was when he sang at the funeral of Enrico Caruso in Naples in 1921. After his retirement, he taught at the Naples Conservatory, where he had, himself, been trained. His pupils included the Hungarian dramatic soprano, Maria Nemeth, and the French tenor, Georges Thill.

De Lucia specialized in his day's "modern" music. From his recordings and the reviews written in that time, his vocal method was not perceived as verismatic; his voice was not particularly dramatic, and his range was not extensive. But he was, it seems, quite a stage actor, compensating for any perceived vocal failings (or idiosyncracies). Another strong point in De Lucia's singing was his musical instinct. His recordings prove that he knew exactly where, and how much, to pull and tug at the music to squeeze the most emotion out of it. He was a master of the art of rubato. One might expect this to have quite an effect on operatic music, but it could also have a devastating emotional effect on his song recordings. What is interesting, is that this very personable manner of singing was a vocal tradition that was all but dead by the early 1900s when verismo singing came into full force in Italy—audiences were beginning to prefer tenors to be forceful and dramatic, rather than artistically delicate. Fernando De Lucia straddled the two worlds of bel canto and verismo and was surprisingly successful.

De Lucia was also a master of ornamental improvisation, gracing, as it was known in his day. One hears this unique art in his creator's recordings of Osaka's aria from Mascagni's *Iris* and in the Cherry Tree duet from Mascagni's *L'Amico Fritz* with Angela De Angelis where he inserts various turns and mordants. He also did this in numerous songs. It is even more apparent in arias from *Il barbiere di Siviglia*.

It is an archaic practice that harks back to the early days of bel canto singing. The little flourishes are meant to add color and grace to vocal lines and make their renditions personal and memorable. It is similar to the way today's popular singers embroider their vocal lines with triplets, ornamental figures, vocal flourishes, mordants, and grace notes. It is a highly expressive and individual form of musical expression that is so integrated into the singer's mentality that it truly becomes a method of interpretation as well as an artistic concept of singing. It is a process that is difficult to explain to a lay person or untrained singer. It is the instinctive knowledge of where an ornament is needed to emphasize a word or the direction of the vocal line. If done correctly, it will seem as if it had always been in the music and a part of what the composer wrote. A number of De Lucia's contemporaries used this flowering of vocal lines including Luisa Tetrazzini, Marcella Sembrich, and Mattia Battistini. To further illuminate this concept, a good example of this type of ornamental writing (on a grand scale) are the variants and ornamention that

Roland Gagnon wrote for Beverly Sills in such operas as *Roberto Devereux, Maria Stuarda, Anna Bolena, Lucia di Lammermoor, I Capuletti ed I Montecchi, La sonnambula*, and many others. In most cases you cannot tell where Donizetti, Bellini, or Rossini left off and Gagnon began.

Composers of the period held varying opinions about DeLucia's gracing of their scores. Mascagni detested it, while Giordano seemed not to mind. It is important to understand that De Lucia used this vocal effect only to grace the vocal line—to enhance the music—not to draw attention to himself.

After listening to a number of his disks, I found them compelling, enjoyable, and satisfying; especially when seen as a window into a long-forgotten mode of singing. So long as the music is sung with honesty and conviction, it doesn't matter whether it is in its original key. In the latter portion of her career, Joan Sutherland regularly transposed the music of *Lakmé, Semiramide, Lucia di Lammermoor* and *Anna Bolena*. Placido Domingo was known to occasionally transpose the music of *Otello*. At one time, transpositions were not only accepted as part of a singer's art, they were expected, and were usually accepted without comment.

It is the rapid oscillation of De Lucia's vibrato that causes problems for today's listener. That, taken with his heavy use of rubati, and the idiosyncratic use of ornaments, makes Fernando De Lucia sound like a kind of musical alien—but what a fascinating, mesmerizing, and beautiful-sounding alien he is.

The fact remains that, throughout the various eras of vocalism, English-speaking countries have always prefered voices that do not flutter like De Lucia's and this must have had much to do with his lack of steady work in both New York and London.

Because of his overt expressiveness and individuality, it is not surprising that De Lucia had quite a large ego. Indeed, his primary reason for beginning to record was to show up the very popular (and younger) Enrico Caruso. De Lucia wanted to demostrate that his singing carried forth the true precepts of bel canto.

No matter the reason that it came into existence, Fernando De Lucia's recorded legacy has left an enduring mark on classical vocal music. Well over one hundred years later, vocal experts continue to argue over his recordings, their correct playback speed, the extent of his notorious transpositon of music, and the effects of his vocal technique. He remains the enigma he has always been.

Michael Scott notes:

> In his lifetime, though de Lucia's histrionic skill was highly regarded, he did not enjoy a reputation, like de Reszké, as a charmer; yet on records it is surely this quality above all that has endeared him to collectors. In the songs of Tosti, Denza, Costa and di Capua, he is irresistible, and when he applies the same affection to a work that never gets it any more, Wagner's *Lohengrin*, the agogic lingerings reveal a quality in the music we had quite forgotten was there. (*The Record of Singing Volume I*, Charles Scribner's Sons, NY, 1977, p. 126,)

Loving the recording process, De Lucia left a huge legacy, about four hundred sides recorded across eighteen years. He began recording with Gramophone, from

1902 to 1909. His partners in duets were such popular singers as Antonio Pini-Corsi (baritone), Maria Galvany (soprano), Giuseppina Huguet (soprano), and Celestina Boninsegna (soprano). His repertoire ran the gamut: *Lohengrin, Luisa Miller, La Favorita, L'Elisir, Carmen, Faust, Mignon, Iris, Tosca, Adriana, Fedora, Manon, Cavalleria rusticana*, and more. In 1911 he recorded thirty sides of Neopolitan songs for Fonotipia and, from 1917 through 1922 (after his retirement), De Lucia recorded an amazing three hundred and one sides for Phonotype Records. His selections included many arias (some, like *Otello*, came from operas he never sang on stage) as well as almost-complete recordings of *Il barbiere di Siviglia* and *Rigoletto*.

John Freestone writes about the unusual situation between the Phonotype company and Fernando De Lucia:

> ...so prolific were his Phonotype recordings that until Dr. Michael Henstock finally unravelled the matter in his biography, Fernando De Lucia, it was for many years widely thought that the tenor owned the company. A few of the titles from this last series are of exceeding rarity since they were made in Naples and may have had only very limited circulation outside that city. (Liner notes for Symposium 1231 The Harold Wayne Collection – Volume 33)

Even more remarkable, Dr. Michael Henstock explains in his biography of De Lucia that the existence of two-thirds of this huge legacy of Phonotype disks is the result of a minor miracle:

> During World War II, Italians were called upon to collect metals, particularly copper, for the war effort. Raffaele and Americo Esposito [of Phonotype] knew that their matrices were threatened. Secretly, largely at night, they built a concrete bunker under the garden behind the factory in Via Enrico de Marinis, and there many of the matrices...passed the war years. A few reappeared when peace was renewed, but most remained underground. Raffaele died in 1945, and Americo in 1956. Astonishingly, neither ever revealed to the family the secret of the garden. In 1961, during work to enlarge the factory, a workman's pick struck the edge of the bunker. As Americo's sons...watched, the vault was opened, and the matrices once again saw daylight. (*Fernando De Lucia*, Duckworth, London, 1990, p.335)

The LP era saw many De Lucia releases throughout the world. The most notable was a Scala release in the U.S. (814) having sixteen operatic selections, as well as releases from Russia and Italy. The U.K. was the leader in producing LPs that included an issue by Belcanto, the budget priced Olympus (ORL 216), and a number of releases from Rubini, including the 1979 critically acclaimed five-disk set of De Lucia's complete G&T recordings. Today's master restorer, Ward Marston studied the Rubini LPs when learning about De Lucia.

In the notes for his own 2013 Fernando De Lucia release (*Fernando De Lucia: The Complete Gramophone Company Recordings 1902–1909*) Marston confesses:

> "(The Rubini)...was a fine set, and like many other music lovers I spent hours listening, enthralled by this fascinating tenor, who sounded as no one I had ever heard, either on records or in the flesh. I was astonished at the number of transposed arias, wondering if

these records had been transferred at the proper speeds. I began collecting the original discs to determine for myself whether or not the Rubini LPs were accurate representations of De Lucia's voice. After years of intense listening, I concluded that the pitches on the Rubini LPs are essentially correct."

Rubini also released at least two other LPs featuring De Lucia's Phonotype recordings.

There is presently no complete Fernando De Lucia collection. This is not surprising. If one one were able to gather all his recordings together at once, they would probably result in a twenty-five-CD set!

The best set circulating today is Ward Marston's collection on four CDs released in 2013. It includes ninety-eight sides, De Lucia's complete Gramophone recordings of 1902 through 1909, and twenty-nine of his three hundred Phonotype records.

If a *full* four-disc set (not one CD is less than seventy-eight minutes) is too much, Nimbus has an excellent seventy-eight-minute overview of his Gramophone recordings.

Symposium has two single-disc issues; one deals with de Lucia's early Gramophone recordings, the other is a part of the wonderful Symposium-sponsored Harold Wayne series, *The Harold Wayne Collection, Volume 33,* a seventy-eight-minute recital offering seventeen of the 1917 to 1922 Phonotype recordings. All but twelve sides can also be found on the Marston set. (Those twelve sides, however, are definitely worth having.)

At the time of this writing, it is rumored that Marston may release another set of De Lucia's Phonotype sides. However, at this time, if you obtain the Marston set and Symposium's Harold Wayne #33, you will have forty-one of the three hundred sides De Lucia made for Phonotype.

There is also an Opal CD (a subsidiary of Pearl) of De Lucia's 1911 Fonotipia's. (Not readily available, you will probably have to search for this one.) From January 10th to the 14th in 1911, he recorded thirty-two sides of Italian songs for Fonotipia (two were not published). A worthwhile set for any library.

Ivan Ershov
(1867–1943)

Ivan Ershov (sometimes spelled Yershov) was one of the finest heroic tenors of his era. Sadly, his name is unfamiliar to most people. He should be mandatory listening for any student tenor. Ershov is a good example of the incorrect belief that if one is not familiar with a singer's name they must not have been very good. There are hundreds of singers who recorded in the pre-LP era who had not only a superb voice and technique but can provide important insight into many aspects of the vocal art. Ivan Ershov is one of these.

He was born the illegitimate son of Maria Stepanova Ershova on a farm near Novocherkaask, Russia. His mother encouraged his interest in music. While in parochial school, he sang in the choir, but in 1883, to help move his family out of poverty, Ershov enrolled in the Alexandrovsky Railway College in Eletz and became a certified engine-driver's mate. During that time he continued to sing, entering and winning amateur singing competitions. Also, he was encouraged to take part in staged operatic productions that were put on by the musical society of Eletz, by the Director of the Railway College. He drew such notice that the citizens of Eletz arranged a benefit for him to travel to Moscow for serious vocal study. However, three months later Ershov went to St. Petersburg where he sang for the composer Anton Rubenstein who recommended he study at the Saint Petersburg Conservatory with Stanislav Ivanovich Gabel and Joseph Palacek. Ershov studied with them for five years on a full scholarship. Between 1891 and 1893 he sang in many student performances. Ershov's climb to fame was slow. Gabel, head of the singing class at the Petersburg Conservatoire wrote about Ershov after his examinations in August of 1890:

> The voice is extremely good. He is talented and has temperament, but he is very nervous, and therefore he is not yet in full command in performance. (Larry Lustig, *The Record Collector*, Volume 42 #4, December, 1997)

Less than a year later Gabel commented:

> I am certain that Ivan Ershov, a pupil of my class, possesses a beautiful voice, studies with great diligence, and has the real possibility of establishing a serious operatic career... (Larry Lustig, *The Record Collector*, Volume 42 #4, December, 1997)

Success did not come easily. When he had finished his studies he was immediately engaged by the Mariinsky Theatre to fill the gap left by the departure of lyric tenor Mikhailov, upon which Gabel commented further, "The reviews were, for the most part, not good, and it was decided that (Ershov) was not yet ready to join the company."

Understandably, Ershov was depressed about the unfavorable reviews but was determined to have a professional career in opera as Gabel continued, "Like many of the finest artists Ershov was mercilessly self-critical. He would agonize almost to the point of neurosis about appearances in new theatres or new roles, often too, when the part was familiar...Ershov would agree to perform in another theatre only when he was aware of just exactly who the conductor, director and other performers would be. He was also insistent on a number of rehearsals..."

At the suggestion of the directors of the Mariinsky, he traveled to Milan in 1894 in order to refine his technique with Cesare Rossi. He returned to Russia that year and was engaged by the Kharkov Opera. Ironically, soon after he accepted that contract, the Mariinsky expressed their interest in having him return. Ershov sent his regrets.

While with the Kharkov, Ershov sang a variety of tenor roles including Romeo in *Roméo et Juliette*, Arturo in *I puritani* (he created quite a sensation with his "clear and clean" high D), Samson in *Samson et Dalila* (critics found him full of great energy and sincerity, acting with fire and great expressiveness), Vladimir in *Prince Igor* and Ernani in *Ernani*. Although successful at the Kharkov, he later accepted a contract with the Mariinsky, making his debut in *Faust* in January of 1895. He remained with that company for thirty-four years, until 1929. However, there were some early problems. On his second appearance as Faust in April, 1895 critic G. P. Kondratiev wrote:

There is no argument that he has a most beautiful voice, but he uses it abominably, rarely producing what I think he really wants to produce.

Later, he wrote:

The production of the voice is far from natural and far from impeccable...but he has temperament and knows how to make a good effect.

Ershov appeared at the Mariinsky in a wide spectrum of operatic works, including Lenski in Tchaikovsky's *Eugene Onegin*, the title roles in *Tannhäuser* (his first Wagner role sung in 1895) and *Lohengrin,* and Faust in *Mefistofele*. The part of Roland in *Esclarmonde* was added in 1897 and, in 1900 he added Tristan in *Tristan und Isolde* and Raoul in *Les Huguenots*. He sang the title role in *Otello* the next year, and *Siegfried* in 1902. He appeared as Radames in *Aïda*, Paolo in *Francesca da Rimini*, John of Leyden in *Le Prophete* and Florestan in *Fidelio*.

In private life Ershov was a reserved, serious-minded individual who disliked the attention he had garnered as a famous singer and was genuinely humble about his accomplishments. He disliked travel, providing one of the reasons why he was not better known to American and English audiences. Other than St Petersburg, he sang only in Kiev and Moscow, and there only occasionally.

He did not seem to be concerned with becoming famous. From all reports, he was a shy, modest man. As Larry Lustig notes in his excellent article, "...he hated any kind of self-promotion, rarely gave interviews and even then would only talk about artistic matters. He suffered terrible stage fright before every one of his appearances...." (Larry Lustig, *The Record Collector*, December, 1997)

Yershov believed strongly that opera was an important art form and not mere entertainment for the wealthy. After the Russian Revolution of 1917, he concentrated most of his energies on producing operatic works and teaching vocal students at the Leningrad (Saint Petersburg) Conservatory, although, in February 1919, he agreed to perform the leading role in a revival of Rimsky-Korsakov's *Kashchey the Deathless*. He also sang Truffaldino in Prokofiev's *The Love for Three Oranges*, which received its premiere Russian performance in February 1926 at the Mariinsky (or the "Leningrad State Academic Theatre for Opera and Ballet" as it had been renamed by the Soviet authorities).

Yershov retired from the stage in 1929, having performed in approximately 55 different operas during the course of his career. In 1938, he was made a People's Artist of the Soviet Union and awarded a doctorate of musicology three years later. He was evacuated to Tashkent in Uzbekistan during the German army's invasion of Russia in World War II. Yershov died in Tashkent in 1943 at the age of 76. His remains were brought back to Russia for reinterment in 1956. (World Public Library, biography provided by his granddaughter, Xenia Krivocheine, http://www.netlibrary.net/articles/Ivan_Yershov, accessed April, 2015)

He was re-buried in the Necropolis of Arts, Alexander Nevsky Monastery (Saint Petersburg). Ershov's wife was a singer and professor at the Petersburg conservatory. His son, Igor Ivanovich Ershov (1916–1985) was a well-known painter and graphic designer.

During his early years at the Mariinsky he became known for his Wagner interpretations bringing an earthy Russian character to Wagner's music. His renown in these roles grew to such an extent that, in 1901, Cosmia Wagner invited him to Bayreuth to perform in her husband's works. Ershov declined, not wanting to relearn his roles in German, but primarily because he feared that he would have to "suppress his own interpretations of the roles in order to fit in with the Bayreuth traditions." (Larry Lustig, *The Record Collector*, December, 1997)

In addition to Wagner, Ershov excelled in such diverse works as *Les Huguenots, Don Giovanni*, and *Ivan Susanin* (his performances of Sobinin's difficult aria with chorus was usually encored—audiences were amazed at his ease and dexterity in singing high C and D-flat.) Ershov's repertoire was vast when one considers that his many concert appearances included such works as Bach's *St. Matthew Passion*, Mozart's *Requiem*, Handel's *Samson*, Berlioz's *Damnation of Faust*, Beethoven's *9th Symphony* and the Verdi *Requiem*.

Throughout his career there seems to have also been an endearing sense of insecurity laced within Ershov's personality as is evidenced by a letter written to his wife in November of 1916: "The entire cast came to me to show how pleased and delighted they were, and I apologized like a fool, in case I had offended anybody."

Handsome, with intense, dark eyes and flexible facial features, like Feodor Chaliapin, he took charge of his own makeup and costuming, and expressed concern for the quality of the productions that surrounded him. Indeed, his acting abilities were often favorably compared to those of Chaliapin. Photographs of Ershov in character show him to be as fascinating as the more famous bass; the two often sang together.

In 1915, Ershov decided to leave the stage and concentrate on teaching voice, taking over students from his teacher, Josef Palacek. He taught for twenty years. In 1922 he transformed the opera class of the Petrograd (formerly St. Petersburg, then Leningrad) Conservatory into the Opera Studio. In 1938, Ershov made a rare singing appearance to perform the Third Act of *Tristan und Isolde* with Fritz Steidry. In 1941 he became a doctor of musicology.

The Voice

While his was one of the great voices of opera, Ershov made only a handful of acoustic recordings, but all are treasures. This is apparent even heard through the dimness of the recording process of that time. It was a finely-spun voice of good size. After analyzing his recordings, I suspect that much of Ershov's dramaticism was carefully planned and had to do with the manner of his utterances more so than his producing huge amounts of sound. He had an excellent command of pitch and diction and knew how to make one work with the other to create the dramatic effects he wanted. This is instinctive and not something that can be taught in the voice studio. Further, his voice had an appealing masculine quality, a virile manner of singing, full of vibrancy.

Michel Scott, usually reticent to praise, noted that:

> Erschov's voice has a resplendent quality entirely of its own; though characteristically Russian it is without the pallid tone and effete manner that is so monotonous and unpleasing in many of his contemporaries. The tone is unusually limpid and brilliant, and he has a complete control over the whole instrument at virtually any dynamic level through a range that extends from bottom C to the D above high C. It would be hard to find a tenor with a better integrated voice, in which the registers are more properly equalized and blended. His singing style is rooted in the messa di voce, and with this as the basis of his effects he has a seemingly inexhaustible range and variety of nuances at his disposal. (*The Record of Singing*, Vol I, Charles Scribner's Sons, New York, 1977, p. 216)

J.B. Steane wrote of him:

> His was a sturdy, ringing heroic voice as we hear in an excerpt from Tannhäuser, but more than that, he could wield this powerful instrument with grace and elegance. (*The Grand Tradition*, Charles Scribner's Sons, New York, 1974, p. 109)

One often finds mention in articles and reviews of Ershov's superlative technique. Considering the vocal trials he had to go through before he could have a professional career, and his almost fanatical preoccupation with the technical aspects of his art, one should not be surprised that he developed one of the finest techniques one will have the pleasure of hearing.

The Recordings

Ershov made only ten recordings (in 1903, on G&T and Columbia), all during his vocal prime. On hearing all of his recordings, one is left with a sense of regret that he did not record more. This is followed by a great sense of relief that he recorded at all! A few selections were recorded for both companies. They reflect Ershov's eclectic repertoire that included arias from Verdi's *Otello*, Meyerbeer's *Les Huguenots* and *Le Prophete*, Wagner's *Siegfried* and *Tannhäuser,* as well as songs by Tchaikovsky and Mussorgsky and a single duet by Konstantin Villebois. All are accompanied by piano. It is disappointing that he did not record with an orchestra. It would have been wonderful to hear this voice with the colors of orchestral instruments surrounding him.

Although tiny, Ershov's recorded legacy is important and invaluable. The recordings show him to have been a solid, versatile musician proficient in all aspects of singing and refined nuance. His finely spun voice was mellow yet capable of tremendous intensity. His low register was darkly tinged yet sweet with a curious, but not unattractive, throaty quality in its lower extremes. His top register blossomed like the more modern Franco Corelli, open-throated and ringing. I am partial to Ershov's timbre, energy, obvious commitment, and emotionally honest delivery. In describing the qualities that make up the Ershov voice, using more modern singers as examples, he had the musical instinct of Jonas Kaufmann, the elegance of Alfredo Kraus, and the thrilling dramaticism of Franco Corelli.

In Russia, during the LP era, all ten selections were gathered onto a single LP (Melodyia M10 45189). At the time of this writing, Ershov's legacy is broken up between two CD labels. The six G&Ts are on volume I of Pearl's massive, five-volume set (15 CDs) *Singers of Imperial Russia*, a superb collection of some of the rarest early Russian recordings. The remaining four Columbias are on a Symposium CD, *Major Vocal Rarities* (Symposium 1350). The Symposium CD also includes three unpublished 1907 Milan sides of Feodor Chaliapin singing unaccompanied folk songs.

Following is the complete list of his disks:

G&T, St. Petersburg 1903 (Pearl)
94y Meyerbeer: Plus blanche (*Les Huguenots*) 022011
95y Meyerbeer: Pour Berthe; Versez! que tout respire (*Le Prophète*) Pastorale & Brindisi (72) 022012
96y Wagner: Hoho! Ho-hei! (Forging scene) (*Siegfried*) 022034
97y Mussrgsky: Death of Field-Marshal (Songs and Dances of Death) 022044
98y Tchaikovsky O child, beneath thy window 022035
99y Villebois: Sailors (w. Sharonov) 024000

Columbia, St. Petersburg 1903/1904 (Symposium)

35469 Meyerbeer: Pour Berthe; Versez! que tout respire (*Le Prophète*) Pastorale
   & Brindisi

35470 Verdi: Ora e per sempre addio (*Otello*):

35472 Wagner: Dir töne Lob (act 1); Dir, Göttin der Liebe (act 2) (*Tannhäuser*)

35473 Wagner: Hoho! Ho-hei! (Forging scene) (*Siegfried*)

Pearl's transfers are remarkable. Keith Hardwick was an aural magician. Even though these recordings are more than one hundred and ten years old, they have astonishing clarity and presence. Ershov's voice emerges as though he was in your living room. Despite initial sharping by Ershov and the low-tech recording, Raoul's Romance from *Les Huguenots* is an excellent introduction to a voice that, in the next moment, can easily deliver Siegfried's Forging Scene with dramatic diction (in Russian), crisp rhythm, and clean floridity. Ershov was more than loud high notes, as his decrescendi and trills in the Pastorale and Drinking Song from *Le Prophete* prove.

Mussorgsky's "Field Marshall" (*Songs and Dances of Death*) has tremendous energy and like Ershov's Wagner is impassioned yet full of nuance. It remains one of the most satisfactory versions of the song that one can hear. Tchaikovsky's "Serenade" is seductive and alluring.

It cannot be stressed how important this small legacy is. For those who think that the "old" singers have nothing to offer us today, Ershov proves that this is untrue.

It is too bad he did not record music by Bach, Berlioz, or from his many other operatic roles. At least Ershov has left us with a small glimpse of his artistry. For that we must be grateful.

(An abridged version of this article appeared in *Classical Singer* magazine, May, 2001)

Amelita Galli-Curci (1882–1963)

Amelita Galli-Curci was born in Milan in 1882. She originally studied piano at the Milan Conservatory (under Vincenzo Appiani) having the intention of becoming a concert pianist.

> In 1905, at the tender age of 23, she won the conservatory's gold medal prize for piano and was offered a professorship. She accepted the position and planned to settle down to a life as a teacher and performer. (http://craton.chez.com/musique/galli-curci/agcbio.htm)

Around this time, Pietro Mascagni, the composer, a friend of the family, heard her sing an aria from *I puritani* and persuaded her to pursue an operatic career rather than the piano. After self-instruction, she made her debut in 1906 at Trani in the role of Gilda in *Rigoletto*. In 1910, she undertook extensive concert tours in South America, and in 1914 she appeared with great success in Russia.

> In 1916 she was a member of the Bracale Opera Company and after concluding a tour of Cuba and Central America decided to go back to Italy by way of New York, which she had never yet seen. Besides she had a letter of introduction to the Victor Company from one of their South American talent scouts. Arriving in New York, she was whisked to Camden and there made her first and tremendously successful Victor recordings. (Aida Favia-Artsay, *The Record Collector*, Vol 4, #10, October, 1949)

Although she intended to leave after making her recordings, a friend persuaded her to audition for the Chicago Opera Company. On her thirty-fourth birthday, (November 18, 1916) she made her American debut with the Chicago Opera, again in the role of Gilda. In 1921, while still on the roster of the Chicago Opera Company, she made her Metropolitan Opera debut in the role of Violetta in *La traviata*. It was during this time that she became an American citizen. During the course of her career she had a repertoire of 23 roles. She remained with the Metropolitan Opera until her final performance (as Rosina) on January 24, 1930.

Due to a goiter operation (it was pressing on her windpipe) she gave up her career in 1936. In November of that year she attempted a comeback in the lyric role of Mimi in Puccini's *La bohème*, but was unsuccessful. She retired in 1937. Galli-Curci married twice, first to the painter Marchese Luigi Curci (1908), from whom she assumed part of her stage name. They were divorced in 1920. In 1921, she married the pianist-composer, Homer Samuels, who accompanied her on many of her recordings. After her retirement, Galli-Curci returned to her home in High Mount, New York, moving in 1948 to Santa Fe, California. When Homer died in 1956, she remained there until 1963 when she moved to La Jolla, California. She died of emphysema on November 26, 1963, after a one-month illness.

The Voice

During her prime, Galli-Curci was considered the epitome of the light, florid soprano, her haunting vocal quality and the pureness of her uppermost tones earning her praise and respect wherever she performed. She remains one of the few sopranos to achieve international fame and a solid niche in posterity through her recordings alone. Her voice was extremely phonogenic and millions of people who never saw her on stage had at least one of her recordings. Her name was practically a household word in New York City years before she ever sang there.

Despite Galli-Curci being unknown when she first arrived on American shores in 1916, she was hardly a novice opera singer. After her 1906 debut in Trani, Italy, she earned quite a reputation through a decade of performances in the Italian provinces, South America, Russia, Spain, and Egypt. Ironically, and to the shame of Milan's La Scala administration, when Galli-Curci auditioned for a production of *La sonnambula* around 1916, she was offered the secondary role of Lisa. Rightfully feeling snubbed, she told its director, Vittorio Mingardi, that she would never again set foot in that opera house, and she never did. La Scala's loss became America's gain.

One of the most controversial aspects of Galli-Curci's career was the unorthodox method of her training. Claiming to be self-taught, according to Galli-Curci, she consulted and reviewed various methods: Lamperti, Concone, and Garcia, as well as Lilli Lehmann's highly respected manual, *Mein Gesangkunst*. She combined the Garcia and Lehmann methods; the Garcia to show her how to produce her tones, and the Lehmann to be aware of the correct sensations that she should feel when singing. Gifted with a naturally light, high voice, she found that sustained singing in the highest regions posed no problems. According to the diva herself, florid singing in the higher regions posed no problems either. The middle voice, especially during legato singing, proved to be more difficult for her—she spent two years working with that register alone. The final result is that her legato is among the smoothest to be found among recordings from that era. After she married Luigi Curci in 1908, her brother-in-law, Genaro, became her vocal coach, working on repertoire rather than vocal technique.

C.E. Le Massena, Galli-Curci's biographer felt that throughout her career Galli-Curci held audience approval to be the most important aspect of her career.

> Her aim was not to measure art in terms of money, but in terms of popularity. She wanted to please, wanted everyone to enjoy her singing and in order to accomplish this, she had

to sing in beguiling tones. If but one thing is preserved of her song career, it will be that her voice caressed the ears. (C.E. Le Massena, *Galli-Curci's Life of Song* – The Paebar Co., NY, 1945)

Although by any standard her technique was impressive, it was not flawless. While coloratura figurations came easily for her, more detailed investigation into the clarity of intervals during her self-studies would have corrected the inaccuracies in her singing that eventually appeared. She tended to gloss over certain types of figurations. Triplet figures, *grupetti*, and trills were often short of the mark in terms of accuracy and clean articulation. Countering this, however, was the inherent beauty of her instrument.

In many respects, Galli-Curci is a study in contrasts. On almost all her coloratura recordings there is a blandness of execution that tends to counteract the brilliance for which she was striving. A kind of odd, indefinable preoccupation robbed many of her performances of clean, accurate rhythmical propulsion and precision. There are instances in which she tends to lag behind the beat. This affected the level of brilliance she was able to achieve. Contrasting this, or maybe because of it, there is a unique and very attractive sense of soft, almost lazy brilliance, much like what is heard on many of Selma Kurz's recordings made around the same time.

Galli-Curci never startles one (as does Luisa Tetrazzini) with pyrotechnics of verve and abandon. Rather, there is calmness, a carefully planned effortlessness that is as aurally appealing as it is spiritual. Her recordings show this clearly. Even on recordings made during her rather rapid decline, there is a most delicious atmosphere of calmness. Given this, after hearing Galli-Curci sing in Boston, the famous soprano, Emma Eames (1865–1952), famous for her *Aïda, Tosca,* and Desdemona in *Otello*, remarked to Max de Schauensee, "My dear, a very beautiful voice, but all I got from her was an aura of great peace."

This sense of "peace" is exactly what audiences loved about this Italian diva. It was an elemental factor in her popularity throughout the years. Despite the occasional technical instabilities heard on her disks, it is to recapture her unique and unprecedented aura of peace and calmness that one returns to her recordings time and again. Of all the Italian sopranos who specialized in her repertoire, only Galli-Curci offers this dream-like quality. Listeners can buy a Galli-Curci record safe in the knowledge that no chances will be taken, that everything will go as planned.

In January of 1927, when Galli-Curci returned to the Metropolitan Opera, W.J. Henderson noted of her performances as Violetta in *La traviata*:

> There is no desire here to belittle the gifts and accomplishments of his pleasing singer, but she has achieved worldwide celebrity in a barren period and with a modest equipment. She has a delightful voice, not one of the great ones of operatic history, but fully equal to the knowledge and requirements of present opera-goers. She sings a fluent cantilena and has a remarkable command of floridity. She delivers recitatives with musical comprehension. She is cool, self-contained and exceedingly careful. One is never swept away by an exhibition of impetuosity. *You admire and cordially applaud this lady, who never disturbs your emotional balance nor her own.* [italics mine] (*New York Sun*, January 6, 1927)

From photographs of the singer in many of her roles, one notices that she was a rather plain woman with a prominent nose set in an oval face. Still, there is an attractive open-eyed innocence that is most engaging, a delicate pride in her bearing and an elusive sadness in her eyes and expression that makes one look twice at her photographs.

And the voice? Max de Schauensee, who heard Galli-Curci in performance many times remembers her voice as lilies floating on water.

He wrote that the soprano "undoubtedly lacked the splendid golden resonance of Melba, the brilliance of Sembrich, or even the spectacular virtuosity of Tetrazzini—but she had other things. Her voice disclosed a rare timbre, a haunting suavity in legato, a delicious ease of utterance in neatly executed florid passages, and that intangible quality that made her a star of her time."

Ronald L. Davis notes:

> Her vocalism was not something that bore rational analysis, for certainly it was no paragon of technical perfection. Its charm was partly her ability to sing the most artificial aria in a simple, straightforward manner, comprehensible even to the unsophisticated listener. (*Opera in Chicago*, Appleton-Century, NY, 1966)

When Galli-Curci sang *Lucia di Lammermoor* in Chicago for the first time, the critic of the *Chicago Examiner* noted that she possessed "...an odd Mona Lisa type of beauty, with a face of olive pallor, that suggests the flesh tint in a painting of the Italian renaissance. She is not a modern personality, her face like her voice would have been understood by our forefathers who loved Garcia and Patti."

Charles Wagner, Galli-Curci's manager noted: "The Mona Lisa story was well-timed— appearing just when the famous masterpiece had been stolen and was on all the front pages." (Charles Wagner, *Seeing Stars*, Arno Press, NY, 1977)

In addition, although Galli-Curci was not a beautiful woman, when she performed on stage it was noted that she gained a physical charm that she did not possess off stage. This, combined with her natural velvet-like voice and her sincere desire to become a "real American" made her irresistible to American audiences. As Wagner wrote,

> All her audiences were made to feel she wanted to please them, and she let them know she wanted to become one of us. She announced her decision to live here permanently. No foreign artist ever having done so before, this single act won enough approval and esteem from our great music-loving country to last her many seasons. (Charles Wagner, *Seeing Stars*, Arno Press, NY, 1977)

Her desire to please was felt by audiences that went to hear her sing. On June 5, 1924 she sang at the Hollywood Bowl with no amplification to an audience of 21,873 that paid a total of $25,935.00.

> ...a record sell out. The New York Times claimed the singer was paid $15,000 for her performance. This figure (which may be a misprint) was the highest paid to a singer for a performance up to that time. Not showing the strains that were to beset her later, she sang a battery of coloratura arias including the "Caro nome" from Rigoletto, the "Bell

Song" from Lakme, the "Polonaise" from Mignon, and the "Mad Scene" from Lucia de Lammermoor. Her enraptured audience cheered with the enthusiasm sports lovers give to successful athletes. (Richard W. Amero, *Amelita Galli-Curci: A San Diego Nightingale* http://www.balboaparkhistory.net/glimpses/curci.htm)

At the time of her New York debut in 1918, W.J. Henderson wrote:

Mme Galli-Curci has a very beautiful voice, one which has a flute-like color throughout, but which excels the flute in the richness of its upper scale. It is a well equalized voice, with a fine welding of registers. It is a voice of abundant power, but the singer with rare wisdom permits it to flow normally and does not force it. It is a voice of unsurpassed elasticity, lending itself readily to gradations of power, which its owner employs with most delicate musical skill and admirable taste.

In the delivery of sustained melodic phrases Mme Galli-Curci shows that she is genuinely musical. Her cantilena is that of a real artist. Her coloratura is continent, well arranged and executed with perfect grace. There is no attempt at mere fireworks. Mme. Galli-Curci apparently is not bent upon performing feats to amaze her hearers, but seems rather to aim at displaying a purely decorative pattern of exquisite beauty and finish. If her future performances confirm this impression the present writer will have lively confidence in her permanent popularity. (*The Art of Singing* – Books for Libraries Press, NY, 1968)

John Ardoin, noted critic, commented that Galli-Curci was "…a diminutive, fragile figure. She was never a tempestuous or whimsical artist, the music came first…There was a beautiful simplicity to both her life and her art, each was indelibly marked by great refinement, gentleness and sensitivity."

Before she reached America, Galli-Curci's performing range included the F above high C. By 1916 she no longer incorporated that note in her work. This is borne out by her earliest recordings on which she only occasionally interpolates a top E. Nonetheless, her range on recordings is quite impressive: from low G# to high E.

Her tonal quality, soft in texture, was remarkably consistent throughout this range, although there were trouble spots where her placement would shift somewhat forward, causing the tone to become white in color. This occurred primarily in the high passaggio area of A to C. Above high C the tone rarely, if ever, spread. This occurred mainly during the last portion of her career (1930–1936) when physical problems were showing themselves. On recordings, it is quite obvious that Galli-Curci strove for pure tone rather than raw power.

Galli-Curci herself supported this in her comment:

It all seems simple to me. Speaking in the technical sense it all boils down to singing without forcing the voice; letting out the breath as it should be let out; never pushing it forth. (Frederick Martens, *The Art of the Prima Donna and Concert Singer,* Arno Press, NY, 1977)

An in-depth study of her recordings shows that she did not always follow her own advice. Even on recordings made in her prime, one finds moments when Galli-Curci applies unnecessary pressure to certain notes using a form of muscular manipulation. The results suggest that the diva may have had an inaccurate concept of how to produce a true crescendo.

In her excellent book, *Philosophy of Singing*, Clara Kathleen Rogers (1844–1931) describes this problem:

> Singers often think they are making a crescendo when, in fact, they are doing nothing of the kind. This is when they press on some of the throat muscles in their ignorance of how a crescendo is made, and associate the physical pressure with an increase of volume of sound.

> They do not really hear an increase of sound, but they take it for granted that there must be one in response to the pressure, which pressure, in point of fact, simply hardens the tone, or renders it tremulous – sometimes both. If we would acquire the skill to swell or decrease the volume of tone at will, we must understand and bear in mind that it is the breath, and the breath alone, that is physically responsible for the increase and decrease of tone, and not muscular pressure or procuring a larger space in the throat for the tone to expand in by depressing the larynx. (*Philosophy of Singing*, Harper & Brothers, New York, 1893)

There is a telling anecdote about Galli-Curci and Estelle Liebling (1880–1970), who was later the teacher of Beverly Sills. Liebling, herself a coloratura soprano, coached Galli-Curci for operatic performances in New York. According to Liebling, when she asked Galli-Curci to describe how she supported her breath— how it felt— Galli-Curci had no idea what she was talking about.

Her misconception of how to accomplish a true crescendo is understandable. It would be easy for a self-taught singer to mistake what they feel and hear as being correct. This is one of the reasons why one studies with a teacher. They possess an objective set of ears that are able to discern what is happening and can help to correct errors; they are an informed individual with whom one can have a discussion.

This technical failing played an important part in the last years of Galli-Curci's career. Mistaking penetration for power, she often hardened her tone to the point where pitch would begin to sag seriously.

Aside from the goiter there have been varying opinions about the early and rather rapid decline of Galli-Curci's voice during the 1920s, when she was only in her forties.

> For two or three seasons it had been evident that Mme. Galli-Curci's fragile voice was yielding to the strain of arduous service. She sang very often in the first years on the stage, doubtless because there was a lively public demand, not to be lightly put aside. (W.J. Henderson, *The Art of Singing*, Books for Libraries Press, NY, 1968)

It cannot be denied that the goiter pressing on her windpipe had a great deal to do with her problems. Reportedly, the soprano had been suffering from throat ailments for 15 years until, in 1935, the goiter was removed.

However, Michael Scott, who can be very perceptive states:

> But this cannot have been the whole story, for even in 1912 we read of her as being not too observant in matters of intonation. The goiter doubtlessly exacerbated the problem, but her method was far from correct. Here was a natural voice, fresh and responsive in her youth but fragile and without proper support. It soon tired, the placing slipped, especially

in the latter part of her career the whole of the lower range sounds dropped. (*The Record of Singing, Volume II*, Holms and Meier, NY, 1980)

As early as February, 1919, debates were being held in American newspapers as to the reasons for Galli-Curci's failure to sing in tune. Ironically (and incorrectly), Fred Gaisberg noted that in the recording studio her handicap was a tendency to sing above the pitch. Her recordings, however, show a definite problem with flatting.

I suspect that the causes for Galli-Curci's flatting were many. I feel that she had a problem in negotiating certain areas of the voice, compounded by the fact she probably did not hear the problem (her ears not being as acute to pitch as they should have been), but I also feel that one of the problems may have been in her initial decision to pursue a predominantly operatic career rather than to concentrate on concert and recital work, something that she was later forced to do because of waning vocal powers. Actually, her voice may have been too fragile to withstand the constant pressure necessary to project over an orchestra, time after time, year after year.

In reviews of that time we read that "her voice rose above the orchestra to fill the largest opera house..." although the recordings she left suggest something different. The voice was obviously Dresden-like, delicate, and unable to withstand great amounts of pressure without hardening. Galli-Curci once told Carl van Vechten that she knew that she sang out of tune, but did not know how to correct it.

In reviews, a surprising number mention that her voice was lost in large auditoriums, some critics making a point of saying that they preferred her in concert where her lack of opulent tonal quality was less noticeable than when she was on the operatic stage.

Galli-Curci was the type of singer who excelled in soft rather than loud singing. She was a more intimate artist than either Nellie Melba or Luisa Tetrazzini. It is not surprising to find that some of her finest work is done with piano accompaniment, chamber orchestras (as are heard on her records), or in duet cadenzas with flute, where the voice was allowed to flow freely.

This tiny Italian diva was not an unintelligent person. Her method of preparing for a performance demonstrates that she was an intelligent musician. If she needed an easy high E, she would make sure that she had at least a high F in private. This sensible stretching of the voice before a performance or a recording session enabled her to sustain her highest tones without overextending herself. This is why her high notes remained pure in quality even when other vocal problems were evident.

The main cause for her vocal instability during the 1920s was the growth of the goiter (which she called her "little potato in the throat") causing her to lose about half of her air volume. By this time it had become an "unsightly tumorous growth on the right side of her neck." (Roland Vernon from liner notes, *Amelita Galli-Curci, Volume II*, Nimbus Records)

In 1935, while in the midst of a concert tour of the Far East, the affects of the goiter became so great that she and her second husband, Homer Samuels, traveled back to Chicago where, on August 10, 1935, the 6 1/2-ounce goiter was removed.

X-rays taken before the operation showed that:

> The trachea was fifty per cent compressed; the larynx was displaced one and one-half inches to the left, tilting to a fifteen degree angle; the esophagus was a whole inch out of line. (C.E. Massena, *Galli-Curci's Life of Song*, The Paebar Co., NY, 1945)

This condition must have been extremely uncomfortable for the singer and explains the noticeable, rapid thinning of the voice and the pinched quality of her lower register.

> Dr. Arnold Kegel performed a thyroidectomy under local anaesthesia on 11 August 1935, at the Chicago Polyclinic/Henrotin Hospital. During the 70-minute surgical procedure, the surgeon asked the patient to sing tones and scales five times in front of several music critics. He removed an adenomatous goitre weighing 185 g that displaced the larynx 4.5 cm to the left and reduced the diameter of the trachea by 50%.

> At the end of the procedure, the soprano sang part of a duet from the Barber of Seville. Immediately afterwards, Galli-Curci was surprised to find her breathing much improved. She performed her first vocal exercises in the hospital ward, and her voice was initially harsh. When one of the nurses commented that she sounded wonderful, Amelita replied bitterly, "Wonderful? It sounds like a circular saw hitting a rusty nail! Amelita was discharged from hospital on August 18 and returned to Los Angeles. …

> Following surgery, Amelita Galli-Curci suffered from hoarseness and told Time magazine, "the operation has pulled my voice way down and I would like to come back to opera as a lyric soprano instead of a coloratura." This transient postoperative hoarseness may have been caused by a unilateral superior laryngeal nerve lesion. After surgery, the singer probably lost the high upper extension of her voice due to EBSLN injury, which is why it took a long period of vocal training before she could return to the stage. Even today, the external branch of the superior laryngeal nerve is known as the "nerve of Galli-Curci.

> (The superior laryngeal nerve injury of a famous soprano, Amelita Galli-Curci; R. MARCHESE-RAGONA, D.A. RESTIVO, I. MYLONAKIS, G. OTTAVIANO, A. MARTINI, R.T. SATALOFF, and A. STAFF Acta Otorhinolaryngol Ital. Feb 2013; 33(1): 67–71. http://www.ncbi.nlm.nih.gov/pmc/articles/PMC3631811/)

Later that year, after rest and recovery, she attempted to resume her career. Unfortunately, many years of laboring under such extreme physical limitations had taken its toll and the soprano never regained her former voice. Of no help was her decision to continue her operatic career rather than do recitals.

Because things felt so different, she mistakenly began to believe that she now had a dramatic soprano voice and would be able to sing *Aïda* and *Tosca*. She chose Chicago for reentry into the operatic scene after a twelve year absence. She appeared as the lyrical Mimi in *La bohème*, on November 24, 1936. It was not a success. Claudia Cassidy of the *Chicago Journal of Commerce* wrote that it was "pathetic."

Galli-Curci abandoned the idea of an operatic comeback and settled for concert appearances. These were not well received either. The throat muscles and voice were too weak to sustain the pressure of constant performing. After a brief series of concerts in 1937, she retired.

Recordings

Galli-Curci began her recording career with American Victor just before her debut with the Chicago Opera Company in 1916. Within six weeks her records were selling in large quantities. From January to June 1917, 460,000 copies were sold. By 1925, her recordings had sold in excess of eleven million copies. Galli-Curci was a prodigious recording artist, making frequent trips for recording sessions at the Victor Studios in Camden, New Jersey where she made 217 masters of 148 selections. In modern comparisons, this would equal about 13 LPs (6 selections per side) or seven CDs. As Gaisberg wrote:

> "She was naturally used to singing in large halls and opera houses, and was plainly cramped in the confines of a small studio, hence she was prone to force. She might therefore have to repeat a number as many as 25 times before a satisfactory 'master' could be obtained. However, the phenomenal sales of her records in America and England more than warranted all this trouble. (Gaisberg, F. W., *The Music Goes Round,* Arno Press (reprint), NY, 1950)

Galli-Curci confessed that she would reject a master due to a problem with a single note. For example, the published version of Rosina's "Una voce poco fa" from *Il barbiere di Siviglia* was the eighth take in that session. Such caution in approving her work for public consumption reflects not the ego of a feisty prima donna, but shows great personal concern for her work and its quality. The many lovely disks she has left to posterity are a tribute to her tenacity in wishing to offer the best performances she could.

It is easy to understand the aural attraction of Galli-Curci's recordings. The voice was well suited to the recording process of that time. Not a large instrument, with its accent on floated purity, it was easier to record than the brilliant edge, and huge top register of Lillian Nordica. Also, Galli-Curci's recorded repertoire included, as well as the typical arias and showpieces, a number of popular songs of the day.

As did many artists of the time, Galli-Curci often made more than one version of a given aria. For some singers it was because they moved to a new recording company. In Galli-Curci's case, it was to redo her acoustic performances using the new electrical recording process. Introduced in March of 1925, this process was a great improvement over the acoustic process and, understandably, Galli-Curci wanted to re-record some of her favorite pieces.

Here are a few that she chose:

Proch: Theme and variations (1917, 1927)
Rossini: Una voce poco fa (*Il barbiere di Siviglia*) (1917, 1927)
Benedict: La Capinera (1918, 1927)
Meyerbeer: Shadow Song (*Dinorah*) (1917, 1925)
Bishop: Echo Song (1921, 1930 – unpublished)
Bishop: Home Sweet Home (1917, 1927 – unpublished, 1928)
Bishop: Lo Here the Gentle Lark (1919, 1927)

There is a final unique aspect of Galli-Curci that we should examine—the peculiar vocal quality that entered her voice during the decade of her decline (1920–1930). Despite technical flaws, some of these records show impressive vocalism. They include the rarely heard aria, "O riante nature" from Gounod's *Philemon e Baucis*, recorded in 1930. What is intriguing about these later disks is a fragility of tone that appeared when Galli-Curci sustained notes between F at the top of the staff and high B. This is especially apparent on disks made with the electrical process as they provide a more accurate impression of her voice. This delicacy of tone was caused by the growing interference of the goiter. Pressing on the windpipe it reduced her volume of air, which in turn made the instrument thinner and weaker in color. This area is most affected as it is a passaggio and needs great breath support to weld it evenly to the rest of the instrument.

This misty, ghost-like quality was evident in soft passages, when the voice rested on a tone of the passaggio during sustained, lyrical phrases, rather than in the midst of coloratura. It was a sound all her own; a variation of her basic tonal quality. As a weak sound caused by physical obstruction, it provided an ethereal quality; a haunting, delicate femininity that is most appealing. This quality added to, rather than detracted from, her palate of expressivity, even if it was unintentional. It is another example of a singer's fault that becomes a successful expressive device. Interestingly, this type of sound can also be found in the soft, pianissimo singing of the Turkish soprano, Leyla Gencer. Although not caused by physical impairment, while floating piano high As and Bs, Gencer would achieve a similar, wispy, fragile sound that contrasted greatly with her dramatic, often guttural, outbursts.

As one can easily tell from her best disks, the effects Galli-Curci was unable to accomplish through virtuosic excitement, she made up for by the exquisite blend she achieved with a flute, the quality of which is quite unique on disk. As her career progressed, pitch inaccuracies became more apparent, especially within the upper passaggio's delicate E (at the top of the staff) to G.

It became evident, too, that certain vowels posed placement problems, especially the more open ones such as "e" of "petto."
Michael Scott noted:

> Galli-Curci made many lovely records. The best of them are usually those that make the least demands of her florid technique. When the going gets hard, as in Dinorah's Shadow Song and the *Mignon* Polonaise, her execution is more of a sketch than a full realization and she not only lacks Tetrazzini's stunning brilliance but she is without her rhythmic brio.

> It should not be thought, however, that there was anything careless in her approach to recording; on the contrary, few great singers took greater pains. Many of her best records were only achieved after four or five different attempts. (*The Record of Singing, Volume II,* Holms and Meier, NY, 1980)

In the LP era, Galli-Curci was generally represented by releases by RCA Victor or Victrola. During the last number of decades the Galli-Curci recordings have been appearing on various labels. In 1993, RCA (BMG) released a good overview of her recordings on a single CD as part of their "Vocal Series." Pearl also has released a CD of this soprano.

Probably the most important is the complete edition on Romophone (which, unfortunately, is now out of print). You can occasionally find them on eBay and other sites, including the online Naxos Music Library site.

They include:

Complete Acoustic Recordings, Volume I (1916–1920) (two CDs)
Complete Acoustic Recordings, Volume II (1920–1924) (two CDs)
Victor Recordings – 1925–1928 (two CDs)
Victor Recordings – 1930 (one CD)

Nimbus has released two CD recitals of this soprano in their Prima Voce series. With a total of 34 selections, Nimbus includes some duets and ensembles that Galli-Curci took part in, thereby offering a rounded vocal portrait. If one is not interested in a complete collection, the Nimbus issue is a good alternative. Their ambisonic technique gives a unique ambiance to old recordings, giving the listener an approximation of Galli-Curci as she might have sounded in an opera house or on a concert stage.

Selected Recordings

According to the *Encyclopedia of Recorded Sound*, after Thomas Edison rejected a test recording in October of 1913, because he felt that Galli-Curci had "too much tremolo," Galli-Curci recorded exclusively for Victor. She made two test recordings on October 28, 1916, the bell song from *Lakmé* and the Queen of the Night's second act aria from Mozart's *Die Zauberflöte*. On October 30th, she recorded Alvarez's "La Partida", and an unpublished mad scene from *Lucia di Lammermoor*.

Galli-Curci's first published aria, "Caro nome" (*Rigoletto*) became one of her most popular recordings. It sold 10,000 copies in its first release, an unprecedented number at the time.

Her discography shows a large number of unpublished recording attempts, often with multiple takes. Sometimes a recording session yielded no acceptable masters. Some arias, like Marguerite's "Jewel Song" from *Faust,* or the Queen of the Night, were simply discarded.

The selection of Galli-Curci recordings that follows is an idiosyncratic list on my part, reflecting my personal preferences within the Galli-Curci legacy. I discuss only solo recordings. This is not meant as a slight to her duet and ensemble recordings or to suggest that they are not wonderful. I urge anyone interested in this soprano to search out those recordings as well. There is much to learn and enjoy from all of her work.

Because Galli-Curci was so particular about what she released to the public, I found that the main problem I had when analyzing her records was to remain objective. Aside from minor, occasional problems, all her recordings are wonderful. The following are some of my favorites.

For organizational purposes, I have arranged the selections chronologically and, beneath that, they are alphabetic, by composer.

1916

Verdi: Caro nome (*Rigoletto*)—1916, 1930

This was one of Galli-Curci's first recordings, made before her debut with the Chicago opera. One can understand why there was such a furor over her voice. Such lovely legato and phrasing; and softly suspended high notes, with a sweetly delicate cadenza at its end that is peaked with a fine D-sharp. Everything is linked together beautifully, and there are nice, gentle nuances. Her crescendo on the penultimate high B is very good with no loss of intensity or pitch.

Listening to the March, 1930 record immediately after her first record is quite a shock. Apart from the better sound in this recording, one gets a sense of the extreme fragility of her voice, as well as the greatly compressed lower regions. Still, the phrasing is exemplary, and she does all she can to link everything together smoothly. Because the technical demands of the aria are not excessive in terms of high notes, she manages an overall lovely reading. Staccati are flung around the recording studio with surprising accuracy. You can tell that she is working very hard to keep everything smooth and beautiful. You can also tell by the end of the aria that she is experiencing difficulties. She sounds tired. The cadenza is sung awkwardly, and without the traditional top D-sharp. After a high B that is close to a wobble, she ends the aria one half-step flat.

1917

Auber: "C'est l'histoire amoureuse" (L'Eclat de Rire) (*Manon Lescaut*)

This is one of the gems of the Galli-Curci legacy. Here is the lambent-voiced singer adored by millions. This laughing song was very popular with recording artists in the early part of the twentieth century. The opera was recorded by EMI in 1974 for the French soprano Mady Mesple. Revivals occurred in Italy in the 1980s with Mariella Devia and in the 1990s with the French soprano, Elizabeth Vidal. This aria (one of many for the lead soprano) is a lively piece sung flawlessly with great charm by Gallli-Curci, and having the hint of a most beguiling naughty smile in the voice.

There are a number of fine things here: pointed, perfect staccati, a running scale up to top D-flat, whipped out with great verve at the end of the first verse, and delicate touches of humor that are never tastelessly overdone. The ending boasts a limpid high D-flat sustained across the entire postlude. This high note (with its indefinable delicacy) is alone worth the price of the record, a classic performance.

Galli-Curci was quite fond of this aria, frequently using it as an encore for recitals, and even using it within the context of the Lesson Scene in *Il barbiere di Siviglia*.

Bellini: Qui la voce (Mad Scene) (*I puritani*)
(with unaccompanied cadenza)—1917
(with voice/flute cadenza)—1920

These recordings of the famous mad scene from *I puritani* are prime Galli-Curci. She made two versions of this aria. One concludes with a voice/flute duet of staggering difficulty; the other ends with a short solo cadenza. This type of elegiac aria suited Galli-Curci's gifts well, enabling her to float her smooth, haunting legato and ornaments with a natural delicacy that speaks of polished refinement. The elegance of her timbre and her manner of singing matches the elegance of Bellini's music.

On the 1917 disk, the cavatina has firm legato and sensitive phrasing. The listener should note the tender, almost pathetic phrasing and vocal coloration of "poi crudele ei mi fugi." There are many cuts so as to allow for the inclusion of the cabaletta, "Vien diletto." To her credit, there is noticeable change in the emotional tone between the two sections. Although only one verse of the cabaletta is included, Galli-Curci's ornaments sparkle with brilliance. The final cadenza has ascending scales and pin-point staccati up to E-flat. Unfortunately the sustained, penultimate high E-flat hardens and sags a bit in pitch as she attempts to increase her air pressure for a crescendo to forte which does not occur. It is only the penetrating characteristic that increases.

Much of the sensitivity and elegance of the 1917 recording is duplicated in the 1920 version. Galli-Curci is at her plangent best and the pianissimi that she suspends are truly lovely. The cabaletta boasts fine musical phrasing and lovely staccati as well as superbly soft D-flats. The extended cadenza with flute is a wonderful playground in which Galli-Curci madly frolics with obvious glee. Sweet blending with the flute during the intricate phrases and the perfect high E-flat are the highlights of the disk.

Bellini: Ah non credea (*La sonnambula*)—1917
Bellini: Ah non giunge (*La sonnambula*)—1924
"Ah non credea" is one of Galli-Curci's loveliest recordings, emphasizing her strong sense of legato and her velvety, sweet tone. Her timbre suits Bellini's soulful music as she imparts many personal touches to make this an unforgettable recording.

An interesting thing is that you hear the soprano clearing her throat just before "potria novel vigore" where she uses Tetrazzini's ornament, rising to a sustained high C. Trills are beautifully spun and there is definite emotion in the soprano's singing. Although it is no longer fashionable, Galli-Curci ends the aria up the octave with a lovely, piano high C that is gently suspended over the orchestra.

Amina's jubilant cabaletta "Ah non giunge," which ends *La sonnambula* contains both verses and was recorded on the same day as the "Bel raggio" from *Semiramide*. It exhibits the same virtues and flaws. The ornamented second verse proves to be cumbersome and heavy work for the singer with rising staccati "sticking" as she lags behind the beat. The short cadenza has some unfortunate glottal clicking (catching) of staccati and trills are so loose as to resemble wobbles. A penultimate high C is approached with a click and followed by an overly bright B-flat.

Buzzi-Peccia: Little Birdies

Recorded in July of 1917, this impressionistic little song has harmonic reminders of Zandonai, as well as other verismatic composers (although one would never call this a piece of verismo). Arturo Buzzi-Peccia (1854–1943) was both a composer and vocal teacher. Unfortunately, his career is very poorly documented.

> He came to the United States in 1898. By 1906, Buzzi-Peccia was living in New York. He came across a singer called Reba Feinsohn and was so impressed by Reba's singing that he offered to give her free lessons. She eventually became famous under the name Alma Gluck (1882–1938) and as the wife of violinist Efrem Zimbalist, mother of the actor Efrem Zimbalist, Jr., and grandmother of actress Stephanie Zimbalist.
>
> Other pupils of Buzzi-Peccia included the poet Dorothy Caruso, wife of Enrico Caruso (he set some of her verses to music, and Enrico sang them), and Sophie Breslau. Given his obscurity, Buzzi-Peccia's songs were widely recorded by such artists as Enrico Caruso, Beniamino Gigli, Carlo Bergonzi, Mario Lanza, Luciano Pavarotti, Giuseppe Di Stefano, and Roberto Alagna. (Wikipedia, accessed December, 2014)

Obviously written for Galli-Curci, this parlor song is a fine framework for her gifts having complicated melismatic material and staccati flourishes. One unaccompanied cadenza is very impressive for her command of pitch and phrasing. While typical of the type of song composed for high sopranos at that time, this one has an interesting hint of the orient that is rather fun. Although not great music, it is interesting enough for repeated hearings.

David: Charmant Oiseau (*La perle du Brésil*)

Zora's Act III aria, "Charmant Oiseau" is rarely heard today. At one time, however, it was a staple of the repertoire for a coloratura soprano. Galli-Curci often programmed this aria for concerts and recitals, although not to the extent as did Luisa Tetrazzini, who adored the aria. This recording presents Galli-Curci's voice vibrantly free, as is shown in the passage, "d'azure et de rubis," with its fermata on a perfectly placed F-sharp. Minus a B natural or two of white quality, the performance could not be finer. Shortened by heavy cutting, Galli-Curci provides an excellent duet with flute. The cadenza is the traditional one sung by Ellen Beach Yaw, Lucette Korsoff, Maria Michailova, Luisa Tetrazzini, Gitta Alpar, Maria Barrientos, Maria Ivogün, and Mado Robin. High staccati are light and free from pressure. The final passage of rising trills to a touched high E is especially brilliant. A penultimate high D is softly suspended alone. Wisely, Galli-Curci does not attempt to increase its volume, and so the note floats ethereally.

Delibes: Bell Song (*Lakmé*)

By the time Galli-Curci recorded the famous Bell Song in 1917, she was no stranger to the aria. She first sang it during a recital in Madrid four years earlier and subsequently performed it frequently in concert, even interpolating it into performances of the lesson scene in *Il barbiere di Siviglia*.

Before the published recording of this aria made on March 5th, Galli Curci had made five earlier attempts to record the piece.

Recorded on the same day as the classic Auber *Manon Lescaut* aria, the Bell Song suits Galli-Curci's technical abilities and temperament. It must have been a good day for Galli-Curci because this recording is a classic performance. She does not offer the heroic, full-throated abandon of Luisa Tetrazzini of almost a decade earlier, but other things instead. Most important is the inclusion of the opening vocalise. Due to time restraints, this is usually omitted on disks that predate Galli-Curci. This version is sung calmly and expressively in a velvety legato; the top E is sung perfectly, left by a strikingly delicate chromatic staccato scale. Lily Pons later adopted this effect, finding it equally effective.

Cuts are, of course, necessary, and only one verse of the bell refrain is heard. The allure of Galli-Curci's voice is undeniable, with special interest focused on the pure, floated pianissimo high B at the end of the first section. The staccato fireworks are pointedly done and lead to a fine climax and top E. Her release of this note suggests that, even as early as 1917, the note was a source of some concern. It is apparent that in the area of high D and E, where her notes were of a naturally gentle nature and floated, Galli-Curci achieved her greatest vocal effects when she was not required to sustain these notes with power over a full orchestra. I believe that this may have been one of the underlying reasons that she chose to close so many of her arias with voice/flute duets; in such instances the climactic effects were assured. Throughout her career, critical reviews mention the beauty of these endings.

> Yesterday according to her custom, she sang a few of her songs with a flute obbligato. To those who have heard her upon numerous occasions, the flute must appear as a symbol both of her voice and of her skill. At every turn, the particulars of her concert contrived to set off her flute-like tones to the best advantage." (*Boston Transcript*, February 14, 1927)

> When we listened to Galli-Curci yesterday at the recital in the Theatre Royal singing 'The Shadow Song' and 'To hear the Gentle Lark' [sic] with flute obligato, the highest compliment we could pay her was that her voice so closely resembled the flute that one might easily suppose that there were two flutes. *(Dublin Ireland Independence*, November 20, 1930.)

When Galli-Curci was required to sustain high notes over a full orchestra she was prone to force her voice. On November 17, 1918 an interview appeared in the *Houston Post* in which she provides a possible reason for the problems she has when sustaining over orchestration. When the interviewer asked the diva whether making her first records had been difficult, she replied:

> "Terrible. I, I knew nothing. I had never made records before—the orchestra seemed so loud I could scarcely hear myself…"

I suspect that the problem existed whether she sang in front of an audience or in a recording studio. Not surprisingly, some of Galli-Curci's best selling coloratura records boast either solo cadenzas or duets with flute at their conclusions: "Caro nome," Mad Scenes from *Lucia di Lammermoor, L'étoile du nord, I puritani,* Proch's Theme and Variations, the Adam Variations, Dinorah's "Shadow Song", Benedict's "La Capinera", and Bishop's "Lo Here the Gentle Lark". In arias such as the Bell Song, Massenet's "Sivillana" (*Don Cesar de Bazan*) and others in which the orchestra plays at full force beneath the soprano, the climax often falls short.

Donizetti: Mad Scene (Ardon gl'incensi) (*Lucia di Lammermoor*)—1917

This was one of Galli-Curci's most famous recordings and a lovely example of her art. Strong, secure legato and beautifully suspended high notes mark this recording as do a few unusual ornaments. As is typical of recordings of this period, the main focus is on the extended cadenza with flute and Galli-Curci does not disappoint. The traditional Ricci cadenza is used for the voice/flute duet and it suits her voice to a tee. One might question the overlong trill on high B-flat which seems unnecessary, but the final E-flat is lovely and worth the wait.

In reviewing the February 2, 1929 matinee of *Lucia di Lammermoor,* Charles Isaacson, in the *New York Telegraph,* wrote:

> Clad in white . . . she indulged in a flow of her most delightful song...For at this moment, Galli-Curci attains to a curious power of acting. Her movements and her gestures, her kneeling and her frightened half look over the shoulders, all take on the simulation of insanity. She is a haunted creature... (Metropolitan Opera Archives, accessed December, 2014)

Meyerbeer: Shadow Song (*Dinorah*)—1917, 1925
Meyerbeer: Dors petite (*Dinorah*)—1924

Meyerbeer's *Dinorah* was Galli-Curci's favorite role and played an important part in her artistic life as it served to present her to the New York public on January 28, 1918 at the Lexington Opera House, under the auspices of the Chicago Opera Company. At that performance more than 3,000 people rose to their feet, cheering the soprano.

This 1917 recording of Dinorah's Act II "Shadow Song" was made the year before that historic night so it provides an accurate aural picture of what all the fuss was about. As are a number of other recordings made in 1917 by Galli-Curci, this is a classic recording. The aria suited Galli-Curci's voice well and her singing of the "no, no, no" is charmingly emphatic, as are the delicate textural touches of staccato. This is a most gracious performance.

Typical of recordings made at this time, the middle section of the scene was cut. The cadenza with flute (found in Estelle Liebling's important book of cadential material, *Coloratura Digest*) remains with us today. Portions of it appear on recordings made by Maria Callas, Joan Sutherland, and others. It was used in its entirety by Galli-Curci's immediate successor at the Metropolitan Opera, Lily Pons.

The final cadence pattern is one that Galli-Curci found particularly attractive. It appears in various forms on at least ten of her recordings and has much to do with their success. In this aria it consists of a leap from high C to a sustained high E-flat which is left by a glissando to an A-flat and then a final leap to high D-flat. Although a small consideration, it played an important part in the success of her work and, I believe, was used for a reason. Its allure is attributable to two features: the illusion of a graceful, stratospheric suspension (the jump from high C to E-flat, a ninth) and her departure from the E-flat by a lively glissando, a quick-catch breath, and a jump to the final high tonic (D-flat).

This pattern gives the illusion of great forward movement and vocal thrust. Galli-Curci generated a considerable amount of intensity during this type of ending, as one can tell from the whip-like release of the final high D-flat.

She was not the only artist to use this cadential pattern. Maria Barrientos (1883–1946) used this formula even more frequently, as her disks for Fonotipia (1906) and Columbia (1916–1920) demonstrate. Barrientos was probably the first to incorporate this cadence (and record it). It is possible that Galli-Curci may have come to the idea of using this pattern from Barrientos' work. Indeed, she was so successful in its use, that her execution of it out-shines Barrientos'. Lily Pons also uses this cadence (in her first, Victor, recording of this aria), but soon discarded it.

The 1925 version is a two-sided disk recorded over two days in December. It is a lovely performance recorded well and accurately reflects her timbre. Especially welcome is the middle section that is usually cut. Galli-Curci provides some of her most interesting and sensitive singing there.

The florid demands of the aria are well met, although more glottal clicks appear than one would like, and some trills are almost comical for their wobbling. The cadenza is more than a minute long and is the high point that one would expect. Lovely phrasing and the floating of higher notes are benefits. There is no sustained high E-flat, but she does touch one in staccato. The final D-flat slips into a soft place where it remains while Galli-Curci sustains the note. This is a bit anti-climactic, but the sound is quite beautiful.

Dinorah's Act I aria, "Si carina," in this Italian translation, is abbreviated, but is successful in confirming Galli-Curci's natural affinity to the role of the gentle Dinorah. This rarely recorded lullaby to Dinorah's pet goat is a delightful aria filled with novel harmonic changes and effects. Galli-Curci's affection for Meyerbeer's music is obvious, as is her ability, with authority, to lead the listener through the many changes found in the piece. Her simple, soft conclusion is lovely.

Proch: Theme and Variations—1917, 1927
Proch's difficult set of variations was popular with coloratura sopranos during the 78 rpm era. In 1917, when Galli-Curci made her first version, the piece had already been recorded by Luisa Tetrazzini, Maria Galvany, Frieda Hempel, and Marguerite Siems. It would soon be followed with versions by Maria Barrientos,

Evelyn Scotney, Elvira De Hidalgo, Luise Szabo, Lily Pons, Miliza Korjus, Mado Robin, and Janine Micheau (among others).

In recent years the piece has been sung by such fine singers as Beverly Hoch and Natalie Dessay.

During her prime, Galli-Curci was fond of performing this piece in recital and concert programs. She also interpolated it into the lesson scene of *Il barbiere di Siviglia*. The variations quite suited Galli-Curci's gifts. As Max deScauensee wrote:

> The caressing legato, the soft brilliancy in ornamentation, the delicious ease of utterance are not the usual bag of coloratura tricks." (Review of Camden LP, High Fidelity, 1958)

It is apparent to the listener that the singer thoroughly enjoys herself. Her phrasing is sensible and the tempo is pleasant. Staccati are pinpointed and clean; scales are accurately sung with ease. Only a few white tones around high B and C show up, but they do not detract from the gracious, refined quality of Galli-Curci's singing. The obligatory duet with flute is short, to the point, and well-constructed. The Galli-Curci "cadence" is present, boasting a fine high E-flat (better than the one in *Dinorah*) that is followed by a sumptuous, sustained high D-flat that conveys a wonderful sense of triumph that is finally released with whip-like action.

The 1927 recording is nowhere near as lovely as the earlier version, although it is better recorded. Galli-Curci's diaphanous top register provides some interesting moments, but the earlier recording is to be preferred. *Staccati* passages in this version are often connected by slurs so as to avoid the clicking that would appear if she did not connect them. She has problems smoothly negotiating the piece. The cadenza is not as successful as one would hope. At the finish a clicked staccato high E-flat is unfortunate and the final high D-flat does not close as dramatically as one would like it to.

Rossini: Una voce poco fa (*Il barbiere di Siviglia*)—1917, 1927

The 1917 recording was one of Galli-Curci's most popular disks. When the diva first sang Rosina at the Metropolitan Opera in 1921, W.J. Henderson wrote that she sang with "daintiness and charm." By that time, Rosina had been in her repertoire for more than ten years. (She first sang this role in Montevideo in 1910.) The character allowed her to be subtly coy and flirtatious which proved to be very effective. According to reviews, in other comic operas (such as Ricci's *Crispino e la Comare*), her comedic abilities were less successful.

When Galli-Curci left the Metropolitan Opera, (January 24, 1930) she chose Rosina for her departure. Photographs show the diva resplendent in costume and mantilla, but unattractive. Her facial features, too thin and sharp, convey an almost vampire look that is most unfortunate. By this time her voice had lost much of its fullness. In 1927, when she sang this opera, W. J. Henderson commented:

> Mme. Galli-Curci was excessively confidential in her utterances. She sang the entire role moderato and most of it piano...She appeared at times to be striving to produce a larger tone, but without result. The quality of her voice, too, was thin and hollow, and there was a complete absence of brilliancy in her delivery. (January, 1927, review, The *Sun*)

Much of what Henderson points out is reflected in the 1927 disk. There is a patina of softness that is initially very pretty, but one soon begins to wonder whether this is caused by vocal limitations. Sung in F major, the high C at the end of the first section is lovely, but one notices that as the tempo increases, Galli-Curci must pluck high notes from nowhere for ornaments and the glottal click begins to appear regularly. She manages to rise to a successful high E-flat near the finish, but the staccato passage immediately following is plagued with clicks. By the end of the aria it is apparent that she is tiring. The final ornamental roulade/flourish is not successful. The penultimate high C is just "so-so" and, because of that, the ending of the aria is anticlimactic.

The 1917 disk, however, dates from her prime, and what a wonderful disk it is! Transposed to the key of F, the voice is limpid and dexterously used. There are technical insights to be gained from this recording. The ornamentation is moderate, (comparing it to earlier disks of Luisa Tetrazzini, Marcella Sembrich, and Maria Galvany), but quite graceful. The area around high A, however, shows placement problems in that notes are not given enough resonating space, resulting in a sound that is white and pale in coloration. This was a recurring problem that often happened when Galli-Curci was in the area between A-flat and high C, requiring that she sing loudly. Later on in the aria, when she sustains a pianissimo high B-flat (right in the middle of this problem area) this does not happen. In forte singing in this range, she tends to move the voice too forward, thereby losing some of the head resonance. Throughout, however, there are many hints of a charming, audible smile of delight as Galli-Curci sings.

The cadenza ending the first part of the aria underscores the problem noted above. She begins the penultimate high C piano, pressing the tone thin, mistaking penetrative power for volume. On releasing this pressure during the decrescendo, the tone warms and overtones reappear, giving incredible height and beauty to the tone, the natural result of her releasing the note. The final cadenza is short and exhibits a technical trick Galli-Curci often used, but few could emulate. She darts up a scale, almost throwing away the final note, much like the crack of a whip. It lends a rhythmic propulsion to her singing; a musical tension that was often missing. The penultimate high C is hard-edged, but secure in pitch.

1919

1918 and 1919 were good years for Galli-Curci. In March of 1919, her manager, Charles Wagner, renegotiated her contract with the Chicago Opera so that she would be paid $2,000.00 per appearance; $2,500.00 when she appeared in New York.

Bellini: Sovra il sen (*La sonnambula*)—1919
Bellini: Come per me sereno (*La sonnambula*)—1920
Galli-Curci recorded the cabaletta to Amina's opening scene before the first cavatina section. It is a bravura performance and, not surprisingly, one very popular

with the public. It has beautiful, sensitive singing as well as spectacular fireworks. The voice is in great shape, the coloratura easy and clean, and the difficult melismas before the finish are nicely handled. She offers a short, unaccompanied cadenza that is remarkable for its vocal fluidity and the beauty of her penultimate high E-flat.

The cavatina, "Come per me sereno" was recorded the following year and is an equally fine recording. It includes a portion of the recitative by Amina, sung with exquisitely soft notes. Her sense of timing is excellent and she wraps her voice graciously around the turns and melismas, making them surprisingly intimate. An unusual ornament or two make their appearance, and more of her beautiful pianissimo high notes before she brings the aria to a fine finish.

Bishop: Lo, Here The Gentle Lark

This is one of Galli-Curci's most famous recordings and one of her best. This concert aria was an audience favorite at the time and although a number of sopranos recorded the piece, Galli-Curci's is among the best. From the time this record was made, this concert aria appears on Galli-Curci's recitals until around 1932. Reviews across the years show that the piece never failed in its effect. In recital, Galli-Curci usually paired it with another aria that uses flute obbligato such as the "Shadow Song" from *Dinorah*.

Another popular recording of this aria was made by Dame Nellie Melba, who made her debut in Brussels in 1887. She was still active during Galli-Curci's prime and the two were not the best of friends. Undoubtedly, when it came to Galli-Curci, Melba felt threatened and feared a loss of power over the public. It did not help that Galli-Curci was becoming famous for her performances of many of Melba's roles and concert arias, such as this one, a piece that Melba considered her personal property!

Melba had little to say about the Italian diva in public. When she did make a comment it was usually couched in very polite tones. In private, however, she was known to make scathing remarks: "That woman sings either flat or sharp. She never has been able to sing." On the other side of the court, Galli-Curci, usually demure and reticent discussing her florid "sisters," aimed her own daggers with equal fine edge: "To hear Melba sing 'Lo, Here the Gentle Lark,' when she has finished you would think it was a turkey." Matters between them never improved.

Chopin: Messaggero Amoroso (Arranged by Buzzi-Peccia)

What a silly, wonderful song this is, a vocal arrangement of Chopin's famous "Minute Waltz." It must have amused Galli-Curci to sing a coloratura arrangement of a piece she once played on the piano. It is two minutes and 47 seconds of fun arranged by Arturo Buzzi-Peccia. Sung with orchestra, it is typical of an arrangement for coloratura soprano composed during the era of the 78 rpm to exhibit their vocal prowess; Galli-Curci certainly shows off. This is great fun, the soprano frolicking up and down scales to high D, presenting great staccati flourishes of charm. At the end she offers a small unaccompanied cadenza of rapid coloratura. For such a short song it packs a wallop that includes a remarkably long, penultimate high E.

Samuels: When Chloris Sleeps

Recorded during the same session as the Chopin/Buzzi-Peccia song, this haunting composition by Galli-Curci's second husband is one of her most lovely recordings. One of the reasons for this is Homer Samuel's great familiarity with her voice and what it can do. Accompanied by orchestra this is a lush, lyric composition with memorable vocal lines (especially "When Chloris sleeps"). The ending is magical, with Galli-Curci rising to a softly sustained *pianissimo* high B.

Interestingly, this song was composed and recorded two years before Galli-Curci and Samuels married. Little information can be found about Samuels. He was a respected accompanist for concert musicians such as the violinist Carl Flesch. Samuels was present during a number of Galli-Curci's recordings. The earliest one I found was "Crépuscule" by Massenet, recorded in October of 1918. He seemed to stay somewhat in the background, but he did arrange "Abide With Me" (recorded in 1925) for her, and accompanied her on her 1927 to 1930 recordings of the more popular literature.

Verdi: Ah fors'e lui…Sempre libera (*La traviata*)

Recorded on March 7, 1919, these are two of Galli-Curci's great records. She had an affinity for this aria as her singing of it is not only first rate, but full of personal touches that are all her own.

The first section, having the "E strano" recitative, is exemplary, and the way she sings the final "del viver mio," with its turn on "mio," has a wonderful sense of desperation and intensity. Only one verse of the aria is included, but it is sung with great sensitivity and no sense of hurry even with a recording's time restraints. Her handling of the peaking high A-flats and the frequent use of diminuendo during rubato is worthy of note. She elects to offer a beautifully interpolated pianissimo high C.

The "Sempre Libera" has a wonderful, if silly, little laugh before it moves on to an aria sung with great verve and élan. High Cs are brilliant and easily held. Ascending scales and coloratura are fleet and clean and she caps things off with a short, unaccompanied cadenza with a fine, long, penultimate high E-flat.

Gali-Curci's debut at the Metropolitan Opera in *La traviata* (November 14, 1921) occurred while she was still appearing with the Chicago Opera Company. It was well covered by the New York newspapers.

> Throughout the evening, to tell the truth, it was not the singing of Mme. Galli-Curci alone that held her audience enthralled, though her coloratura achievements in the "Ah, fors e lui" and "Sempre Libera" brought forth, of course, the expected storm of applause. Hardly less potent the influence of her gentle portrayal, so human in its appeal, so artfully yet so naturally elaborated in its histrionic detail, in gesture, in play of mien and features. She was nervous at the outset, obviously so, and this brought the natural consequence, a shortage of breath. Carefully at times, almost gingerly, she spun out filaments of resonant silver. Now and again, too, despite evident efforts to avoid her most conspicuous shortcoming, her tones would sag, especially when she rose, to loftier altitudes. (Max Smith, *The New York American,* Metropolitan Opera Archives, accessed November, 2014)

1920

Dell-Aqua: Villanelle

This was once a favorite plaything of coloratura sopranos. Almost all the greats recorded it at one time or another. It fell out of favor after the 1940s. Among the most famous recordings are those by Frieda Hempel, Maria Ivogün (contemporary with Galli-Curci), and Lily Pons (who recorded an outstandingly virtuosic version in 1940). Sung in its original French, Galli-Curci gives a lovely performance, surprising the listener with *two* cadenzas with flute.

This is one of those concert pieces that has vocal challenges that can be expanded depending on the ability of the singer. Galli-Curci is wonderful in this piece, offering lovely phrasing and coloratura. Trills are much tighter than usual, and after a very long high B-flat trill (about 12 seconds), there is a final, interpolated high E-flat that has more body than one expects. Oddly, although one of her best, this record is among her lesser-known recordings.

1921

Adam: Ah Vous Dirais je Maman

Adam's pyrotechnical variations on "Ah Vous Dirais je Maman" is a great introduction to the voice and the art of Amelita Galli-Curci. Recorded two months before her Metropolitan Opera debut as Violetta in *La traviata* (November 14, 1921), it is a fine example of the condition of her voice at the time.

J.B. Steane wrote of her performance:

> Her breath control and the ease with which she could pass over the whole instrument of the voice are evident…the last variation before the cadenza having beautifully clear arpeggios sung in a series on a single breath. The musical content of the piece is slight, yet it would be a very austere listener who could not find some delight in sounds of such rare delicacy. (*The Grand Tradition*, Charles Scribner's Sons, NY, 1974)

From the first phrase, the listener is aware of a timbre and style of singing that is individual. The number of variations is abridged, but those sung are spun out easily. In its finest moments Galli-Curci's coloratura is a sparkling waterfall in brilliant sunlight. There is the sense of a sunny disposition that reflects from her easy way of performing such virtuosic feats.

At the end we come to an important feature of Galli-Curci's art that we touched on earlier: the voice/flute cadenza. Many of this singer's recordings use this type of cadential flourish. Like many other light-voiced coloratura sopranos, she found this to be a most appealing and suitable conclusion to a bravura aria that allows her to concentrate on tonal quality rather than quantity. It is also an attractive device because of her voice's flute-like high register.

These delicate contests with flute allow Galli-Curci to achieve some of her most impressive and lovely vocal effects. During the early days of her career, Galli-Curci found that, of the available (and traditional) ornaments and cadenzas, many did not suit her voice. Armed with the confidence of ten years of conservatory work in theory and piano studies, she decided to write her own. Many are so well written that they are still in use today, having become "traditional" more than one hundred years later.

The cadenza for "Ah Vous Dirais je Maman" is typical of the Galli-Curci formula, feather-light staccato with top Ds that create a liquid blend with the flute. Especially lovely is the jump to a penultimate high D while the flute sustains a lower F-sharp. The aural effect of this blend is exquisite and unique among recordings.

Bishop: Echo Song—1921
Bishop: Echo Song—1930 (unpublished)

1921 saw the creation of some very nice Galli-Curci recordings, and this is definitely one of them. Once a popular concert aria for coloratura sopranos, this piece was last recorded by Galli-Curci's successor, Lily Pons, in 1940. Pons, however, transposed the aria up a minor third in order to display her high F and left posterity a particularly brilliant rendition. In this recording Galli-Curci almost matches Pons' brilliance. Her arrangement in D major has less althleticism than does Pons' arrangement by Frank La Forge, but Galli-Curci has a good time running among the twisting lines and fioriture. Her top notes are pure and easily reached; the staccati are wonderfully pointed. The obligatory voice-flute duet appears, cleverly constructed with echo effects and one passage having a long-held high C-sharp that is very impressive for Gallli-Curci's breath control. The final high D is matched perfectly to the flute's F-sharp, giving the aria a lovely and sweet ending.

The 1930 version went unpublished, although the disk is not that bad. Obviously suffering from the effects of the goiter, Gali-Curci presents a delicate version. Despite her vocal condition, she is not vocally hesitant. The final high D is accomplished only with great pressure and it is squeezed into a thin line. Also, because of the physical problems she was experiencing, the lower register is pinched, causing her to slide coarsely through this segment.

Similar ornamentation to the 1921 version is sung, but the florid phrases are now choppy and broken due to her waning breath capacity. Particularly difficult passages show pauses for preparation. I suspect that these difficulties displeased Galli-Curci and were the reasons for the recording remaining unissued.

1923

Bellini: Polonaise (*I puritani*)

This is another "fun" Galli-Curci record. Although some of the trills disintegrate into wobbles, Galli-Curci's sense of style, and her pointing of the tops of staccato phrases, is excellent. Her sense of rhythmical momentum is solid and although this is primarily a bravura number, she does not let it descend into mindless chatter. The staccati, including those that rise to high D, are clean and click-free. Especially notable is her building of tension as she moves to the finish. Unfortunately she trills too long on the penultimate high A that seems to tire her so that her final D is preceded by a glottal click.

Massenet: Sevillana (*Don Cesar de Bazan*)

This aria from Massenet's third opera is rarely recorded. Written in a period of six weeks, the score was premiered on November 30, 1872, in Paris. As the original score was destroyed by a fire at the theater in 1888, Massenet rewrote and re-orchestrated the work. The opera seems not to have been performed since the nineteenth century.

This aria is a lightweight and buoyant piece that is perfect for a recital or concert encore. Despite its appealing Spanish flavor and engaging tempo, it seems not to have been very popular with artists. Nellie Melba and Galli-Curci made recordings, as did the Egyptian, Goar Gasparyan, and the Russian, Valeria Barsova. Korean soprano, Sumi Jo included the aria on a showpiece CD. One of the reasons for the aria's neglect is that the range is great, from low C-sharp to high E. Technically, Massenet's score demands fluid triplets, easy high staccati, an excellent rhythmical sense, rippling coloratura, and clean, rapid diction.

Galli-Curci's recording surpasses Melba's version, although to be fair, Melba was considerably older when she recorded the piece and was unable to illuminate the elegance inherent in Massenet's music. Galli-Curci's version is quite fine. There is no clicking during the many staccato measures and only indistinct triplets mar an otherwise excellent performance. She sings Massenet's original ending, not altering the final measures as did Valeria Barsova. Unfortunately, Massenet's finish is insipid. At the end, because it is marked fortissimo in the orchestral parts, Galli-Curci's final high D seems understated and anti-climactic.

Verdi: Tacea la notte (*Il trovatore*)—1923, 1930
Verdi: D'amor sull ali rosee (*Il trovatore*)—1924

One does not usually think of Galli-Curci in relation to the *Trovatore* arias, but she gives a surprisingly beautiful rendition of both. These are curiosities in her recorded legacy, not valid artistic statements. Nonetheless, her 1923-24 recordings are a pleasure.

In the 1923 "Tacea la notte placida" Galli-Curci's voice is lightweight but, commendably, she includes a portion of the preceding recitative and presents beautiful upper-register singing; the difficult top D-flat is easily plucked from the air. The one verse of the cabaletta is expectedly fleet and Galli-Curci is one of few to sing Verdi's low A-flat in the run before the short coda. She adopts Luisa Tetrazzini's brilliant finish, interpolating a pure, penultimate high E-flat (a tradition revived in 1950, by Maria Callas in Mexico City).

In 1930, when Galli-Curci re-recorded this aria, she phrases similarly, but leaves out the high E-flat, using her favored cadence formula, this time a high B-flat to A-flat. Cleanly recorded in the electrical process, this performance underlines the serious problems the soprano was having, including the thin timbre she was left with at the time. A high D-flat at the end of the cavatina, however, is quite good. Overall, her voice seems too lightweight for Verdi's music.

The "D'amor sull alil rosee" of 1924, includes the recitative, "Timor di me?" Although Galli-Curci's voice lacks the necessary heft one usually associates with this aria, her naturally plaintive timbre suits the music and its mood, plus, she is an experienced Verdi singer. Some notes are just shy of pitch and Verdi's long phrases sometimes defeat her breath control, but, on the positive side, high phrases exploit Galli-Curci's velvet upper extension. The high D-flat is easily reached and she changes Verdi's cadenza to rise once again to that note. She did not remake this aria for the electrical process.

1924

Rossini: Bel raggio (*Semiramide*)—1924

Galli-Curci never performed the role of *Semiramide* since it had left the repertoire of most international opera houses during Nellie Melba's reign. Luisa Tetrazzini kept the aria alive by including it in her recitals and concerts around the time that Galli-Curci made this recording. It suited Tetrazzini's authoritative, energetic style of singing. It does not, however, lend itself quite so well to Galli-Curci's gentle style.

Dramatic vocal accentuation does not seem to have been in Galli-Curci's artistic temperament. A difference between this recording and Galli-Curci's earlier recordings is a progressing weakness in the area of E, F and F-sharp at the top of the staff (an important passaggio point for soprano voices). It is here that the ghost-like quality enters her voice. Unfortunately, one also notices slight pitch discrepancies as well. Certain vowels, as the "o" in "brillo," and "a" in "renderà" present placement difficulties for this soprano since the larynx must be slightly more open for these vowels and the goiter was beginning to press against her windpipe. Overall, there seems to be a diffusion of power throughout the range. Even so, the core of the tone is beautiful, if of an ultra-delicate quality—warm and appealing.

Despite the time cuts for recording purposes, there are wonderful things to be heard. One is her superb phrasing of "geme, tremor, langui, oh come respirò." "Dolce pensiero," is sung as written with no ornamentation. The intricate passages give Galli-Curci a moment or two of discomfort, but the coloratura is sensitively phrased in her distinctive "whip-like" manner. She inserts a short, unaccompanied cadenza at the conclusion. Stylistically, it is not at all out of place. Although brief, it is quite a tour-de-force with a vocal flourish that travels over two and one-half octaves, ranging from low G-sharp to the top D. She crowns it with a beautifully sustained, penultimate high E.

Problems, however, continue to show themselves. A muscular click (glottal stroke) is quite audible when Galli-Curci attacks the high E. Unfortunately, this becomes a permanent flaw in her high notes on disks made after 1921. It also becomes commonplace in her staccati work. It is simply the muscular intervention of smooth vocal emission.

As W. J. Henderson wrote:

> This attack begins what is called the stroke of the glottis which in plain English means the flying together of the two vocal cords. If the singer thinks of the tone apart from its motor, the air column, he will fall into one or two vices: either his vocal cords will come together before the air strikes them from below or afterward. If they do the former the air will forcibly open them and a little clicking sound will be caused. (*The Art of Singing*, Books for Libraries Press, NY, 1968)

This is what plagued Galli-Curci, caused mainly by the effects of the goiter. Aware of her waning air supply and so as to compensate for its loss, she apparently attempted to thrust forth more air in order to facilitate her singing of notes in the higher regions. This muscular activity began to interfere with her staccato work and the voice would catch, click, or even split. (This can be heard on many of her florid recordings after 1925.) The consistent friction eventually robs the voice of limpidity and slowly erodes the highest range.

As Michael Scott notes:

> "She continued to sing in opera in Chicago until 1924 when she left in a huff over being kept to the letter of her contract. The management declined to switch...opening night from *Lakmé* to *Dinorah*; by that time E natural was a chancy note and in *Dinorah* she needed to go no higher than D-flat. (*The Record of Singing, Volume II*, Holms & Meier, NY, 1980)

The 1924 *Semiramide* recording demonstrates, however, that even if the high E could be a chancy note when Galli-Curci was able to sing it, the tone was still pure and beautiful in texture.

The clicks became more and more obvious and troublesome as time went on. A number of electrical recordings (such as the 1927 "Una voce poco fa" remake) show that the diva is clearly working against serious technical deficiencies having waning resources and a rather raspy instrument. As time passed, she found it necessary to revise most of her ornaments and cadenzas to match fading range and technical resources.

Galli-Curci's voice was not, by nature, placed too forward. Originally, it lay securely in the middle, exactly where it should be. As the goiter grew, her placement was forced and edged forward, at first subtly, then quite dramatically. This thinned much of the middle and upper compass. One notices on this disk of "Bel raggio," Galli-Curci's tendency, while in the throes of intricate fioriture, to change from a covered "awh" vowel to a more open (almost spread) "ah."

1925

Thomas: Mad Scene (*Hamlet*)

The lengthy mad scene from Thomas's *Hamlet* was necessarily shortened during the 78 rpm era. Galli-Curci solved some of this problem by spreading the aria over two sides of a record. She was able thereby to offer more music than was customary, as well as a gift to her listeners at its conclusion, a duet with flute. She was fond of this scene and used in it frequently in concert and recital programs.

Sometimes it did not produce the result she wanted.

> The program concluded with the Hamlet aria, a remarkable exhibition of trills, roulades and high staccato notes, which, however, brought no insistent demands for an added number. (Philadelphia Bulletin, 1-22-19)

She came to record the aria six years later, electrically, in December of 1925. This occurred after a vocally strenuous year of concerts in America, Hawaii, Australia, and the Far East. From the first note it is evident that the voice has undergone considerable change, specifically in the middle register and in transitional areas. In hindsight it becomes apparent that the goiter was making itself known. This, combined with overwork, made her tonal quality thin and dangerously sheer. Certain technical failings are now more than obvious. Her trill now tends to descend an interval of a third during oscillation and resembles a pronounced wobble rather than a trill. Certain pitches are merely hinted at, especially in the upper passaggio of F-sharp and G. The pitch of a few of the numerous high Bs is highly suspect, while the lower register is pinched and obviously not comfortable.

As with many of Galli-Curci's disks recorded in the 1920s, coloratura is often suggested rather than defined. The muscular click appears not only on staccati within a certain range, but also during her general attack or emission. With all these problems, one might ask whether this record is worth hearing? Absolutely!

Despite its problems, this is a surprisingly lovely recording, having much to do with the quality of Galli-Curci's voice. Because of its defects, the voice now sounds even more fragile and feminine. The pale high notes have an aura of innocence that is surprisingly successful in creating a sense of Ophelia's character. The recording is bright and clean, giving the listener a true aural representation of the Galli-Curci voice as it must have been. The wispy delicacy of the upper register is like a soft breath—and what a sweet, tender breath it is.

In spite of unpolished, florid vocalism, there is an uncommon sense of vocal refinement due entirely to the soprano's inherent tonal quality. This refinement is found on all of her disks, even those laden with problems. This demonstrates the suavity that critics and musicians frequently speak of, and the reason for her continued public appeal even during her decline.

The elaborate cadenza with flute that Galli-Curci uses to finish the aria does not stylistically belong with the piece, neither is it particularly well constructed. But it is an interesting addition, if only for another opportunity to hear Galli-Curci match tones with a flute. Unfortunately, there is a grotesque "click" preceding the high C-sharp near the ending. That note, however, is a good, solid tone with all its necessary upper harmonics. The final high B is even better, solidly round having the unique Galli-Curci quality. The note is held for the entire postlude.

This ending is a good example of the diva's innate understanding of exactly when to release a sustained high note so as to provide the most rhythmically exciting effect. Had she held the note for one second more, or one less, the effect would have been ruined. The natural musical tension that had been building would have been lost as well. This was something Lily Pons, her successor, never quite understood. Pons had no inner sense of timing; how long to sustain her high notes. She frequently ruined climaxes by overly long high notes that often dissipate the excitement.

A sense of inner timing in singing cannot, unfortunately, be taught. One can explain and demonstrate to a student at what point a note should be released when sustained at a climax, or within a fermata, but, unless it is sensed internally, it does not work. Maria Callas possessed this ability to a striking degree as her superb Bellinian recitatives and dramatic outbursts show. Luisa Tetrazzini also possessed this inherent skill, as did Galli-Curci.

1927

Arditi: Parla Waltz
Not often heard today, as late as the 1950s and 1960s this gracious waltz was recorded or sung from the stage by such singers as Erika Köth, Joan Sutherland, Ingeborg Hallstein, Mado Robin, Erna Sack, Rita Streich, Sylvia Geszty, and in more current time by Edita Gruberova and Anna Netrebko.

When Galli-Curci recorded this piece in 1927, it was a staple of the florid concert repertoire and was even sung and recorded by a number of lyric artists as well, including the delicious Alma Gluck. Comparing three performances of this waltz by Marcella Sembrich, Amelita Galli-Curci, and Joan Sutherland, J.B. Steane felt that Galli-Curci "has her own individuality, a smiling gracefulness and unfussy exactness that makes the record one of her most charming." (*The Grand Tradition*, Scribners and Sons, New York, 1974)

One of the rewards of this disk is its excellent sonic qualitiy. The voice is cleanly and accurately reproduced. The delicacy of her voice is immediately apparent as is her unique tonal quality—one that diffuses around F-sharp at the top of the staff. This disk exhibits the unique Galli-Curci contrasts quite well.

Although the song is cleanly articulated, it is lazily sung. Despite the brilliance of the vocalization, there is a detachment from what she is doing, almost an air of disinterest, and because of this there is practically no rhythmic excitement. There is also a tendency to lag slightly behind the beat. Yet, the timbre of the voice, and her vocal poise makes this a haunting performance, one that you will return to repeatedly. High As are soft and floated purely, while the final high D is emitted without the click one tends now to expect in the soprano's career. It is a softly sustained high note with many overtones.

Gretry: La Fauvette (*Zemire et Azor*)—1927
This wonderful aria was yet another favorite Galli-Curci concert piece, who was the first to record it. She left us a charming disk. *Zemire et Azor* was first heard in Fontainebleau in 1771. It has a plot similar to *Beauty and the Beast*.

This is a dynamic, colorful aria that Galli-Curci zips through with great ease and charm. Admittedly, some of the more ornate passages are skimmed, but the staccato work is of the first order. Even with its heavy cuts, this is an enjoyable disk having a minute-long duet with flute at its ending. Although the use of a voice/flute cadenza is incongruous within this aria, as an exhibitionistic platform it is quite successful and enjoyable. She revels in the demands of the harmonic complexities of the cadenza and offers lovely singing, that includes a penultimate top D. Light in spirit and heavy on grace, this is a joy to listen to—even if Lily Pons surpassed it with her 1940 disk.

1928

Bishop: Home Sweet Home (*Clari*)

This piece has an unusual history. It is pretty much forgotten that it is an aria from a three-act opera by Bishop: *Clari, or the Maid of Milan*, composed in 1823. It has a libretto by the American, John Howard Payne, The aria became enormously popular, so much so that in 1852, Bishop revamped the song as a parlor ballad. It was popular in the United States throughout the Civil War and after.

> On page 112 (of the score) "Home, Sweet Home" first appears entitled merely "Song, Clari," with the caption in the upper right hand corner "adapted from a national melody and arranged by Henry R. Bishop, 1823." The fiction that the melody was adapted from a Sicilian air has persisted to this day...
>
> "The music is mediocre but Bishop evidently thought well enough of the one particular tune to write the whole opera around it. It appears first in the overture, then is sung, as we have said before, by Clari in the first act, then it serves as the climax to an interpolated playlet. In the third act, it is sung by the peasants welcoming home the penitent Clari, and finally, at the very end, by a chorus behind the scenes." (Barbara Duncan, "Home, Sweet Home," University of Rochester Library Bulletin, Volume IV. Winter 1949, Number 2) https://www.lib.rochester.edu/index.cfm?PAGE=1307

This was one of Galli-Curci's most famous encore songs and recordings. She invariably ended her recitals with this song, adding a wonderful touch by accompanying herself on the piano. She also had a penchant for including it in the lesson scene in Rossini's *Il barbiere di Siviglia*.

> But the climax came in the singing lesson when after the 'Shadow Song' from Dinorah had been exquisitely sung, the singer demurely took her seat at the spinet and, playing her own accompaniment, sang 'Home Sweet Home,' most affectingly, but wholly without affectation. At the word 'like' she upsoared to a dizzy altitude in that still small pianissimo which is all her own. (*Philadelphia Public Ledger*, March 7, 1919)

Galli Curci made a number of versions of this popular concert song, but probably the most famous is the 1928 electrical recording, in which she is accompanied by her second husband, Homer Samuels (who played all of her recitals after their marriage in 1921).

The changes in the voice from the recording a decade or so earlier are very apparent. The tone is thinner, occasionally fighting for freedom from the goiter's interference, and now full of shadows. As in many of her later recordings, despite these problems, they seem to underline a nostalgic poignancy in the song. Although her vocal resources are waning, the phrasing and subtle diminuendi are exquisitely done. A few variants appear at the conclusion, but they are not obtrusive. The chief merit of the disk is her unaffected simplicity.

Scarlatti: Io Vi Miro Ancor Vestito (Cantata)

This is a fascinating record, a real rarity when Galli-Curci made it. It was still a rarity when Roberta Peters made her excellent version on an RCA Victor LP in 1958.

Despite waning resources, Galli-Curci gives a lively performance full of dash and verve. From her manner it is obvious that she has a special place in her heart for this obscure piece. It is one of the singer's loveliest recordings from this late period in her career. Although heavily cut, she manages to give one a taste of the cantata and Scarlatti's music. Both her phrasing and her diction are sensitive. One hears an issue with pitch in her middle register, as if she is hanging onto the pitch by a thread, but this is not enough to detract strongly from her lovely performance. As is expected, she adds a voice/flute duet that lasts just over a minute. Although it is superfluous, it is rather interesting. She brings back some of the major thematic material, managing to traverse the fioriture with grace. One flourish over a slightly uncomfortable high E-flat travels down more than two octaves to low A. She finishes with her favorite cadence that jumps to a high C, and finishing on a lovely B-flat.

1930

Gounod: O Riante Nature (*Philemon e Baucis*)

Another surprise is this aria from *Philemon e Baucis* that is rarely recorded or performed. The most recent revival of the complete opera took place in the 1950s with Renata Scotto; the most recent recording of this aria was made in 2000 by the soprano Elizabeth Vidal. Galli-Curci's cut version is lovely, with brilliant staccati and swaggering verve. Her pitch is excellent, as is her sense of correct style and manner.

The opening, "O riante nature," has lovely legato and soft top notes, The necessary cuts progress smoothly into the transitional phrases that lead into the fast section. One particular octave jump to high C is especially lovely. In many ways this aria seems like an exercise in staccato work. The waltz-like fast section has some wonderful phrasing (aside from an occasional suspect pitch) and wide-sweeping phrases. She is obviously enjoying the music and herself. Few clicks appear. A duet with flute tops off the aria and, other than an undisciplined trill, it is one of the best records she made at that time. A sweeping ascending scale to a staccato high C-sharp is brilliant. Once more, she ends the aria with her favored cadence, this time with a sustained high B followed by a high A.

Meyerbeer: Prayer and Barcarolle (*L'etoile du nord*)—1922
Meyerbeer: Mad Scene ("La, La, la, Air cheri) (*L 'etoile du nord*)—1930

Although Meyerbeer's *L'etoile du nord* was not in the repertoire during Galli-Curci's era, she made a recording of Catherine's two main arias.

The disk of "Catherine's Prayer" and "Barcarolle" which ends act I of the opera was recorded in 1922. It has long, lilting legato phrases, and only a few pitch discrepancies appear within the upper passaggio area. Most of these are forgotten, however, with the arrival of the wonderful barcarolle with its snake-like coloratura and the diva's easy, whip-like singing. The concluding duet with flute is in an echo format and quite wonderful. Except for a few labored ascending staccato scales it could not be bettered. To conclude the piece she offers a penultimate top D that, although prefaced by a muscular "click," is a full, luxurious tone.

The mad scene is an impossible extravaganza. A moody tour-de-force of coloratura difficulties, it is one of the most ornate of all existing mad scenes. Not content to use just one flute during this scene, Meyerbeer incorporates two. All the battery of the florid soprano are called into play—trills, arpeggios, staccati, ascending and descending scales, and various melismatic patterns.

Irving Kolodin writes of Galli-Curci's recording:

> There is fabulous singing on this disc, limpid in quality, undeviatingly accurate. The recording is a trial, but the reward of the sounds that emerge is considerable. (*The Metropolitan Opera 1883-1950*, Alfred A. Knopf, NY, 1953)

We might judge this recording a bit less kindly today. Thankfully, very little clicking is heard in the many staccato passages. Because of the very good recording technique, one can appreciate the precise point of these tiny notes. Unfortunately, some of the trills are more like wobbles and Galli-Curci's tone is thin so that, in the middle register, it tends to veer toward flatness. Her phrasing is exemplary, however, and she is clever in her manipulation of passages that tax her abilities. Her cadenza is inventive and includes not only some interesting high staccati work and lyrical restatements of one of the themes, but a wonderful two-octave descent from high D as well. Galli-Curci wraps the aria up with a high D that is solid but is sung with more pressure than grace.

Three quarters of this cadenza was adopted by one of Galli-Curci's modern admirers, Dame Joan Sutherland, when she made her own 1969 recording of the aria.

In Conclusion

During her years at the Metropolitan Opera, Galli-Curci was greatly loved by the American audience. She retired from the Met in January of 1930. By December, a new coloratura had arrived at that house, one who inherited the Galli-Curci mantle and carried it for many decades, Lily Pons. During her retirement, Galli-Curci returned to her loves: painting, the piano, and reading.

> Galli-Curci was a student of the Indian meditation and yoga teacher Paramahansa Yogananda. She wrote the foreword to Yogananda's 1929 book *Whispers from Eternity*. (Wikipedia, accessed 12-14-2014)

After retiring, she would occasionally sing an aria for guests. A favorite was "Suicidio" from *La Gioconda*. Two of her most famous guests were Joan Sutherland and Richard Bonynge, who visited her in Rancho Santa Fe in 1961. Commenting on that visit, Sutherland said that Galli-Curci was "the most enchanting lady I ever met in my life, so full of vitality and personality—and so warm. So often one's idol does not meet one's expectations when the time comes. But we can in all honesty say Lita surpassed our dreams."

Galli-Curci remained a gracious woman and did not seem to mind retirement, enjoying the quiet and its peace. True to her philosophical bent, she spent time delving into occult philosophy and many felt that she was abandoning the world that had given her such success and glory. Her motto for many years was "simplicity, sincerity, serenity,"—what she most desired after her vigorous career. She once candidly remarked, "It is unwise to plague tomorrow with backward glances to yesterday—you cannot play with the same toys all your life!" True to her word, she preferred not to dwell on her past career and its glories, but to spend time learning of other things and enjoying her well-deserved rest.

Amelita Galli-Curci was not a great actress, but, from reports and reviews, it is clear that a grace marked her work on stage. As with her singing, her dramatic work was guided by the three Ss: simplicity, sincerity, and serenity. This is not meant to imply that she was not acutely aware of her operatic characters or did not strive to portray them as honestly as possible.

> …when I first was to sing Mimi and Violetta, I went to a physician to learn the correct use of the hands, the quick, almost jerky gestures and incessant fidgeting that are characteristic of the consumptive. The doctor impressed upon me that in the last stages of tuberculosis there is no cough, only a terrible stabbing pain in the lungs. So in the last act of *traviata* and *Boheme* I did not cough, but clutched my chest as if to tear out the pain. (William Seward, "A Conversation with Amelita Galli-Curci," *High Fidelity Magazine*, 1964)

Despite good and bad reviews, the physical medical issues, and the anecdotes, it is the recordings that she left to posterity that we must use to judge Amelita Galli-Curci.

When analyzing and discussing recordings that are almost one hundred years, or even older, and the product of a different period and style of singing, one must tread lightly. These are not modern digital recordings or studio-perfected performances. These are moments that accurately reflect the abilities and faults of the performer. Galli-Curci, who took such care in the quality of her recordings, and who left such a fine, large legacy, created a remarkable number of recordings that are valued treasures.

Shortly before her death, Amelita Galli-Curci commented:

> If I listen to those records made so many generations ago in relation to that tantalizing musical horizon I sought to achieve, I am very humble, but if I compare them to the records of other sopranos, I am very proud. (William Seward, "A Conversation with Amelita Galli-Curci," *High Fidelity Magazine*, 1964)

Maria Galvany
(1875-1927)

Maria Galvany, one of the most controversial of vocal virtuosi, was born in Mancha Real, Andalusia, Spain in 1875, but was raised near Granada. She studied at a private music school in Madrid run by Napoleone Verger, a well-respected Italian baritone. After a short, but intensive period of study, she made her operatic debut in 1896, at the age of twenty-one, at Cartagena as *Lucia di Lammermoor* and soon became a favorite with the Spanish public, singing such operas as *La traviata, Les Huguenots, Linda di Chamonix,* and *La sonnambula.*

While traveling in Spain, around 1898, she met and married a lawyer, Carlos Tejada. The next year she gave birth to a son, Carlos. Although she sang in Milan (1901) it was not at La Scala, but the Teatro Del Verme. In 1903, she sang in Parma, in *La sonnambula* and in 1905 she toured Belgium, Holland, and France. During 1908, she sang Ophelia in Thomas's Hamlet in Venice and in 1909 traveled to London as part of a touring company, singing *La sonnombula, Il barbiere di Siviglia* and *Dinorah.*

Throughout that decade Maria Galvany became very popular with provincial Italian and Spanish audiences. She was also greatly admired in Russia, particularly in Moscow and St. Petersburg, as well as in Brazil, Portugal, and Argentina. Despite her popularity, she never performed in first-string opera houses, never having appeared at the Paris Opéra, Covent Garden, Teatro Colon, the Metropolitan Opera, or La Scala. Most of her career was spent in touring groups travelling to the provinces to offer nights of opera. The closest thing she got to being part of an ensemble was her (almost) annual appearances at the Coliseum of Recreations in Lisbon, Portugal, a 4,000 seat, circular venue that usually offered sporting and circus events; in spring they offered an "Opera Season." It was there that Maria Galvany reigned between 1900 and 1916.

She performed in the United States only once, a three-week engagement in 1912, two weeks at the Orpheum Theater in San Francisco, and one week in Oakland, singing in vaudeville rather than opera. In Oakland she shared the program with a "short sentimental play, a Scottish ventriloquist and French conjurors…" (Robert Bunyard, *The Record Collector*, March 2012, Vol 57, #1.)

By 1918, she had retired. Completely forgotten by the time of her death, her passing was not even noted in the press at the time. As a matter of fact, the circumstances of her death remained a mystery for more than five decades. According to most reports, she settled in Rio de Janeiro, taught voice, and occasionally gave concerts. Until 1990, it had been assumed that she died in Rio on November 2, 1949 in a San Luis retirement home. It seems, however, that this was not the case. In the English magazine, *The Record Collector*, Dr. Jaques Alain Leon of Brazil stated that the death information usually accepted about this soprano was false:

"The person who actually died there in Botafolgo, in Rio, was another soprano, Fanny *Maria* Rollas *Galvani*. who was born on 25th March, 1859. She was a dramatic soprano and never recorded. She met the French tenor Rene Talba well into her eighties. He told me this story himself and he was sure that Galvany, the coloratura, was killed by influenza in 1918 as there is no trace of her after that." (*The Record Collector,* Volume 35, 1990, p. 250)

In his very well-researched article for *The Record Collector* (Vol 57, #1, March, 2012) Bunyard provided evidence that the reality was less mysterious and more mundane. Maria Galvany died "not in solitude, but surrounded by her family" on August 3, 1927, at the young age of 52, suggesting that she died due to some illness.

The Voice, Career, and Recordings

Thanks to Robert Bunyard and his exhaustive article for *The Record Collector*, we now realize that there is much more to Maria Galvany than was originally thought.

Maria Galvany was born four years after the famous Luisa Tetrazzini, and seven years before the equally famous Amelita Galli-Curci. She never attained their renown, due to various factors that contributed to this situation. Firstly, she never performed on American operatic stages, and only a few times in England (not at Covent Garden). Secondly, in other countries she rarely performed in first-rate houses, or under first-rate conductors. Her fame today rests solely on the recordings she left us.

Other issues worked against this singer—serious issues. According to Bunyard, Maria Galvany was on the roster of the Teatro Real in Madrid, a highly respected national opera house, for two years (an opera house that her teacher, Napoleone Verger, was associated with). This occurred after a very successful year touring as a star attraction. In 1900, when her contract was up with the Real, she had to make a decision whether to renew her contract or to set out on her own again. This decision was to have a profound impact on her career and her artistry.

The twenty-four-year-old soprano chose to go out on her own. As Bunyard notes, "It was clear to her, possibly also to her advisers, that she could capitalize on the enduring attraction that many people had of the music of Rossini, Donizetti, Bellini and early Verdi." This could be interpreted as a desire to capitalize on her merits or, as an already demonstrated "easy way out."

Bunyard states that Galvany was "a very determined and assertive woman..." This could translate as egotistical and stubborn. From her recordings one gets the impression that Galvany was certainly an extrovert and loved to show off. Traveling allowed her to sing the way she pleased. So in 1900, it appears that Maria Galvany became a one-stop soprano—a touring singer, an artistic gypsy who traveled throughout the provinces offering her ten operatic roles.

One must be careful in interpreting an artist's reasons for making such an important decision without an ability to consult with the individual. In this case I will risk a chance and state my thoughts about this. Having been a professional singer for many years, I feel I can bring some insight about the psyche of artists.

Part of her decision was probably due to insecurity and the preference to be a big fish in a small pond. Association with a single house often results in a competition to constantly prove one's self artistically; this probably did not appeal to her. Also, it would be easy for Galvany to be overshadowed by more famous or more popular artists. That may already have been happening as she was regularly put against the very popular Regina Pacini, an artist who had already established herself at the Real. It is interesting that in the annals of the Real, their names frequently appear sharing roles. Used to being the center of attention on her tours, one wonders how Galvany might have felt about this.

When traveling on her own, appearing as a guest artist, Galvany could play the prima donna all she liked. Indeed, most of the time she would be the shining star because the artists surrounding her were competent, but not first rate. Bunyard puts forth a good argument that Maria Galvany preferred to continue as a free lance artist who specialized in bel canto. I feel, however, that one also needs to take into consideration the mental set of a performer.

Because of the overt nature of her art and the audience adulation that Galvany received, she probably decided to take the easy (lazy?) way out—where the most money could be made. So she took to the road, joining touring companies in which she could call the shots. There is no shame in that decision. Unfortunately, a vagabond operatic career contributes almost no growth potential as an artist.

Also limiting her international appeal was the natural timbre of her upper register, a sound that did not generally appeal to English or American audiences. It is a vocal placement (pinched back to the soft palate, rather than closer to the hard palate and frontal) that even today does not reproduce well on recordings. Maria Galvany was typical of the type of coloratura soprano being produced in vocal studios of Latin countries at that time; Maria Barrientos, Elvira De Hidalgo, and Mercedes Capsir had similar placements.

This compact placement should not be confused with the white, tight-jawed Italians: Toti Dal Monte, Margherita Carosio, and Anna-Maria Guglielmetti. Galvany's high register was probably heavy with overtones that could not adequately be captured on recordings. This can be proven to some extent by comparing commercial and live recordings of similarly timbred singers closer to our time; Roberta Peters, Renata Scotto, and Ruth Welting. Each has a similar placement when moving into the upper extreme, as if they were trapping the sound far back in their throats. Listening to these singers in an opera house proves that their high notes have many overtones that float with warmth and height as they are conveyed by the hall's acoustics. On recordings, however, these same high notes are often not captured and come through as wiry or thin.

While this seems a lot to do about nothing, this must be understood before a new listener approaches Maria Galvany's recordings. Combining these circumstances with the rapidity of her execution and the quality of the recording process at that time, the result often produces an unfortunate comical edge that attaches to her more virtuosic selections.

John Steane judged Maria Galvany as "...a Spanish soprano who most notably on records could sound like a whistling kettle on a high E flat." Although he admitted that she "...had a pleasant middle voice, and her facility in rapid staccato was extraordinary." (*The Grand Tradition*, Charles Scribner's Sons, NY, 1974)

Michael Scott also found little merit in Galvany's recordings:

> On these we hear a hard little voice of no particular quality, the tone fluttery but secure, the range extending easily to the high F, and with quite an extraordinary facility in staccato which she takes the opportunity to show off whenever she can, no matter how inappropriate; it is surprising to find a cadenza at the end of the Bell Song, outrageous in the Queen of the Night's aria, the staccati chattering away like machine gun fire. Her records are amusing party pieces. (*The Record of Singing*, Charles Scribner's Sons, NY, 1977, p. 163)

Nina Morgana Zirato (1892–1986), the wife of Bruno Zirato, Enrico Caruso's secretary and Lily Pons' first manager, was, herself, a well-respected coloratura singer. Morgana was discovered by Caruso while a teenager and frequently sang in Chicago, Milan, and with the Metropolitan Opera. She offers a different perspective.

> In 1909, when I went to Milan to study with Teresa Arkel, I heard one of the greatest of all coloraturas, Maria Galvany. After Patti it was Galvany, not Sembrich or Melba (whom I heard when I was young and considered a bore), who was the *soprano leggiero* ideal among the young Italian sopranos of my own generation. Galvany's technique was absolutely stunning! (*Lily Pons A Centenial Portrait*, James A. Drake and Kristin Beall Ludecke, Amadeus Press, Portland, Oregon, 1999, p. 50)

Morgana goes on to say that Lily Pons' staccato technique reminded her in many ways of the rapid-fire staccati of Maria Galvany.

A factor that played another part in Maria Galvany remaining a provincial artist is that, at least on her solo recordings, she seemed to grasp every opportunity to show off her agility rather than to use artistic discretion in her work. This served to emphasize the circus tent qualities of her artistic gifts.

There is an occasional carelessness on her recordings that is not attractive and her self-indulgent manner of singing can become tiresome. This would have been tempered by exposure to artists of greater stature. With Galvany (as with many true virtuosi such as Miliza Korjus and Luciana Serra) it is best to sample her art in small doses.

The fact remains that Galvany was a virtuoso technician, pure and simple. She had an inherent love for, and an understanding of, complicated florid work much like the finest instrumental virtuosi. Her technical battery was astonishing; like a human violin, she darted through intricate coloratura and staccati with a rapidity and accuracy that is not equaled in the history of recorded voices. No technical challenge was beyond her abilities.

If one listens through the background noise of her disks, concentrating on the sound of her voice, it was well-produced with an attractive, warm middle register contrasted by a focused, ringing top to F in alt.

I disagree with Michael Scott. I find Galvany's timbre easy to distinguish from other sopranos of that era. Galvany must have felt, at times, that the music did not sufficiently display her virtuosity. To remedy this, she simply tacked on a cadenza. (Of the fifteen solo selections offered on the only CD presently available [Preiser], at least six feature voice/flute contests.) It is of note to today's listeners to realize that, even in the prime of her time, Galvany's concentration on the virtuostic aspects of her singing was anachronistic. She did not fit in with the forward-looking artists of her day, such as Melba, who spent much of her career promoting the lyrical merits of the new, modern music of Puccini and others. This makes Galvany's decision to restrict her artistic focus all the more regrettable.

Despite her "negatives," I confess that I have always championed Galvany. I feel that most contemporary listeners misunderstand Maria Galvany's particular art. Critics often lose sight of the primary motivation behind her singing. She was a virtuoso, nothing more, nothing less. She never pretended to be anything else. Because of this, there is a fitting sense of daring and the spectacular that is found on her disks. She is the type of technician (in vocal terms) that one finds mirrored on the recordings of such idiosyncratic instrumental artists as pianists Alfred Cortot, Vladimir de Pachmann, Simon Barere and violinists Zino Francescati and Michael Rabin. Like them, Galvany revels in the most outrageous intricacies of fioriture and she obviously enjoyed presenting this to the listener with a nonchalance of execution that is wholly unique.

Selected Recordings

Galvany recorded for five companies. Her first disks were in 1899–1900 for Sociedad Fonografica Espagnola, Madrid (34 cylinders), 1903 for G&T and Pathé. She returned to G&T in 1906, moving again to Pathé in 1907, pre Red Dog, 1907–1908 (who produced her most famous recordings). From 1910–1911 she made cylinders for Edison. The discography by Paul Steinson and David Mason in *The Record Collector* (Vol 57 #1) lists an amazing 110 disks (or cylinders) with 15 unpublished, including a group of Edison records procuced in 1911.

I find this number remarkable because most collectors know her work from about forty selections that were released by various LP labels throughout the decades. For many years it was primarily Club "99" who kept Galvany's singing before collectors. Most of the Club "99" album selections are duplicated by the twenty selections on the CD issued by Preiser in 2003.

Missing are the scintillating "Ouvi dizar," a Fado Portuguez by Neuparth, a remarkable tour de force written for Galvany, the infamous Queen of the Night aria, (she made at least three versions between 1903 and 1911) and Galvany's take on the Tetrazzini warhorse, "Io non sono piu l'Annetta" from Ricci's *Crispino e la Comare.*

Shortly after the Club "99" LP, OASI released their Galvany LP (574) which did not have any important duplicates, but concentrated on the Pathé and the rare 1903 G&Ts. An important selection from that group makes its appearance on the Preiser CD, the Dufau "Maggio" waltz, a nimble frolic that rivals Arditi's display waltzes.

For those interested, the second volume of Ward Maston's *The Edison Legacy* (Marston 53014-2, three discs, December, 2012) has three Galvany Edisons: a duet from *La sonnambula* with Umberto Macnez, the "Proch Variations," and the "Incantatrice Waltz." All were recorded in October of 1910 and have excellent sound.

Unfortunately, few of her discs were made with first rate colleagues. Sessions with Fernando de Lucia, Francesco Marconi, and Titta Ruffo find Galvany to be a thoughtful and considerate partner having a recording decorum that suggests that all she needed was a bit of discipline and guidance. Whether this was offered to the singer at some time, but was declined, is not known, but it is obvious that she was not totally without musical instinct, or discipline. Her work during duet sessions earned her the nickname, *Maria Gentile*. A few of her duet discs with Titta Ruffo still command attention. For many decades their version of the comic duet, "Dunque io son" from Rossini's *Il barbiere di Siviglia*, was considered the finest of the early recordings. Their version of the Act II duet "Dite a la giovane" from *La traviata* is still regarded as one of the finer early renditions.

Had she been able to work with conductors who might have carefully guided her artistic growth, it is possible that Maria Galvany's legacy would have been quite different. Left to herself, she did what she did best, and in doing so she limited herself, often showing a wanton disregard for stylistic proprieties. It is almost as if she thought that the more showy her singing was, the more impressive and important she would become.

There is an undeniable probity about some of her disks; a non-apologetic honesty about her virtuosity that can be found to be refreshing. Her florid capabilities were so staggeringly advanced that today's listeners may be made uncomfortable by her freakish ability to sing so rapidly and cleanly. This ability was joined to a sense of joy and freedom in the upper fourth of her range that is rarely heard in any era of vocalism. Galvany's voice must have held up well. According to reviews, she sang a good high F in public in 1909 when she was 34 years old, after thirteen years of professional singing.

Unfortunately, it is also true that some of her records make it difficult to approach her art with seriousness, having much to do with the extremely fast tempi chosen to frame the arias.

Some of her recordings are marred by odd and disappointing mistakes, often orchestral rather than vocal. Then there is Galvany's penchant for swooping to her highest tones—as at the end of the *Hamlet, La traviata*, and *Lakmé* selections—which often makes these flourishes sound wildly undisciplined and shrill. These high notes emerge as more piercing on recording than they would have sounded in an opera house.

On the other hand, moments like the end of "Spargi d'amaro pianto" from *Lucia di Lammermoor*, with its clean attack on a final high E-flat, are quite brilliant. One notes however, that Galvany, at times, overshoots her pitch in the area of high E-flat and E. Rarely is this sharpness offensive, indeed, in some instances it adds a moment of excitement. These problems are consistent enough to suggest that she may have had problems in judging pitch when within that area, or had trouble controlling her performance adrenaline. In analyzing some of her recordings for *The Record Collector* (Vol. 57#1), Michael Aspinall puts it rather nicely: "Excessive enthusiasm often seems to thwart her best intentions."

A few arias are surprisingly unimpressive. One of these is Rosina's "Una voce poco fa," the first selection on the Preiser CD. Sung in the raised key of F major, the humor never emerges. The aria is peppered with many high Ds and rapid roulades, but the whole thing is too determined and coarse. The frothy waltz song from *Romeo et Juliete* is another casualty. It has no hint of the Gallic charm it should have. Surprising are the Proch Variations; although lightweight to begin with, in this case they are largely unsuccessful as Galvany simply sings the music too fast. The listener does not have enough time to register all that she is doing.

A disk that I thoroughly enjoy is the "Carcelleras" (The Prison Song) from Chapi's zarzuela, *Las hijas del Zebedeo*, recorded in 1907. In this piece, a then-favorite with sopranos, Galvany shows the solidity and warmth of her lower register to great effect. It also highlights the kind of smooth transition that she could call upon between the middle and lower registers.

The duets are especially instructive. They prove that with a first-rate partner, Galvany could be just as artistic as any. The *La sonnambula* duet with De Lucia and piano accompaniment is a lovely bit of work from both artists, the blend between the two voices is excellent and it is apparent that Galvany is following de Lucia's every move.

Arditi – Incantatrice Waltz –1907, Edison 4-Minute Cylinder 1910

What can one say about such a record? Surely there is nothing in the annals of vocal recordings to match such a display. If I could have only one Galvany recording it would be this one. As well as great fun, it serves as an excellent demonstration of what the human voice can accomplish in rare instances. Alongside the Queen of the Night disk, this 1907 side is probably Maria Galvany's most famous recording.

The ending of this "Incantatrice" is a remarkable piece of singing no matter what vocal standard is held to as an example. Even when the music is teeming with coloratura and multiple vocal tricks, including rapid staccati figurations, roulades, trills, wide leaps, octave glissandi, and attacks on repeated high Ds, Galvany's vocal attack is invariably immediate and clean. She seems never to tire, her stamina absolutely prodigious. Blessed with what must have been overly developed diaphragm muscles, she tossed off high staccati passages with complete clarity three or four times faster than anyone else. Complimenting this was her remarkable sense of pitch.

Maria Galvany re-recorded this showpiece for Edison during her final (published) recording session in 1910. These takes are available for download from the Cylinder Preservation and Digitization Project of the Donald C. Davidson Library at the University of California in Santa Barbara (http://cylinders.library.ucsb.edu).

Luckily, two takes were preserved and are available: Cylinder 2335 (Take 1) and Cylinder 2336 (Take 2). What I mean by "luckily" is that it is rare that one has the opportunity to make a side by side comparison of recordings that were made within minutes of each other. They confirm her consistency as a singer, along with her ability to tirelessly spin out repeated coloratura with commendable accuracy. Of the two takes, I prefer the first. During the last half of the piece I counted at least twelve high Ds!

In comparing all of the versions, I prefer this four-minute Edison over the others. Oddly accompanied by brass, the soprano weaves her aural magic, providing a truly remarkable rendition. She is comfortable with Arditi's challenges, and she adds to them with additional fioriture and cadenzas. The second take is similar to the first except that it is sonically more distant and the caressing of a few phrases more overt. The coloratura is amazingly consistent.

Bellini – Come per me sereno (*La sonnambula*), 1910, 4-minute Edison Blue Amberol 28123 (http://cylinders.library.ucsb.edu)

This is one of the few recordings of this soprano on which her intonation is not quite on target, suggesting that she was not fully warmed up for the recording session. At the end of the aria an unaccompanied cadenza appears that Galvany dispatches with aplomb. "Sovra il sen" is given a bravura performance, although there is inconsistency in the placement of the high A-flat. Staccati flourishes are offered with obvious enjoyment, and not content with the difficulties of Bellini's original composition, she adds additional roulades near the finish.

Bellini – Ah non giunge (*La sonnambula*), 1908

Undoubtedly, the disks that will most interest today's listeners are Galvany's pyrotechnical displays. Within that group there are special renditions, including the 1908 "Ah non giunge" from *La sonnambula* which is given a dashing, bravura performance. In her 1903 piano-accompanied version for Pathé she ends the aria with a penultimate high F. Here she contents herself with typical ornaments up to high E-flat, and the ending has a brilliant final flourish.

Bellini – Mad Scene (*I puritani*), 1908

Galvany sings this with more sensitivity and lovely tone than one might expect from such a virtuoso. This is one of her more successful records although it is riddled with cuts; only a fraction of the cabaletta is included. She ends the aria with a brief staccato flourish and an immediate leap to a brilliant, penultimate high E-flat.

Delibes—Bell Song (*Lakmé*), 1908

Many snicker at Galvany's recordings—the rapidity of her execution and the quality of the recording process at the time lend an unfortunate, comical edge to her records. This Italian-sung recording of the Bell Song is not one of her better efforts. There are careless errors, no sense of character, and the chime that is struck preceding the bell refrain is comically sharp in pitch. To further exhibit her prowess, Galvany chooses to interpolate a cadenza with flute. By itself, this is a brilliant florid effect and a marvel of rapid execution that one can enjoy for her miraculous sense of pitch. In the context of this aria, however, it is stylistically deplorable, having nothing to do with Delibes. The final swoop to high E is secure, but a bit shrill.

Donizetti – Mad Scene (*Lucia di Lammermoor*), 1908

Lucia's famous mad scene is typical of recordings of the time except that purists will be horrified by Galvany's decision to include two duets with flute, one at its usual place and another at the end of "Spargi d'amaro pianto". Occasional register shifts are evident, but these are countered by a surprising sincerity of performance.

At times, Galvany resorts to the "bamboleggiante" or "doll-like" vocal effect that Michael Aspinall discusses in his notes for EMI's 3 CD set of Luisa Tetrazzini's London recordings. This is an effect meant to convey either youth or madness that is better merged with Galvany's vocal technique than others who use it.

Between the verses of "Spargi d'amaro pianto" Galvany takes off in a surprising staccato flight to the high D. The rest of the aria is nicely done with sensitivity. The second duet with flute is cleverly constructed and not at all offensive. The final high E-flat is brilliantly sustained, although she sits on the sharp side of the note.

Gounod – Waltz Song (*Mireille*), 1906

Although more than forty years ago, I remember the first time I heard Maria Galvany. It was a T.A.P (Top Artists Platters) LP, *20 Coloratura Sopranos*, and the selection was "Mireille's Waltz." I recall being shocked, but I also remember that I giggled. I would like to think that it was because I was dizzy from the inhuman rapidity of Galvany's execution, but I am not sure. Galvany darts through the aria in under three minutes, even with an additional voice/flute cadenza! It makes most listeners think the recording is being played at twice its normal speed or that the transfers were above speed. An interesting aside: if you listen carefully to the end of the aria, you can hear the remarkable "ping" of Galvany's penultimate high D as it rings through the membrane of the recording horn.

Mozart- Der hölle rache (*Die Zauberflöte*), 1906, 1910 (sung in Italian)

Maria Galvany's most famous recording is the Queen of the Night's Vengeance Aria from Act II of Mozart's *Die Zauberflöte*, a 1906 Red G&T record—

for all the wrong reasons. In this Italian-sung recording she dashes through high staccati with a rapidity that defies description. As if Mozart's infamous aria were not brilliant enough, she adds a cadenza with flute at the conclusion, capping it with a strong, brilliant high D. Because of the staggering rapidity with which she throws off the aria, one almost overlooks the fact that she does not make one of the high Fs asked for by Mozart. It is this recording that is most prized as the ultimate party recording.

In 1910, she made an even better recording for Edison (Amberol 35012). It is available for download from the Cylinder Preservation and Digitization Project from the Donald C. Davidson Library at the University of California in Santa Barbara (http://cylinders.library.ucsb.edu).

Aside from better sonics, the difference between the recordings is that Galvany has extended the voice/flute cadenza and shows unusual attention to artistic detail during its delivery. Although this recording is in questionable style and taste, it is a fascinating exercise in the singing of interpretive cadenzas. There is a fascinating and deliberate change of tempo after the rapid staccati on high C and A. The next passages which include the high Fs are brought back to a more normal tempo suggesting that her "three times as fast" delivery was being used as an effect, not just as the momentary showing off of her machine-gun high staccati. As in all of her other recordings of this aria, Galvany does not make one of the high F's that Mozart asks for.

Not all serious musicians find Galvany humorous. In an illuminating interview with William Braun for *Opera News*, the renowned conductor, Nicholas Harnoncourt, made some startling remarks concerning Galvany's recording of the Queen of the Night's second aria. During the interview Braun comments:

> Galvany makes huge, sudden accelerations each time the coloratura comes in, then adds a relentless cadenza with flute before the last phrase. Harnoncourt not only knows the recording, he loves it. 'I would jump four meters in the air to hear her. Forget the cadenza at the end—it was the style at the time. But what she does with the coloratura is absolutely unique. The meaning of the coloratura when she starts that! And the whole tempo is already fast for this aria, which is very convincing. I think this maybe is exactly what Mozart meant, because the coloratura becomes a new dimension of aggression... (William Braun, *Opera News*, October 2003, p. 43)

Thomas – Mad Scene (*Hamlet*), 1907 (sung in Italian)

Another successful recording is the mad scene from Hamlet. The quality of Galvany's performance suggests that she may have had an affinity for Thomas's music.

Not all critics agree with me. In an April, 1938 issue of Gramophone, A.W. commented about this record:

> Ophelia's struggle with her mind exhibits both good and bad singing.

During the ballade section Galvany carefully creates the appropriate mood of sorrow and nostalgia. Her rendering of the lines: (in Italian) "Sul cor della sposa tien lo sposo il cor. L'alma e gelosa d'un si dolce amor" (On his lady's bosom the knight rests his heart. My soul is jealous of such a love.) is surprisingly potent and affecting. Her warmly hued lower register contributes much to the success of this section, which is then brilliantly contrasted by the pyrotechnics that follow. There is a feeling of desperation in the second half of the aria that is appropriate, including the long run up to high E. Galvany swoops to an additional sustained top E during the final cadence, bringing the aria to a brilliant finish. An interesting note: at times one can hear Galvany clearing her throat.

Verdi – Sempre libera (*La traviata*), 1910

Recorded during the same sessions as the other Edisons discussed earlier, this disk was recorded with a brass band. The tempo is fine, not too rushed and allowing the listener to hear Galvany's musical inflections. One of these is a remarkable decrescendo sung on a long high C on "mi ritrovi." Both verses are included on the 4:16 minute record with Alfredo's lines being played by a trumpet. One notices occasional problems with pitch placement, but, on the whole, this is a nice recording. Like Tetrazzini, Galvany adds additional high Cs near the end of the aria, then swoops to a very successful high E-flat.

The Preiser CD

In 2003, the Austrian firm, Preiser, released an excellent representation of this soprano's special gifts while minimizing her shortcomings (PR89578). It offers a generous sampling of her staggering pyrotechnical abilities which helps to balance out negative notions held about her musicianship.

Thanks to Preiser's care, Galvany's unusual technique emerges clear and brilliant. They should be commended for their concern in the preparation of this album, including the dignity of its graphic presentation that is appropriate. The transfers are excellent; the quality clean and clear with the voice well forward. I am very familiar with her LP issues. The CD release was revelatory, particularly in regard to Galvany's middle register.

This disc is not for everyone. Each listener will have a judgment. I have always found it less than sporting that, in a world where instrumental virtuosi are invariably treated with respect and, sometimes, awe, that same virtuosity in singing is often ridiculed.

That said, if you love the human voice, are interested in virtuosi, or are fascinated by vocal phenomena, Maria Galvany's unembarrassed eccentricity is quite for you. I, for one, would hate to be without at least a few of her records. I would rather applaud Maria Galvany's recordings and her audacious pyrotechnics than be bored to death by over-cautious, carefully sanitized singing.

Author Note: Although not yet on CD, go to YouTube (www.youtube.com/watch?v=v0NvYqxVjYc) for the piece by Julio Neuparth, "Ouvi Dizar" a Fado Portuguez. This pyrotechnical song was written for Maria Galvany by Neuparth. She premiered it in public in 1903. The work was recorded for Victor (87061) on May

12, 1908. For some reason the 78 rpm disk was never released in the United States. (As mentioned earlier, it is included on the Club "99" LP.) "Ouvi dizar" is a brilliant display piece perfectly suited to Galvany's temperament and voice. It fully exploits her voice's capabilities and is worth seeking out.

Galvany did have admirers among other singers. The Chilean soprano, Sofia Del Campo (1884–1969) admired Galvany enough to "lift" a portion of Galvany's flute cadenza at the conclusion of Lakmé's Bell Song, using it in her own recording. Del Campo also attempts to emulate Galvany's rapid staccato technique, but often with not good results.

(An abridged version of this chapter was published by *Opera Quarterly*, Summer, 2004.)

Maria Ivogün
(1891–1987)

When it comes to the traditional coloratura soprano voice, it is Hungarian-born Maria Ivogün who seems to best represent this voice type; heady sweetness, accurate, graceful, elegant execution, and a delectable manner of performing. Indeed the one word that best describes this remarkable artist is "delicious."

Maria Ivogün was born Maria Kempner in Budapest on November 18, 1891. Her professional name comes from a clever contraction of her mother's name, Ida von Gunter, a famous operetta singer. Maria was educated in Switzerland and trained as a singer at the Imperial Academy in Vienna, studying under Irene Schlemmer-Ambros. Bruno Walter hired Ivogün out of the Academy, making her debut in Munich in 1913 as Mimi in *La bohème*. The twenty-two year old followed this with a substitution for an ailing Queen of the Night in *Mozart's Die Zauberflöte*. She was immediately popular with audiences and remained loyally at the Munich Staatsoper for twelve years (1913–1925), carefully guided and guarded by Bruno Walter.

At the Staatsoper her roles included Nanetta (*Falstaff*), Ighino in the world premiere of Pfitzner's *Palestrina*, the Nightingale in the world premiere of Braunfels' *Die Vögel*, Oscar in *Un ballo in maschera*, Norina in *Don Pasquale*, Rosina in *Il barbiere di Siviglia*, Gilda in *Rigoletto*, Constanza in *Die Entführung aus dem Serail*, Frau Fluth in *Die lustigen Weiber von Windsor*, Olympia in *Contes d'Hoffmann*, Zerbinetta in *Ariadne auf Naxos* (chosen by Strauss himself), Violetta in *La traviata*, *Manon*, and the Queen in *Les Huguenots*. In addition to performances at Munich, she frequently guested in Vienna, Salzburg, London, Chicago, and Berlin. (In 1925, when Bruno Walter went to Berlin, the ever-loyal Ivogün followed.) Ivogün never sang at the Metropolitan Opera, probably because Amelita Galli-Curci reigned over their florid repertoire at that time, and was quite possessive of her roles at that house. Ivogün did, however, tour the United States in 1920, and again in 1924.

It is clear that despite the acclaim accorded her, Ivogün never behaved like a "star," but remained refreshingly modest and was a considerate colleague. In 1921 she married the German tenor, Karl Erb (1877–1958), often singing and recording with him, although most of their work remained unpublished for decades. Despite her being the occasional international guest, it appears that Ivogün preferred to be associated with a single house; first Munich, and then Berlin. In 1932, she and Erb divorced and she married her (and Karl Erb's) accompanist, Michael Raucheisen, the following year. She had been giving recitals from as early as 1921, but under her new husband's guidance she developed into a lieder artist of the first order.

Ivogün gave her final stage appearance in 1934. Her retirement, at age 43, left many curious as to the reasons for her decision, especially as she seemed to be at the peak of her powers. Apparently, the reasons were many. While some of it lay in the sense of responsibility Ivogün felt in serving her art, she was also subject to depression. Most photos of the singer, when out of costume, show her to be a fragile-looking woman who seems to be perpetually tired. She had problems with her eyesight, and the failure of her marriage to Karl Erb undoubtedly did not help matters. Perhaps even more devastating, in 1928 her only sister drowned at sea. It seems that she was never able to rid herself of the guilt she felt, as it was she who had persuaded her sister to make the trip. She cancelled engagements for an entire year and returned to the stage only at the insistent urging of Bruno Walter in 1929. She retired for good five years later. Her career lasted just over twenty years.

After her retirement she concentrated on teaching. In 1948 she accepted a position at the Vienna Music Academy. In 1950 she was appointed Professor at the Academy of Music in Berlin. During her career as a teacher, her two most prominent pupils were Elisabeth Schwarzkopf (1915–2006) and Rita Streich (1920–1987).

Among the finest tributes paid to Maria Ivogün, one comes from Elisabeth Schwarzkopf. Early in her career Schwarzkopf was taken to Ivogün. Schwarzkopf had just finished performing Zerbinetta and was tortured by serious doubts about her voice and repertoire. Ivogün agreed to take her as a pupil only if Schwarzkopf agreed that they would go back to the beginning and rebuild her voice from scratch.

This was the beginning of a relationship that produced not only one of the greatest artists of the 20th century, but fostered a respect for Ivogün that endured throughout Schwarzkopf's life. Ivogün's regard for Schwarzkopf went beyond the typically formal teacher-student relationship. When Schwarzkopf came down with tuberculosis it was Ivogün who took her to a sanatorium. It was Ivogün and her husband, Michael Raucheisen, who introduced Schawarzkopf to the lieder repertoire and encouraged her to investigate its vast richness. Throughout her life, Schwarzkopf's resolute deference to Ivogün's vocal advice never abated. This veneration is quite a remarkable testimony, especially considering the strong, independent personality from which it springs.

As John Steane commented:

"Through Schwarzkopf's singing, Ivogün's art remained a living force within a new generation; and it is so still, for the pupil is now herself a professor. Her ultimate reference is still to that legendary 'Ariel of the opera world', the one whose reputation would be defended (in extremis) at the cost of a bloody nose, and who recreated Schwarzkopf's voice giving it this time a firm technical foundation. In Schwarzkopf's studio discussion ranges far and wide, but there comes a point where debate, for the time being, must rest: a point which is signaled, as often as not, by the two words 'Ivogün said...' (*Opera Now*, January 1992)

The Voice

Ivogün's voice was one of sunlight, grace, and delicacy. Her voice was small and pure, with a top register that was a bit segregated from the rest of the voice; her timbre was sweet, her manner elegant, and her method of phrasing of the highest order. Her top range went all the way to an easy high F and her middle and bottom registers were solid and full of color. She was able to generate considerable carrying power up to about high A or B flat. Past that point, however, careful negotiation with the passaggio into a pure, sweet, head voice had to be made. Like Selma Kurz and other high, German-trained artists of the time whose voices were physiologically based on the "float" rather than the "spin," her top register was kept somewhat segregated from the rest of the voice, and after the high C had to switch to a more easily negotiated whistle-voice. Today, listeners may find her high register lacking in impact because of its delicate, bird-like sound. Ivogün worked very hard on the adjustment between registers to assure that her voice emerged smooth. She became quite adept at acrobatic arabesques and the florid devices—tightly knit trills, pointed, high staccato, and aspirate-free coloratura.

Ivogün cleverly turned what could have been a deficiency into a virtue by making her musical points with the use of (my term) high note brevity. Many of her recorded arias end with top E-flats or Fs that are cleverly incorporated into the rhythmic framework of the piece, thus emerging as ornamental or pointed exclamations rather than grand flourishes. It is a potent effect and quite successful. By 1932 and her final recordings, the top register had strengthened, but high F was no longer available.

The Recordings

From 1916 to 1932 Maria Ivogün made 74 sides for four companies: Odeon (1916–1919), Brunswick (1923), Gramophone (1924–1925) and HMV (1932).

During the LP era she was well represented with releases by Preiser (three volumes), Club "99", Court Opera Classics, and Scala.

In 1992, the budget-priced label Nimbus released a disk (NI7832) that includes eighteen recordings of which only five are Odeons. It provides an excellent cross section of her recording career, including a few lieder selections. In reviewing this release for *Gramophone*, J.B. Steane wrote:

> Here is one of the loveliest of all the century's sopranos, heard in a fine selection of her best recordings. Immaculate copies of the originals have been used here, and they respond well to Nimbus's methods of transfer. It is a disc which every lover of singing should rejoice in.

In 2000, Preiser scored a major point with collectors by releasing a complete CD edition (thirty-five selections) of her earliest recordings, the Odeons (two CDs, 98237), including seventeen unpublished recordings. It is a treasure; a remarkable collection that includes four previously unreleased duets with Erb. It offers the listener great opportunity to study and compare published disks with unpublished disks. Gilda's "Caro nome," for example, was recorded four times (two times with a final top E), but not one was deemed fit for publication. Three versions of the mad scene from *Lucia di Lammermoor* were made, but only one was published.

The Preiser two-disc set of the Odeons has many wonderful examples of Ivogün's beautiful timbre and remarkable facility. One of the most interesting recordings is the "Ah non giunge" from *La sonnambula*. Her rhythmic accentuation of staccato high Fs at the conlcusion resembles the joyous laughter that Amina would have felt at her reunion with Elvino. This is a very clever effect on Ivogün's part. There are fascinating versions of "Caro nome" and arias from *Lucia di Lammermoor, Die Zauberflöte, Die Entfuhrung aus dem Serail, Il barbiere di Siviglia, La traviata* and duets with her first husband, Karl Erb. It is an indispensable set for those interested in this soprano's work.

Unfortunately, at the time of this writing, very few of the twelve 1923 U.S.-made Brunswick records are available on CD. Some of the repertoire was not recorded for other companies; arias from *Manon, La perle du Brésil* as well as showpieces by Bishop, Eckert, and Strauss.

Ivogün and Zerbinetta

Ivogün's most famous recording is the 1932 HMV disk of Zerbinetta's aria from Strauss's *Ariadne auf Naxos*. It has been a classic since its release. On numerous LP compilations, the only CD on which it presently can be found easily is Volume II of Nimbus's *Great Singers* (NI 7812). Preiser offers it on a difficult-to-find compilation of Strauss works (Preiser 89950). As if being heard in a concert hall, the Nimbus transfers enable Ivogün's smiling voice to shoot into the warm acoustics with great luster and beauty.

Irving Kolodin ranked her recording as "the classic version" and in the third issue of the *H.M.V. Connoisseur Catalogue*, Herman Klein wrote:

> The gifted young singer, Maria Ivogün re-enters the field with a triumphant display of fireworks in Zerbinetta's difficult Recit. and Aria from Strauss's *Ariadne auf Naxos*...a veritable *tour de force* that none but the 'elect' may dare attempt (*Herman Klein and the Gramophone*, Amadeus Press, 1990, pg 543)

There have been many great recordings of this aria since the opera was composed, including such singers as Erika Köth, Rita Streich, Roberta Peters, Edita Gruberova, Natalie Dessay, and Diana Damrau. Maria Ivogün's celebrated recording remains the archetypal rendition. When she recorded the aria, the 1916 version of the opera was only sixteen years old and Zerbinetta's difficult scena had rarely been recorded. The composer, Richard Strauss, described her Zerbinetta as "simply unique and without rival." and whenever possible he would make a point of hiring her. (*The Grove Book of Opera Singers*, edited by Laura Williams Macy, p. 234.)

Ivogün's recording takes only nine minutes (there is a tiny cut in the recitative section). Even up to today, it remains the performance by which all others are measured. Superbly conducted by Leo Blech, Ivogün provides a marvel of virtuoso singing and subtle humor. Everything on this disk is in balance.

Legato and fioriture are phrased with a sensitivity to the music and style at hand, and breathing spots are carefully plotted and never obtrusive, a component of her art that was quite advanced and modern for her era. Because of the time restraints of recording at that time, tempi are rather brisk, but not once does one get the sense that Ivogün is rushing through the music. Indeed, there is a sense of composure throughout this difficult music that one misses in most other recordings. Although there are minor glitches, these do not detract from Ivogün's delicious, smiling manner, sassy interpretation, and virtuostic delivery. She whips through Strauss's convoluted music with disarming ease, excellent pitch, conversational diction, and few intervallic errors.

By the time of this recording, her voice had settled into a homogenous, integrated column of sound. Following Strauss's wishes, she provides a reasonable trill on the long, high D. No coarseness mars this recording. There is only her sweet, sunshine-bright timbre, and artistic, fluent coloratura, all dispatched with spirit and crowned with brilliant top notes, including a fine high E. Subsequent generations will find singers who play more with dynamics and tempi, but few have matched Ivogün's direct, no-nonsense delivery, and sunshine-bright charm. This belongs in every library.

Other Recordings

In 1916 and in 1925, Maria Ivogün made a number of versions of "Una voce poco fa" (*Il barbiere di Siviglia*). Although Ivogün's voice seems a bit uneven to us today, it had a most appealing timbre and was an instrument that was beautifully and elegantly handled.

The most interesting Ivogün version of "Una voce poco fa" is a 1916 unpublished disk now on Preiser CD (89094). One questions it going unpublished as it is a wonderful performance. Aside from one or two notes that fail to make their mark, the coloratura is a model of artistic perfection. Her ornamentation, of which there is quite a bit, is distinctive and different in composition and effect than those of her colleague, Frieda Hempel. As if bursting into laughter, for the repeat of "Io sono docile," Ivogün bounces back and forth around high C, crowning the phrase with a top F. Although today's critics might consider her elaborate version to border on bad taste, all her ornaments are aural depictions of laughter or humor. Like many soprano Rosinas, this is a playful rather than determined character. Determination was left to the mezzi.

In listening to the re-releases of this soprano, I found myself returning time and again to the Nimbus issue which has some truly classic renditions. High on the list is Handel's "Sweet Bird" (*L'Allegro*). It should be pointed out that this is the archaic and overly ornamented version of the aria used by coloratura sopranos before the piece was indignantly reclaimed by the early music movement of the 1970s. Ivogün's recording is an eloquent testimonial to her smooth legato, dewy, fresh tone, and beautiful phrasing. Delicate trills and high staccati pepper her (mostly discrete) ornamentation.

Norina's aria from *Don Pasquale* remains one of her most engaging recordings, full of humor and superb top notes up to high F. Another comic gem, and one perfect for Ivogün's gifts and timbre is the great aria of Frau Fluth from Nicolai's *Merry Wives of Windsor*. Here superb diction and an ironic comic sense permeate the piece, but never cheapen the music. Recorded in 1917, the top voice is vibrant and easy and the difficult, ornamental run up to top F is whipped out with verve.

The Preiser CD set: *The Complete Odeons* (89237) includes Ivogün's famous early recordings of the arias of the Queen of the Night (*Die Zauberflöte*). The first aria, "O zittre nicht", originally recorded in 1916, went unpublished for many decades. 1916's "Der holle rache" was her first published recording. She remade both arias for Gramophon in 1925 (once available on Preiser LP: LV 69). Although the 1916 recordings find her in somewhat fresher voice, either set of disks is worth hearing and owning, the climactic high Fs just as potent in 1925 as in 1916.

Lieder was important to Ivogün. The Nimbus release offers the only two orchestrally accompanied selections by Schubert that Ivogün recorded. They were made for Brunswick in 1923 during the time she was singing Rosina with the Chicago Opera. They are notable for her classic, direct phrasing and attention to beauty of sound and subtle nuance. Ivogün had definite ideas about this repertoire and she executes them brilliantly, easily taking the listener along with her.

One of her greatest recordings is of a silly piece, a vocal adaptation of Fritz Kreisler's violin solo, "Liebesfreud." This is a classic of its kind for Ivogün's superb pitch, and almost tangible joy in singing. Her beautiful middle voice is complimented by graceful, high coloratura arabesques and some superb pointing of staccati passages. Contrasting this are the four folk songs arranged by Grund that were recorded in 1932. These are among the most moving of all her disks for their simplicity and exquisite phrasing. (One of them, "Z'Lauterbach," was later made famous as a recital encore by soprano Montserrat Caballe.)

In 1932, Ivogün wrote an article for a book called *We From the Opera* (Verlag F. Bruckmann A.G. Munich) in which she offered advice to young singers:

> One has often said that I have made my way thanks to my natural gifts. Here let me tell you for once, in black and white, that I have worked day and night with endless pains, with hot tears of despondency and even despair, with giving up other interests that could divert and use up strength....Not fame, high fees or titles should be the initiative, they are not worth by themselves that you sacrifice your life blood...The selfless love for this, our profession, must be the motive.

The recordings of Maria Ivogün prove that she lived by her own words. They also prove that, no matter what the repertoire, it is dedication to "the art" and not to one's self that enables singers to attain the spiritual height they aspire to.

(A shorter version of this chapter first appeared in *Classical Singer,* November, 2001)

Miliza Korjus
(1909–1980)

Miliza Korjus was born in Warsaw in 1909 where her father, Artur Korjus, an Estonian of Swedish descent and a colonel in the Imperial Russian Army, was posted. Miliza's mother, Anna Gintowt, was descended from Lithuanian-Polish nobility. Miliza had one brother, and four sisters. Her mother and father separated during the Russian revolution and in 1918 she moved to Kiev with her mother and sisters.

While still in her teens, she joined the Dumka Choir in Kiev and toured the Soviet Union. In Estonia, Miliza studied with well-known voice teacher, Barbara Malama, whom she credited for teaching her superb breath control. Miliza regularly emphasized how much the recordings of Tetrazzini and Galli-Curci had influenced her technique.

She met Dr. Kuno Foelsch, a physicist, and married him in 1929. The couple moved to Germany where she continued her concert career throughout Europe. In 1933 she was engaged by Max von Schillings for the Berlin State Opera. Her opera roles included Gilda in *Rigoletto*, Rosina in *The Barber of Seville*, Violetta in *La Traviata*, Lucia in *Lucia di Lammermoor*, and her greatest success, the Queen of the Night in *The Magic Flute*." (adapted from http://www.korjus.x10host.com/biography.htm)

Her debut at the Berlin Staatsoper in 1933 was as Gilda (*Rigoletto*). She remained there for three years, during which time she made a number of guest appearances in Vienna, Paris, Brussels, Stockholm, and Munich. While associated with the Berlin Opera Korjus made a series of recordings that became legendary.

Irving Thalberg of Metro-Goldwyn-Mayer Pictures, hearing one of her recordings, offered her a part in the film, *The Great Waltz,* about the life of Johann Strauss (with musical adaptation by Dimitri Tiomkin). Korjus moved to Hollywood in 1936 to make the film. It was released in 1938, becoming an immediate critical success. Miliza Korjus was nominated for an Academy Award as Best Supporting Actress. In reviewing the film, the critic for the *New York Herald Tribune* wrote: "… it is however, Miliza Korjus' picture throughout. Her personality was magnetic. Will there ever be another to sing waltzes with such bravado?"

A second film, *Guns and Fiddles*, the story of Sandor Rozsa (an Hungarian Robin Hood), was to begin production in 1940, but was never made. Miliza was to play Sandor's gypsy love. The music for the film was derived from Liszt and arranged by Emmerich Kalman. Two weeks before production was to begin, however, Miliza was seriously injured in an automobile accident.

After nine months in the hospital she moved to Mexico, where, in 1942, she made the film, "Caballeria del Imperio." Korjus left Mexico in 1944 making extensive concert tours (1944–1945) in North America, Canada, Jamaica, and Puerto Rico.

Her Carnegie Hall debut during that tour in October of 1944 was well received, although it was evident that her top register was rapidly deteriorating due to the manipulative abuse it had sustained over the years.

Even so, when reviewing the concert, Virgil Thompson of the *New York Herald Tribune* wrote:

> She has a voice with coloratura work that seems almost unbelievable for beauty of tone, accuracy of pitch, musicianly rhythm and phrasing, and a velocity unknown since the early days of the century.

Time Magazine noted:

> Among vocal connoisseurs Miliza Korjus' silvery, agile recordings of such challenging arias as the Bell Song from Lakmé and the Queen of the Night Aria from The Magic Flute had roused admiration and curiosity. But until this week, almost none of her phonographic fans had heard her in the flesh. When she walked on Carnegie Hall's stage and launched into Lucia's Mad Scene and an assortment of Mozart and Verdi fireworks, they lent attentive ears. Soprano Korjus flatted on a couple of high notes, sang a phrase or two off pitch. Her high Ds and Fs were a little strident. But she handled most of her arias with grace and ease. By the intermission, her fans had already reached a verdict: Miliza Korjus is not quite as good as her recordings, but she is one of the best coloraturas U.S. concertgoers have heard in a decade.(*Time Magazine*, October 30, 1944,)

Her public performances dwindled during the next few years, making only occasional concert appearances during the late 1940s.

In 1952 she married her second husband, Dr. Walter Shector, a physician, and retired from the stage, ending a career that lasted less than twenty years. She was a bright light in southern Californian society, sought out by visiting artists such as Joan Sutherland, Beverly Sills, Rudolph Nureyev and Maya Plisetskaya. She died of heart failure in August 1980.

Although greatly admired in Berlin for her operatic performances, elsewhere she was primarily known as a concert artist who specialized in music of a lighter vein. In Britain she was known as a "gramophone soprano" as her recordings lacked the glamour of a celebrity label.

Miliza Korjus was considered a bit odd. According to her, the great Wagnerian soprano, Frida Leider (1888–1975) active during the 1920s and 1930s, told Korjus that she heard Wagnerian tones in her voice. This comment spurred the coloratura to perform the Forest Bird in *Siegfried* and then Helmwige in *Die Walküre*. According to Korjus, she had trouble finding her entrance during the famous Ride of the Valkyries, so she learned all the parts and sang along with the other Valkyries. They were not amused. She was asked by the management to desist.

Of the many coloratura singers who have recorded since 1900, Miliza Korjus is a rare virtuoso. Like Maria Galvany and Luisa Tetrazzini, she left recordings that sparkle with florid work of sometimes staggering perfection. These recordings are all the more impressive having been recorded before the art of splicing notes and passages was developed. Each disk is a live performance in that it is a product of that moment, containing no retouching or alteration. It accurately reflects what the artist was capable of at that moment in time.

Different from many other florid specialists, Miliza Korjus coupled her coloratura technique with an instrumental timbre and precision in her upper register. Although her idiosyncratic way of singing high notes as "straight tones" has drawbacks both pedagogically and aurally, few singers have equaled her accuracy of pitch when singing above high C. Her abilities are remarkable for absolute clarity of arpeggios, ascending and descending chromatic scales, high, rapid staccati, and intricate, multi-note variational patterns. Complimenting these technical feats is an intuitive grace of execution, a charming, yet assertive personality, and a lovely, distinctive timbre.

Miliza Korjus never attained international renown as an operatic artist of the first order. Also, her vocal prime was very short. She made her debut in Berlin when she was 24 and by the time she was 30 she was experiencing serious vocal problems.

Although her performing career was brief, Korjus managed to make quite a few recordings, some of them excellent. From 1934 to 1936 she made forty-two published 78 rpm sides for HMV in Berlin. After that, she recorded sporadically for RCA Victor (eleven sides). Her last major commercial recordings (two sets of four Strauss Waltzes) were recorded for Victor in May of 1945 and September of 1947.

Always an eccentric, in the middle 1960s she founded her own recording label, "Venus," and began to release new recordings. Korjus continued to record privately and to work on her music until her death in August of 1980.

The Voice

During her main recording years (1934–1947) the Korjus voice was distinctive for its clean, clear timbre—rich and full in the middle and bottom, instrumental at the top—and the unaffected charm of her singing. Her performing range was broad; just under three octaves: low A to the A-flat above high C. Her florid technique (excepting trills) was flawless. It was a sizable voice for its type and capable of great vitality and decisive thrust. The voice had a subtle vibrancy up to about high B-flat. After that, the emission underwent a radical change and muscular manipulation took over. The notes above high B-flat took on a straightness of emission completely devoid of natural vibrato.

This unusual method of singing undoubtedly contributed to the instrumental success of her many showpieces. In her performance of operatic music, however, this threatened to remove a sense of the human element.

I have found in the literature, only one mention of teachers, Barbara Malama, although it would seem that she must have had some other kind of guidance. In most articles, Korjus maintains that she taught herself to sing by listening and imitating recordings of her idol Luisa Tetrazzini, and other famous singers. It is important to understand that, despite her phenomenally clean coloratura singing and her instrument's inherent cool beauty, the voice was a manufactured instrument. Instead of riding freely on breath support, her voice was controlled by muscles surrounding the larynx. This goes against all pedagogical methods of vocal production which emphasize the complete absence of laryngeal tension. Korjus held (or pressed down upon) the larynx using muscular control, thus enabling her to sing (and to control) her highest tones in an absolutely straight manner.

Undoubtedly, Korjus had an unusual larynx construction that allowed her to sing runs in such a manner and ascend to such heights (aside from manipulation). Her coloratura technique included a method of articulating each note without resorting to aspirates. This is a different technique from the yodeling-like coloratura of the Dutch soprano Christina Deutekom (1931–2014), who sang in the 1970s and 80s. Korjus' coloratura has wittily been called "cluckeratura" or "flutter-stitch." There have been other artists who have displayed a similar technical method. For example: Ada Sari (1886–1968), during the 1920s, Laurel Hurley (1927), active at the New York City Opera and the Metropolitan Opera in the 1950s, Italian soprano, Luciana Serra (1946–), and Edita Gruberova (1946–), who made her operatic debut in 1968 and is still active. Each of these women shows partial usage of this florid technique, although none of them uses the great amount of manipulation that is found in the work of Miliza Korjus.

Although her high register was noted for its facility and tonal accuracy, her "laser-beam" style of emission when sustaining notes above the staff was better suited to showpieces, where the instrumental quality of these sounds dovetail nicely with the technical requirements of the music. In operatic selections, the cool control of Korjus' upper register tends to detract from the emotional content of the music.

Unfortunately, Korjus' tremendous muscular manipulation in high register work rapidly took its toll. Even though her coloratura facility remained exceptional, by 1942 (when she was 33), her high A-flat and high F had disappeared; her D and E-flat had hardened to excruciating brittleness.

Oscar Thompson reviewed her Carnegie Hall debut on October 22, 1944. For the concert, Korjus included the first aria of the Queen of the Night (*Die Zauberflöte*), the bolero (*I Vespri Siciliani*), the mad scene (*Lucia di Lammermoor*), Delibes' "Pizzicato Polka," and Proch's "Theme and Variations." He noted:

> …one thing was evident – a house had been assembled that expected a sensation. This was in fair measure provided, though Miss Korjus sang many of her high tones off pitch. One of them—at the close of the 'Mad Scene' from Donizetti's 'Lucia di Lammermoor' – was a good half tone flat, and through the first part of her program notes in alt went generally awry. Some tones were coarse in quality and her bravura singing was by no means of impeccable accuracy….At its best, the voice shames the two-penny pipes that have been heard in opera here in recent seasons….Her highest tones were her most powerful. Though she apparently could not shape a syllable on them, she hurled them out into the

auditorium with prodigality. Whether they were on pitch or not, and whatever their quality, they were reassuring in their vitality. (*The New York Sun*, Monday, October 23, 1944)

By 1966, when Korjus began to make new recordings for her own vanity label, Venus, her voice had lowered considerably. Of a projected fifteen discs, only six appeared: *Golden Voice, Divine Music, Viking Nightingale, Night in Venice, Queen of Melody*, and *Jenny Lind Festival*. The albums sported a color painting of Korjus and the inner record sleeves noted, "The Venus Recording Company of America presents the golden voice of Miliza Korjus."

The performances were unfortunate. For unknown reasons, Korjus sang French arias in Russian or German and there were disgraceful lapses in artistic taste. Her famous agility was still much in evidence, but the tonal quality had hardened, becoming greatly constricted and unpleasant. The liner notes are embarrassing—"Korjus (rhymes with gorgeous)"—and show an over-indulgent hand in praise of the renditions that are offered. In preparing the listener for the treats to be found in the *La perle du Brésil* aria, the liner notes boast: "an interpretation to be compared with the brilliance of colours one sees in the orchids of Brazil." (*Viking Nightingale*, LP 969)

As for the Act II gypsy song from *Carmen*, sung in Russian, the listener is told, "when Bizet composed his operatic masterpiece, he created this melody to display the verve and fiery temperament of the Gypsy. To sing CARMEN as the composer intended, MILIZA KORJUS interprets the refrain in bolero tempo." (*Golden Voice of Miliza Korjus,* LP 963-M)

What the over-zealous liner notes do not tell the listener is that much of the eclectic repertoire found on the records had to be lowered considerably to meet the soprano's declining range—in some instances as much as a third or a fourth. Even with this lowering of vocal altitudes, high As and B-flats are pinched and constricted.

Korjus was just 57 when she made the Venus recordings, a not very advanced age for a singer. Many artists sing professionally well into their sixties. At the time of this writing, Edita Gruberova (who made her debut in 1968) is still performing her famous repertoire of *Roberto Devereux* and *Anna Bolena* in key. Most operatic careers last between twenty and forty years. Lily Pons, Korjus's contemporary, sang professionally from 1928 to 1962. She even came out of retirement in 1972 to appear in a New York Philharmonic concert. As a whole, her career lasted forty-four years.

Despite her vocal issues, Korjus's 1930s recordings exhibit her lovely voice and manner at its best; excellent legato and diction, rare authority in florid singing, and the obvious enjoyment she takes in the most impossible vocal challenges.

Selected Recordings

Not surprisingly, a number of Korjus's recordings are classics of their kind. Taken as a whole, her discography makes for more satisfying listening than the discographies of many other singers. Part of this has to do with the degree of her tonal accuracy. This, coupled with the sweetness of her middle register, makes a number of her more lyrical arias very ingratiating. No other singer manages to so successfully combine the accuracy and fluidity of instrumental precision with the coloratura soprano voice.

During the LP era, Korjus's singing was preserved on releases by OASI (three volumes), Electrola (a famous two-LP set that presents an excellent cross section of her talents) Voce, and RCA Camden.

In the late 1980s, two CD releases were issued at almost the same time, "The Legendary Soprano Miliza Korjus" on Legendary Recordings, CD 1019, and "OASI Presents Miliza Korjus," OASI 7005. Pearl released a compilation of Korjus in 1996.

In 2004, Hänssler Classic released a compilation called, "The Art of Coloratura" which included eighteen of her most famous disks.

Preiser released a number of volumes: Volume I in 1992, Volume II followed in 1998, and Volume III (Strauss and other waltzes, as well as an unpublished *Die Entführung aus dem Serail* aria) in 2006. These volumes are probably the best representation of this singer, offering fifty of the sixty-one sides she made. They run from operatic arias to concert fluff and movie-musicals, dating from her first in January of 1934, to her last Victor in 1947. As a whole, the three volumes are an excellent edition, offering clean, rich transfers that fortunately temper Korjus's inherently brilliant timbre.

Miliza Korjus's art is an acquired taste. One listens to her recordings for flawless, instrumentally precise singing. It must be cautioned, however, that her pyrotechnical recordings need to be sampled in small doses. When approached in that way, they prove to be very satisfying and have considerable impact.

Live Recordings

There are a number of live examples of Korjus's singing. One is a performance of the opera portion of Richard Strauss's *Ariadne auf Naxos* (Preiser CD) that took place on June 11, 1935, when Korjus was guesting in Stuttgart. She sings Najade. (Erna Berger sings Zerbinetta while Viorica Urseleac is Ariadne.) Korjus has brief moments in the opening trio that are plagued with problems of sharpness and she seems hampered by her own singing process.

During the 1970s OASI released an LP (#552) that included a live performance of Lucia's "Spargi d'amaro pianto." Although the date of the performance is not stated, it probably dates from her stay in Mexico between 1942 and 1944. Some things are apparent: her high, bright, frontal placement, and a definite fondness for the use of Italian-like white vowels. She probably adopted these kinds of vowels to help her tonal focus and penetration in the middle register. Problems with her vocal production are apparent. The top of the voice is pinched and not comfortable. Between the two verses she interpolates a high D that she should have avoided. It is no surprise that she does not attempt a final high E-flat. This is rather sad, as the soprano was only about thirty-three years old at the time.

One of her last documented public appearances was in 1950, when Korjus consented to return to New York to sing Strauss's "Kaiserwalzer" during the party scene in *Die Fledermaus* in a performance given by the Metropolitan Opera House. The well-known critic, Irving Kolodin stated it to be outrageous that the Met never hired Korjus to sing the role of the Queen of the Night in *Die Zauberflöte*. Edward Johnson, then-general manager of the Metropolitan, stated that it was felt that the Korjus voice was "too small" for the house. A possible real reason that Miliza Korjus never appeared at the Met may have been due to her already pronounced eccentricities, and, perhaps, the behind-the-scenes political machinations of Lily Pons, the Met's then-reigning coloratura soprano.

In the 1980s, Voce LP Records released a disk (#52) of Miliza Korjus and Lily Pons in live performance that included portions of a 1950 Hollywood Bowl concert in which Korjus took part. The selections include a very fleet "Alleluia" by Mozart from his *Exsultate Jubilate*, as well as three Strauss waltzes that she had recorded for RCA Victor in the 1940s ("Artist's Life," "Blue Danube Waltz," and "Emperor Waltz"). Most illuminating about these live recordings (in surprisingly good sound) is that Korjus was quite consistent in her performance practices, whether live or in the studio. Although she goes no higher than a very stiff high D, her agility remains astounding as does the sweet wistfulness of her timbre. What shocks the modern listener, however, is the power of the upper middle register. Hers was no piping little soprano voice. Its clarity in the high register more resembles the pure brightness of a clarinet than a human voice.

Thanks to YouTube, many of her 1939 radio broadcasts of "Good News" shows are available for all to hear. About twenty songs/arias can presently be found, including a mad scene from *Lucia di Lammermoor* broadcast on March 2, 1939 with a male chorus and a fine showing of her lower register with solid technical battery on high. So, too, there is a vibrant "Sempre libera" (*La traviata*), a wonderfully intricate vocal arrangement of Mozart's "Turkish March," Strauss's "Vienna Woods," Bizet's "Tarantella," Benedicts' "Gypsy and the Bird," and a lovely Schubert "Serenade".

Selected Commercial Recordings

Adam: Theme and Variations

Considering her technique, it is not surprising that Korjus excels in variation pieces. This March, 1934 recording is a classic, outshining the famous 1921 disk made by Amelita Galli-Curci. Korjus exhibits an easy, secure, intuitive sense of style and phrasing in these athletic variations. Despite the "lightness" of the content, this is incredibly poised and artistic singing. Evenly controlled fioriture is rolled out with a sensitivity and subtle use of nuance not usually encountered in this type of music. The acrobatics are so perfect and instrumental in quality that one does not miss text. Of special note are the wide, octave leaps done without pause and without a note out of place. Korjus's middle register is lovely and appealing throughout. Because of the technical nature of the piece, this is one of those recordings where her straight, vibrato-less high register seems appropriate. There is also another of Korjus's main vocal effects here—sustaining a high penultimate note (the D in this piece) as piano through a gradual crescendo to forte (while maintaining an absolutely straight emission). It is quite effective.

Delibes: Blanche Douga (*Lakmé*)
Delibes: Bell Song (*Lakmé*) (sung in Italian)
Surprisingly, Korjus's pallid, cool tones sound quite appropriate in these selections from *Lakmé*. Recorded in January of 1936, the atmospheric Act I prayer to Dourga (Lakmé's entrance) is sung in Italian and has firm, round tones linked by a fine legato line. Her customary use of straight tone is rather appealing in this exotic piece. It lends a credible illusion of chasteness. The slow, graceful coloratura is sung without fault and Korjus's voice weaves nicely throughout the surrounding textures and instruments. Her accuracy during rapid figurations is impeccable, the voice glittering through florid devices and high notes.

If accepted as an "instrumental" approach to an operatic aria, Korjus's Italian performance of the bell song is magnificent. The use of the Italian translation is not ideal, but this was a typical practice at the time. Because the vocalise was sung, half of the central aria is cut to allow room for a single bell refrain. Korjus's slightly cool timbre suits this music. The opening is phrased with bravura, the central aria has an appealing, youthful quality, and one immaculate bell refrain gains in momentum (and intensity) as the aria draws to a close. Her coloratura work is uncannily accurate with pointed, full staccati and fluent scales (with every note in place). The final straight-tone high E (as clean as a clarinet) fits in well with Korjus's instrumental manner and is easily sustained.

Max de Schaunsee (1900–1982), the critic for the *Philadelphia Evening Bulletin* praised Korjus's voice in this recording for its "pallid almost indolent tones in legato passages," marvelously contrasted by her rapid scale passages "which have the breathtaking speed of a flash of lightning." (*Opera News*, November 18, 1946)

Interesting comparisons can be drawn between contemporaries Lily Pons and Miliza Korjus. Both were somewhat monochromatic, but each represented an opposite pole of vocal coloration: Pons, warm and sweet; Korjus, silvery and placid. Korjus's recording is technically sure with staccato, runs, and high E's shining forth with ridiculous ease. Stylistically, her singing is accurate and aurally rewarding. In comparing Pons' RCA Victor recording with this one by Korjus, the American music critic, Irving Kolodin (1908–1988) wrote:

> Though the experience of America with Korjus has been largely in the misuse of her talents by Hollywood, she is a vocalist of considerable accomplishments, as this impeccable, beautifully articulated performance attests. Bruno Siedler-Winkler conducts the orchestra in the pre-war European recording and Mme. Korjus uses an Italian text, but the

results are closer to the intent of Delibes than the light-voiced singing of Pons. (*The New Guide to Recorded Music International Edition*, Doubleday and Company, Inc., 1950, p. 136)

Dell Aqua: Villanelle

This 1935 disk is unusual for the inventive arrangement that is used, most probably by Seidler-Winkler, the conductor. During the early part of the twentieth century, Dell Aqua's charming song was a favorite with high sopranos, many of whom made recordings. These include Gitta Alpar, Sofia Del Campo, Frieda Hempel, Maria Ivogün, Selma Kurz, and Lily Pons. Although Lily Pons' recording reigns supreme for the imagination and beauty of her singing, Korjus's version is one of the most daring and inventive. The cadenza is spectacular as the voice seems to ascend higher and higher to play with the birds, going to high E-flat and F—evocative, if a bit hard in texture. Rita Streich (1920–1987) adopted the first half of the Korjus cadenza for her own 1958 recording of Villanelle. The flights of high staccato in Streich's version are quite beautiful.

Donizetti: Mad Scene (*Lucia di Lammermoor*)

Technically, this eight-and-one-half-minute recording is amazingly accurate. Korjus's recording starts with the beginning of the mad scene, ends with the duet with flute, and includes a male chorus. A January, 1936 recording, it shows no change in the Korjus voice from two years before. Although she is musical and the scene emphasizes the sweet timbre of her middle register, the contrast with Donizetti's emotional score and her straight high register sets up odd conflicts in this Italian music. Cuts are necessary and well-planned. Unfortunately, apart from technical facility, this is a dramatically un-affecting recording. Some ornamentation during the cadenza is a bit wayward; at its worst, just plain odd. After continued listening to multiple of her operatic recordings, it becomes apparent that, although her technical facility was immense, it was that very aspect of her art that limits her appeal in operatic music. The final straight-tone high E-flat is easily sustained over a subdued male chorus. The note is absolute in pitch, but lacks resemblance to a human sound. With such a straight-tone technique, coloration on highs becomes impossible. The instrumental sound and quality, virtuous in one respect becomes a liability, impeding the possibility for interpretive characterization.

Donizetti: Die Zigeunerin

This is a good example of the difference between Korjus's singing of operatic music and light, concert pieces. Because of this music's technical demands one would assume the piece comes from one of Donizetti's operas. Actually, it is the concert setting of a poem by Carlo Guaita that, unfortunately, is rarely programmed or recorded. Korjus's recording was one of the first made of this music (raised a full tone). YouTube has a recording with Ingeborg Hallstein and another with Montserrat Caballe, both in key.

This was Korjus's last recording in Berlin in March of 1936. A wonderful bit of froth, this cheerful Donizetti song about a gypsy girl is enhanced by a male chorus, the use of tambourines, and Korjus's seemingly endless upper extension (to a sustained high E). Her sense of playfulness is infectious and the coloratura roulades are delicate expressions of joy. The only drawback is her inability to offer finely rolled trills.

Gounod: Waltz Song (*Mireille*)

Recorded in March of 1935, Mireille's waltz song to the birds is given a remarkably brilliant and inventive performance by Korjus. From about 1900 to 1950 this was a very popular recording item for sopranos. In more recent years, Joan Sutherland, Edita Gruberova, and Renee Fleming have revived this piece for recordings or concerts. There are a number of excellent recordings of this aria and the reasons for its popularity include it being well written and that it has ornamental passages that have become traditional. Although Korjus's trills are barely formed, and there is an occasional scoop, the high register is very responsive and she provides volleys of staccati patterns that travel into the stratosphere. As if for fun, she inserts a final cadenza, duet with flute, that has some incredibly pointed flights of high staccati reaching high E five times.

Mackeben: Warum? (*Student von Prague*)

Originally written for a German musical film, this is an exquisite recording made shortly after the film's premiere in August of 1935. In contrast to the surrounding pyrotechnical pieces, the simplicity of "Warum?" is welcome. Written for Miliza Korjus by the composer and conducted by him, the song is transformed into a gem of haunting beauty by a combination of Mackeben's gentle composition and the soprano's expressive legato and misty tonal quality.

Mackeben: Es zogen zwei spielleut (*Student von Prague*)

Recorded at the same time as "Warum?," this theme and variations is quite impressive and one of my favorite Korjus disks. For some reason, it is rarely included in compilations of this singer's work. I find that odd as it is one of her most impressive bravura efforts.

I grew up with an original 10-inch 78 rpm disk of this, the other side being "Warum?." This bit of froth could not be more different from the sentimental "Warum?." Accompanied by a male chorus and piano, Korjus chirps and weaves some wonderfully intricate variations and high staccati through the progressively more complicated strophic verses. There is a staccato ascent to a sustained high F (near the beginning) that is especially stunning. Another special moment occurs when Korjus jumps up an octave to hum a lovely high C followed by a high D that she picks out of the air. While it is a great deal of fun, Korjus's technical mastery and accuracy is astonishing. Less than three minutes long, Korjus offers more and more brilliant ornaments until she finishes with another perfect high F.

Meyerbeer: Shadow Song *(Dinorah)* (sung in Italian)

Dinorah's famous aria was recorded by almost every coloratura of any note during the early twentieth century including Maria Michailowa, Josefina Huguet, Maria Galvany, Luisa Tetrazzini, Selma Kurz, Eugenia Bronskaya, and others.

Unfortunately, the tempo on Korjus's December, 1934 disk is too fast, making the runs and echo effects distracting rather than exciting. Some of her frantic singing is almost humorous. I suspect the problem with tempi was due to the fact that she and the conductor, Schönbaumsfeld, chose to include what is usually cut in the central part of the aria, so time had to be allotted for its inclusion. This is the best part of the recording. Korjus's handling of Meyerbeer's gentle music in this section is charming. The traditional duet with flute is not included. Instead, Korjus ascends to a piercing A-flat above high C. The merits of this must be left to the individual listener to decide.

Moszkowsky: Liebe kleine Nachtigal (Serenade)
This piece has always been on the fringe of the repertoire for Germanic high sopranos. Moritz Moszkowsky (1854–1925) was famous for his instrumental compositions and considered by many to be the best composer for piano after Frederick Chopin. This light piece is an arrangement of his "Serenada," Opus 15, #1. This song has not often been recorded, the last singers to record it having been Erika Köth and Ingeborg Hallstein, both of whom give exemplary renditions. It is probable that Korjus's rendition was one of the song's first recordings. It was perfect for her voice and wide-eyed, breathily innocent singing and interpretation. Recorded in February, 1936 and conducted by Siedler-Winker, it is lightly buoyant. Its bird-like ornaments (up to high F-sharp) are sung with grace and infectious enjoyment.

Mozart: Ach ich liebte (Die Entführung aus dem Serail) – unpublished
Volume III of Preiser's Korjus series includes an unexpected treat, an unpublished (October 2, 1934) recording of Costanza's act I aria. This is an amazingly beautiful recording that causes one to wonder why it was never published. Korjus's tone is sumptuously beautiful and her technical control is outstanding. There is much sensitive tapering of phrases and her clean manner of singing perfectly suits Mozart's music. The difficult roulades near the end are sung with perfect articulation and admirable ease.

Mozart: Martern aller arten (Die Entführung aus dem Serail)
Recorded in October of 1934, this is a highly successful, lightly dramatic performance of the aria. Traditional cuts for 78 rpm recordings of that time are imposed so that the 11-minute aria fits onto a 4-minute side. Korjus's first full, clear notes are immediately brilliant. There is dramatic vocalism here, no matter how subtle it may seem to listeners familiar with recordings by Joan Sutherland, Maria Callas, and Edda Moser. The unusually large range of this aria (from low B-flat to high D) is easily embraced. Firm, round tone, accurate, glistening scales, and brilliant high notes are sung with technical assurance. Her diction is exemplary. Especially apt is Korjus's sense of drama in the lines: "lärme, tobe, würte, zuletzt befreit mich doch der Tod." All is couched in secure musicianship as Korjus easily matches the

orchestra note for note in the final runs up to high C. Typical of early recordings of this aria (Lilli Lehmann, Maria Ivogün, and Frieda Hempel), Korjus interpolates a final high C. In her case, the instrumental approach and quality of the note blend perfectly with the surrounding instruments and give a fine sense of finality to the phrase and the aria.

Mozart: Der hölle rache (*Die Zauberflöte*)

Miliza Korjus's March, 1934 disk of the Queen of the Night's second act aria is considered by many to be one of the best early electric recordings of this aria. Although Korjus does not display great power or vocal thrust in her singing, she generates an unusual amount of musical tension and vocal brilliance. She effectively displays a smoldering, suppressed fury rather than out-and-out rage. Each note clearly audible, there is no cheating on the intricate figurations (especially before the repeated staccati high As and Cs). Korjus is one of few singers able to easily negotiate the difficult triplet figures that Mozart asks for near the end of the aria, not to mention the icy, spiked, high Fs. It wasn't until 1964, thirty years later, and the Klemperer recording of *Die Zauberflöte* on EMI with Lucia Popp, that one experiences a similar icy chill. Despite her easy ability to do so, Korjus sings the final of the aria without an extra final high D that others have interpolated, taking only an "unwritten" high A. Her phrasing is artistic throughout and the end has a wonderful sense of the malevolent.

Müller: Coloratura Variations on Drei Röslein

This record is less familiar, but more staggering than other of Miliza Korjus's variation pieces. It is the impossible tour-de-force "Variations on Drei Roslein," written for Korjus by Johannes Müller, a frequent conductor of her recordings. Recorded in February of 1934 it is her third recording and an awesome achievement, a marathon of intricate, multi-note patterns, excessively wide leaps, complicated runs, arpeggios, trills, and high staccati, all framed by music created to fully exploit the Korjus technique. It is a field day for Korjus who seems to truly relish singing the intricate music. Although light in weight, the piece and the recording are charming due to Korjus's vocal nonchalance. The tessitura is quite high, sitting regularly around high A. A segment near the end should be especially noted for the energetic weaving of intricate coloratura passages through the fabric of the chorus. After an exhausting series of roulades, Korjus repeatedly picks high F staccati out of the stratosphere, repeating the main melody up the octave in the range of high D, E and F.

Proch: Theme and Variations

Although a number of sopranos recorded this concert piece before Korjus, including Luisa Tetrazzini, Amelita Galli-Curci, Lucette Korsoff and Frieda Hempel, none is more suited to this music than Miliza Korjus. Her performance is a lesson in the sensitive phrasing of difficult fioriture. She shows a well-judged, relaxed tempo, and an authoritative vocal poise. As in the Adam Variations, in this piece

Korjus's unorthodox emission of her high register never offends. She intuitively understands how to present such pieces without making them seem more important than they are, but without denigrating them. Her delivery is serious, never coy or arch. The ending is especially fine. Korjus incorporates Galli-Curci's final flourish, leaping to a high E-flat that she gradually gives more power to before descending to A-flat to finally jump back to D-flat.

In comparing her recording to that of Lily Pons, Irving Kolodin writes:

> The slighter voice of Pons is outstripped by the meatier one of Korjus both in vocal brilliance and controlled exhibitionism. Korjus performs the required stunts with firmly centered tone and crisp articulation. Pons with gasps and clucks, grotesque swoops and slides. (*The New Guide to Recorded Music International Edition*, Doubleday 1950, p. 307)

Rossini: Una voce poco fa (*Il barbiere di Siviglia*)

Rosina's famous aria was recorded in June of 1934. It is a technically polished, very poised, and surprisingly uninteresting performance. Sung in German, Korjus's method of emission clashes badly with the inherent humor of Rossini's Italian music. Her clockwork precision tends to detract from the main, humorous objective of the aria. As one would expect, the coloratura figurations and high notes are sung with consummate ease and absolutely no vibrato. While there is perverse fascination with such technical precision, the mechanical accuracy of the fioriture detracts from the humanity of the aria. It must be noted, however, that taking an immediate, final high F with no preparation is an impressive feat.

The Strauss Waltzes

Strauss: Voci di Primavera (Voices of Spring)

Made in January of 1934, this is Korjus's first published recording, a good, healthy "sing" with little extraneous ornamentation. Rhythmically alert with dynamic energy, it is Miliza Korjus at her best. The technical demands of the vocal arrangement are met with precision that Korjus caps with an immediate, brilliant, vibrato-free high F. When first released, this recording must have stunned listeners with its beauty and accuracy. There is much nuance and many vocal touches that make this rise above that of a mere show piece.

Strauss: 1001 Nights

In May of 1935, Korjus made one of her most virtuostic recordings, a vocal adaptation of Strauss' *1001 Nights*. Wonderful, full tone, good simulations of trills and some excellent thrusting into the upper regions of her voice highlight this record. It is likely that the arrangement was made for Korjus by the conductor, Seidler-Winker. At the three-minute mark there is a fascinating chromatic climb that takes her to high E. What is interesting is that the listener easily hears the changes in Korjus's emission as she climbs up note by note. This is followed by an intense section that builds as Korjus repeatedly soars up to high A to begin a minute-long cadenza that rises in impossible figurations through intricate staccati figures to high E, F, and F-sharp before she finishes with a grand (and notably intense) flourish of triplets that lead to a powerful, penultimate high E.

Volume III of Preiser's Korjus CDs includes the four waltzes that Korjus recorded in May, 1945, conducted by Giuseppe Bamboschek and another four conducted by Antol Dorati in September, 1947.

The eight waltzes are:

(Conducted by Bamboschek)
Wein, Weib und Gesang (2–19–45)
Kaiserwalzer (5–1–45)
1001 Nacht (5–1–45)
An der schönen blauen Donau (5–1–45)

(Conducted by Dorati)
Künsterleben (Artist's Life) (9–19–47)
Rosen aus dem Süden (Roses from the South) (9–19–47)
Wiener Blut (Vienna Blood) (9–19–47)
Schatzwalzer (9–19–47)

This series of excessively florid Strauss Waltzes will probably have its greatest appeal among true florid aficionados. Sung in English with an odd accent, I have a great personal fondness for these waltzes. Much of this has to do with the staccato work. In 1981, I corresponded with musicologist, William Ashbrook (1922–2009). In a discussion about Miliza Korjus he wrote:

> It was clearly her unreliable intonation and her sustained acuti that sounded like the noon-whistle which so severely limited her public career in the U.S. That New York concert (in spite of the kind review) was really a disaster. I had interesting talks with Giuseppe Bamboschek about Korjus, because he had what he regarded as the thankless task of making those Strauss-waltz arrangements for her Victor recordings and strove to eliminate any opportunities for sustained high-notes (the normal coloratura's stock-in-trade) and was reduced to writing those peculiar staccati passages for her because only they represented her in her best light, and yet they are tiresome in their monotony. (from a private letter of March 6, 1981)

The arrangements that Ashbrook mentions are overly embroidered and abound in intricate staccato work, although rarely does Korjus travel above high C. One lone, piercing E-flat displays the precariousness of her high register. The waltzes are innocuous enough and one or two at a time make for fun listening. There is a fascinating "out-take" (test recording) of "Artist's Life" on YouTube that shows Korjus at work with Antol Dorati during the RCA sessions in 1947. From a 16-inch shellac disk, this is a different take from the one issued by Victor. It is likely a test cut that includes an interrupted session. She becomes quite defensive when a musical error causes the session to be interrupted, displaying this readily by accusing the flautist of playing an unwanted sforzando.

Originally the eight waltzes were housed in two separate 78 rpm albums, and recorded in two sessions of four, two years apart. In 1958, RCA merged both albums and an additional waltz, "Vienna Woods" (December, 1938), on *Vienna in 3/4 Time,* a Camden LP, (CAL 427).

Recorded late in her career (even though she was only thirty-six years old), these eight waltzes have always been considered controversial. When Miliza Korjus made these recordings, many sopranos had recorded Strauss waltzes—Luisa Tetrazzini, Maria Ivogün, Melitta Heim, Irene Eden, Marcella Sembrich, and of course, Lily Pons. The success of each had much to do with the quality of their arrangements. The arrangements composed for Korjus are saccharine and athletically over the top.

There are problems with the arrangements that demonstrate why Bamboschek, who created them, complained. Most of the arrangements are written in C major to allow Korjus to take a final high C (half of the eight arrangements end this way). One, "Wein, Weib und Gesang," ends with the soprano taking an excruciatingly tight (and obviously uncomfortable) high E-flat. The "Blue Danube" remains in the traditional high soprano key of D major. At its end, Korjus offers her own version of high D. One of the most ornate, a new recording of "1001 Nights," is in B-flat. This last is a flamboyant staccato arrangement by Bamboschek having a minute-long duet with flute that touches high D twice. The finish is intense.

Irving Kolodin, generally a supporter of Korjus' art, did not care at all for her Strauss waltzes. Writing about her 1945 version of the "Blue Danube Waltz" he notes:

> The filigree version of Korjus is not recommended except to be played as punishment for some Straussian who has been naughty." (*The New Guide to Recorded Music International Edition,* Doubleday 1950, p. 404)

Of her "Roses from the South," he refused to comment.

Korjus recorded other waltzes during various phases of her career, including a few from the 1938 movie, *The Great Waltz,* that are included on Volume III of Preiser's Korjus series.

Taubert: Der Vogel im Wald

Taubert's "Bird in the Wood" was a favorite of Selma Kurz. It was a popular Victorian salon piece that was often used by sopranos as a recital encore. It must have been something to hear, especially by Kurz, who was famous for rolling her trills for inordinate periods of time.

Korjus does not trill. Therefore, the rather modern-sounding arrangement of this little song, recorded in March of 1936, becomes a coloratura extravaganza of staccati. It is one of the most pyrotechnical versions one can hear on disk, replete with a duet with flute. Korjus does actually trill. It is just that her trills do not have the effect they should, due to their lack of formation.

Much of this song's charming simplicity is lost in a vocal scramble as Korjus spins out roulades, staccato figurations, trills, echo effects, and high notes (up to high E-flat) with disarming ease.

Verdi: Ernani Involami (*Ernani*)

This 1936 recording uses German text that disrupts the natural flow of the Italian vocal line as it was originally composed. Verdi's music is a stretch for the Korjus voice. Her singing up to high B-flat is quite fine, but high Cs are approached with a sense of caution that is noticeable. The recitative that comes before has full, rich tone and there is an appropriate sense of thrusted urgency. There is an appealing smoky, almost smoldering, sensual intensity that is quite individual. Unfortunately, Korjus's ending (a trill on high A, moving to high D, followed by a descent to C, to a final B-flat) is anything but stylistic, the emission mannered and awkward.

Verdi: Bolero (*I Vespri Siciliani*)

When Miliza Korjus recorded this aria in 1935, only a handful of singers had recorded it before. (Luisa Tetrazzini, Sigrid Arnoldson, Rosa Raisa, Claudia Muzio and Rosa Ponselle.) Among them, Korjus provides the most bravura performance. Different from the *Ernani* aria, this florid music suits her voice and technique quite well. It displays to perfection her accurate coloratura singing within a true allegro (though not "bolero") tempo. At times the aria seems a bit frantic, but there is dazzling singing here. While purists might rail at the questionable (and un-stylistic) cadenza that Korjus inserts, it certainly serves its purpose, underlining Elena's joy at her upcoming marriage. With laughter-like, repeated staccati high Es and F-sharps, it is a memorable rendition. During these last few measures there are no fewer than five high Es and three F-sharps.

Weber: Invitation to the Dance

Recorded in October of 1934, this concert piece is known primarily as a piano or orchestral work. It is presented here in a monstrously difficult, quite exciting vocal arrangement, proving yet again that it is in extroverted bravura pieces such as this that Korjus prevails. Her secure technical resources, vast range, sure intonation, and sensible, yet imaginative phrasing make it an interesting confection, enjoyable for its verve and virtuosic audacity. Furthermore, her naturally volatile personality helps to exploit the virtuosity required of the piece. Her instrumental high register fits in perfectly with the surrounding instruments. Of special interest is the chromatic climb over two octaves at the conclusion.

After listening to much of the legacy of Miliza Korjus it becomes evident that, while she vacillated between opera and concert showpieces, it was in the concert repertoire that she excelled. In almost all of her performances there is an appealing aura of natural charm and artistic honesty. One may not agree with her ideals or her musical taste, but she promotes them without shame, the strength of her conviction always evident. This, and her technical facility, tends to cause one to return to her recordings. Sincere and immediately endearing, her charm gives her best recordings a delicate femininity that is most appealing.

Although she does not always perform with impeccable musical taste, her recordings are always interesting and show personality. That said, many of Korjus' cadenzas and ornaments would not be tolerated today. No matter the style of ornamentation of that time period, Miliza Korjus was an eccentric singer, not only because of her singing method, but also in her choice of ornamentation.

This eccentricity of the Korjus personality never abated. She was known to sing an aria from *Carmen* in Russian, an aria from *Die Fledermaus* in Spanish, and before her death she stated that she planned to compose an opera called *Nefertiti,* based on Egypt's famous queen. In her own words:

> …because story is not really essential in an opera, I am not going to have words. It will all be humming, using every possible note in the human voice, from high to low and orchestral music. It will be very educational. (*Opera News*, November 21, 1970)

Another project that was never realized was a recording of Isolde's "Liebestod" employing seventeen harps. She (obviously) loved the harp and perceived this aria as a lullaby of love. She would sing Brünnhilde's "Immolation Scene" from *Die Götterdämmerung* with organ. "It is a funeral, you see, and at funerals they play the organ." The diva admitted that she could never do this in an opera house, but on disk she could do whatever she wanted.

When interviewed by Florence Stevenson for an article in the November 21, 1970 issue of *Opera News* she was asked which of her careers it was that she had she enjoyed the most. (According to Korjus she had had seven careers: church singing, dancing, musical comedy, recordings, opera, film, and the "new" 1960s recordings she was then making.) Korjus replied with her characteristic bluntness: "The records. It is the only way to become immortal."

Miliza Korjus's recordings, made eighty years ago in Berlin, will serve her legacy well.

Dame Nellie Melba (1861–1931)

Among famous historical singers, Nellie Melba has always been controversial. She is a paradox. On one hand her name stands for vocal perfection and on the other her recordings disclose something quite different.

Everyone should hear at least one recording of the famous Melba. She reigned supreme throughout the English-speaking world for decades, and was one of the most important and influential operatic divas in the history of classical music. Toast and desserts were named after her making Melba a name to be revered.

Like Enrico Caruso, many books have been written about her to which I refer readers for greater in-depth biographical information. There are excellent books by John Hetherington, Joseph Wechsberg, Ann Blainey, Thérèse Radic, and others.

Nellie Melba was born Helen Nellie Porter Mitchell in Mebourne, Australia in 1861. When young, she studied with Mary Ellen Christian (a former pupil of Manuel Garcia) and Pietro Cecchi, an Italian tenor and a well-known teacher in Melbourne. In 1886, Melba went to Paris to study with Mathilde Marchesi. She made an inauspicious debut in London in 1888 as *Lucia di Lammermoor*. When Augustus Harris, the general manager of Covent Garden offered her only the small role of Oscar in *Un ballo in maschera*, she left England in a huff to sing elsewhere. She did, however, garner the support of Lady de Grey, a very influential member of English society. Melba had good success in Brussels and in Paris, and due to the machinations of Lady de Grey, returned to Covent Garden in 1889, to eventually become their reigning prima donna until her operatic retirement in 1926. Her debut at the Metopolitan Opera in 1893 made her their darling as well, and she sang there until 1910. Her final performance was a charity concert in London on June 10, 1930. She died in Sydney, Australia in 1931. Her most famous roles were Marguerite in *Faust*, *Lucia di Lammermoor*, Mimi (*La bohéme*), Ophelia in Thomas' *Hamlet*, Nedda in *Pagliacci*, Juliette in *Romeo et Juliette*, Gilda in *Rigoletto*, Desdemona in *Otello*, and *Lakmé*.

In 1918 Melba was appointed Dame Commander of the British Empire for her charity work during World War I, and was elevated to Dame Grand Cross of the

British Empire in 1927. She and Dame May Whitty were the first entertainers to be awarded the honor of Dame Commander of the British Empire.

One divatic stunt almost ruined Nellie Melba's voice and her career. In December of 1896 she decided that she would sing Brünnhilde in *Siegfried* at the Metropolitan Opera. By that time she had sung Wagner's Elsa in *Lohengrin* (in French) and Elizabeth in *Tannhaüser* (in Italian) and had had some success in both roles. At that time, Wagner's music dramas were the rage so Melba decided that she should sing the most famous of Wagner's heroines, Brünnhilde. It was a big mistake.

> ...under the influence of Jean de Reszke, whose enthusiasm for The Ring she caught, Melba took advantage of her box-office power to persuade the management of the Met to reserve the role for her...Lillian Nordica, enraged at being shut out of a part that would naturally have fallen to her lot at the Met, spread rumors that Melba had intrigued with de Reszke to see she was not engaged for that season...The performance was a near disaster. (Thérèse Radic, *Melba*, Macmillan Australia, 1986)

The other five scheduled performances had to be cancelled and Melba fled to Europe to recuperate. Her voice recovered, but her ego was severely bruised and from that time on she had a dislike for sopranos capable of singing Wagner roles.

> Melba believed that her voice and personality were of a kind that came together only once a century. Certainly she drew the admiration of other singers, and even had the capacity to make them sing better. But not everyone rated her so highly. Whatever the case in London and New York, and to a lesser degree the Francophone countries, her standing was not quite so high beyond: Sir Thomas Beecham believed this to be because she was 'wanting in genuine spiritual refinement', while others spoke of her coldness. George Bernard Shaw, then a music critic, initially found Melba 'hard, shallow, self-sufficient and altogether unsympathetic', but by 1892—after the break with the duke of Orleans—he acknowledged her as not merely a brilliant singer but a dramatic soprano. Shortly afterwards Melba's limitations were made painfully apparent: her Brunnhilde in *Siegfried* at the Metropolitan in 1896 was a disaster, and her singing of the title role in *Aida* a few years later was scarcely more successful. Similarly, although Melba claimed that Puccini wrote the part of *Madame Butterfly* for her, and she studied it with him, something in the role eluded her and she never sang it. (Jim Davidson, *Australian Dictionary of Biography*, Volume 10, (MUP), 1986 http://adb.anu.edu.au/biography/melba-dame-nellie-7551)

The Records

Melba made 150 sides during sixteen recording sessions between 1904 and 1926. Although she originally recorded in England for Gramophone, by 1907 she was also recording for American Victor. Her recordings have always been available and beginning in the LP era, they could be found on releases by EMI, Scala, TAP, Rococo, and many smaller labels.

In 1994, Romophone released a three-CD set of her complete Victor recordings (1907–1916) made when she was forty-six and older. The set has sixty-three sides, some of which are now considered classic early recordings, such as the two-sided mad scene from Thomas' *Hamlet*. Transferred by Ward Marston, the sound is about as good as you can get.

In 1995, the small label, Phonograph, released her "Farewell Concert" at Covent Garden on June 8, 1926, along with other arias. In 1997, Nimbus released a single disc of Melba sides that duplicates many of the Romophone selections.

Finally, in 2002, Ward Marston began a project to transfer all of the Melba sides onto seven CDs for Naxos. His work is exemplary, and if you are to explore this soprano's work, I suggest starting with Naxos.

Truesound Transfers (http://www.truesoundtransfers.de/) is run by Christian Zwarg in Berlin. They have produced a series of CD-R issues presenting rare recordings from the acoustic era (1888–1930) as well as some early electric recordings from the 1920s and 1930s. Zwarg has released a Melba CD that includes the famous 1904 sides. I do not like to recommend CD-R discs as I have found they have a declining shelf life, but Zwarg has managed to present the Melba voice in a way that is remarkable. They are worth looking into.

Often, when recommending a singer's legacy, one suggests that a novice start with the early recordings, when the singer's voice is fresh. With Melba, however, I propose the opposite. I believe one should start with her famous "Farewell Concert" at Covent Garden given on June 8, 1926, which, remarkably, was captured live. At the time, Melba was sixty-five years old. She sang excerpts from Verdi's *Otello* and Puccini's *La bohème*. The reasons I suggest starting with that concert is, that when it took place, the recording process was electrical rather than acoustic. The microphone was better able to capture the unique Melba timbre. She may have been sixty-five, but her technique was excellent. More importantly, however, because of the technological advances, one gets a very good idea of the special Melba sound. Above all, it was the Melba sound that made her such a famous singer.

Unfortunately, for many modern-day listeners Nellie Melba is a conundrum. Her early records do indeed display a remarkable voice and technical facility, but they also reveal an almost coarse vocal attack. Her training with Marchesi occasionally lent an unattractive laser-like edge to the higher notes that does not translate well in the acoustical recording process. The most common complaint is that Melba sounds like an English boy soprano. Amusingly, Melba prided herself on this: Melba herself said to Percy Colson:

> My voice is like a glorified boy's voice. (Charles Nelson Gattey, *Queens of Song*, Barrie and Jenkins, Ltd, London, 1979)

Her sense of a fluid legato often differs from what we consider "flowing" today. Notes are often presented individually, or as little spikes, rather than as sounds linked within a smooth phrase. I have always felt that Melba was an inconsistent singer. Her approach to music seems to vary, depending on what she is singing. She often layers emotional meaning onto second-rate material while merely "going through the paces" on more complex operatic arias. She, at times, sounds sublime; and, at others, truly vulgar. This is unsettling when listening to her recordings. Oddly, her legato is more refined in the 1913 recording of "Comin thro the Rye," and the 1916 disk of "Annie Laurie," than it is in the 1910 disk of Verdi's "Ah fors e lui" from *La traviata*.

Of Melba's "studio" recordings, I prefer the first sides made in 1904 and various selections from later years. By 1904 she had been a major international star for fifteen years. The recordings were made in the drawing room of her London residence at 30 Great Cumberland Place, in Mayfair, London. These were most probably test records. They include arias from her most famous roles of that time: *La traviata*, *Lucia di Lammermoor, Hamlet, La bohème, Le nozze di Figaro,* and *Rigoletto* as well as *L'Allegro, il Penseroso ed il Moderato, and* songs by Tosti, Arditi, and others— all accompanied by piano. It is here that one hears her vibrant freshness and at least part of her famous upper extension (up to high D).

The five 1904 selections that best show her technical battery include Bemberg's "Nymphes et sylvains" (with some remarkable trills and scale work) and the waltz by Luigi Arditi, "Se saran rose" (known as "The Melba Waltz") which has always been one of the great Melba sides. Arditi (1822—1903) was an Italian composer and conductor. He conducted a number of the early Verdi premieres in America in the 1840s. His vocal waltzes were extremely popular with high sopranos during the acoustic era. "Il Bacio" and "Parla!" are still sung in concerts and recitals. Arditi originally wrote "Se saran rose" for Adelina Patti, but Melba seized the music as her own. A very special moment during the Arditi waltz is a dynamic high A trill that Melba sings between the two verses of the piece—once heard, it is not forgotten. Beyond some craggy approaches to higher notes, it is an infectious piece of music; the final high D is *great* fun.

The mad scenes from *Hamlet* and *Lucia*, and the Handel showpiece from *Il Penseroso*, all show remarkable coloratura: arpeggios, roulades, staccati, and trills of incomparable glitter. An amusing and human moment occurs during a take of the voice/flute cadenza from "Sweet Bird" (*L'Allegro, il Penseroso ed il Moderato)* when Melba (or the flautist) makes a wrong entrance. Melba says exasperatedly: "Now we'll have to do it again." When she sings the cadenza again, it is a marvel of coloratura and bird-like trills that she caps with a fine high D.

I have always been fond of her 1909 recording of Hahn's "D'une Prison" with its simple, but persuasive, vocal line. The song's requirements are deceptive, however. Contrary to what the listener might think, this is not an easy song to sing or to interpret. It requires restraint, but also an eloquent handling of the vowels and text. Melba sings it just the way it should be sung. It is a very special recorded moment.

Another of my absolute favorite Melba records is the piano-accompanied, bittersweet "Le temps des lilas" by Chausson, recorded in May of 1913. There are no brilliant displays here, just the sound of the Melba voice and her apparent love for the music. This is evident by her intimate pronunciation of the French text. One can hear the ring of her upper register in the recording studio's acoustics in the phrase *"Et nous n'irons plus courir."* Especially moving is her singing of the final line: "Avec notre amour est mort à jamais" (Along with our love, [that] is dead forever) which she sustains within a finely graded decrescendo until the tone disappears into surrounding harmonics. The amount of musical detail in this song and the fact that it is so recognizable is quite remarkable. This is a Melba record that I can listen to over and over. I have always felt that it is one of her great recordings.

Very interesting is a "distance test" that Melba recorded in May, 1910. Thankfully this was preserved. It shows the impact of the singer's voice at various distances from the recording horn.

J.B. Steane writes (in liner notes for the Melba Nimbus CD):

> She was a singer who could achieve perfection in a way that was beyond the capability of practically every other comparable singer both in her own and in later times; yet she was always spoiling things.

It is the paradox of her recordings!—and what is so frustrating about Melba.

Famous for her Ophelia, her 1910 (or 1904) eight-minute mad scene from *Hamlet* is one of the most complete versions up to that time. A two-sided release, it has beautiful singing and some atrocious cackling as well.

The two sides of the *Otello* Willow Song and "Ave Maria" done in August of 1910 find the soprano offering beautiful renditions—except for the unmusical punching of various syllables and notes, and, at times, her relentless mezza-forte dynamic. But, beneath this, there is a defined understanding of, and an obvious affection for, the music. (Melba reputedly studied Desdemona with Verdi himself.)

As a modern-day trained singer and listener, I find her recordings to be occasionally annoying enigmas. With her contemporary, Luisa Tetrazzini, it is obvious why she became famous and loved; with Melba one often scratches one's head, wholly mystified.

Not helping this puzzle are the many sides of second-rate musical material that Melba released. One must weed through them to get at the good recordings. This chaff includes the songs of Herman Bemberg (1859–1931), an Argentinean composer and friend of Melba. He studied under Massenet, but if not for the records Melba made of his songs, he would be completely forgotten today.

From the writings of the day, one might assume that the extreme contrasts in Melba recordings may have been unintentionally provided by the recording process.

For instance, according to the famous critic of the day, W J Henderson:

> The Melba attack was little short of marvelous. The term attack is not a good one. Melba indeed had no attack; she opened her mouth and a tone was in existence. (W.J. Henderson *The Art of Singing*, Dial Press, 1938, p. 421)

But this is not what we hear on her recordings. What we hear is much more percussive and, in a sense, crude. Part of this may have been inherent in the soprano's personality.

Within his remarkable and excellently detailed liner notes for the LP set *Nellie Melba: The London Recordings 1904-1926 (EMI),* Michael Aspinall notes:

> The ruthless stamp of her driving ambition is clearly revealed just by the sound of her records; *Caro nome*, for instance, is destitute of feminine charm, and the aggressively assertive Gilda seems bent on bullying her audience into submission with cascades of

dazzling runs, brilliant staccati and vibrant, flawless trills. At times she wields her angelic voice like a club to stun her hearers.

This was part and parcel of who Nellie Melba really was.

Adelaide Lubbock, the young daughter of Lord Stanley (who gave the address during Melba's farewell concert at Covent Garden) met Melba in her youth and remembers the soprano vividly:

> Madame Melba often came to the house. She and my mother became great friends, although I don't think my father cared for her too much. He was bored by her aggressive prima-donna airs. We loved her as she was kind to us and gave us wonderful grown-up presents...She was a stocky woman of middle height, rather coarse complexioned, with an imposing singer's bust. With men she was inclined to be tom-boyishly flirtatious, and she had an arch habit of pirouetting round on her heel when she wished to be specially fascinating and which I believe used to embarrass my father. She had a jolly sense of humour and an impulsive and basically generous nature...Her speaking-voice as I remember it was rather strident and gave no hint of the pure and flute-like quality of her singing. (Thérèse Radic, *Melba*, Macmillan Australia, 1986)

No matter what, Melba was truly a "monstre sacré":

> Sometimes she came and practiced her roles in the drawing room at Government House, and we were allowed to listen...But what we liked best was when she lost her temper with Mr. Caruthers, the accompanist. She would scream abuse at the wretched, squirming creature in between roulades and trills, and sometimes even box his ears. She used to walk about the room gesticulating and acting as she sang, and we would gleefully watch the accompanist flinch as she approached the piano during these peregrinations. (ibid)

W. J. Henderson was one of the great New York critics from whose book, *The Art of Singing* (1938), I often quote. His astute writings stand beside those of Herman Klein and J.B.Steane as among the most perceptive reflections on the art of singing that have ever been written. He knew singing and the art of singing. His comments suggest that it is, perhaps, the recording process that exacerbates certain vocal blemishes that ordinarily are not noticed in the opera house.

Of her debut at the Metropolitan Opera as *Lucia di Lammermoor* on December 4, 1893, he writes:

> If she is not the foremost coloratura soprano of the day, she is certainly in the very front rank. Nature has gifted her with one of the loveliest voices that ever issued from a human throat. It is simply delicious in its fullness, richness, and purity. Some of the notes sound like some of those of Mme. Patti in her prime, but the voice as a whole resembles no other...It is perfectly equalized in all its registers, and its placing is a model of voice production. Indeed, Mme. Melba's whole method is a constant tribute to the veteran teacher, Mme. Marchesi. It so happens that Mmes. Eames and Calvé are also pupils of Mme. Marchesi, who thus gets a splendid advertisement from the present company. It is only fair to say that Mme. Melba shows the results of more extended vocal training than either of the others. Her voice comes out in that smooth, spontaneous manner that is found only where the "automatism," as the teachers call it, is perfected. If there is anything in the method of singing that Mme. Melba does not know and does not employ without conscious effort she

failed to betray it last night. Those who really love good singing will get more pleasure from the beautiful quality of her voice and its exquisite production than from her clean exectution of those ornaments which seem to the best taste to be generally out of place in the lyric drama. It should be added that her style is less cold than reports from abroad had led us to expect. (Metropolitan Opera Archives, accessed January, 2015)

Melba sang at the Metropolitan Opera until her final *La traviata* at that house on November 29, 1910. During those years she sang 210 performances of 17 roles: 116 in-house and 94 while on tour. Her repertoire ranged from *Semiramide* to the *Siegfried* Brünnhilde (one performance only in 1896). Her most performed role was Marguerite in *Faust* (forty-seven times). *Lucia di Lammermoor* followed closely with thirty-one.

Melba knew many of the composers whose music she sang—Gounod, Thomas, Massenet, Delibes, Verdi and Puccini, having worked with many of them personally. Delibes worked with Melba on *Lakmé* and, although she was criticized for her abominable French, it was reported that Delibes said he didn't care how badly she pronounced the text, so long as she sang the role.

Different from many other florid artists of her time, Melba was very much a modern singer in that she promoted contemporary works. Recognizing Puccini's gifts, she sought him out in order to work on Mimi in *La bohème*. She first performed Mimi in Philadelphia and in the first performance of the opera given at Covent Garden in 1899. (One must remember that *La bohème* premiered in Turin when Melba was only 35 years old.) Considering her determination, it is not surprising that, at Covent Garden at least, the role of Mimi remained Melba's personal property until her retirement in 1926.

Writing for *Gramophone* in 2009, J.B. Steane notes:

> The most common complaint about her as an artist was that she was cold. The voice itself was admitted to be of exceptional purity, and her technique might be judged near to perfection in matters of placement, evenness, accuracy in tills and fluency in scale-work. But (critical opinions would then say) it was too impersonal, lacking in variety of coloration, to be effective as an instrument for the expression of feelings. Moreover, she could not act, or she simply would not try. And in an operatic artist that was some limitation, even in the Golden Age.
>
> Now, I write as one addicted. I hear in Melba's records many things I wish were otherwise but still treasure them. As the years go by I find the sound of that 'cold' voice curiously moving, often surprisingly and sometimes alarmingly so. It's partly, and primarily, the recognition of a unique timbre, which brings an unbidden thrill. It might be in a quite simple phrase – the last notes of Mimi's 'Addio, senza rancor', for instance – sung well within any singer's range. But when she does soar aloft—think of Ophelia's 'A vos jeux' – the effect can be breathtaking, like Hopkins's windhover ('the achieve of, the mastery of, the thing'). Her trill, as in 'Caro nome', is utterly precise, like a great pianist's. Her scale ('Sempre libera') is perfection – and there is something moving in the mere fact of such perfection. Or there is when it is found in company with such a rare purity of tone.

W. J. Henderson probably said it best:

> There is one quality (her voice had) …and which may be comprehended even by those who did not hear her; it had splendor. The tones glowed with a starlike brilliance. They flamed

with a white flame. And they possessed a remarkable force which the famous singer always used with continence. (W.J. Henderson, *The Art of Singing*, Dial Press, 1938, p. 420)

If I am asked to introduce someone to the Melba voice, I invariably turn to her farewell concert—especially the *La bohème* excerpts like "Donde Lieta Usci." One gets a good idea of the special quality of her youthful timbre (even at age sixty-five) and the soaring, fiery beauty of her voice. It is that special "flame" that one hears hints of during her 1926 Farewell Concert.

When Melba died, her son, George, was by her side, as was her faithful flautist, John L Lemmone, who was also her accompanist, manager, and opera company impresario. She was buried next to her father as she had wished.

"The war had depressed the value of her shares, otherwise she would have left far more than the quarter of a million pounds she did. In her will there were legacies to acquaintances as well as friends she knew to be in need." (Charles Nelson Gattey, *Queens of Song*, Barrie and Jenkins, Ltd, London, 1979)

There truly was no one like her.

Nellie Melba Addendum:

The Dame Clara Butt Scandal

Only once did Melba shake the Australian people's devotion to their star. When Clara Butt and Kennerley Rumford were about to tour Australia for the first time...the Rumford's asked Melba's advice. What sort of programmes, they wondered, would Australians like? 'Sing 'em muck,' said Melba, bluntly, 'It's all they understand.'

Forty years later, when Clara Butt wrote her *Memoires*, she recalled the advice she had been given by the greatest musical personality Australia had produced, and caused an uproar. ...'How could I have said that?' asked Melba plaintively of the Australian press. 'I have always had the greatest admiration for the taste and discrimination of my Australian audiences.' A mutual friend asked Melba if it were true that she had really given Clara Butt this dangerous advice. 'Of course not,' retorted Melba; 'in Clara's case it wasn't necessary.' (Ivor Newton, *At the Piano*, Hamish Hamilton, London, 1966)

Nellie Melba and Stella Power (1896–1977)

Stella Power was a lyric coloratura born Tertia Power in Richmond, Melbourne who originally studied with Dame Nellie Melba's teacher, Elsa Wiedermann. She became one of Melba's first students, working closely with her at the Albert Street Conservatorium in East Melbourne. Power's studies were so successful that she earned the blessing (or curse) of being known as "The Little Melba." While meant to be a compliment, the course of Power's career (as a concert singer) was quite different from Melba's (as an opera singer) and thus set up unfair comparisons.

Power began her career with a recital in Melbourne in 1916. In 1917 she toured the United States with Melba for six months. In 1918, she married William Francis O'Rourke, a commercial traveler, and their son Billy was born in 1920. During 1918, Power was back in the United States for concerts with the violinists Eugène Ysaÿe and Mischa Elman. Also at this time (1918–1919) she took part in an extensive tour with Melba as an associate artist, recording eight sides for Edison (one of which was Arditi's "Se saran rose"—the Melba Waltz). She made her official London debut at the Royal Albert Hall on November 23, 1919, in a concert conducted by Sir Landon Ronald. During the time of her pregnancy, she lost the support of Melba who was furious and felt betrayed by her protégé, feeling that Power should have taken her career more seriously. While in Britain, Power appeared with such luminaries as John McCormack, cellists Jean Gerardy and Lauri Kennedy, pianist Wilhelm Backhaus, and violinist Jan Kubelík. It was around this time that she made ten sides for HMV where she was actually entitled, "The Little Melba." Power returned to Australia in 1923 to perform in picture-palaces. In 1926, she returned to the United States with a nine-year contract to perform as a featured singer in popular revues, appearing with such personalities as Will Rogers and Mae West. Billy, her young son, traveled with her. When she returned to Australia in 1935, she lived with her brother, Cyril, suggesting that either her husband, William, had died or that they had divorced. Power spent four months in New Zealand. In 1946 she was the voice of Melba in the radio serial, *Melba—The Life Story of a Great Australian*. She retired from singing in the 1950s but taught voice throughout the 1960s. Power rarely appeared in opera, once as Micaëla in *Carmen* in 1924, and then later, in 1938, she sang the role of Norina in *Don Pasquale,* and the title role in *Martha*, both with Dino Borgioli, in "condensed" radio versions of both operas for the Australian Broadcasting Commission.

The Nellie Melba Estate

On August 23, 2014 Melba's home (Coombe Cottage) was opened to the public by the Melba Estate. Located at 675 Maroondah Highway, Coldstream, Victoria, Australia, it includes seven acres of stunning gardens.

> Pamela, or Lady Vestey, Melba's only grandchild who lived here for 40 years until she died in 2011, wanted the estate to remain in the family, to perpetuate Melba's legacy. Melba's great-grandsons Lord Samuel Vestey and the Honourable Mark Vestey are spending millions converting outbuildings into a cafe-restaurant, gallery and cellar door, which will open on August 23.

> Estate Manager, Daniel Johnson said opening the estate was a way for Lady Vestey's sons to keep it viable while educating new generations about the "amazing" Melba. 'She was a very driven, single-minded woman from Australia who conquered the world.'" (Carolyn Webb, *The Age*, http://www.theage.com.au/victoria/dame-nellie-melbas-retreat-set-to-embrace-a-new-public-20140719-3c7vx.html

Nellie Melba and Food Honors:

Four food items created by the famous French chef Auguste Escoffier of the Savoy Hotel in London: Peach Melba is a classic dessert, invented in 1892 or 1893, to honour the Australian soprano. It combines two favourite summer fruits: peaches and raspberry sauce accompanying vanilla ice cream. In 1892, Nellie Melba was performing in Wagner's opera *Lohengrin* at Covent Garden. The Duke of Orléans gave a dinner party to celebrate her triumph. For the occasion, Escoffier created a new dessert, and to display it, he used an ice sculpture of a swan, which is featured in the opera. The swan carried peaches which rested on a bed of vanilla ice cream and which were topped with spun sugar. In 1900, Escoffier created a new version of the dessert. For the occasion of the opening of the Carlton hotel, where he was head chef, Escoffier omitted the ice swan and topped the peaches with raspberry purée. Other versions of this dessert use pears, apricots, or strawberries instead of peaches and/or use raspberry sauce or melted red currant jelly instead of raspberry purée. Melba sauce is a sweet purée of raspberries and redcurrant. Melba toast is a very dry, crisp and thinly sliced toast often served with soup and salad or topped with either melted cheese or pâté. Its name is thought to date from 1897, when the singer was very ill and it became a staple of her diet. The toast was created for her by chef and fan Auguste Escoffier, who also created the Peach Melba dessert for her. The hotel proprietor César Ritz supposedly named it in a conversation with Escoffier. Melba Garniture is chicken, truffles and mushrooms stuffed into tomatoes with velouté. (http://operafresh. blogspot.com/2011/02/commemorating-dame-nellie-melba.html)

Antonina Nezhdanova (1873–1950)

Antonina Nezhdanova was born near Odessa, to parents who were school teachers. Both were themselves amateur singers, and her father had formed a local choir in which young Antonina sang, even as a small child. She was a good and diligent student, and after studying at Odessa, attended and graduated from Umberto Masetti's famous class at the Moscow conservatory in 1902. (She was to continue studying with Masetti until his death in 1919.) She was immediately engaged at the Bolshoi, where she remained for more than thirty years, singing leading roles in Russian and West European operas, most frequently opposite the great tenor Leonid Sobinov… Some outstanding roles of her huge repertoire were: Ludmilla in Glinka's *Ruslan and Ludmilla*, Tatyana, Lakmé, the Snow Maiden, Volkhova, Elsa, and Rosina.

My grateful thanks to Edmund St. Austell for allowing me to quote the above directly from his wonderfully informative blogsite: http://greatoperasingers.blogspot. com.

"She embraced the Communist era with enthusiasm, having been taught by her parents that it was the duty of middle and upper class Russians to help the less fortunate, and support their legitimate claims to a decent life. So strong was this belief in her that she would often sing in provincial theaters for food, or even for nothing at all. This earned her the great and ever-lasting affection of the Russian people…In the USSR she was among the most honored singers and teachers. The government bestowed upon her the prestigious title 'People's Artist of the Soviet Union,' for her great artistry, and 'Hero of Labor' for her life-long efforts on behalf of socialist reform. From 1936 on, she taught at the Stanislavsky Opera Studio, later at the Bolshoi Opera Studio, and finally at the Moscow Conservatory, from 1943 until (her death in) 1950.'" (Natalia Bukanova at sergeilemeshev.blogspot.com)

Although Nezhdanova is not well known today, this soprano is one of the most important artists of the early 20th century. Some of the reason for her importance may be because she studied with Umberto Masetti. While still in school, Nezhdanova went to St. Petersburg and Moscow with friends. In St. Petersburg she sang for a Professor I. Prianishnikov:

. . . who told her that she did not have the voice for an operatic career. On October 24, during her stay in Moscow she went to the Moscow conservatory and although she was told that she was too late to enroll, and that there no vacancies, she managed to get an audition and was accepted as a supernumerary pupil in the class of Professor Umberto A. Mazzini [sic], a specialist in the Italian school of bel canto. (John W. Robertson, *The Record Collector*, Vol 24, #1 & 2, January 1978)

Masetti (1869–1919), who had taught such renowned singers as Riccardo Stracciari, had just arrived at the conservatory from Bologna. Masetti's teaching was to have a profound impact on Nezhdanova's artistry. Another reason for her expertise is the type of person Nezhdanova was. Not content to rest on her laurels after becoming famous, she maintained her studies with Masetti until his death in 1919, continuing to grow and refine her art.

After singing the role of Constanza in Mozart's *Entführung aus dem Serail* as part of her final conservatory exams, she made her formal debut in April, 1902, at the age of 29, as Antonida in Glinka's *A Life for the Czar*. She quickly became one of the most popular and important lyric coloratura artists performing in Russia. Nezhdanova rarely appeared outside of Russia, being content to remain at the Bolshoi as well as having a serious fear of sea travel.

Offers to sing in Europe and the United States were regularly presented to the soprano, but she rejected them all. She did, however, decide to accept an offer from the Paris Opéra. In April of 1912, Nezhdanova sang three performances of Gilda in *Rigoletto* with Enrico Caruso and Titta Ruffo at the Opéra; otherwise, she remained in Moscow.

She retired from the stage in 1933, but continued to give concerts, often accompanied by the composer, Sergei Rachmaninov, who held her art in high esteem. It was to Antonina Nezhdanova that he dedicated his now famous "Vocalise." A frequent performer on the radio, her last appearance was in August, 1943. A favorite recitalist in Russia as well, her recitals helped educate the public to the works of Beethoven, Mozart, Gretchaninnoff, and Rachmaninov.

Perhaps a reason for her initial acclaim as well as her ability to maintain that acclaim over her entire career has to do with being a late starter, having begun her career after she had reached both vocal, physical, and emotional maturity.

The Voice

Nezhdanova was a superb artist who was obviously quite serious about her art and maintained an unusually high level of artistic consistency through at least thirty years. This was attributable to two factors: her thorough training with Masetti, and her innate vocal intelligence. Of the Russian sopranos of this period, it is Nezhdanova who shows herself to be the most eloquent; the most artistically refined.

Her solid, Italian–based training is evident on her recordings, as is her smooth legato and perfected technique in all manner of fioritura, showing much patience in their preparation. (During her early studies she was offered a number of opportunities to make her professional debut but she declined, preferring to complete her studies.) This is not to say that this preparation was not without its obstacles, the most difficult one being the highest register.

When Nezhdanova began her studies with Masetti in 1899, she had the range of a mezzo-soprano (up to about high B) and the timbre of a lyric soprano. It was only after a year of extensive, concentrated study that she was able to attain high E. High F did not come until she had been performing on the stage of the Bolshoi for a number of years (probably somewhere around 1910 or 1911 as her recording of the Queen of the Night aria was not made until 1912).

Nezhdanova continued to study even after she was a successful artist, the purpose being the further refining of her vocal emission. Even so, her disks show an occasional caution in singing notes above high C. In the early recordings of 1906–1911 there is the clear avoidance of finishing on a high note. By 1912, at the age of thirty-nine, she had reached her prime and her earlier problems in the placement of high notes had been corrected.

The voice is a vibrant, warmly colored one that, on recordings, occasionally becomes somewhat white in its upper reaches. The middle register is solidly produced and quite lovely, while the lower, although not exceptional, is also well produced. Not once, on the forty or sides that I have listened to, does she become shrill.

As J.B. Steane wrote:

> Probably no soprano is more readily enjoyable on pre-electrical records. Her voice sounds fresh and young, clear and firm, her technique is always admirable, often dazzling, and she sings with heart and intelligence…One of the loveliest of all sopranos in this early period of the gramophone, she seems also to approximate more nearly than others to the mythical condition of the singer without faults. (*The Grand Tradition*, Charles Scribner's Sons, New York, 1974, p. 109)

Selected Recordings

During the LP era in the U.S. (1950s–1970s), a number of LPs of this soprano were released by such labels as Rubini (2 volumes), OASI, Court Opera Classics (Preiser), Club "99" and, of course, Russian Melodyia. Today, her work can be sampled on CD reissues on Nimbus, Pearl (*Singers from Russia*, Volume IV) and Preiser. Despite this, much of her recorded legacy is presently unavailable. Guessing that someday much of it *will* be available, I will include evaluations of some records that may not yet be on CD.

One Rubini LP disk (GV 42) is especially missed because it collects Nezhdanova's recordings of six of *Lakmé*'s main moments. Because she was a famous *Lakmé* in Russia at that time, these disks are an important heritage of the style and taste prevalent then in Russia. Rubini presents them in a logical and instructive grouping.

During her recording career (1904–1940) Antonina Nezhdanova made more than 170 sides, of which at least twenty-five remain unpublished. For example, although Nezhdanova released two recordings of the Bell Song from *Lakmé*, (1906 and 1912), at least three other versions remain unpublished. There are also some titles that she never re-recorded and remain unpublished including:

Meyerbeer – Shadow Song (*Dinorah*)
Meyerbeer: "Robert toi que j'aime" (*Robert le Diable*)
Saint-Saens – Vocalise (*Parysatis*)
Tchaikovsky – Aria from *Mazeppa*
Verdi – "Saper voreste" (*Un ballo in maschera*)

An oddity about her recording career is that during 1911 the only month in which she recorded was May. In two sessions she made thirteen sides that included arias from *La bohème, Lakmé, Peer Gynt*, Del Aqua's "Villanelle", *The Tsar's Bride* and Delibes' "Fille de Cadix." Of all of these, only one side, an aria from Rubinstein's *The Demon* was published. She was dissatisfied with those recordings and those sessions for some reason, and no other attempt to record was made until a full year later. That year, 1912, brought forth some of her most classic recordings.

Of certain pieces, a number of her recordings are among the finest you can hear. They include an idiomatic and expertly sung "O beau pays" (*Les Huguenots*) and Alabiev's "Nightingale." The arias from *Lakmé* are notable despite that they are sung in Russian with not ideal tempi. The second act aria from Bizet's *Les pêcheurs de perles* is a wonderful exercise in vocal control and expressivity.

All of her recordings show an art reflective of high, international quality. Much of this is attributable to her florid technique that boasts clean scale work (no aspirates), firm, centered staccati, excellent, evenly-rolled trills and very effective morendi. Nezhdanova's use of the breath is excellent as is demonstrated by her firm, tremulous-free legato, and smooth, yet vibrant, vocalization.

The secret of Nezhdanova's success is there for all to hear. Her persistence in achieving the smoothest vocalism possible as well as taking extreme care with sensitive phrasing are simply demonstrated and presented without fanfare.

Nezhdanova recorded for about thirty-six years. Her first disks were four titles recorded in St. Petersburg for Pathé in 1904. From 1906 to 1908 she made over thirty titles for G&T and, in 1910, signed a five-year contract with the Gramophone company. During that period she remade a number of her earlier efforts, halting her acoustical recording in April of 1914.

Due to the approaching 1917 Revolution in Russia, and its resulting political problems, production of records was stopped in 1915. Seven years later, in 1922, classical recording in Russia was resumed. Nezhdanova, however, did not record again until mid-1934. By this time the electrical process was in use and recording was done at the State House of Recording in Moscow. Because Nezhdanova was sixty-one years old her new recordings were primarily of the song literature and Russian folk material.

Alabiev – "Nightingale"—Preiser
Accompanied by piano, this fascinating work was recorded in 1908. Nezhdanova starts off tame, but secure in offering the main melody. Before too long she

presents coloratura arabesques of great beauty, including long trills of even texture. She is very aggressive in this song, making for much intensity.

There is great Russian tradition about this song among Russian high sopranos, and Nezhdanova is one of the best. Around the halfway mark she treats the listener to a remarkable high D that is part of the arch of a phrase. This is followed by an unusual break into chest register that is almost affectionately sung. Her trills are superb, including a very long, penultimate trill on high A. The final high D is held long after the piano accompaniment ends. During this three-minute song Nezhdanova offers the listener no fewer than three excellent high Ds.

Arditi – "Parla Waltz"—Preiser

A wonderful record! Produced in 1912, and accompanied by orchestra, it is one of the great recordings this singer produced. Sonically clear and clean, the Nezhdanova voice is well-highlighted. Her sense of rhythm is spot on, as is her sense of fun. An unusual variant has her ascending a scale to a top D with obvious enjoyment. Her trills are beautiful and full, and the top of the voice is fully responsive to her demands. The finish is brilliant with an excellent high A trill that swoops to a sustained high D.

Auber – "Or son sola" (*Fra Diavolo*) – Preiser

This aria was borrowed by Auber from his own opera, *Le Serment*, and inserted into *Fra Diavolo* for Zerlina somewhere around 1858. About the original aria in *Le Serment*, Robert Letellier writes:

> The most famous piece in the opera is Marie's *grand air à vocalises* for the soprano ('Dès enfance les mêmes chaînes') in which all the most arduous difficulties of the art of singing are displayed. It was a triumph for Madame Damoreau, and served for a long time as a test piece, *le morceau de concours,* dreaded by young aspirant virtuosi. It was later introduced into the beginning of act 2 of the Italian version of *Fra Diavolo* as a more substantial and challenging alternative to Zerline's aria as she prepares the room for Lord and Lady Cockburn. (*Daniel-François-Esprit Auber: Le Serment*, Edited and Introduced by Robert Ignatius Letellier, Cambridge Scholars Publishing, 2011, Newcastle upon Tyne, UK, http://www.cambridgescholars.com/download/sample/58478)

Despite that this is a wonderful and inventive aria, it has never been part of the standard repertoire for the coloratura soprano. It is a difficult, rather complex aria to sing, rarely appearing on records or concert programs. The few who have recorded or sung the aria in concert, or in a staged production, include Maria Barrientos, Lina Pagliughi, Roberta Peters, Mary Costa, Dame Joan Sutherland, Isobel Buchanan, Angela Denning, Luciana Serra, and Sumi Jo. Its neglect is no doubt due to its excessive technical demands. A number of its passages are extremely difficult to accurately navigate.

Nezhdanova's recording was made in 1910 and is sung in Russian. One immediately notes the bright freshness of Nezhdanova's voice and her sensitive handling of the long lines of the cavatina. The voice is well-integrated and she appears fearless when traveling into the upper regions, including one ascent to a sustained high C-sharp. Although she avoids traditional interpolations that rise to high D, it is beautifully sung. A portion of the allegro is included that is prefaced by a wonderful trill that Nezhdanova rolls forth beautifully. There are some very tricky triplet passages, but the intricate fiorture and staccati are brilliantly dispatched as is a final unaccompanied cadenza. A penultimate high E is missing, but the leading trill to a final high A is superbly rolled. Then, as now, this alternate aria for Zerlina is a recording rarity, most sopranos preferring the original and less strenuous "Quel bonheur."

Bellini – "Mad Scene" (*I puritani*) Nimbus, Preiser

The mad scene from *I Puritani* was recorded in 1912, highlighting Nezhdanova's beautiful middle and lower registers that pour out with great finesse and control. This is one of her most lovely records as the nature of Bellini's style of composition suits her extremely well and she shows great affection for this music. A good portion of "Qui la voce" is included, and one verse of the cabaletta is delightfully ornamented with many individual variants. The record is a pleasure from beginning to end with Nezhdanova inserting high staccati with ease, taking a penultimate E-flat to conclude. Its only flaw is that the high E-flat is slightly under pitch because of a misjudged connecting swoop.

Bizet – "Comme autrefois" (*Les pêcheurs de perles*)—Pearl

This is another Nezhdanova gem of lyricism that is supported by a fine legato line. With good reason, this has long been considered one of Nezhdanova's finest recordings. Especially beautiful is her return to the main theme. Bizet's cadenza is well done which Nezhdanova caps with a lovely penultimate high C.

Cui – "Bolero"—Pearl

Given the perfection of Nezhdanova's 1907 recording, it is too bad that Cui's wonderful "Bolero" is not better known to American listeners. It has always been a favorite piece for Russian high sopranos. Nezhdanova's recording lacks some of the infectious abandon found on Valeria Barsova's later recording, but it still has much verve, charm, and elegance. During the final phrase, a staccato top D is perfectly picked from the air, a most impressive feat.

David – "Charmant Oiseau" (*La perle du Brésil*)—Pearl

The only drawback to this 1907 recording is that it is piano-accompanied. It would have been wonderful to hear Nezhdanova sing this with an orchestra. Even so, it is an unusual piece in this soprano's legacy as she appears to have never recorded any other aria with a duet with flute.

Only one verse is sung, but Nezhdanova shows smooth legato despite the rather craggy Russian translation of the French original. Her duet with flute is truly lovely as she shoots off high staccati like child's play. Compared to some of her contemporaries, she plucks a penultimate high D from the air quite successfully and brings the aria to a fine close.

Dell Aqua – "Minuet"

Not often recorded, Dell Aqua's Minuet is one of this soprano's most charming discs. Recorded in April of 1912, the day before recording her excellent bell song and about a week after recording the Queen of the Night's "Der hölle rache," this is a special treat. Like Dell Aqua's other pieces of this kind, "Villanelle" and "Chanson Provençale," this is a lovely Victorian parlor song for a high soprano. During this era it was probably sung often during "at homes," performances held at the homes of wealthy patrons of opera.

Nezhdanova displays firm tone and brilliant frontal placement of the French text. It has quite a number of difficult spots, not the least of which are wide staccato leaps (all cleanly sung) and measure upon measure of high staccati that lead to the finish on a triumphant high D.

Typical of Slavic sopranos, Nezhdanova often uses a connecting swoop to access final high notes. This approach continues to be used by modern day sopranos despite its dangers and the occasional stylistic impropriety. A singer must be very careful as Nezhdanova herself demonstrates in recordings. If a singer's breath support is not solid, and if the penultimate (the approaching note) is not placed high enough, it will pull the pitch of the final high note down until the artist corrects its placement.

The Arias from *Lakmé*

One hopes that some enterprising CD label will eventually release a compilation of these pieces Rubini did on LP. The original recordings were not made sequentially, ranging from 1906 (act I Prayer, "Blanche Dourga") to 1914 ("Tu m'as donné le plus doux reve.") Of her thirty-seven roles, *Lakmé* was one of Nezhdanova's favorites. She first sang the role in October of 1903 and sang it well into the 1920s. It is obvious that she had great affection for Delibes' opera as she made a point of recording all of Lakmé's set pieces (except the act III Lullaby) at a time when it was usual to record only the act I prayer to Dourga or the act II "Bell Song."

An interesting thing about these disks is that those with piano feature her teacher, Masetti, accompanying. Not surprisingly, the bell song occupied a special place during Nezhdanova's recitals and concerts as she would usually end the evening with this aria. These sides show that Nezhdanova's Lakmé was a character of dignity and gentle femininity. The lyrical aspects of the music are highlighted by her excellent, strong legato, while the two pieces needing florid mastery are sung easily, with accuracy.

Writing for the liner notes of the Rubini LP, Eric Rees notes:

> The excerpts from *Lakmé* are a study in themselves. The virtuoso flights of the Bell Song are delivered with an enchanting vivacity and mastery – but that is only to be expected.

What is less predictable is the sense of character development manifested in the course of the opera. The early scenes are characterized by the serene dignity, the rapt innocence of a dedicated priestess. But in the later scenes we find ourselves confronted by a woman of warmth and noble pathos. Not every coloratura soprano has had the vocal resource and psychological insight to encompass such shades of expressiveness. (Rubini LP, GV 42)

"Blanche Dourga" – Act I

The opening "Prayer" in act I of *Lakmè* is her entrance. Despite a noisy background, the absence of an accompanying male chorus, and clunky piano accompaniment, this recording immediately establishes the caliber of this artist. Although sung in Russian, all phrases are smoothly linked, ornaments are sensitively phrased, and there is no obtrusive scooping in its many jumps. Staccati are delicately sung within the line and are not punched. The final high B-flat has a lovely diminuendo.

"Dôme épais, le jasmin" Act I Duet

The published recording of this lovely duet between Lakmé and Mallika (E. Popella-Davidova) was successful on its first take on November 24, 1912. A second take is unpublished. This is a fine performance by both artists who achieve a nice blend.

Its only flaw is the initial entrance, which is too loud and punched, as if the singers had been surprised. The difficult blending of the close intervals is clean with nice pianissimo touches. One is immediately aware of Nezhdanova's command of the passaggio area, especially the F-sharp and G at the top of the staff. These tones are round and firm yet pliable enough to allow a superb, spinning diminuendo. During the bridge between the two verses, Nezhdanova gets off the track a bit, but recovers well. (Remember that, back then, a recording session was essentially a live performance.)

Although this recording is a bit too heavy-handed to be idiomatic, it is still one of the best versions of that period—despite the use of a Russian translation of the French text. The ending is lovely.

"Pourquoi dans les grand bois" – Act I

Tinged with melancholy, Lakme's introspective act I aria is perfect music for Nezhdanova's brand of lyricism. Recorded in 1914, the piece is taken at a sensible tempo, having very nice phrasing. One gets the opportunity to enjoy Nezhdanova's lyric abilities as well as it being an excellent recording for students seeking to understand how to accomplish subtle dramaticism within a lyrical framework.

"Où va la jeune Hindoue" (Bell Song) – Act II

The following two versions of the "Bell Song" are sung in Russian and show Nezdanova's growth during the six years between the recordings. Counting three unpublished takes, this aria was the most recorded in her repertoire.

1906

This 1906 version, with Masetti at the piano, shows that Nezhdanova already had a wonderful, authoritative delivery. She had been performing the role for three years. Despite the voice's freshness, this recording is not as well presented as the later 1912 recording. There is similar phrasing, but the high B at the end of the first section is not as good as it will become (although there is a nice diminuendo). The high staccati emerge a bit white, suggesting that she has not yet completely mastered the highest range. Only one bell refrain is offered, framing an excellent trill, but, like her colleague, Maria Michailova (who recorded the aria a year before), she eschews the high E.

1912

The 1912 recording, made on April 24, 1912 (and now on Preiser CD), is with orchestra. One immediately hears that Nezhdanova's voice is more comfortable negotiating the highest register as is witnessed by a variant she incorporates before the bell refrain. There are a few special moments that include her individual textural phrasing (in Russian) of "Quand la lune se joue dans les grand mimosas." Another is her note-for-note clarity of the difficult ascending run that concludes the first section of the aria, a very difficult segment. Most sopranos find that these measures present the most difficulty, more so than the staccati or the high notes that follow.

Welcome in this recording are the wonderful octave staccato jumps that she offers just before the bell refrain. The single bell refrain is sung with great authority and clean, pointed staccati. There is an excellently rolled trill on G-sharp and, like many other singers, she uses the variant that imitates the bells rather than sing Delibes' original scale work. The final staccato statement rising to the top D-sharp is done on a single breath and without hesitation. The high B trill is propulsive and tight-knit and, in this version, Nezhdanova swoops to a very successful high E.

"Dans le foret pres de nous" – Act II

Recorded in 1907, we are provided quite a contrast to the pyrotechnics of the bell song. Both verses are sung. Although a russian translation is used, everything is connected with a firm, flowing legato. Nezhdanova pays special attention to the chromaticism of the vocal line and, when appropriate, highlights those notes.

"Tu m'as donné "—Act III

If "Dans le foret pres de nous" was an unusual choice to record, then Lakme's final aria, is a true curiosity. This record, made in September of 1915, is extremely rare. During that year Nezhdanova recorded approximately twenty sides. This appears to be the only one that was released. The other masters are said to have been lost in the chaos of the 1917 Revolution. This is a very fine recording and one is grateful that it exists. Both verses are presented, the second being especially suitable to Nezhdanova's soft singing and pathos. The high B near the close of the aria is especially lovely, begun as a lilting piano tone that grows to a vibrant forte. The finish is very moving.

Donizetti – "Regnava nel silenzio" (*Lucia di Lammermoor*) – Preiser

Recorded in 1913, Lucia's "Regnava nel silenzio" is given a wonderful performance. In order to include the complete cabaletta, only one (severely cut) verse of "Regnava" is sung. Even so, Nezhdanova treats the listener to a wonderfully firm legato and subtle nuancing. A harmonically abrupt cut leads into the two verses of "Quando rapito." This is wonderful singing, a Nezhdanova recording that stands beside Luisa Tetrazzini's presentation as one of the best recordings to come out of that era. Its ornamentation is fresh and individual, with much staccati that lead to a wonderful passage up to high E. After a few more roulades, Nezhdanova presents an excellent trill before swooping to a fine high D. This recording stands up well to repeated hearings.

Goldmark – "Schmucket Euch mir Rosen" (*Wintermärchen*) – Preiser

Perdita's act II aria in B-flat is an unusual piece of music. It was a rarity when it was recorded in 1910, and it remains so today. It is typical of Goldmark's brand of exoticism, giving a singer much chromaticism to negotiate, some awkward intervals, and a leap from C in the staff to a high D. Although sung here as a solo, in the score it is accompanied by a full chorus.

Nezhdanova uses full lyrical tone with a good use of the lower mixture for the first part. Much of the aria lies quite high, the singer being regularly near the F at the top of the staff. There is also a difficult sequence of rising passages that lead to high B-flat. Even so, Nezhdanova's high notes are easy and full.

The second section is introduced by a long, excellent trill on the F at the top of the staff that is followed by a difficult unaccompanied cadenza that conjures up an eerie atmosphere somewhat similar to the effect of the "Lockruf" vocalize from Goldmark's *Königin von Saba*. Ranging up to high D, this section is vocalized masterfully. Nezhdanova finishes with a flurry of triplet figures, another ascent to high D, and a final, triumphant high B-flat (one among many that have appeared in the course of this aria). Like a number of Nezhdanova's recordings, this one bears up very well to repeated hearings.

Gounod – "Waltz Song" (*Mireille*) – Pearl

This 1908 recording is a pleasure. It is a silly trifle of a thing, but in the hands of a Nezhdanova it becomes special. There is a wonderful smile in the voice and vocal fluidity as she glides through some intricate fioriture. Sung in the lower key of F (rather than its original G major) Nezhdanova has a field day with the coloratura, phrasing everything with élan and sensitivity. Never once does she lose her propelling energy. Unusual here is that Nezhdanova sings the aria in its original French. The penultimate high C is a beautiful note.

Meyerbeer – "Noble Seigneurs" (*Les Huguenots*) – Preiser

One of my favorite recordings of Nezhdanova is Urbain's aria from Meyerbeer's *Les Huguenots*. Recorded in 1914, the sonics of this disk are excellent and Nezhdanova's voice suits the aria quite well. Usually sung by mezzo-sopranos, the role of Urbain is occasionally undertaken by high sopranos. Sung in a Russian translation, the repeated "nyet, nyet, nyet," could be comical, except that Nezhdanova carefully downplays those phrases. This recording is one of very few examples of Nezhdanova making a slight placement error (in the lower register). Of little consequence, it does not detract from the dignity and fluid grace of her performance that includes an excellent trill on F at the top staff that leads to a lovely high B-flat that Nezhdanova tapers to a fine piano.

Mozart – "Der hölle rache" (*Die Zauberflöte*)—Preiser

This 1912 recording occurred on the same day as Zaremba's "Nightingale." She first sang The Queen of the Night at the Bolshoi in January of 1906. It is notable that, by the time she made this recording, she had completely integrated the high F into her voice. It emerges clean and pointed; not at all a squeak as so often happens. Using a sensible, moderate tempo, the soprano offers a subtly menacing performance that relies on agogic accent rather than overt dramaticsim. The high staccati Cs and Fs are crisp and true to pitch. The infamous triplet figures are not as clean as one would want, but, overall, this is a respectable performance and better than many others. She elects to end on a high A.

Proch – "Theme and Variations"

This 1913 recording is hard to find and has yet to appear on CD. It was recorded on the same day as the *Hamlet* mad scene and "Una voce poco fa." It is an exceptional demonstration of Nezhdanova's coloratura. The criticism I have is that the tempo is a bit too frantic. She sings the piece (cut, of course) in under four minutes.

Nezhdanova offers glistening trills and clear, clean coloratura work, pointed staccati and her agility is impressive. High D-flats are perfectly placed and the ending cadenza is worthy of note because the finish is the one used by Maria Galvany. This suggests that Masetti may have been familiar with Galvany's recordings, or her singing, and gave the flourish to Nezhdanova.

Puccini – "Si mi chiamano Mimi" (*La bohème*) – Preiser

This 1912 disk is a welcome entry in Nezhdanova's legacy since it is one of the few arias of its type that she recorded. She first sang the role a year earlier in January of 1911. From it one can tell that she was probably a lovely Mimi. Although in Russian translation, Nezhdanova's control of her vibrato and consonants make the legato flow as freely (and beautifully) as if she had sung it in Italian. Her voice is full and the higher notes are all in control. The phrases are tapered and all is framed in a solid musicianship that is as welcome as it is rare. She finishes before Mimi's usual final narrative lines excusing herself. It is a fitting and graceful finish.

Rachmaninov—"How Fair this Spot," Rimsky-Korsakov – "The Nightingale and the Rose"—Pearl

Recorded in April of 1914 with piano accompaniment, this is a very special record. Both songs are perfect for Nezhdanova's voice. In fact, "How Fair this Spot" sounds so perfect that one wonders if the dedication to "N" in the score refers to Nezhdanova. It is a short song in A major, having only two pages of music written in the tempo of moderato. It may take but two minutes to perform, but those minutes are magical. Especially beautiful is Nezhdanova's way of achieving the written pianissimo high B near the end.

Many sopranos have sung and recorded this piece, but in my experience, the finest of these was Roberta Peters, who in recitals in the United States during the 1980s showed her great musicianship and exquisitely floated high B to great advantage in this song. It is most unfortunate that she never recorded it commercially.

The Rimsky-Korsakov little gem of a song has also long been a favorite and recorded many times by various types of sopranos (and tenors), including such singers as Dimitri Smirnov (1913), Xenia Belmas, and Rosa Ponselle, as well as more recent singers, Beverly Sills and Anna Netrebko. Its exotic appeal is not hard to understand. One can tell from Nezhdanova's recording that the song was obviously an enjoyable one for her to sing and it gives back much of what the singer puts into the music. Like many, she takes the final phrase up the octave to great effect.

Rimsky-Korsakov – Hymn to the Sun (*Coq D'or*)—Pearl

Nezhdanova first sang the role of the Queen of Shemakha in the Bolshoi premiere of the opera in November, 1909, two months after its world premiere in September. In this 1910 recording Nezhdanova starts off a bit edgy. She struggles initially with the high tessitura of the opening phrase, but quickly gets things under control to deliver one of the great early recordings of this difficult aria. Needless to say, her understanding of Rimsky-Korsakov's idiom is perfect and she handles the chromatic writing with great clarity. Only a slightly off pitch top D mars an otherwise superb recording.

Rossini – Una voce poco fa (*Il barbiere di Siviglia*) – Preiser, Nimbus

Rosina's famous aria from *Il barbiere di Siviglia* (in Russian, of course) was recorded in April of 1913 and, considering Nezhdanova's background and training, it is not a surprise that she gives a wonderfully idiomatic performance. Ornamentation is tastefully done and shows valid artistic purpose. Sung in F, during the second section ("Io sono docile"), some of the ornamentation is quite complicated. All is delivered with ease, the finish boasting a fine trill on high C.

Of Nezhdanova and this aria, Edmund St. Austell notes on his website:

> As a general rule…bel canto singing tends to produce whiter, open phonation that reveals the more characteristic tones of the speaking voice of the singer. Chaliapin is a particularly striking example of this kind of singing, so much so that some refer to him as a singing actor because of the extremely clear enunciation that is part of bel canto training. Nezhdanova, however, does not go to that extreme. Her singing style was pure bel canto, with an emphasis on lyricism and beauty, reflecting her lifelong study with Masetti…a superb example of (this is) the great soprano singing a classic Italian aria, 'Una Voce Poco Fa.' I call your attention to the extraordinary flexibility of the voice, and the immaculate, almost understated style, which is actually more respectful of the tradition of

great singing—and Rossini's intentions—than the often self-indulgent bombast that can accompany this particular showpiece aria. (http://greatoperasingers.blogspot.com)

Taubert – "Vogel in Wald"—Nimbus

This 1910 disk of Taubert's slight "Vogel in Wald" is less ornamented than many other versions, but it is better sung. It is a parlor song often sung for effect, to display the singer's ability to trill. It was very popular with sopranos in the last century and like Selma Kurz (who made probably the most famous recording of this piece), Nezhdanova offers a finely-rolled trill at the end of the song, in this instance for 13 seconds.

Thomas – "Mad Scene" (*Hamlet*)—Preiser

The famous mad scene from Thomas's *Hamlet* (a 1913 recording) is truncated, but is given a wonderfully sensitive performance. Especially nice is the round fullness of Nezhdanova's middle and lower registers that speak very well on the recording. Although not one of her most famous records, it is grand. In the brief cadenza with staccati, Nezhdanova manages to ride nicely over the high E. The difficult, high tessitura of the last section is handled well; the coloratura is cleanly articulated with style. Although she avoids the high E in the darting run near the end, the finish is excellent.

Verdi – "Bolero" (*I vespri Siciliani*) – Preiser, Pearl

In 1914, Nezhdanova chose to record her version of this bolero from Verdi's *I Vespri Sicliani*. Not a repertoire piece, nor as well known then as it is today, it was an interesting choice for recording. Taken at a very quick tempo, this is quite a brilliant showpiece, even if most of the trills do not speak. Nonetheless, the coloratura is clean and delivered with flair. Some unusual cuts are made to allow for an odd, short cadenza that makes its appearance at the end, giving the soprano a chance to better develop her trill during a series of rising passages. There is no "traditional" penultimate high E but she takes a nice, final A.

Verdi – "Ah fors' è lui..sempre libera" (*La traviata*)—Pearl

Violetta was an early role for Nezhdanova. She first sang it in December of 1904. Pearl cleverly put together her 1906 disk of "Ah fors' è lui" sung with piano, pairing it with a 1912, orchestrally accompanied, "Sempre libera." The sonics are quite good, presenting Nezhdanova's voice nice and forward. "Ah fors' è lui" is aggressively performed with some glorious high notes. This must have been one of her great roles. She manages to get the right mood and atmosphere within just a few minutes. She adds a brilliant ending cadenza that takes her to a beautiful, sustained high C.

"Sempre libera" is as stunning as one might expect. Accompanied by orchestra it shows off Nezhdanova's dramaticism. Some of the lower fioriture doesn't speak quite so well due to the very rapid tempo. Only one verse is included, but the recitative preceding the aria was included. Nezhdanova offers a fine leading trill and sings with nice abandon. The two ascending scale passages to high A-flat (and then to C) near the ending are offered first as staccato and then legato, a very nice touch. She finishes with a swoop to a fine penultimate high E-flat while the orchestra tacets.

Wagner – *Lohengrin* – Nimbus

Nezhdanova was versatile. In December of 1908, she sang her only Wagner role, Elsa in *Lohengrin* with Leonid Sobinov. She was quite popular in that role, recording three selections in Russian translation in January and February of 1910. Totaling thirteen minutes, they are wonderful records and should be part of every Wagnerian's library.

"Einsam in Trüben Tagen" shows what a strong, lyrical Elsa she must have been. Especially nice is her subtle accenting of the chromaticism of her vocal lines. She builds the intensity gradually to successfully bring the aria to an exciting finish. Elsa's Act II aria, "Euch lüften," is also excellent. It is one of my favorites, especially its sweet, floated ending—such wonderful overtones. Nezhdanova's strong lyrical line is grounded with excellent breath support. She is so successful in this music that one would never suspect that she could follow it with the Queen of the Night's aria with its high Fs.

The Act III duet "Das Süsse Lied verhallt" with Leonid Sobinov (a frequent partner of hers at the Bolshoi) is another special recording. Sobinov's clean timbre blends well with Nezdanova's rounder tones. One of the great early Wagner recordings, Nezhdanova proves to be an excellent partner, building on Sobinov's gradually created intensity. This 4:17-minute excerpt is just wonderful. It is unfortunate that the two made only two recordings together, this and a disk of the duet from *Les pêcheurs de perles*.

There are many more wonderful recordings by this soprano, so one hopes that a comprehensive Nezhdanova set will appear one day. Until then, seek out the Nimbus or the Preiser single-disk issues, or the Pearl *Singers from Russia* (Volume IV). There are very few duplications between Nimbus and Preiser, so both are worth purchasing.

Rosa Ponselle (1897–1981)

Born Rosa Ponzillo in 1897, in Meriden, Connecticut, this soprano originally planned on an instrumental career. Under her sister Carmela's influence, however, Rosa began to perform with her in vaudeville. At that time, sister acts were very popular. From 1915 to 1918 they were known on the circuit as "Those Tailored Italian Girls." Not your usual vaudeville act, they were part of the Keith Circuit. The Keith Circuit had some of the highest-paid performers in all vaudeville, and being part of that company was prestigious. They sang opera arias (and duets), popular Italian songs, and ballads typical of the day.

After requesting a pay raise in 1918, they were dropped from the Keith Circuit. Coincidental with this, Carmela was studying voice with William Thorner in New York City. Thorner, a well-respected and connected teacher, had Carmela and Rosa sing for Caruso, the then-reigning tenor at the Metropolitan Opera. Caruso was impressed enough with Rosa that he arranged an audition for her with Giulio Gatti-Casazza, the general manager of the Met who offered Rosa a contract beginning that same year.

After a successful debut in *Forza del destino* opposite Caruso in November of 1918, she immediately became a darling of the Met and sang a surprisingly diverse repertoire of twenty-three operas including roles in *Cavalleria rusticana, Oberon, La Juive, William Tell, Ernani, Il trovatore, Aïda, La Gioconda, L'Africaine, Don Carlo, Le Roi D'Ys, Don Giovanni, Andrea Chénier, La Vestale, Norma, Luisa Miller, La traviata, Carmen, Eugene Onegin*, and *The Love of Three Kings*. She also sang performances of the *Verdi Requiem* and Rossini's *Messe Solennelle* and *Stabat Mater*. Preferring to remain with the Metropolitan Opera, Ponselle rarely traveled abroad. She did sing in London, at Covent Garden, for three seasons: in 1929 as *Norma* and *La Gioconda*; in 1930 she sang *Norma* again, *L'amore dei tre re*, and *La traviata* (her first); in 1931 she sang *La forza del destino, Fedra* by Romani, and a repeat of *La traviata*. In May, 1933 she traveled to Florence, Italy for two performances of *La vestale*. During the 1930s at the Met she continued to broaden her repertoire with Violetta in *La traviata* (1930) and *Carmen* (1935). Despite her success with audiences, Ponselle received scathing criticism for her Carmen in the New York press at the time.

In November, 1936, she married Carle Jackson, the son of Howard W. Jackson, a four-term mayor of Baltimore. By this time her only roles were in *Cavalleria Rusticana* and *Carmen*. Disillusioned by the management's refusal to mount Cilea's *Adriana Lecouvreur* for her, she did not renew her contract with the Metropolitan. Her last appearance on the operatic stage was in April 1937, as *Carmen* in a Metropolitan Opera tour performance in Cleveland. As Wikipedia accurately notes:

> Ponselle did not consciously or purposefully retire after her Cleveland *Carmen* in 1937, she just let her career slip away.

She and Jackson moved to Hollywood around 1938 for the purpose of promoting Rosa in film work. Unfortunately, because of her excessive fee demands, the project fell through. They settled in Baltimore after building Villa Pace in Green Spring Valley a project designed by Palmer and Lambden, architects, of Baltimore. Villa Pace, a seventeen-room estate, was patterned after an Italian villa. It was cross-shaped, had stucco masonry, and a red tiled roof; each interior room was differently designed.

> From its name to its cross-shaped design, the home was an enduring testament to the significance of La forza del destino in Ponselle's personal life. The name came from the fourth-act aria "Pace, pace, mio Dio." On one of the two columns bordering the villa's main entrance, the first four notes of the aria were etched in the shape of roses. The floor plan of Villa Pace, a cruciform of four separate sections, each with an ambience and function all its own, had been inspired by the crimson cross that adorned her fourth-act costume in Forza. (James Drake, *Rosa Ponselle – A Centenary Biography*. Amadeus Press, 2003)

Her general nervousness at having to perform, and a specific (obsessive) fear of high notes coupled with a receding top register had much to do with Rosa's self-imposed retirement. Not surprisingly, once Ponselle retired she did not miss performing. She continued to sing, privately, for certain guests and at her whim. In the 1940s she became involved with the new Baltimore Civic Opera and helped coach singers that came there to perform. Among them were Placido Domingo, Beverly Sills, Gilda Cruz-Romo, Sherrill Milnes and James Morris. Rosa and Carle divorced in 1949. During her career at the Metropolitan Opera Rosa Ponselle sang a total of 366 performances at the house and on tour.

The Voice

Throughout the decades there have been certain voices that defined the merits of preserving singing on disc: Enrico Caruso, Feodor Chaliapin, Maria Callas, Joan Sutherland and Rosa Ponselle. Her voice was individual and unmistakable, a dark column of sound. It was a luscious and velvety soprano voice that, in youth, was well supported on the breath and full of rich harmonics. Although, like Marilyn

Horne and Regina Resnik, Ponselle began singing as a soprano when young, as she matured she became closer to a mezzo soprano. It is also true that after about ten years of performing on the operatic stage her top register began to recede rather quickly.

In her prime, her voice had a range from at least middle C to high D-flat (sung in the *Trovatore* aria and on stage at the end of the act I trio). On recordings and in live performances, the Ponselle voice was a thing of beauty with unified registers and a consistent timbre whether in the high or low register.

It seems that, from the beginning, Ponselle had a fear of high notes. She had such a fear of high Cs that she confessed that before she took a new role she would check the score to see how many high Cs there were. This was a serious phobia, but a not uncommon one. Ponselle's concern about high notes underlines the fact that singers are not automatons. Singing is a mental process that is governed by very human emotions. A singer has to hear and feel a note before they sing it. The act of singing is a constant personal monitoring of what the singer is doing. It can take just one time, one "crack," for fear to take over—the fear of wondering whether it will happen again. "Will I make that high note?" Stage fright can be quite debilitating.

A singer must know her music inside and out. She must know when the next high note is coming in order to prepare. If one's technique is secure one need not put much thought into what is needed—one just does it. Training, rehearsal, and split second instinct take over. If there is fear about what one is doing or whether it will work, that is when problems can arise. Fear can make the throat close, the breath to become shallow, and instill a sense of paralyzing panic that can come on within seconds.

This only needs to happen once. Singing is a difficult process because you cannot see the process; you can only go by how it feels. That is why singers train so arduously, to know exactly how the music should feel in the voice when it is sung correctly, and to know how to deal with mishaps as they occur. For instance, by the time Ponselle came to sing *Norma* in 1927, all high Cs had to be transposed down.

Artistically, Rosa Ponselle was a study in contrasts, a curious blend of refinement and vulgarity. Although her singing and florid technique was elegant, her taste in repertoire and her delivery was often crude. In two complete live operas, *La traviata* and *Carmen,* Ponselle shows a shocking disregard for the written score as she inserts spoken dialogue where none exists and by playing well over the top in her vocal theatrics. Although there is some aural appeal in this (there is much "face" to her singing) repetition finds such effects tedious. As theater of the moment, however, these exploits are undeniably exciting.

On recordings, Ponselle hid her fear of high notes well. For a self-taught singer, her voice was well placed, her vocal concepts and instincts advanced, and her scale was seamless. Her approach to high notes would sometimes be abandoned or even propulsive (although they were always controlled). Her skills in florid singing were, for her type of soprano, prodigious. As one easily hears in arias from *Ernani,*

L'Africaine, Mlle Modiste, and her unique version of "Comin' Thro' the Rye," her ornamental trills, staccati, and roulades were almost flawless and are phrased with the mastery of one who completely understands the inner workings of florid music. Although modern critics tend to downplay her florid abilities, when comparing Ponselle's singing to contemporary sopranos one quickly realizes that it is only the coloratura sopranos who have similar florid brilliance. Her technical facility contributes much to her fluidity of phrasing and suavity of legato.

There have always been questions about the true nature of Rosa Ponselle's voice.

In reviewing the books: *Rosa Ponselle: A Centenary Biography* by James Drake and *Rosa Ponselle, America Diva* by Mary Jane Phillips-Matz, for the New York Times on December 7, 1997, Terry Treachout makes a fascinating (and I feel accurate) statement about the reality of Rosa Ponselle's voice:

> The gifts lavished upon her by nature did not include the rock-solid high notes of a true soprano, and within a few years of her spectacular debut, Ponselle's voice began gradually to settle into the lower tessitura of a mezzo-soprano. Trained singers learn to cope with the changes that the human voice undergoes as middle age approaches, but the self-taught Ponselle lacked the technical savvy to adjust; by the late 1920's, it was clear that she was no longer comfortable above B flat. Unfortunately, B and C are a dramatic soprano's money notes, and Ponselle's growing inability to produce them on demand took its psychological toll: she developed a crippling case of stage fright, dropped roles which contained exposed high C's (she gave up "Aida" early on) and started secretly transposing her big arias into lower keys.(http://www.nytimes.com/books/97/12/07/reviews/971207.07teachot.html)

Selected Recordings

I should preface this section by saying that there are many wonderful Ponselle recordings available. Because of that, this is a very subjective selection of recordings, chosen because they mean something to me. Someone else would choose others.

To dissect Rosa Ponselle's recordings in such detail is unfair. Indeed, it is unfair to *any* singer who made 78 rpm recordings because records do not necessarily reflect what that singer could do interpretively on stage. Ponselle, herself, often complained of this. She preferred broadcasting. The time constraints of 78s are like a straight jacket when it comes to nuance and interpretation. Despite this, there is much to be learned from a singer's recorded legacy. During the era of the 78 no splicing was possible, so each side is a small slice of truth, especially as to a singer's consistency.

In 1918 Ponselle signed a five-year contract with Columbia and, between 1918 (two weeks after her Metropolitan Opera debut) and 1923, made forty-four sides. Of those, forty-one are available at the time of this writing. These are extremely important documents that demonstrate the Ponselle voice in its youth; at the time of her Metropolitan Opera debut, and in roles she never performed on stage. They include arias from *Lohengrin, I Vespri Siciliani, I Pagliacci, Sadko, Manon Lescaut,*

Tosca, and *Madama Butterfly* as well as some of her early vaudeville duets that are priceless in the coupling of the Ponselle sisters. It would appear that the powers to be at Columbia chose what Ponselle recorded. These sides are now available on a two-CD set from Pearl.

Her move to Victor in 1923 came too late for her to record duets or scenes with her mentor, Enrico Caruso, but it did pair her with the equally imposing Giovanni Martinelli in selections from *Aïda* and *La forza del destino.* From 1923 to 1929 she made seventy-four records. Fifteen of these remained unpublished until the Romophone editions of 1993–1995 appeared. She did not record again until after she moved to Hollywood. In 1939 she made eight sides of selections from the song literature.

Persuaded by baritone John Charles Thomas to sing at the Republican National Convention in 1952, the event was broadcast on radio bringing her to the attention of executives at RCA who convinced the soprano to consider making new records. Not willing to make the trip to New York, she, in turn, convinced RCA to send recording crews to Villa Pace, her palatial estate outside of Baltimore. In five days in October of 1954, she made fifty-one selections with pianist Igor Chichagov. RCA released thirty-two of these selections on two LP records. The entire output of those sessions, along with eight 1939 Hollywood-recorded sides were released by Romophone in 1997 on three compact discs. When reviewing them, Alexander Morin comments:

> …all (the selections are) sung with musical intelligence, subtlety of phrase and inflection, and an exquisite mezza voce that is unmatched today. There is more vocal opulence and excitement in the earlier recordings, but in these later performances, Ponselle's artistry is compelling as ever. (*American Record Guide,* May/June, 1997)

When it comes to Ponselle, and many other singers, the most important service that Romophone provided was the ability to listen to, absorb, and compare a singer's unpublished sides. In Ponselle's case there are nine unpublished sides in volume one and eight in volume two that represent her in her artistic prime (1923–1929). In 1939, two sides were unpublished and in 1954, twenty-one sides. For the curious listener and the historian, these forty unpublished takes are invaluable glimpses into Ponselle's artistry. They show much about her consistency and demonstrate how seriously she approached the making and then release of her recordings. For instance, combining the Columbia and the RCA records together, both published and unpublished, she actually made:

six disks of Verdi—"Pace, pace" (*La forza del destino*) her famous,
signature piece
five disks of Verdi—"Ernani involami" (*Ernani*)
five disks of Verdi—"Ritorna vincitor" (*Aïda*)
three disks of Verdi—"O patria mia" (*Aïda*)
three disks of Meyerbeer—"Figlio del Sol" (*L'Africaine*).

One can easily spend hours listening to and comparing the various takes of these arias.

Re-pressings of Ponselle's recorded legacy have always been popular. In the LP era there were many that promoted her work admirably, but none so well as a two-disk set on RCA Camden that was released in 1957, *The Art of Rosa Ponselle*. It is still available on eBay. This was a wonderful document of Ponselle's merits. All Victor recordings, it contains arias from *La Vestale*, *L'Africaine*, *Ernani*, *La Gioconda* and major chunks from *La forza del destino*, *Norma*, and pieces from the song literature. Although the Camden set does not include the Columbia discs, the set gives an accurate portrait of her voice during its prime.

Not surprisingly, Ponselle's art has appeared on many CDs.

Among the most important, and the first to appear was, fittingly, a BMG (RCA) CD of sixteen selections ranging from *Ernani*, *Norma*, *Aïda*, and *La Vestale*, to folk songs released in 1989,

Forty-one Columbia Acoustics were released by Pearl in 1992 (GEMM 9964).

For the most part, however, Ponselle's legacy was faithfully documented in three volumes (7 CDs) on Romophone (with restorations by Ward Marston):

Victor 1923–1925 – Romophone 81006 (1993)
Victor 1926–1929 – Romophone 81007 (1994)
Victor 1939 and the Villa Pace recordings – Romophone 81022 (1996)

With the demise of Romophone, it apears that Naxos (having begun in 2006) is releasing new Ward Marston restorations of all the Ponselle Victors.

Within its *Prima Voce* series, Nimbus released three volumes devoted to Ponselle (1989, 1993, 1996) which offer forty-nine selections available separately or boxed together as a set. (NI 7805, NI 7846, NI 7878). These offer refreshing programming and the opportunity to experience a different take on the Ponselle voice.

In 1999 and 2000, Ward Marston released two 2-CD sets of "Rosa Ponselle on the Air," comprised of various broadcasts the soprano had made between 1934 and 1937. Offering a total of eighty-three selections, with many selections that the soprano never recorded commercially, these two sets are indispensible for those interested in this soprano's art.

The preference of one re-issue over another is a matter of personal preference. All of Ponselle's records are worth owning if only for the ability to revel in the scrumptious sound of her voice and the intimate manner of her art. Although I prefer her in operatic arias, many enjoy her songs.

Although Ponselle recorded a number of songs, I have mostly avoided analyzing them. I will let the reader listen and make his or her own judgments about those records. Considering how glorious Ponselle's voice is, it never ceases to amaze me why she seemed to exert so much effort to record and promote so much second-rate material. When it came to operatic music, her style was (for the most part) impeccable. Music from the song repertoire, however, was always sung in "Rosa Ponselle style" whether it came from the French, German, Spanish, or English literature.

Bellini – "Casta Diva" (*Norma*) – Columbia 1919, RCA Victor 1928–29
Many singers had recorded "Casta diva" and its cabaletta before Ponselle: Giannina

Russ, Ester Mazzoleni, Marcella Sembrich, Lilli Lehmann, Elise Elizza, Ines de Frate, and Emma Calve. For many, Ponselle's RCA Victor electrical recording made in 1928–29 stands as a benchmark. She sang thirty performances of *Norma* with the Metropolitan Opera; twenty in-house, and ten while on tour. Although applauded for her courage in undertaking such a taxing role, some imperfections are noticed.

After the first night, (November 16, 1927) Lawrence Gilman writes in the *New York Tribune:*

> ...Her singing of certain fioriture was not entirely free from raggedness. Some of the passagework was blurred. And in her moulding of the long, expressive lines of Bellini's cantilena there was phrasing that might have been questioned by other than merely fanatical purists...(http://archives.metoperafamily.org/archives/frame.htm)

W. J. Henderson in the *New York Sun* feels that, although sung well, a major part of the role was lacking in definition:

> ...(Ponselle's) 'Casta diva' was a genuinely beautiful piece of singing. To be a great Norma is more difficult in these days of specialized singing than it was in those of Pasta and Grisi, when every operatic artist was expected to be thoroughly grounded in the technics of florid song. Miss Ponselle proved last evening that she has given much time and labor to the practice of vocalises, although there was much simplification and curtailing of the time-honored cadenzas. She had also given study to the Bellini recitative. We are bound to confess, however, that in the recitatives, not only Miss Ponselle, but every one else in the cast was heavy and monotonous. (Metropolitan Opera Archives, accessed July 2014)

Columbia, 1919

Because Ponselle's 1928–29 electrically-recorded version of this scene is so famous, many forget that she recorded "Cast diva" for Columbia in December of 1919, eight years before she sang the role on stage. Although the Columbia disk misses much of the nuance Ponselle would bring to the music in ten years, there is some fabulous singing on this record. The voice is full of rich head tones and although only one verse is sung, the cabaletta is offered as well. This last has some remarkable, fast singing with clean scales and melismas; the penultimate high C is quite beautiful. In *Opera on Record* (Hutchinson & Co, London 1979) Andrew Porter rightly judged:

> This is an astonishing disc. It *is* 'just vocalize', with little interpretive feeling, but the voice has a fleetness and brilliance very different from the lustrous and more darkly burnished timbre that came later.

Victor, 1928–29

With the arrival of LPs, the two segments of this scene (recorded in different years by Victor) were able to be sewn together to form a whole. The cabaletta was recorded in

1928 and "Cast diva" with its preceding recitative was done the year after. There are many things to extol about these sides—the use of a chorus, the excellent electrical recording, and Ponselle's coming to maturity as an artist. There are a few minor problems, however. Much is made of the high A-flat that Ponselle sings at the end of the recitative, but to my ears it lacks the heady overtones that I would expect from a voice that could encompass a high C. It is a lovely note, but it does not appear easy. Later, the difficult passage of repeated high As that lead to the high B-flat sound as difficult as they are and, technically, Ponselle should not have scooped to the B-flat. Doing that tends to pull the pitch down so that the note sits on the line that is between being on and under the pitch.

The twining melismas over the chorus are wonderful for their clarity and gentle phrasing. The finish of the aria is beautiful for her pure head voice on the F at the top of the staff. The cabaletta, recorded in 1928, has a nice stately tempo and one can hear Ponselle moving around in the room's acoustics. Most of the coloratura is impressive for its clarity, but the first high C is barely reached. The penultimate high C is scooped and held, but it has few overtones and surprisingly little impact. It does not ride over the chorus and orchestra as it should.

Gluck – "Divinites du Styx" (*Alceste*) Chesterfield Hour radio broadcast, December 3, 1934

Ponselle performed on The Chesterfield Hour thirty-four times. Thirteen broadcasts were preserved and are on two Marston *Rosa Ponselle on the Air* CD sets. Transposed down one-half step, this aria suits Ponselle's voice at that time, and her classical sound. She is quite dramatic and the low Bs are rich and obviously comfortable. This probably would have been a good role for her as would have Orfeo in *Orfeo ed Eurydice*, also by Gluck.

Halevy – "Il va venir" (*La Juive*) – Columbia, 1924

Although originally recorded for Columbia in 1923, after her move to Victor, Ponselle returned to Columbia in early 1924 to remake this aria and the "Ballatella" from *Pagliacci*—neither of which were originally deemed succcessful.

This has always been my favorite Rosa Ponselle record. Aside from the music being extremely affecting, Ponselle's handling of the (heavily cut) aria is nothing short of spectacular. She sang a total of seventeen performances of the role of Rachel with the Metropolitan; twelve in-house, and five on tour.

After a November 22, 1919 performance, James Huneker writes in the *New York World*:

> ...there are only two beautiful voices in the Metropolitan company, and Rosa Ponselle is the other one. As for Caruso and his impersonation of the old Jew, Eléazar, we may say that he has seldom demonstrated his vocal artistry or his dramatic gifts in such a striking manner. His make-up is that of Shylock curls, gabardine and the racial nose... Rosa Ponselle's artistic development grows apace. Her singing and acting are surer, better coordinated than last season. The role of Rachel is wholly conventional, one of the "O ciel" kind, but she easily compassed it. Her solo in Act II was effective... (http://archives. metoperafamily.org/archives/frame.htm)

Despite the popularity of the *La Juive* revival in 1919, Ponselle did not record this aria until 1924. She immediately establishes its mood. (Rachel is filled with apprehension over her impending meeting with Léopold.) Ponselle's wonderful head voice is promoted as is a propulsive dramaticism. Although cut, Ponselle knits together what is left and traverses occasionally awkward lines with ease. Pianissimo is used craftily and the upper register is rich and gleaming. There are nice, even, delicate textural touches during the aria, and the ending is sumptuous; one of the best for this aria. The finish is very exciting with its climactic rise to high B, followed by a final "il va venir!"

Herbert – "Kiss me Again" (*Mlle. Modiste*) – Columbia, 1920

This was clearly a vaudeville favorite and, as it turns out, one of her best recordings for Columbia. She actually auditioned for vaudeville with this aria. She had already been singing it in appearances at the San Carlino theatre and at Café Mellone, both in New Haven. When Rosa and Carmela did their fifteen to twenty minute act, this was Ponselle's solo piece (a Fritzi Scheff arrangement). The first half of the aria is great fun and Ponselle obviously enjoys showing off the coloratura and staccati flourishes. It is a slight abridgement of the original, longer aria. The "Kiss me" waltz is presented well, especially the phrase, "tenderly pressed." A final high G is full, rich, and solid. Making comparisons are fun and often illuminating: Lily Pons often programmed "Kiss me Again" (only the waltz, not the florid earlier section). She, however, sang the piece up a minor third so that her final note was a high B-flat.

Lohr – "Where My Caravan Has Rested" – Columbia, 1922

I confess to an irrational love of this duet that Rosa sang with her sister and recorded in the summer of 1922. It is not first rate music, but there is something about the piece that makes it attractive. I suspect it has something to do with the close twining of the sisters' voices whose timbres are so similar. Undoubtedly this is one of the pieces from their vaudeville days. Like "Comin' thro' the Rye," I am grateful that they recorded this duet. The blend of the two voices in simple harmony is exquisite; Ponselle's high voice is glorious. A nostalgic piece of fluff, the ending is (for me) sublime as Rosa slides to a beautiful, round, high A-flat. Sometimes the most affecting music is not necessarily the greatest.

Leoncavallo – "Stridono lassu" (*I Pagliacci*) – Columbia, 1924

One of her last records for Columbia, this is one of her best. The role of Nedda was not in her performance repertoire, but this record shows that it might have been a good choice. Her gentle entrance in the moderato, on the dolce high A is absolutely beautiful and the bird effects with trills and staccati up to high B are charming. So often these passages come off heavy-handed and coarse. Not so with Ponselle. Everything is carefully gauged and birdlike. Unfortunately, the strings at the beginning of "Stridono lassu" are ragged and out of tune. Ponselle knits the phrases together in the central aria, but there is a sense of control rather than abandonment. It is as if she is carefully monitoring her voice while in the aria's rather high tessitura. The finale with its swoop to high A-sharp is excellent.

Mascagni – "Voi lo sapete" (*Cavalleria rusticana*) – Columbia 1919

Recorded in January 1919, *Cavalleria rusticana* was Ponselle's second role at the Metropolitan Opera and her most-performed role. This aria sat well for Ponselle so she is able to concentrate on drama rather than vocalism to offer a highly dramatic performance. Like huge organ pipes, her higher notes emerge round and full. She is relaxed so that pianissimo nuances add to the vividness of her portrayal.

Considering how important the role was in her stage repertoire it is odd that, not only did she not record this aria for Victor, but she also did not record any of the duets.

Unfortunately, no Metropolitan Opera broadcast survives of Ponselle singing the role of Santuzza, but there is a live radio broadcast from March 11, 1936 (the Chesterfield Hour) in which she infuses the short aria (3:17) with great drama. The character of Santuzza appealed to Ponselle as a dramatic figure and she offers an exciting reading. There are some wonderful pianissimi contrasted by strong, dramatic lunges into her higher register.

Meyerbeer –"Figlio del Sol" (*L'Africaine*) – Columbia, 1923; Victor, 1925

The revival of *L'Africaine* at the Metropolitan Opera on March 21, 1923 proved to be a popular ticket item during the next few years. Ponselle sang the role thirty-five times: twenty-six times in the house and nine tour appearances in Atlanta, Baltimore, and Philadelphia. There was also a broadcast (unfortunately not preserved) on January 13, 1934, with Nina Morgana as Inez, Fredrick Jagel, and Armando Borgioli; conducted by Tullio Serafin. Selika, like Rachel in *La Juive*, was not one of Ponselle's favored roles. Even so, the records she left of their respective arias are among her best.

When Ponselle sang Selika on April 2, 1923, P. Charles Rodda in *Musical America* wrote:

> Miss Ponselle was regal in voice and gesture as the captive queen, Selika. Her air "In grembo a me" in the second act was finely sung, and she was effectively dramatic in the subsequent encounter with Nelusko… (Metropolitan Opera Archives, accessed July 2014)

Two years later in 1925 she sang the role on November 21. Oscar Thompson wrote in *Musical America*:

> Miss Ponselle's superb organ is worthy of better music than that of Selika, though this tends to emphasize the volume of tone and the very good trill she has at her command. Her characterization still lacks physical repose and her dusky make-up could be improved. (http://archives.metoperafamily.org/archives/frame.htm)

Ponselle made three recordings of this aria: one for Columbia and two for RCA (one of which was unpublished until the release of the Romophone set)

The 1923 Columbia recording is an excellent rendition of this challenging piece although it is not as finished and poised as the later version for RCA. There are some wonderful, light touches and the cadenzas are all well taken, the descending triplets being especially fine. She does a bit of gentle swooping into the top register, but it does not offend and her trill is quite spectacular. The aria is, of course, cut, and despite the rather extroverted nature of the music, Ponselle successfully presents it as a lullaby. The leap to high B near the end is excellent, round and pure. In this recording she sings the aria as it was written and does not interpolate a final high A.

The 1925 RCA Victor recording is one of Ponselle's great records. The aria may not be the greatest music, but the performance is. Phrasing is magisterial with gentle touches like caresses on higher notes. The short duet cadenza with flute is beautifully done with the repeated high B staccati delicately done and followed by a wonderful trill on E. Obviously Ponselle was in good voice this day, the numerous high As are all taken with ease and the swoop to high B is firm and secure. Different from her earlier Columbia recording, Ponselle decided to end the aria by interpolating a piano high A.

Ponchielli – "Suicidio!" (*La Gioconda*) – Columbia, 1923; Victor, 1925

After a performance in Philadelphia on December 9, 1924, Linton Martin writes of Ponselle's *La Gioconda* in the *Philadelphia American.* He was not impressed with the role:

> The color and volume of her voice make it unique among the dramatic soprani, at least when she doesn't soar too high. She carried no great conviction histrionically, but could any singer in such an absurd role? (Metropolitan Opera Archives, accessed July 2014)

That said, what a wonderful recording this Columbia disk is! Ponselle is immediately imposing with a fine, dramatic outburst and good exploitation of her chest register. The middle section is gently ethereal with a beautifully floated high A. The build up, "vinsi 'l'infausta," with it's exposed G-sharps to "geloso febbre" is grand and she sings a fine "fra le tenebre" on middle C-sharp in a well-mixed chest voice. Throughout this recording there are lovely nuances. This is another aria that suits her gifts, including a climactic swoop to high B that is very successful. As is true with many of her records, Ponselle's rendition is a model of poised, expressive singing with well-modulated registers that is recommended for study by today's students and listeners.

The 1925 Victor recording is similar to the Columbia of two years earlier. If anything, the middle section is even more gentle—softer—the high A almost a whisper. There is a bit more drama and (perhaps because of it) the swoop to high B is not as free as it was two years before.

Of the fifteen selections she recorded in 1925, only two of the operatic records were published and eleven were recordings of material that could have been left out of her legacy without any consequence at all.

Rimsky-Korsakov – "The Nightingale and the Rose" – RCA Victor, 1939

One of the six recordings released while the soprano was living in Hollywood, this song has always been a favorite among sopranos, including very high sopranos.

Ponselle offers her own unique take on this exotic song. Although she tends to try to make this song more important than it is, and her pronunciation is a bit off, she offers many compensating pianissimo effects, including an eerie moment when she hums up to high A-flat. No matter how artistically imbalanced this recording is, it is a lovely memento.

Romani – "O divin Afrodite" (*Fedra*) Chesterfield Hour radio broadcast, March 18, 1936

I wish I could say some nice things about this piece. I tend to support obscure "written-for" arias and usually support the efforts involved. This, however, is just terrible. It is derivative music having no recognizable melodies or direction. I hear echoes of Cilea, Massenet, and Zandonai throughout. Written for Ponselle, the range is rather restricted, although it does call for a low A and she goes to G at the top of the staff. There are a preponderance of E-flats (in the staff) in declamatory phrases and she uses a fine and rich chest voice on an F on the staff, but, overall, the piece is a loud mess and completely forgettable.

Rossini – "Bel raggio" (*Semiramide*) Chesterfield Hour radio broadcast, May 21, 1936

This is the only existing example of Ponselle singing this great aria. Introduced by Milton Cross (of Metropolitan Opera broadcast fame), this is a valuable broadcast as she never recorded the aria commercially. Within the first minute, Ponselle offers a cadenza to a brilliantly sustained high B. Her handling of Rossini's florid music is excellent and she shows an innate understanding of phrasing within coloratura. (Not all singers get this important facet of the florid art.) The second half, "Dolce pensiero," is given less than two minutes and is therefore taken at a very rapid tempo which causes some of the coloratura to be a bit sloppy. The finish is nicely done: a slight cadenza, followed by a series of trills on E, F-sharp, and G-sharp that rises to a strong final high A.

Saint-Saens – "Printemps qui commence" (*Samson et Dalila*) Chesterfield Hour radio broadcast, October 29, 1934

At first I was amused by Ponselle's mispronunciation of "Dalila" but once she began to sing I forgot all about that. What a role this would have been for her had she decided to undertake it. Through a lot of background noise, one hears a beautiful and expressive rendition of this aria. Her middle and lower registers are well highlighted and her legato is flowing. There is some beautiful pianissimo work. Unhampered by the constraints of a 78 rpm disk, Ponselle provides a natural ebb and flow of the aria. The ending is thoughtful and very expressive.

Schubert – "Erlkönig" Chesterfield Hour radio broadcast, March 14, 1936

Although one might consider this German lied a curiosity of Ponselle's repertoire, it turns out that she occasionally programmed it on recitals. For the radio broadcast, the piece is accompanied by orchestra. This will not be to everyone's taste, especially lieder purists, but it is clear that Ponselle has put a lot of thought into her interpretation and she delivers it with great authority. Her German is serviceable and all is kept pretty much under control until near the end when the "child" becomes rather wild. Actually, it fits in well with her interpretation. The huge dramatic gasp after "war tod" (low C-sharp and D) is a bit much, but if it is accepted as a part of her theatrical interpretation, it works.

In writing about Ponselle for *The Sun* on May 20, 2001, Tim Smith comments about her version of *Erlkönig*:

> …some of Ponselle's interpretive ideas raise eyebrows. In two performances of Schubert's "Erlkonig," a radio broadcast from 1936 and a Villa Pace recording from 1954, she adds the same little histrionic cry of horror at the very end. It's about as far removed from Schubertian style as you could get, absolutely wrong stylistically. And yet, it works somehow.

Spontini – "Tu che invoco" (*La Vestale*) – Victor, 1926; Chesterfield Hour radio broadcast, April 1, 1936

Ponselle first sang *La Vestale* at its Metropolitan Opera premiere on November 12, 1925. She sang eight performances in the house and one while on tour.

Irving Weil of the *Evening Journal* makes the judgment:

> Her singing and acting of this role was the high spot of her career on the Metropolitan stage. She has never done anything else even approaching it. She has not always been notable for the discretion, to say nothing of the beauty of her singing, and her acting at times has been not much better than operatic windmill gesticulations. But her Vestal last night completely wipes out everything we have ever had against her. No other woman now at the Metropolitan can sing like this. It was pure, limpid, lovely tone, always completely within suave control, never striving for more than legitimate and needful effect, continuously expressive of the textual line. There was both superb power and delicate restraint in the handling of the voice, the power never forced, the restraint skillful and unobvious. (Metropolitan Opera Archives – Accessed July 2014)

She recorded nothing from *La Vestale* until the next year, 1926. From the quality of her singing, one wishes that she had also recorded the second half of the aria with its dramatic florid demands. Ester Mazzoleni recorded the whole scene (admittedly abbreviated, but over two sides) in 1909, and even interpolated a spectacular high C at the end.

In this, the main aria, Ponselle offers classically sculpted legato lines and a gentle handling of many dips into the chest register, quite appropriate to this style of music. The tiring build to the repeated high A's is exemplarily done and followed by a telling pianissimo passage leading into the reprise of the main theme.

I find it interesting that the timing of the original Victor recording clocks in at 4:32 and the Chesterfield broadcast of 1936 at 4:36, there being no difference in the time she takes to sing the aria, whether on disk or live. Her interpretation is also similar and it is very nice to hear her sing this music live. Her lower register is quite beautiful.

Spontini – "O nume tutelar" (*La Vestale*) – Victor 1926

Recorded on the same day in May as "Tu che invoco," this is also quite beautiful. One is grateful that Ponselle recorded these arias, rarities when she sang them, and rarities today. I believe that this was the first recording of this aria. Classically pure phrasing and solid legato predominate. Her pianissimo repeat of the phrase at the end is a stunning effect. I prefer this recording to her "Tu che invoco."

Strauss – "Blue Danube Waltz" – Columbia, 1921, Chesterfield Hour radio broadcast, October 15, 1934

A lot of people laugh at this 1921 Columbia recording, but one must remember that many sopranos sang and recorded vocal arrangements of this piece at that time. Although Ponselle's version goes no higher than B, it has some of the same attributes as recordings sung by coloratura sopranos. What most people find amusing is her rather stilted English diction and the use of a silly-sounding "Tra-la-la." However, I find this a fun recording with some wonderful vocal flourishes and artistically phrased coloratura and trills. Ponselle certainly seems to be having a good time. High notes ring out with conviction, and awkward leaps are perfectly executed.

The Chesterfield broadcast, made thirteen years later is even more elaborate and more fun. Ponselle opens with a wonderful cadenza of trills and staccati. Unfortunately, the English text is horrible, but if you can ignore that, it is quite fun, There is a good sense of occasion and Ponselle obviously enjoys singing the roulades. The arrangement is much more ornamented than the earlier Columbia version and there is a great trill on high A-flat that Ponselle sustains easily. There is a notable swoop to high B in the coda that is quite elegantly sung.

Traditional – "Comin' thro' the Rye" – Columbia, 1919

This was one of the duets that Rosa and her sister, Carmela, sang on the vaudeville circuit. I am glad that they decided to make a recording of it as it is quite something to hear. It was Rosa who created the coloratura arrangement. The Columbia record undoubtedly reflects exactly how they performed the piece on the vaudeville stage. Not only is it a wonderfully shocking surprise, it is great fun. I have always felt that it is one of the great coloratura recordings.

There is much beautiful singing, a simplicity of style, humor, and technical dazzle. For those not familiar with this rendition, the beginning is sung simply, as a duet between the two sisters who show great blend and delivery. In the second verse things change in a big way. Rosa and Carmela suddenly take off in unaccompanied cadenzas that are full of high staccati, flourishes to high B, roulades, trills (even a brief echo of part of the *Lucia di Lammermoor* cadenza) all resembling the famous cadenzas in Bellini's "Mira O Norma". Both singers easily fulfill the florid requirements and although the record is short, it is two minutes and twenty seconds of delight.

Verdi – "Ritorna vincitor" (*Aïda*) – Columbia, 1923; Victor, 1923 and 1928; General Motors radio broadcast, September 27, 1936

Although Ponselle had a love/hate relationship with this role, she made a total of sixteen sides of music from the opera as compared to only twelve sides of *La forza del destino.* "Ritorna vincitor" was not recorded until September of 1923. It suits Ponselle so well that one wishes that it had been spread over two sides rather than a version drastically cut for one side. Tempi tend to be on the fast side, but her diction is excellent and her voice glorious. She knits the phrases together with a fine legato and a sense of forward movement. There are some lovely touches on higher notes and an appealing delicacy.

The next version was for Victor in December of the same year, after she had moved to Victor. It shows more nuance and interpretation than does the Columbia recording. This aria is less challenging than act III's "O patria mia" and is therefore often more satisfying. "Numi pieta" has some flipping through register breaks during one or two phrases.

The unpublished version (recorded a few days later) is about thirty seconds longer and was sung on a day when all the arias (*Aïda* and *Forza* selections) were rejected. No matter, Ponselle's singing is excellent and I think this is a wonderful performance. I actually prefer it to the published version.

After another unpublished recording in 1926, she recorded the aria for Victor in 1928. This "Ritorna vincitor" is well-recorded electrically and is the "famous" version. It highlights Ponselle's rich, warm voice. One notices that in all her versions of this aria the climactic high B-flat is never sung as Aïda's moment of desperation; it is too segregated from the rest of the phrase to be effective. Once past that note, though, the aria is wonderful. "Numi pieta" is especially moving and is, I feel, the glory of this recording. Using poised piano phrases with believable thrusts into her high register she manages to create a very magical moment. One wishes that the aria was not abbreviated.

During the General Motors broadcast of 1936 we get a chance to hear a complete Ponselle interpretation of this aria, and, even better, it is live. There are some subtle nuances in this performance. As one might expect in a live situation, the climactic high B-flat is held longer than it is on the records and, consequently, it better reflects Aïda's emotions and has more dramatic impact. No matter the deficiencies in sound, it is good to hear her in the rest of this aria's music. The famous "Numi pieta," always a special Ponselle moment, is exquisitely floated.

Verdi — "O patria mia" *(Aïda)* – Columbia, 1918; Victor, 1923

It is interesting that Ponselle sang only fourteen performances of this role with the Metropolitan Opera Company. I say interesting, because musically and temperamentally, the role suited her so well although it had a built-in inhibitor for her. After a mishap during a performance in Brooklyn, she became very nervous about the exposed high C in this aria. As she and her voice matured, that note became a thing of terror and she eventually was forced to drop the role because of her fear of that note.

Luckily, she made some wonderful records of Aida's music, including "O patria mia," during her first Columbia recording sessions in 1918. Here she is fresh in her youth, the voice beautifully produced, with high notes gleaming. Her naturally dark timbre twined through the chromaticism of the aria beautifully; a heart-felt and lovely rendition, even if only one verse of the aria is included. The difficult ascent to high C is done well, Ponselle taking a breath before. The note is lovely, held bravely, and is pure in tone. It is not piano but a gentle mezza-forte; it works well within her interpretation. The final high A is sustained beautifully.

The later "O patria mia" in 1923 shows little difference from 1918 except that both verses are included and the ascent to the high C does not include an extra breath so that the C does not sound as comfortable. John Steane put it best when he noted that the high C in this recording "…is a good solid note but not comfortable in its resonance…" (*Voices, Singers & Critics*, Amadeus Press, 1992, Portland Oregon, p. 140)

Verdi – "Pur ti riveggo" and "La tra foreste" (*Aïda*) Victor, 1924

This central section of the Nile scene was recorded in 1924, with Giovanni Martinelli. These are very exciting sides. Their voices blend well and after so much solo work, it is good to hear Ponselle interacting with another singer. "Fuggiam gli ardori nospiti" is lovely for her twining her voice around the accompanying oboe. Martinelli is attentive to Ponselle and his frontal buzz is well-tempered by Ponselle's lush timbre. Ponselle's ascent to a final high B flat is beautiful and is sustained as a quiet mezza-forte.

Verdi – "La fatal pietra" and "O terra addio" (*Aïda*) Victor, 1924

Also recorded in February, 1924, this has been considered, for decades, one of the great historical recordings of this final scene. It still holds it place well and commands respect. Ponselle's "Vedi l'angelo," with its accurate, pointed staccati, is a marvel of delicate execution along with beautiful pianissimo high B flats. "O terra addio" finds both singers transcending the score to provide a magical moment. The top B flat sung by both is quite a climax.

Verdi – "Ernani involami" (*Ernani*) – Columbia, 1922; Victor 1923, 1924, 1928

Ponselle sang Elvira in *Ernani* twenty times for the Metropolitan Opera: sixteen times in the house and four while on tour. It was a popular role for the soprano and most of that popularity rests on the merits of her singing of Elvira's act I aria. Although she enjoyed singing this aria, Elvira was not one of Ponselle's favored roles.

The Columbia record (minus the recitative) was recorded in June of 1922. A few times during this recording (and in others) you can actually hear Ponselle's high voice ringing in the acoustics of the recording room. Her voice is rich and smooth with an excellent F at the top of the staff (often a perilous passaggio note for the soprano voice). At one point she executes a beautifully molded decrescendo on that note. She glosses over a few of the highest notes in melismatic passages, but counteracts this in the cabaletta by performing excellent scales in rapid tempo, and a magnificent, finely rolled trill on the top F. This is followed by a beautiful and surprisingly delicate high staccato flourish. The cabaletta shows great energy and the final B-flat is triumphant.

The unpublished 1923 Victor recording is very interesting. I always find it fascinating to hear and compare such discs. In this case a gracious 3:00 is allotted to the main aria. But, because of this the cabaletta "Tutto sprezzo" is very fast. Even so, Ponselle manages all the notes and some nuances as well.

The published 1924 disk includes the recitative and her lower register is strong, her pianissimo singing is secure, and the messa di voce on the top F is especially well presented. The aria is well-negotiated, which is remarkable as some of the phrases are quite challenging. Only 1:42 is allotted to the cabaletta so some of the coloratura is a bit rushed. The trill on the F and the following volley of staccati is wonderful; there is even a slight decrescendo during the trill. No matter the technical challenges of this aria, when it comes to the trill on F and the staccati that follow (touching high B-flat) Ponselle always delivers perfectly.

Her most famous recording of this aria is the 1928 electrically recorded disk. The many merits of this recording include a well-delivered recitative. The Ponselle specialties, including a lovely messa di voce on the F at the end of the recitative, are all here. There are some fresh nuances in this recording, but one notices that the cadenza with the high C is not ideal. The cabaletta has an explosive trill that is made even more exciting by the tiniest pause before her attack. The staccati that follow are on the mark. The ending seems a bit difficult, but the added trill on F before the final B-flat is excellent. To this day one rarely hears such a melding of legato and coloratura within the same framework, and few singers can emit a staccato flourish as Ponselle does in this recording after her remarkably rolled trill on the top F. This is a marvelous recording that is full of panache and brilliance, as well as full, weighty tone.

Verdi – "La Vergine degli Angeli" (*La forza del destino)* – Columbia, 1918; Victor, 1928

Leonora in *La Forza del destino* was not only Ponselle's debut role at the Metropolitan Opera on November 15, 1918, it was also the premiere of the work at that house. At that time, performances of this opera were quite a rarity. It was a role that she would sing twenty-seven times in-house and eight times on tour.

Because this role was so crucial to Ponselle's career, and because the reviews that appeared are so interesting, I quote two by Max Smith. His astute observations show that from the beginning, her voice and its classification were controversial:

Of the 1918 premier, he writes in *The New York American*:

It was difficult to believe that Miss Ponselle's earlier stage experiences had been confined to vaudeville, so much assurance she exhibited yesterday while facing a gathering that might well have unnerved her. To judge from her demeanor and her acting one would have taken her to be a youthful singer well versed in the routine of lyric drama. Always in gesture, in pose, and in facial expression did she seem to have perfect command of herself. And this gave cause for quite as much surprise as did the quality of her voice, the control she exerted over it while supporting her tones on an ample supply of breath, and the dramatic intensity she so spontaneously infused in her singing.

...There may be difference of opinion regarding the exact character of the new singer's voice. It has the mellow opulence and warmth of a mezzo in the lower register and responds easily below C natural. Yet, has her voice the range of a dramatic soprano? Only her middle tones are slightly throaty and her high tones not quite free and round in their resonance... (Metropolitan Opera Archives, Accessed July 2014)

Even more surprising is his review after hearing the second performance on November 28:

Another hearing of Rosa Ponselle as Leonora in 'La Forza del Destino' tended to encourage the belief that this young woman, whose star rose so suddenly from the horizon of vaudeville into the operatic firmament, is in reality a mezzo-soprano with voice artificially elevated to an altitude somewhat above its normal range.

Nature has provided her with excellent material. But despite the power and expansiveness of her vocal organ the strain of sustaining a high tessitura is distinctly to be observed in her emission. Her high tones, which she frequently approaches with a scoop, become pinched when she attempts to reduce them to a mezzo-voce, and in full-throated utterance they often assume a hardness of timbre very different from the mellow vibrancy of her low tones. They are inclined, moreover, under pressure, to overtop the correct pitch.

Taking everything into consideration, Mr. Gatti-Casazza's new prima donna sang surprisingly well last night. One marveled again at her poise and assurance. But her singing in such an exacting aria, for example, as the "Madre, Pietosa Vergine"—can hardly be described as finished. It was potent, it was persuasive; it had the vigor and the strength of youth. But it had crudities that not every one in the auditorium could overlook

Interestingly, Ponselle's first recording of music from *La Forza del destino* was not what would become her signature tune, "Pace, Pace," but "La Vergine degl'angeli." Recorded in December of 1918, it reflects what she did with the music at the time of her debut. Sung with accompanying chorus, her gentle entrance is magical, with beautiful legato and firm, round tone. This is not only one of her great recordings, but also one of the best of this aria.

Ten years later, in 1928, she re-recorded the aria for Victor with chorus and bass, Ezio Pinza. Pinza, who opens the scene, is wonderful, authoritative and solid. The Victor recording offers more of the scene than the earlier Columbia record and Ponselle's gentle entrance is, again, striking, her legato firm and the G at the top of the staff shows good control. Because of the electric process there is better balance among all of the singers, giving the scene more impact. There is little change in Ponselle's interpretation. Ponselle did not like this recording, feeling that someone had turned up her microphone, thereby distorting the sound of what was heard when she sang it in an opera house.

Verdi – "Pace pace mio Dio" (*La forza del destino)* – Columbia, 1920; Victor, 1924, 1928

Finally, in 1920, Ponselle records Leonora's act IV showpiece. Later, as if to make up for a lack of foresight, she makes five more recordings, published and unpublished, for Victor. One questions why some of her unpublished recordings went unpublished, except that the singer was extremely particular about her recordings, reflecting well on her standard of quality. Although not as refined as it was to become (for Victor), there is definitely an interpretation at work on the Columbia recording. Understandably, because of time constraints, the aria is abbreviated and the tempi are not ideal. The infamous high B-flat pianissimo asked for by Verdi is mezza forte, but it is a beautiful note, controlled and freely produced. so it works in this context. All through the aria Ponselle phrases with authority and familiarity and the final "Maledizione!" is full and exciting; the final high B-flat is attacked separately and easily sustained.

The 1924 published Victor has her famous messa di voce on the top F and her gentle handling of phrases is unique to this recording. Her head voice is especially telling here. The crucial high B-flat is taken well and sustained easily. The finish is quite exciting.

The most famous Ponselle recording of this aria remains the 1928 electrical disk with its especially melting messa di voce on the sustained F of the opening "Pace." Ponselle was one of those singers who was remarkably consistent, but rarely provided spontaneous expression. Her drama was scripted and she rarely strayed from that plan. My point is that the Columbia recording is just as good. The top B-flat (pianissimo) has to be sung mezza forte, with no nuance. It works, and the following "Maledizione!" is more darkly heavy. In this recording, different from others, she uses a springboard note to access the final high B-flat.

Verdi – "Willow Song" and "Ave Maria" (*Otello)*—Victor, 1924

This is another role that was not in Ponselle's repertoire that she was obviously fond of. From her singing, one can tell it would have been a good role for her. Although she recorded the "Ave Maria" in 1923 for Columbia, she recorded the entire scene for Victor a year later: there are nice touches and fine pianissimo singing. As one would expect, the "Willow Song" is heavily cut to allow it to fit on a single side of a 78 rpm disk. Even so, the repeats of "Salce" are very effective as is her grand farewell to Emilia. Recorded on the same day, "Ave Maria" is quite beautiful with firm legato and a bit of drama. The final "Pregha" is sung with a gradual decrescendo on the E until her voice blends in completely with the surrounding instruments. This is a clever effect that is not often used by other sopranos. The arpeggiated rise to high A-flat on "Ave" is very beautiful, although she cheats a bit by leaving out the "v" of "Ave." She did the same thing when she sang the aria live.

Verdi – "Bolero" (*I Vespri Siciliani)* – Columbia, 1920

Although *I Vespri Siciliani* was never a part of Ponselle's performing repertoire, this aria was. She sang it a number of times at Metropolitan Opera Galas and obviously enjoyed the challenges of Verdi's florid music. The Columbia disk, recorded in March of 1920, is a wonderful display of her virtuosity. During that era, performances of *I Vespri Siciliani* were a rarity, much more so than today. Although, by the time of Ponselle's recording, it had already been recorded by Celestina Bonnisegna, Marcella Sembrich, Luisa Tetrazzini, and Selma Kurz. Ponselle happily performs this florid music and negotiates the coloratura well with excellent diction and delicate touches. The tempo is good and she shows a good integration of the registers. The trills are not quite formed, but Ponselle's manner is both graceful and elegant. Near the end there are occasional placement slips as she travels through the low register in the midst of melismas, but this is a very successful performance of the aria.

Verdi – "Tacea la notte placida" (*Il trovatore*) – Columbia, 1922
Verdi – "D'amor sull ali rosee" (*Il trovatore*) – Columbia, 1918

Ponselle's Columbia recordings of "Tacea la notte placida" and "D'amor sull ali rosee" are archetypes for those that follow. Her timbre is like a column of solid, dark chocolate and her head voice is pure. There is seamless legato and the artistic tapering of phrases provides unforgettable performances, each aria having its own, distinct mood.

In "Tacea la notte placida" the smooth integration of her registers is as evident as her innate sensitivity in phrasing Verdi's music. This is elegant singing, full of hints of the tremendous passion Leonora harbors. Although Ponselle avoids Verdi's high D-flat, the single cabaletta verse has clean coloratura, pointed staccato, and superb trills. Her finish is especially notable for her instinctive understanding of the workings of inner rhythms. The release of the final, high A-flat is perfectly timed for maximum impact.

"D'amor sull ali rosee" is memorable for Ponselle's lilting phrasing, overt sense of yearning, and beautiful, softly grained high notes. She provides cleanly poised, majestically phrased singing that is so securely worked into the voice that the listener is unaware of the difficulties of Verdi's music. The sustained high C is floated exquisitely as Ponselle then gently touches a top D-flat within Verdi's phrase structure. The finish boasts a superb high G trill that resolves to a softly floated A-flat. (There has been some question as to whether Ponselle lowered this aria. She has always insisted that she had not.)

Wagner – "Einsam in trüben tagen" (*Lohengrin*) – Columbia, 1923

This is another great Columbia disk and curiosity in Ponselle's legacy. Although not a role that one would have expected Ponselle to have undertaken on stage, the aria is beautifully suited to her voice and is given a fine, sculpted performance. As a matter of fact given her singing here, one wishes that she had recorded "Du bist der Lenz" from *Die Walküre* or Elizabeth's "Dich teure Halle" from *Tannhäuser*. She would often include the latter during her early concerts. Ponselle's very formal, beautiful handling of Wagner's jumps and her rich columnar voice are eloquent in Elsa's dream. Having a range only to high G-sharp this worked perfectly for

Ponselle, enabling her to easily infuse the music with drama. You can hear her top register pinging in the room's acoustics.

Complete Live Operas:

Although a performance of *Don Giovanni* with Ponselle does exist, the sound quality is so poor that I will forgo its discussion.

Carmen three performances (on Eclipse, Arkadia, and Gala):
Boston – March 28, 1936
New York—January 9, 1937
Cleveland—April 17, 1937

Although Carmen was Ponselle's last role with the Metropolitan Opera company, her last performance on that stage was during a concert on March 14, 1937, in which she sang "O divina Afrodite" from Romano Romani's *Fedra,* conducted by the composer. In that concert she also sang Schubert's "Erlkönig" and Rimsky-Korsakov's "The Nightingale and the Rose."

Her first performance of *Carmen* at the Metropolitan Opera on December 27, 1935, was met with strongly worded criticism. The costumes, however, designed by Valentina, were lauded. Rosa Ponselle sang fifteen performances of Carmen; nine in the house and six on tour.

Danton Walker writes in New York's *Daily News*:

...It is this reporter's happy privilege to tell you in no uncertain terms, that as the castanet-playing, hip shaking she-devil of Merimee's tragedy, our Rosa went to town in as high, wide and handsome a production of the Bizet opera as it has ever been my joy to witness. The more pedantic among the critical fraternity may, and probably will, tell you this morning that our Rosa's characterization was a bit vulgar. So what? If Carmen wasn't vulgar, what was she? ...She was a roughneck first to last, with a bawdy wit and a native gayety which most of the Carmens miss, but which our Rosa suggested superbly.

She was, in short, somewhere between Calve and Castagna, and the best Carmen I've seen and heard since Maria Gay, some of whose business she had absorbed. Not surprising since La Gay was seated in Ponselle's dressing room during the opera, egging her on. [Another Carmen, Geraldine Farrar, was applauding her from the first row.]" (Metropolitan Opera Archives, Accessed July 2014)

Feeling differently about what he experienced in the opera house, Olin Downes writes in *The New York Times*:

We have never heard Miss Ponselle sing so badly, and we have seldom seen the part enacted in such an artificial and generally unconvincing manner. Her first act was more carefully composed than what followed. It had less exaggeration, fewer mannerisms, some interesting detail and clean diction. She used a little of the spoken dialogue of the original version of the opera with good effect, but already showed a cheerful disregard of laws of good singing for which she has won richly deserved eminence. She also played fast and loose with time and with rhythm, and to this to an extent unnecessary for any genuinely expressive purpose.

It appeared that Miss Ponselle had determined at any cost to quality of tone, to pitch, to vocal style, to be 'dramatic'. This unfortunate intention only served, of course, to defeat the very ends it was designed to promote. Especially from a voice and such an artist are these methods unnecessary and inadvisable, for Miss Ponselle is primarily a singer and secondarily an actress, and not all her efforts put her in the dramatic frame.

Her dancing need not be dwelt upon, although in the inn scene it raised the question whether Spanish gypsies preferred the Charleston or the Black Bottom as models for their evolutions. The sum of her acting was affected, overdrawn, often inept. There was bad vocal style, carelessness of execution, inaccurate intonation. (ibid)

After a January 6, 1936 performance, Marcia Davenport writes the following in the March, 1936 issue of *Stage* magazine:

The eagerly anticipated Carmen of Rosa Ponselle met with such disastrous disapproval that its virtues—of which there are some—passed largely unnoticed…Her finger-snappings, eye-winkings, and hip-slingings were not the trouble with her performance. Her costumes were magnificent, if too exotic, and her vivacity all to the good. The trouble with her Carmen was vocal, and that, for the voice of a Ponselle, is really regrettable. Somebody had coached her badly, with a meretricious conception of Bizet's thrilling music, and had urged upon her deviations from good singing of which it is hard to believe her capable…

La traviata Met broadcast, January 5, 1935

Like *Carmen*, Ponselle sang fifteen performances of La Traiviata at the Metropolitan Opera; ten in house and five on tour.

When Ponselle sang her first *traviata* at Covent Garden, Herman Klein writes in the July, 1930 issue of *Gramophone*:

Musically speaking, the American soprano's reading of the part was extremely original; too much so at many points for the liking of those who knew how Verdi wanted his music to be sung.

An in-depth analysis of the details of Ponselle's live recordings of *La traviata* and *Carmen* could be book length. I urge the reader to seek out these recordings and then to listen and decide for one's self. They are fascinating documents of a most individual performer.

Joseph Schwarz (1880–1926)

One of the most unjustly neglected artists from an earlier era is baritone, Joseph Schwarz. Although internationally praised during the early years of the twentieth century, today he is virtually unknown to most listeners.

Schwarz was born on October 10, 1880, in Riga, Latvia, then a province of Tsarist Russia. He was one of ten children born into a poor, German-Jewish family and originally apprenticed to be a tailor. Fortunately, some wealthy entrepreneurs happened to hear Joseph sing, recognized the inherent vocal ability of the young man, and sponsored his music studies. After studying in Berlin with Alexander Heinemann, he went to Vienna and studied with Adolf Robinson at the Vienna Conservatory. He made his operatic debut in 1900 in Linz as Amonasro in *Aïda*. After tours that took him back to his home town of Riga, to Graz, and to the Imperial Opera in St. Petersburg, he settled at the Vienna Staatsoper where he was a member from 1909 to 1915. After the death of Leopold Demuth, Schwarz took over most of his roles. He was very popular, especially when partnered with Caruso, who guested often at the Staatsoper.

Although initially a restrained interpreter, he soon grew to be an impassioned artist with a wide repertoire. His roles included the Wagnerian Amfortas, Wolfram and the Wanderer as well as the Italian Rigoletto, Iago (*Otello*), Germont (*La traviata*), Scarpia (*Tosca*), Tonio (*Pagliacci*), the French Valentine (*Faust*), Athanael (*Thaïs*), Escamillo (*Carmen*), and the four villains in *Contes d'Hoffmann*. During a guest appearance at the Berlin Opera in 1915, Schwarz was hailed as a second Battistini. Because of the phenomenal response of Berlin audiences, he decided to terminate his contract with the Vienna Opera and move to Berlin. While there he was acclaimed as a singing actor who excelled equally in the French, Italian, and German repertoire. He was especially famous for his incomparable Rigoletto and searing interpretation of Verdi's Iago, both of which were held as yardsticks for all German interpreters that followed.

During the early 1920s, Schwarz concertized throughout the United States and Europe, including Covent Garden and the Civic Opera of Chicago (1921–1925).

In 1921, Schwarz made his New York debut in recital at Carnegie Hall. The February, 1921 issue (page 36) of *The Musician* (The Music Teacher's Magazine, Henderson Publications, Inc., New York) notes:

But lest we forget the vocalists, we must record the New York debut of Joseph Schwarz, a Russian baritone, who has sung much in Europe. Mr. Schwarz selected for his first appearance works of Handel, Verdi, Rachmaninoff, Tschaikovski, Massenet, Liszt, Walter Kramer and Grieg. While the press was somewhat reserved in its praise, it was generally recognized, however, that here was a singer of distinction. Mr. Finck of the *Post* said: 'He shows a real dramatic temperament, but his sentiment quite frequently degenerates into sentimentality. He is evidently a man of intelligence, and, gifted as he is with a really beautiful voice, he should be very successful here.' The *Brooklyn Daily Eagle* called the singer 'an artist to his finger-tips,' whereas the *Tribune* said: 'His voice is of unusually beautiful quality, but his singing is of so conventional an order that his really magnificent organ is not always displayed to its fullest advantage.' (J.T.H., Jr.)

Also giving recitals that year were sopranos Frieda Hempel and Yvonne de Treville, as well as tenor Hipólito Lázaro.
In March, *The Columbia Daily Spectator* notes:

Joseph Schwarz, the Russian baritone, is making his first appearance with the orchestra in this country at the Philarmonic concert on Sunday afternoon, March 12, at Carnegie Hall. He will sing "Wotan's Farewell" from "The Valkyrie," and the aria from "The Masked Ball. (Volume XLIV, Number 96, March 3, 1921)

In December of 1921, after having sung performances as Wolfram and Rigoletto for Chicago audiences, he performed Giorgio Germont in *La traviata* and caused quite a stir:

Joseph Schwarz sang Germont pere for the first time here. It scarcely needed the 'Di Provenza' aria to confirm and strengthen my already profound and sincere admiration for the art of this great singer. Even at the risk of repeating myself, I must say that Schwarz's singing is a lesson in the art of shading, nuance, expression. After his duet with Madame Galli-Curci he lived the role to the minutest detail. The audience gave him such an ovation after the aria that the 'no encore' rule trembled in the balance. (Herman Devries, *Chicago Evening American*, December 21, 1921)

On December 28, 1922, Schwarz gave another recital at Carnegie Hall, this time with orchestra, singing music by Handel, Brahms, Liszt, and Dvorak, as well as a number of popular operatic arias.

Although most biographies of this singer mention that he performed with the Metropolitan Opera in New York, I found no mention of his name in the on-line annals. This suggests that he may have been engaged to appear at the Metropolitan Opera, but died before the contract was to begin.

Unfortunately, by 1925, because of personal pressures and an alcohol addiction, Schwarz's health declined rapidly. He died the next year, on November 10, 1926, at the age of forty-six. He was buried in the Jewish cemetery in Berlin-Weissensee:

His mausoleum bears the inscription, 'Lord, you are my refuge for ever and ever.' Those works took on a literal meaning for many Jews, because the mausoleum served many of them as a refuge during the period of Nazi terror. (Bernhard Press, *The Murder of the Jews in Latvia: 1941–1945*, Northwestern University Press, 1992).

Despite his short life, he proved to be one of the finest baritones to have graced the lyric stage. In addition to the exquisite timbre of his lush voice, Schwarz was a darkly handsome man carrying much intensity to the stage.

Schwarz was an intermittently active recording artist from 1907 through 1925. He left seventy-six published sides for Zonophone, Edison, Pathé, Parlophon, and Grammophon. His Pathé sides are rarities and have not yet been transferred onto either LP or CD formats.

During the LP era, Preiser was the primary custodian of Schwarz's art, releasing a number of volumes.

In 1991 (and 1999), Preiser put their Schwarz material onto two generous CDs (89033 & 89184) containing thirty-nine selections of both operatic and song repertoire.

In 2004, Hänssler Classics released a CD of eighteen selections, more or less mirroring sides already released by Preiser. Either is to be recommended.

Schwarz's recorded selections are wide-ranging, including arias from *Il barbiere di Siviglia, Zar und Zimmermann, Das Rheingold, The Demon, Il re di Lahore, Herodiade, Hans Heiling, Tannhäuser* (2), *Faust, Il trovatore, La traviata, Un ballo in maschera* (2), *Otello, L'Africaine* (2), *Contes d'Hoffmann, Pagliacci, Zazà, Xerxes,* and *Elijah,* as well as songs by Grieg, Liszt, Beethoven, Mendelssohn, Giordani, R. Strauss, and Lewandowski's "Kol nidre."

From his recordings, it is obvious that Schwarz's training had been extensive and based on Italian bel canto. He seems to have eschewed the typical veristic mannerisms that most baritones of that era favored. Because of this, there is an elegance to his singing, no matter the dynamics.

His voice was of sufficient size, with a very mellow, lush timbre supported by solid breath control technique and an ease in the top register that allowed for some unusual nuance. Despite everything being sung in German, Schwarz's sense of line is so firmly rooted in the Italian style that one is almost deceived into believing that he is singing in original languages. Not content to just sing the music, Schwarz imbues each piece with personal touches that remain with the listener long after the recording is over.

Especially important are the excerpts from *Rigoletto* that include three duets with the exquisite Claire Dux (found on Preiser's Volume I). Rigoletto was probably Schwarz's most famous role. He offers a fascinating, multifaceted interpretation of great vocal allure, as well as much psychological insight. The most unusual aspect of these recordings is that, although they were not recorded in sequence, one is still able to trace the growth and change in the character through Schwarz's interpretation. They also prove that, despite the limitations of the recording process at the time, and without the benefit of an audience, Schwarz was a singer who always gave one hundred percent. Each piece receives his complete artistic attention, as everything is phrased with imagination and originality.

To elaborate, the first selection, "Pari siamo," introduces us to Schwarz's Jester, a proud, somewhat stodgy character, yet one who has moments of introspection; moments that he carefully keeps hidden from others. The aria moves back and forth between these two traits with unusual smoothness. When Gilda enters, and he deals with her, the edge of pride is still there, but it becomes softened because of her proximity and his obvious love for her. He is gentle and sweet and Dux responds accordingly. Hers is close to the ideal voice for a Gilda, sweet and lyrical. Schwarz begins both sections of the duet with a sweet pianissimo that perfectly sets up what is to follow. The "Deh non parlare" duet is very moving, attributable to the nuance that Schwarz lends to the simple lines, even gracefully ornamenting one of the important cadences, as is the old custom. So natural does it sound, that it almost appears that it were a spontaneous improvisation. I was especially taken with certain tempi choices. For instance, the ritards Schwarz and Dux incorporate into the "Ah, veglia oh donna" duet make sense. And, in the case of Dux's difficult lines (which rise to peaking Cs and B-flats), they help to maintain the concept of a private exchange between two people rather than a virtuosic singing display.

By "Cortigiani," Schwarz's proud Rigoletto is almost completely shattered. Although he begins the aria with a touch of the pride first displayed in "Pari siamo," it is obviously a defense of his character and it quickly disintegrates. By the time he begs Marullo for the whereabouts of Gilda, he is completely broken and desperate. Interestingly, Schwarz ignores the score's marking of forte at "tu taci," singing instead a high pianissimo that says so much more about what is happening to his character internally than the written forte would have done. The aria proper is sung with great intensity, but always a strong legato line and one does not notice that the aria is being sung in German, not Italian.

The final selection is the "Piangi" duet after Gilda's act III confession. Here, some of the pride that Schwarz's character had, returns, this time tempered by a pity for both his and his daughter's situation. His singing of "Weine" (Piangi) is a command to Gilda to mourn their combined betrayal. During the duets, Schwarz always provides a strong, impenetrable legato line for Dux to play against. Metaphorically, it could be interpreted as a vocal depiction of the impenetrable strength of a father's love for his daughter. The decrescendo they both use during the final ritard in the final cadence, will break your heart. These selections alone are worth the price of the CD.

Other selections on Volume I include arias and duets from *Il trovatore* (2), *La traviata, Ballo in maschera* (2), *Otello, L'Africaine* (2), *Hoffmann* (be sure to listen to his decrescendo at the end of this aria!) and a Liszt song.

The selections from *L'Africaine* are refreshingly different and thrillingly sung. Although Dux does not have the correct vocal weight for a *Trovatore*, Leonora, the act IV duet is successful due to the extreme musicality of both artists. Preiser has also included the famous recording of Iago's Credo from *Otello*. This (with

Rigoletto), was a role for which Schwarz was renowned. It is masterful and beautifully sung, while a strongly interpreted performance. Of special note is an extremely moving, "Oh quand je dors" by Liszt, and an idiomatic, gorgeous "Kol nidre."

In reviewing the Hänssler Classic CD (94507) on April 18, 2005, Jan Neckers on the website, Opera Today (http://www.operatoday.com) writes:

…The older collector will probably have the originals, the Preiser LP's or the 2 Preiser CD's with most of Schwarz's output on Parlophone and Gramophone. As far as I know no one has ever put young Schwarz's records on Zonophone (2), Edison (1) or Pathé (12) on CD. The CD under review gives us 18 tracks, all recorded for Gramophone and is very much duplicated by the Preiser CD's. Therefore this is meant for either the new collector or for someone who doesn't need to have the complete recorded output of a particular singer. Not that Schwarz doesn't deserve to be remembered by every note he ever sang for the horn. In his *magnum opus* German critic Jürgen Kesting (*Die Grossen Sänger*, 3 vols., 2089 pp.) writes: " though he never recorded electrically his recordings show us the best German baritone of the century."[1] High praise indeed though probably well-deserved. Kesting still tells us that Schwarz died at the early age of 46 due to kidney insufficiency. However the sleeve notes on this latest issue bluntly say the baritone was an alcoholic who by the time of his death had become a sad wreck. Therefore it was Schwarz's own behaviour that caused the tragedy which resulted in us having no electric recordings.

Still, these acoustics give a formidable portrait of the singer and we can understand British publisher Victor Gollanz who put Schwarz's Rigoletto on the same height as Caruso's Duca. As Schwarz was Jewish, his records were not available in Germany for a whole generation and this may be one of the reasons he is less well remembered than he deserves."

(An abbreviated version of this article first appeared in *Classical Singer*, October, 2001)

Marcella Sembrich (1858–1935)

Marcella Sembrich was born in 1858, as Prakseda Macelina Kochaska in Wisniewczyk in Austrian Galacia, now part of Ukraine. She first studied piano at the age of four and violin at the age of six, with her father, a professional violinist. She excelled at both instruments. At the age of fifteen, on the advice of her future husband, the pianist Wilhelm Stengel (1846–1917), she went to Vienna in 1873 to study under the famous pianist Julius Epstein, a pupil of Moscheles, who, after hearing her sing, advised her to concentrate instead on vocal studies. (As did Franz Liszt.) This she did, studying with Victor Rokitansky for a year, then moving to Milan to study with Giovanni Battista Lamperti.

She made her operatic debut in Athens at the age of nineteen in Bellini's *I puritani*. It was at the time of her debut that she chose to use her mother's maiden name, Sembrich, as her stage name, and married Stengel. After her debut she sang performances of *Dinorah*, *La sonnambula*, *Robert le Diable* and *Lucia di Lammermoor*. Slated to make her debut at the Vienna Staatsoper, she broke the contract when she found that she was pregnant. After her son, Wilhelm, Jr. was born, she continued her studies in Vienna and was hired to guest at the Dresden Royal Opera in 1878 (debuting as *Lucia di Lammermoor*). Her success was such that she was immediately engaged as a member of the company and remained there until 1880. By this time her roles had included Gilda in *Rigoletto*, Marguerite in *Les Huguenots*, Catherine in *L'étoile du nord*, Rosina in *Il barbiere di Siviglia*, Violetta in *La traviata*, Constanza in *Die Entführung aus dem Serail*, Susannah in *Le nozze di Figaro,* Zerlina in *Don Giovanni*, Lakmé in *Lakmé*, Norina in *Don Pasquale*, Marie in *La fille du regiment*, and The Queen of the Night in *Die Zauberflöte*.

In 1880, she debuted at Covent Garden in *Lucia di Lammermoor* and, in 1883 at the Metropolitan Opera Company (on the second night of its inaugural season) again in *Lucia di Lammermoor*.

An unusual event occurred during a Metropolitan Opera gala the next season, on April 21, 1884. It was a testimonial benefit for Henry E. Abbey, the first general manager of the Metropolitan Opera. (The gala was to help to balance the budget of the new opera house.)

Sembrich sang in the second act of *Il barbiere di Siviglia*. During the lesson scene she sang the "Theme and Variations" by Proch and the Russian National Anthem. Then, after a break (when act II, scene 2 of *Aïda* was performed), Sembrich returned center stage to perform:

De Beriot: Concerto No. 7: Adagio and Rondo Finale (played by Sembrich on the violin)
Chopin: Waltz in C sharp minor (an encore she played on the piano)
Bellini: "Ah non giunge" *(La sonnambula)* (a second encore, this time sung)

She appeared with her violin once more . . . the Bach-Gounod "Ave Maria," . . . sung beautifully by Mme. Nilsson.

As W.J. Henderson notes in *The New York Times*:

Mme. Sembrich carried off a large share of the evening's honors. Her singing of Proch's air and variations in the lesson scene of "Il Barbiere" was admirable for smoothness and ease of execution. She was twice interrupted by applause in the staccato passage and made to return to the beginning. Subsequently she made her first appearance as a violinist, playing the adagio and finale from De Beriot's seventh concerto. Her playing was a surprise. She possesses a delightfully clear and sweet tone, her stopping is accurate, and her bowing strong. Above all, she plays with the sentiment of an artist. A storm of applause followed her performance, and for an encore she played, on the piano, Chopin's waltz in C sharp minor, proving herself to be also an accomplished pianist. Again recalled, she came before the curtain, sang once more, and retired laden with flowers. She appeared with her violin once more, when she played the obligato to the Bach-Gounod "Ave Maria," which was sung beautifully by Mme. Nilsson. (Metropolitan Opera Archives, Accessed 1-13-15)

Considering her accomplishments, it is not surprising (but still disappointing), that political machinations at the Metropolitan Opera caused Sembrich's contract not to be renewed. She was gone from that house for fourteen years.

In 1885, Marcella had another son, Marcel, who died in 1901 at the age of sixteen of complications from a childhood illness. During the following years, Sembrich made guest appearances in Paris, Brussels, Milan, Berlin, Vienna, Stockholm, and from 1890 to 1897 was a huge success at the Italian Opera in St. Petersburg. Sembrich was invited to return to the Metropolitan Opera in 1898 and remained with that company for the next eleven years. She retired from the stage (and the Metropolitan Opera) on February 6, 1909 with a huge gala to honor her final appearance in opera.

For the gala she sang selections from *Don Pasquale (*a duet with Antonio Scotti*)*, *Il barbiere di Siviglia* (act II, including the lesson scene), the "Voices of Spring Waltz," the act II duet from *Don Pasquale* with Alessandro Bonci, "Ah non giunge" from *La sonnambula*, and Chopin's "A Maiden's Wish" (accompanying herself on piano), and act I of *La traviata*, with Enrico Caruso. A presentation was made to

Sembrich by George J. McClellan, the then-mayor of New York City. The Metropolitan Opera Archives note:

> During the farewell ceremonies, the soprano was escorted onstage by general manager Giulio Gatti-Casazza. At the final curtain, a shower of rose petals fell on the diva and the many guests assembled onstage to pay her homage.

While at the Metropolitan Opera, Sembrich sang some five hundred performances of twenty-six roles that included forty-one Lucias *(Lucia di Lammermoor)*, sixty-five Rosinas *(Il barbiere di Siviglia)*, forty-nine Violettas *(La traviata)*, twenty-seven Mimis *(La bohème)*, twenty-eight Gildas *(Rigoletto)*, and twenty-seven Queen of the Nights *(Die Zauberflöte)*.

Sembrich continued to perform in recital (where she was extremely popular) until the death of her husband in 1917. After his death, Sembrich devoted her time to teaching. She was a favored teacher at both the Curtis Institute in Philadelphia, and the Juilliard School of Music in New York City. After the outbreak of World War I Sembrich remained in the New York area. In 1922 she purchased a 14-acre lakeside estate in Lake George and built a home with a caretaker's cottage as well as her vocal studio—a Spanish revival stucco building that is now on the National Register of Historic Places.

> Three years after the diva's death...the Opera Museum was opened by her daughter-in-law, Julliette deCoppet Stengel. Four scenic acres remain on this parcel that boasts Mme. Sembrich's prized rhododendrons and gardenias, a thousand-foot shoreline path that wends its way to a structure called the University of Modern Languages and on to a scenic overlook, interpretive signage, and cozy woodland nooks with comfortable benches. Everywhere lies the grandeur that is Lake George...
>
> Mme. Sembrich's studio now serves a dual purpose, with one area housing the Sembrich collection of memorabilia, art and costumes, and the acoustically fine teaching room that now functions as an intimate setting for chamber music performances, allowing audiences to experience the music as it was originally performed in the salons and parlors of Europe. Mme. Sembrich's 1905 Steinway piano, completely restored, reigns over all. The museum and grounds are open daily from June 15th through September 15th. (http://www.lakegeorge.com/business/marcella-sembrich-opera-museum-6344)

Sembrich died in 1935 at the age of 76. A remarkable musician, during her career she continued her studies of the piano and violin (as well as periodic vocal study) and often played or accompanied herself in public. She gave her first song recital in 1900 and was one of the few divas of the time to promote art song recitals. Indeed, she did much at the time to educate the general public about the works of Franz Schubert, Johannes Brahms, Hugo Wolf, and Richard Strauss.

There is a mystery about the Sembrich family. In the 1999 liner notes for the Nimbus CD of Sembrich selections, David Alexander Terry notes:

> Sembrich's daughter-in-law, Juliette de Coppet, the wife of her son Wilhelm lived with Mme. Sembrich and served as her assistant in professional and business matters. Wilhelm seems to have been estranged in later years not only from his wife but from his parents. In the extensive Sembrich collection in the archives of the Music Division of the New York

Public Library there is very little in the way of photographs, letters or papers dealing with Wilhelm, and it is said that Juliette expunged whatever material may have been in Sembrich's private papers before it was bequeathed to the Library.

This peculiar attempt by his former wife to erase the existence of the younger Wilhelm from the family's history (and the family) suggests some sort of scandal or personal issue concerning Wilhelm that was felt to be too humiliating to acknowledge.

The Voice

Herman Klein, who heard such legendary singers as Adelina Patti, Ilma di Murska, and Terese Tietjens, included Marcella Sembrich in his book *Great Women Singers of my Time*. Klein heard Sembrich many times throughout her career and noted that in 1881:

> (Her voice) was singularly entrancing. I was immensely struck with the vibrant quality and bell-like purity of her tone, her impeccable intonation, and the faultless accuracy of her scales. She had a perfect shake, and the masterful ease and facility of her execution was displayed over a compass extending to the F in alt. (*Books for Libraries Press*, Freeport, New York, 1931)

He also felt that there were similarities between Adelina Patti and Sembrich.

> The resemblance between the voices of Patti and Sembrich…lay not so much in actual timbre as in identical mechanical method, coupled with tonal features that were the outcome of a certain amount of imitation, conscious or unconscious on Sembrich's part. (*Books for Libraries Press*, Freeport, New York, 1931)

Interestingly, critical reviews of the time give the impression that Sembrich's voice was not admired for its tonal warmth, but, rather, its virtuosic capabilities. Much of this had to do with her manner of singing.

According to Max de Schaunsee, between 1883 and 1898, Sembrich developed hearing problems that led to a kind of deafness that evidenced itself in occasional pitch problems and a more dry, reedy tone.

J.B. Steane also writes of certain problems with this voice:

> To (W.J.) Henderson she was, in fact, the singer most beloved of all, and his essay on her, published shortly after her death in 1935, is one of the most precise and convincing appreciations of a singer ever written. We really need to have that article in hand as we listen to her records, for the impression they give is sometimes rather different.

> For example, Henderson speaks of the emotional quality of her singing and the magic she exercised 'in purely lyric music embodying tender pathos.' Records give little indication of this. As we listen carefully, there is tenderness in 'Qui la voce'…but this is not a quality that the records would normally have brought to our attention. (*The Grand Tradition*, Charles Scribner's Sons, New York, 1974)

Sembrich's voice was rapidly spun with a narrow but brilliant and shimmering vibrato, remarkable virtuosity, and a particularly fine trill. The recordings demonstrate an ingratiating crystalline timbre and an obvious commitment to any music she sings. On records, however, hers is a voice that is seemingly produced with little phrase-tapering or dynamic shading. Everything is "held" in an instrumental manner that, although admirable for its clarity of pitch, lacks a quality of refinement in execution and phrasing that true legato requires. It is as if phrases are presented to the listener in blocks of sound, almost everything delivered in a relentless mezza forte. There is the occasional flicker of unstable vibrato during legato, suggesting faulty breath support; that her support was fighting against muscular restrictions. There is often the sense, too, that Sembrich is holding back when attacking the highest tones.

> But what is really disturbing in the records is something which must surely be a basic effect of her method of voice production. Very often, an outstanding and marvelous characteristic of Sembrich's singing is the absolute purity of a held high note; perfectly round and even, so that one feels it could be drawn, as a regular, unflawed column or tube. But sometimes the column wavers, uneven vibrations appear as a flutter upsetting the firmness, and there are many examples of this on record. The 1903 Columbias have it: in the *traviata* and *Ernani* arias the flutter is so marked that one would swear that the records were playing high, yet the pitch is correct and transposition seems unlikely. (*The Grand Tradition*, Charles Scribner's Sons, New York, 1974, p. 68)

After hearing a number of the Sembrich records, one realizes that the acoustic recording process emphasized inconsistencies in this singer's voice, whereas the acoustics of a theatre or concert hall might have masked them from listeners.

I suspect that recording was an ordeal for Sembrich. Initially one is impressed by her splendid virtuosity, but after a few instances of an unstable flow of legato one becomes alarmed. She seems only to release her voice when she is in the midst of coloratura figurations and the voice is not being rigidly held in place. More unattractive is her lack of artistic portamento (or at least what we today consider to be "artistic") that is replaced by a surprisingly vulgar scooping. For instance, the finish of the "Jewel Song" from *Faust* is ruined by her pedestrian way of handling the final cadence. In her day she was considered an excellent Mozart singer. Today, our tastes have changed. To us, her Mozart shows a very unmusical way of handling vocal phrases and a surprising disregard for Mozart's score. In some cases, however, it is more a matter of prevailing taste and the fluctuating priorities of vocal style. Many gasp at Sembrich's audacity to interpolate a high D at the end of the Queen of the Night's vengeance aria from act II of *Die Zauberflöte*. In her day, however, this was a generally accepted alternate finish for the aria.

I suspect that her voice was difficult to record and this may have had to do with her method of singing. I never get the feeling that the high notes she chooses to interpolate are beyond her, but that she is being cautious with their emission; as if she is afraid to let her top register soar.

Selected Recordings

Including both published and unpublished disks, Sembrich made a total of one hundred recordings. In 1900, she made a few disks for the Bettini Phonograph Laboratory and a few years later (1902–1903) was featured on some of the infamous Mapleson Cylinders, non-commercial recordings of actual performances recorded in the Metropolitan Opera House in New York. I say infamous because it is well known in music circles that these recordings are extremely difficult to listen to because of their age and condition In 1903, she made three 10-inch disks for the Columbia Phonograph Company. Most of her recording was done, however, for the Victor Company, beginning in 1904.

For many years Marcella Sembrich was one of the singers most conspicuous for her absence on CD. With the assistance of the Rodgers and Hammerstein Archives and the New York Public Library in 1997, the British label, Romophone, provided listeners (and collectors) with the ability to explore the legacy of one of America's most beloved artists, a favorite with critics and audiences alike. Although Romophone exists no longer, copies of the two Sembrich releases can be found on line.

Differing from her contemporary, Nellie Melba, Sembrich's recording career was confined to America. Not beginning until the diva was forty-two, and after she had been performing on the operatic stage for twenty-seven years, her recording career lasted nineteen years. She continued to record (privately) until her sixty-first year, two years after her retirement from the recital stage. Recordings that she made in 1919 were not intended to be sold to the public, but recorded for Sembrich's private use and as gifts for family and friends.

Sembrich's recordings are not those of a debutante, or a singer in her prime, but a seasoned artist who was beginning her decline. It was not until 1904 that Sembrich seriously undertook her recorded legacy. By then she was forty-six and had been singing for more than twenty years. Even so, she could still call on an occasional high D, as in Arditi's "Parla Waltz," the great aria from *Halka*, or Alabiev's "Nightingale." Although Sembrich made recordings of the Strauss waltzes "Voices of Spring" and "Tales from Vienna Woods," and frequently scheduled them on concerts and recitals, the main issue in these recordings is their uninteresting arrangements. One hearing of either waltz is enough—especially with the occasionally unstable vocalism.

During the LP era in America and England, Sembrich's work was only to be found on smaller, independent labels: Rococo, Preiser, Delta, Cantilena, and IRCC. Single selections could also be found on Olympus, Scala, TAP (Top Artists Platter) and Belcantodisc. Today her work can be found on two Romophone releases (81026 and 81027) with a total of ninety-seven selections (her entire output for Victor as well as the infamous Mapleson cylinders, and privately recorded sides made in 1919).

There is also a single Nimbus recital of twenty-one well-chosen selections. If one is not interested in a multi-disc collection of this singer, the Nimbus is an excellent choice as it is a generous program (seventy-seven minutes) that includes some of her best operatic recordings and song selections. The

Nimbus technology and their manner of transfer provides a fascinating take on the Sembrich voice.

For newcomers to the Sembrich voice, I recommend starting with the Nimbus issue. While I usually prefer more "normal" transfers when it comes to providing initial exposure to historical singers, in the case of Marcella Sembrich, I feel the Nimbus program is the better way to go. The vocal issues mentioned earlier are still evident, but they are less obtrusive due to the ambisonic method of transfer that Nimbus uses. In some cases the negative impact is lessened quite a bit. Overall, Nimbus is more "Sembrich-friendly."

MP3 files (which can be downloaded free) of about fifteen Sembrich sides are available on line, including some of her most famous recordings. This archive is a great place to hear and sample many singer's voices before deciding who and what to buy. (https://archive.org/search.php?query=subject%3A%22Sembrich%22)

Bellini – "Ah non giunge" (*La sonnambula*) 1904, 1906

Sembrich's 1904 piano-accompanied disk of "Ah non giunge" has long been held up as a holy relic of pyrotechnical singing. I find it rather lumpy; the vibrato-shifting makes me uncomfortable. It was quite famous at one time, but today one can all too easily hear the faults, especially when compared to the many recordings that have been made since then. I prefer to suggest her recordings of arias from *Norma, Ernani, I puritani* and *Il barbiere di Siviglia*,—all having unusual variants—to best demonstrate her art and that era's manner of decoration. (Many of Sembrich's ornaments come directly from Adelina Patti.) The Nimbus presentation makes this recording more palatable.

The orchestrally accompanied 1906 recording is better than the 1904 recording; much of the singing is under better control. One notices her rather brutal attack on higher notes and trills that sometimes lends a unappealing coarseness to her singing. There is still an occasional taste of an unstable flicker of vibrato, but things are more smoothly delivered overall. She takes her time with the staccati ornaments and they go much better. The final unaccompanied cadenza is well done with brilliant scales and a nice lead-in to the final B-flat.

Chopin – "Zyczenie" (*The Maiden's Wish*) 1904

Recorded in November of 1904, this is a delightful record. Sung in Polish, with some wonderful rubati, this is a fine showing of the Sembrich talent. The final wordless obbligato (imitating the piano accompaniment) is very nice with Sembrich flicking a top D-flat in a wonderful staccato flourish. Oddly, the next (and final) note is awkward.

Donizetti – "Mad Scene" (*Lucia di Lamermoor*) 1906

Lucia di Lammermoor was an important Sembrich role and no matter what faults are found here, it is good to be able to hear her voice in this music.

Accompanied by orchestra, it is unfortunate that Sembrich begins with a rather unattractive singing of the initial phrase: "Ardon gli incensi" having a complete lack of portamento between notes. Too much of Donizetti's vocal line is presented note by note rather than in flowing phrases. Not until "Alfin son tua" does she let up on this clumpy effect. There are, however, some wonderfully imaginative ornaments. The cadenza with flute is prefaced by lumpy staccati, but a portion of the cadenza with flute is an original composition by Sembrich and highlights her voice's merits. Only a clumsy staccato flourish near the end (with a high D) is unfortunate. As one might expect, there is no final high E-flat.

W.J. Henderson reviews her 1883 debut as *Lucia di Lammermoor* at the Metropolitan Opera:

> No singer ever won the recognition of a New York audience more easily than Mme. Sembrich did. The very first note she uttered seemed to establish her in the favor of her hearers, and before the curtain had been lowered upon the first act the new prima donna's triumph was complete...Mme. Sembrich's voice is a light soprano, and, to judge by her impersonation of Lucia, she has nothing to fear from the few popular rivals she now has. The new favorite's tones are singularly clear and brilliant, and she encompasses, without seeming effort, the highest notes in the music. In addtion to this her execution is absolutely faultless, and she sings with a facility of expression and a perfection that are alike most gratifying to the sensitive listener. (Metropolitan Opera Archives, accessed 1-10-15)

Donizetti – "O luce di quest anima" (*Linda di Chamonix*) 1908

Linda was not one of her roles at the Met, but Sembrich certainly knows this music and gives it a rousing performance. She does not include the preceding recitative. Her use of rallentando is clever and her ornamentation, although tame by today's standards, makes its point. Most interesting is her delivery of the florid measures that display the art of the virtuoso. Only about three minutes in length, this is a very direct sing-through of the aria. The double climb to high C is obviously not easy for the soprano, so she uses an ornamental flourish to replace one climb, but manages the other well, the high C displaying no shifting of vibrato. There is no final cadenza but there is a fine, final high C.

Hahn – "Si mes vers" 1908

This is considered by many to be one of Sembrich's greatest song disks, and with good reason. Gone is the sense of huge blocks of stolid notes. There is flowing, sweet legato and a gentle, unforgettable interpretation. Despite its minimal range requirements, this is not an easy song to sing. The legato phrasing and subtle integration of the higher notes demand much control from the singer. Schubert's "Wohin is on the same disk, and is just as good. Musically sung with excellent diction, the song is presented with great forward movement, yet is never rushed, while there is much use of telling rubati.

J.B. Steane writes:

> This is beautifully sung, and especially interesting because it shows more persuasively than her other records how good a concert singer she could be...Still, the outstanding

feature of Sembrich's records remains their brilliance in fioritura...So the gramophone presents another paradox: that to this most musical of virtuosi we come essentially for the virtuosity. Other singers, far less musical, have left more of purely musical interest behind them. (*The Grand Tradition*, Charles Scribner's Sons, New York, 1974 p. 70)

Lehar – "Dolce amor" (*Die Lustige Witwe*) 1908 (second take)

This is another wonderful recording from 1908, the Merry Widow Waltz (sung in Italian). One of the few to record this piece, Sembrich enhances Lehar's gentle melodies, offering wonderful coloratura during the course of this four-minute song. Trills are well-rounded and flow with elasticity. One does notice (here as well as in many other recordings) that Sembrich tends to aggressively "attack" a trill rather than to roll into it elegantly. Romophone's CD volume I has both takes of this piece. A comparison of them is most interesting; I prefer the second.

Moniuszko – "Gdyby Rannem Slonkiem" ("If By the Morning Sun") (*Halka*) 1907

During the 1980s this remarkable aria was beautifully recorded by the lirico-spinto sopranos Teresa Kubiak and Teresa Zylis-Gara. Sembrich's recording was the first. Sung in Polish it has always been a favorite with collectors and not hard to understand why. It is a beautiful composition that suits the Sembrich voice and temperament well. Despite the occasional rasp that appears when the soprano travels through her middle register, this is a delicious recording. (Listen, too, to the Nimbus transfer. It is wonderful.)

The opera deals with the "tragic love of the title character, the highlander girl Halka, for the noble Janusz, who abandons her to wed the daughter of the Esquire. It is a tale of jealousy and sacrifice." (Wikipedia) A two-act version was premiered on January 1, 1848 and a four-act version was premiered in Warsaw on January 1, 1858. Shortly after, the opera was produced in the United States, Canada, Mexico, Japan, Turkey, Russia, and Cuba. The opera is still occasionally revived. Sembrich's recording of Halka's act II (scene 1) aria is one of her best. It is so good that one wonders why the aria is not performed more often in concerts and recitals. Capped by an interpolated, vibrant top D, one is left with the desire is to hear more.

It is too bad that Sembrich never recorded Ewa's "Italian Aria" from Moniuszko's 1860 opera *Hrabina* (The Countess). It would have been a spectacular showpiece for her. It appears that only Bogna Sokorska has recorded the aria (brilliantly in fact) on a 1964 LP record of highlights from the opera that was released by Muza. Katarzyna Dondalska has performed the aria in concert (electing to end the aria on a rather unattractive A above high C). It can be heard on YouTube. Anna Kutkowska-Kass, gave a brilliant performance of this aria (with piano accompaniment) during a Moniuszko Festival in Białystok in 2012.

This is one of the hidden glories of the florid literature that deserves to be heard more than it is. It is a gracious and elegant piece of music that is reminiscent of the Mozart and Bellini styles.

Rossini – "Una voce poco fa" (*Il barbiere di Siviglia*) 1907

Irrepressible, Marcella Sembrich made a pyrotechnical version of this aria in 1907. She was a famous Rosina, having performed in the first production of *Il bariere di Siviglia* that was given in the inaugural season of the Metropolitan Opera in 1883. When she came to record this aria she was past her prime, but even so, this is a remarkable performance.

This impossibly ornate version is in the "Patti style," the voluminous flourishes sounding decidedly odd to modern ears. Gone is Rossini's marking, "moderato," that is instead sung presto. Sembrich's version is probably the apex of the virtuosic tradition in the performance of this aria. There is much to learn from this disk. One is the manner in which she sings. There is a remarkable, controlled energy that is coupled with a theatrical dash governed by polished technique, a rare combination. Sembrich's bright, fastly spun voice glistens through the impossibly rapid ornamentation with dazzling speed and, while we might strongly disagree with her over-ornamented performance today, her execution is a marvel.

Rossini – "Bel raggio" (*Semiramide*) 1908

This aria was used by Sembrich only in concert, because by the time she made the recording, *Semiramide* was considered "old-fashioned" and rarely revived. Typical of that time, the six-minute-plus aria is cut to four minutes.

Unfortunately, her initial phrase is extremely awkward. Except for the usual faults, an odd use of a very tight "eee" vowel for "lu*sing*hier" along with extreme cuts, this is an excellent demonstration of her rapid scale work. A crudeness of attack when singing certain types of phrases is noticed. Her ornaments and her manner of singing Rossini's music harks back to earlier eras and, different from many of her contemporaries, Sembrich elects to end the first section with a sustained high A. There is an unusual use of rallentando throughout and the cabaletta, "Dolce pensiero," has some unusual ornaments. She brings it to a close with a fine trill on G leading to another final high A.

Strauss – "Ständchen" 1904

This song demonstrates a problem Sembrich has when trying to scale back her voice for simple songs. One hears her attempting to sing some phrases piano, but one also hears the muscular manipulation that prevents the voice from flowing smoothly. Only when she lets her voice out without trying to soften its volume, can you hear her true, soaring sound (as in the climactic high B-flat). She seeks to convey sensitivity, but this backfires for the most part, due to her unyielding method of vocal production.

Verdi – "Bolero" (*I Vespri Siciliani*) – 1908

Sembrich shapes and molds an uninteresting aria (except for its florid demands) into a personal expression of joy, making it quite unforgettable. There is an unusual and fascinating use of rubati. Her command of the florid measures, including trills, is better than on many of her other recordings. There is an interpretation at work here, but one wonders at the odd columnar sustaining of some notes that sound distinctly out of place in this music. Because of time restraints, the final measures of coloratura are a mess, as is the penultimate trill on G-sharp (the vibrato shifts in and out of focus). Even so, this is very interesting singing.

Verdi – "Ernani Involami" (*Ernani*) 1906, 1908

The 1908 record (like the *Semiramide* aria, "Bel raggio") begins tremulously. Some surprises occur, including an unusual use of rubati and the ornamenting of Verdi's flourish at the beginning of the cabaletta (which is rather nice). Heavily cut, we find the soprano dipping coarsely into the lower register and some of the music is a bit awkward. At the end she offers another unstable trill, this time on A, going to a good B-flat. The trill finds her throat muscles trying to interfere with her production.

The 1906 recording is more enjoyable and her ornaments speak better. Her finish of the cavatina, "Ernani involami" with its interpolated high B-flat is a minor tradition at the time and very successful; the top of the voice seems firmer than it would be two years later. Both the ending and Sembrich's vocal abandon are quite exciting. Sembrich demonstrates the subtle art of "gracing" (ornamental improvisation), adding various turns and mordents that "sweeten" Verdi's line. This tradition was dying out by this time, although Luisa Tetrazzini, Fernando De Lucia, and Mattia Battistini (and others) still incorporated it into their work.

Verdi – "Caro nome" (Rigoletto) 1906

This 1906 "Caro nome" begins quite vulgarly with a straight-tone "Caro nome" followed by so little use of correct portamento that one is left with a very unpleasant response. Portamenti are replaced by unattractive swoops and solid, chunky notes. The cadenza has dropped notes, an awkward climbing of the scale, and a trill that does not form easily. Not one of her better efforts. I also do not like the (very abbreviated) "Tutte le feste" and following duet with Mario Sammarco. Both singers sing with unyielding stolidity in an unattractive straight tone manner. Sembrich's voice often becomes raspy in her attempt to be dramatic within the lower register.

Verdi – "Ah Fors'è lui...sempre libera" (*La traviata*) 1904, 1908

This is one of Sembrich's most famous roles, but one immediately notices an unstable sustaining of the high A-flats. Her sense of the text is excellent though, and her projection of the various moods is very clear. "A quell'amor ch'è palpito" is excellent in its soaring intensity. A lightening of "mysterioso" and a thrust on "Croce" are both apt. There is an unusual cadenza that I am sure is of Sembrich's making, and a trill that finishes the first half.

This is one of her most satisfactory records. Unbelievably, "Ah Fors'è lui" takes only two minutes and forty-four seconds to present to the listener.

The "Sempre libera" has solid lower trills and the middle C speaks quite well. The sustained high C is not as good. The ending roulades are done with abandon and excitement and the finish on a final high A-flat is quite good. This record can be listened to many times.

A 1904 piano-accompanied "Ah! Fors'e Lui…Sempre libera" has the soprano dropping both text and notes in a careless manner while adding ornaments and somewhat altering Verdi's vocal line. As is often the case with Sembrich recordings, the trill on G is good, but the approach is coarse.

Conclusion

Despite blemishes, the Sembrich legacy is worthy not only of serious study, but it is also entertaining and mostly enjoyable. This is especially true of some of her recordings of the songs of Schumann, Schubert, Brahms, Arne, Hahn, and Chopin. Sembrich accompanies herself on two of the Chopin songs proving that reports of her pianistic abilities were not just publicity hype. (Unfortunately, no recordings exist of her violin playing.) In addition to the arias and songs that I have detailed, another of my song favorites is her simple (if a bit stiff) rendition of Schumann's "Der Nussbaum." Another most impressive track is Arditi's "Parla Waltz" (Sembrich's signature tune) that boasts not only an excellent sense of moving rhythm, a fresh, clean timbre, a charming, unapologetically bravura delivery, but, also, a telling high D at its conclusion. With about ninety tracks available of this singer, I have only touched on a handful.

Typical of the Romophone series, and what sets it apart from the other labels (except Marston), is the inclusion of unpublished sides and alternate takes. Between the two Romophone Sembrich volumes there are seven unpublished sides and various additional takes: three versions of the act I *La traviata* scena (one unpublished), two versions of the "Voices of Spring" Waltz, Chopin's "Zyczenie" (The Maiden's Wish), Alabiev's "Nightingale," "The Last Rose of Summer," and the "Jewel Song" from Faust (in Italian and French) and others. The alternate takes demonstrate that Sembrich took her art seriously and was obviously concerned about the product she offered to the public. That does not take into account nineteen unpublished disks from 1919 or the Mapelson cylinders. All these sides are important since they not only provide us with the opportunity for direct comparison, but offer an even fuller portrait of the artist at work.

Although Sembrich could be stiff dramatically, she displayed a tremendous verve for cascades of brilliant, often inventive fioriture. This sense of vocal abandon, combined with her vibrant, fresh-sounding voice, are the two main factors that repeatedly bring the listener back to her recordings.

Despite my analytical nit-picking, there is much to enjoy and admire in the Sembrich legacy. I remember my wonder at her ornaments and manner of singing the first time I heard her sing such arias as "Una voce poco fa" from *Il barbiere di Siviglia* and the "Bel raggio" from *Semiramide*. Few listeners will listen as critically as

I had to in creating this appreciation. And that is as it should be. My job is to point out both the good and the bad and although there are problems or issues about a singer's legacy, this does not mean that it is not important or valuable. Through her training and the recordings that she has left posterity, Marcella Sembrich remains an important link to the generation of singers and artists who came before.

(An abbreviated version of this first appeared as a review in *The Record Collector,* December, 1997)

Luisa Tetrazzini (1871–1940)

Secrets of Coloratura: The Art of Luisa Tetrazzini

Born in Florence, on June 29, 1871, this artist first studied voice under her sister, Eva Tetrazzini-Campanini, a successful opera singer. Later, she studied with professor Ceccherini at the Liceo Musicale in Florence. In 1892, at the age of 21, she made her operatic debut in Florence as Inez in Meyerbeer's *L'Africaine.* Her rise to stardom was slow. After many performances in smaller Italian opera houses, she toured South America in 1898 and performed in San Francisco in 1903.

Her first great success was her debut at Covent Garden on November 2, 1907 as Violetta in *La traviata.* She was thirty-six years old. She earned twenty curtain calls from a half-full house (as it was off-season). The newspaper reviews the next day insured that that would never happen again. She sang nine more performances that season. From 1908 to 1912 she sang every summer season at Covent Garden, performing such roles as Lakmé, Rosina, Violetta, Amina, Lucia, Leila and Gilda. From that time on, her success was assured and she appeared with great acclaim in most of the musical centers of the world.

In January, 1908, she made her New York debut, again as Violetta, with Oscar Hammerstein's Manhattan Opera Company. She sang with that company until it became defunct in 1910. With Mary Garden, she was one of Oscar Hammerstein's greatest attractions, drawing a full house whenever she appeared. Her roles included Dinorah, Lucia, Marie (*La fille du regiment*) Elvira (*I puritani*), Anetta (*Crispino e la Comare*) and Gilda (*Rigoletto*). On December 27, 1911, she made her Metropolitan Opera debut as Lucia di Lammermoor. She sang only eight performances during a single season with the Met. All performances were sold out. More than 2,000 people were turned away from the box office for her final performance as Gilda (*Rigoletto*).

Although she married three times, Tetrazzini was unlucky in her choice of men. During her thirty-two-year career, Tetrazzini earned more than five million dollars. Unfortunately, most of it was lost in unwise investments attributable to her trusting nature. During her career, she appeared in Russia, Mexico, Spain, Italy, North America, South America, Vienna, and England, gathering much success until her retirement in 1934, when she taught voice in Rome and Milan, making occasional appearances in order to earn money. Her most famous pupil was Lina Pagliughi, whom Tetrazzini considered her protégé. She died in Milan, on April 28, 1940, of a cerebral hemorrhage. She was sixty-nine years old.

In 1921 she wrote her memoirs, *My Life of Song* (with the help of Fred Gaisberg). *How to Sing* came in 1923, and, in 1924, she published a treatise called *The Art of Singing*, which, along with a similar one by Enrico Caruso, has been reprinted by Dover publications. Concise but astute, it demonstrates her abilities as an author and educator.

Critics and Admirers

In the pantheon of famous coloratura sopranos who have committed their art to disks, Luisa Tetrazzini is unique. Her florid technique was governed by a strong, active imagination and an exuberant, rhythmically potent delivery. She sang coloratura with the grace of a florid specialist and the natural thrust of a dramatic soprano. Chronologically, Tetrazzini fits neatly between Nellie Melba (who was in her decline) and Amelita Galli-Curci (who made her operatic debut in 1916). After the placidity of Melba's perfected coloratura, Tetrazzini's vibrant, almost reckless abandon was like a shot in the arm. Coupled with her charming personality and naivete she quickly endeared herself to the hearts of audiences wherever she sang. She was an irresistible performer.

As Edward C. Moore wrote:

> ...she came and laid everyone low. With the most disdainful ease she made the art of coloratura to glow as it never has since. Physical illusion was not in her line at all; she was the size of three or four Maggie Teytes. But what a voice. Even after all these years one can recall the warm reediness of its qualities, the joyous certainty with which it swooped into all the cascades and fireworks of coloratura display, the piercing intensity which somehow or other never became shrill. (*Forty Years of Opera in Chicago*, New York, 1930)

At the time, critics spent gallons of ink describing this coloratura's allure and criticizing her faults. John Pitts Sanborn, an eminent critic, wrote several descriptive articles about Tetrazzini around 1912. He notes that when she first sang with the Manhattan Opera Company:

> ...she was chiefly admirable for her extraordinary upper octave. In it the tones were perfectly produced, pure, dazzling in their flame-like play of color. When she sang a thing like the Carneval of Venice variations, her staccati, her chromatic runs, her echo effects, her swelling and diminishing of a tone, the ravishing curve of her portamento showed a vocal

virtuoso in that excelled region without a peer. The feats of Sembrich and Melba paled in comparison. After a year's absence she returned to sing in concert. Then the voice was almost perfectly equalized, a glorious organ from top to bottom. Even in the lowest register she was ready with a firm rich tone as in 'Voi che sapete' (Nozze di Figaro). She not only sang great florid arias with perfect command of voice, technique and style, she sang Aida's 'Ritorna vincitor' as scarcely a dramatic soprano has sung it here; she sang Solveig's song from Peer Gynt like a true lieder singer and the page's song from Figaro with an adorable Mozartean simplicity. (*Liner Notes* from ASCO A-109, *Luisa Tetrazzini*)

It was not a perfect voice, however, and most criticism centered around the disparity between her upper and lower registers. Indeed, it was her lower register that elicited the most controversy. The famous critic W. J. Henderson wrote an in-depth review, not only of her voice, but also her use of it when she made her debut with the Manhattan Opera Company on January 16, 1908. Although it is long, because of its excellence I quote a large portion of that review:

Mme. Tetrazzini has a fresh, clear voice of pure soprano quality and of sufficient range, though other roles must perhaps disclose its furthest flights above the staff. The perfectly unworn condition and youthful timbre of this voice are its largest charms, and to those must be added a splendid richness in the upper range. Indeed, the best part of the voice as heard last evening was from the G above the staff to the high C. The B flat in 'Sempre libera' was a tone of which any singer might have been proud. The high D in the same number was by no means so good, and the high E flat which the singer took in ending the scene was a head tone of thin quality and refused to stay on the pitch.

In coloratura Mme. Tetrazzini quite justified much that had been written about her. She sang staccato with consummate ease, though not with the approved method of breathing. Her method is merely to check the flow between tones instead of lightly attacking each note separately. But the effect which she produces, that of detached notes rather than strict staccato, is charming. Of her shake less can be said in praise. It was neither clear in emission nor steady, and the interval was surely at least open to question.

Descending scales she sang beautifully, with perfect smoothness and clean articulation. Her transformation of the plain scale in the opening cadenza of 'Sempre libera' into a chromatic scale, though a departure from the letter of the score, was not at all out of taste, and its execution fully sustained its right to existence.

The ascending scales in the same number were sung in a manner which would not be tolerated by any reputable teacher in a pupil of a year's standing. They began with a tremulous and throaty voce bianca and ended in a sweep into a full medium, with the chest resonance carried up to a preposterous height.

The most notable shortcoming of Mme. Tetrazzini's singing as revealed last night was her extraordinary emission of her lower medium notes. These were all sung with a pinched glottis and with a color so pallid and a tremolo so pronounced that they were often not a bad imitation of the wailing of a cross infant. This style of tone production she carried into most of her recitative, til she seemed to be inclined to think that Violetta ought to show that fondness for 'baby talk' which is sometimes accepted as a charm among her kind.

In cantilena the new soprano fell furthest below the demands of supreme vocal art. Her cantabile was uneven in tone quality, the breaks between her medium and and her upper notes coming out most unpleasantly and her tricks of phrasing in short and spasmodic groups, with breath taken capriciously and without consideration of either text or music, were serious blots upon her delivery. For example, in beginning 'Ah fors e lui,' she deliberately made a phrase after the u, and, taking a leisurely breath, introduced the i as if it belonged to the next word.

The continued employment of cold color in cantabile quite removed the possibility of pathos from 'Non sapete,' while a pitiless description of her infantile delivery of 'Dite alla giovane' would read like cruelty... (*The Art of Singing*, The Dial Press, NY, 1938.)

The famous Irish tenor, John McCormack, felt that the weakness of Tetrazzini's middle and bottom registers was the result of overwork and uncongenial repertory in her youth. Michael Scott, and others, maintain that during the early years of her career Tetrazzini sang such out-of-fach roles as Fidelia in Puccini's *Edgar*, Musetta in *La bohéme*, Leonora in *La forza del destino*, and *Aïda* (in Mexico she reputedly ended the Triumphal Scene with a top E-flat.) Although I feel that this last should be taken with a grain of salt, Tetrazzini, herself, claims that she performed *Aïda* many times: "... I was invariably successful (as) Aida. I have sung this famous work many hundreds of times." (*My Life of Song*, Cassell, London, 1921)

I find no mention of such heavy roles in the excellent chronology of Tetrazzini's appearances in Charles Neilson Gattey's acclaimed biography, *Luisa Tetrazzini, The Florentine Nightingale*, (Amadeus Press, Portland, Oregon, 1995), or in the list of her operatic repertoire compiled by Charles Neilson Gattey and Thomas G. Kaufman. The only roles like this that do appear are Musetta (*La bohème*) which she only sang occasionally, and Micaela (*Carmen*) which she sang many times during her career. It is entirely possible, however, that she sang arias from such dramatic works in concert as she often programmed Santuzza's "Voi lo sapete" from *Cavalleria rusticana* but she never performed that role on stage.

Other critics felt that the disparity between her registers was simply a matter of late maturing. This is supported by her unpublished recordings, made in the 1920s, when the lower registers seem to better blend into the rest of the voice and are darker and firmer. This is often the case with higher voices, the lower reaches are the last to develop. Part of this is due to training and a concentration on the quality of the top register, and part of it is just the process of the natural growth of the vocal apparatus.

The Voce Bianca

I suspect that all of the above probably played a part in her register inequalities as did the fact that the soprano was fond of using voce bianca, the white voice, in much of her middle and lower register singing to help depict youth, madness, childishness, illness, and so forth. During this era, this was an Italian vocal method used by high sopranos as an interpretive device. While not the only one of her generation to use this method, she often used it ad nauseam and its use would strip the natural richness from her lower register.

Tetrazzini defended her use of this method:

This is a voice production where a head resonance alone is employed, without sufficient of the apoggio or enough of the mouth resonance to give the tone a vital quality. This 'white voice' should be thoroughly understood and is one of the many shades of tone that a singer can use at times, just as the impressionist uses various unusual colors to produce certain atmospheric effects. For instance, in the Mad scene in Lucia the use of the white voice suggest the babbling of the mad woman, as the same voice in the last act of Traviata or in the last act of Boheme suggest utter physical exhaustion and the approach of death. (*The Art of Singing*, The Metropolitan Company Publishers, New York, 1909)

In his excellent notes for the EMI Tetrazzini London Recordings release, Michael Aspinall explains further:

Italians call this sound 'bamboleggiante' (doll-like), and it can be found in recordings of Tetrazzini's contemporaries Regina Pacini, Regina Pinkert, Isabela Svicher, Maria Galvany, Rosina Storchio and Josefina Huguet. From the next generation, even so lovely a singer as Amelita Galli-Curci has more than a hint of the doll; others, like Mercedes Capsir, Elvira de Hidalgo or Nunu Sanchioni, are painfully shrill... The fashion seems to have completely died out in Italy since the war, though Renata Scotto occasionally reminds one of the 'child' school...

Even Maria Callas, in some of her portrayals (*La sonnambula*, *La traviata*, and *Lucia di Lammermoor*, for example) resorts to a variation of the voce bianca to help promote the illusion of illness, youth, or madness in her characterizations.

Tetrazzini is different from the others because she uses this method only in her lower registers. The rest of the voice is produced with a healthy ring and often golden lushness. On recordings, at least for the modern listener, this creates some startling contrasts. Once one becomes accustomed to the sound of this method and understands what Tetrazzini is doing, her effects become clear. It is then one notices that, contrary to belief, her low register is not weak at all, but solid and quite strong. It is true that she occasionally pinches (or squeezes) her tone when in that area, but, generally, it is her use of voce bianca that gives the false impression of a weak lower register.

Florid Technique, Vocal Poise and "Gracing"

All of her many florid recordings reflect the happy, almost child-like quality that seems to have been so much a part of Tetrazzini's nature. It is this youthful excitement in her singing, evident even in her later years, that attracts the listener. Also contributory is her uncommon poise when delivering impossibly intricate fioriture. On no other records can you find such joyous, full-throated abandon in the midst of cadenzas and intricate ornamentation. Indeed, she seems to relish their challenge. This sense of enjoyment is such that one almost envisions her smile of delight as she moves full force into cadenzas and fioriture. Undoubtedly, one of the reasons for this is that her technical basis is so solid and secure. This may have been attributable to her slow rise to stardom and her many years honing her craft in the provinces. Those important, formative years solidified her technique so that nothing could throw this soprano, allowing her to grow into a vocal virtuoso of the first order.

Tetrazzini's memory was excellent. Most of her roles were learned when she was very young, hammered into her head by a répétiteur because, we are told, she could not read music. They were never forgotten. Not only that, but Tetrazzini's knowledge of ornamental patterns, cadential formulae and variational possibilities was as extensive as her inventiveness in putting them to use. During her early years of touring she would study with any Italian teacher she found, soaking up information and cadenzi. She had even compiled a small booklet of cadenzas and ornaments during her travels in Spain, Russia, Poland and South America. She always kept the book with her. Being immersed and comfortable in the art of ornamentation, she soon found the kinds of embellishments that best suited her voice.

She was an instinctive performer and her art was based on that intangible rather than study and a well-rounded education of vocal method and style. Because of this, improvising was of paramount importance in Tetrazzini's work, lending an air of individuality to everything she sang.

A fascinating glimpse of this (one of the few I have come across) is from a review of a concert Tetrazzini gave at the Coliseum in Saint Louis, Missouri on February 6, 1920. The concert included:

Thomas: "Mad Scene" (*Hamlet*)
Eckert: "Swiss Echo Song"
Tate: "Somewhere a Voice is Calling"
Tosti: "L'Ultima Canzone"
Benedict: "Carnival of Venice Variations"
Haydn-Woods: "Bird of Love Divine"

According to the critic in the Globe-Democrat (February 7, 1920) some variations in the Carnival of Venice were especially spontaneous:

> It seemed that Tetrazzini at one time during the rendition was improvising and roulading and trilling ad libitum; for pianist Cimarra kept gazing at the diva over the note rack, moving his head to and fro as if trying to improvise an accompaniment.

In her autobiography, Frieda Hempel considered this ability as one of the things that she most admired about Luisa Tetrazzini's art:

> I considered her way of singing magnificent, and I admired her art above that of Sembrich and Melba... Her elegance in singing, her dashing way of composing new cadenzas on the spur of the moment on the concert stage, her absolutely perfect breath control, her brilliant coloratura fireworks, and her magnificent high tones were all part of her consummate artistry. (*Mein Leben dem Gesang,* Argon Verlag, GmbH, Berlin, 1955),

It is clear from Tetrazzini's recordings that her phrase ornaments, grace notes, mordents and triplets, were improvised at her whim. Part of this ability was due to her complete immersion in the "old" tradition of ornamental improvisation or "gracing" as it was known at the time. It is a form of personalized interpretation typified by Mattia Battistini, Fernando de Lucia, and Adelina Patti—a style of singing in which the singer adds various ornaments to a vocal line. It is an interpretive art based on the flow, direction, and harmonics of the musical phrase, rather than the content of the text and is used to add grace and elegance to the musical line. An example of this personalization can be heard in Lillian Nordica's 1906 recording of "Tacea la notte placida" from *Il trovatore*. Her ornamentation (or "flowering") was originally used by the Hungarian soprano, Teresa Tietjens (1831–1877), and was given to Nordica by the famous critic, Herman Klein.

Tetrazzini was an instinctive performer.

Although a simplistic explanation, there are two types of singers: the analytical and the instinctive. The analytical singer is very precise in the approach to music, preferring to dissect it almost mathematically, so, for example, that they understand exactly where to put the "i" of "lui" when confronted with two eighth notes. Nellie Melba, Joan Sutherland, Elisabeth Schwarzkopf and Dietrich Fischer-Dieskau are examples of that type. The instinctive singer (like Luisa Tetrazzini, Maria Callas, Renata Scotto, Franco Corelli and Luciano Pavarotti) approach music more emotionally. It would not occur to any of them to use such precise dissection; they simply intuit how it is to be done. This does not suggest that one type of singer is better or more musical than the other; there are good and bad points to either—they just approach music in different ways.

But, of the two, it is only the instinctive singer who can improvise ornaments on the spur of the moment. (There are, of course, always exceptions.) This ability comes not only from the knowledge of ornamental patterns, but an inherent sense of where and how they can be used within a vocal phrase.

What makes this so complicated is that there is no road map for how this is to be accomplished. Certainly, a knowledge of ornamentation is crucial, but doing it springs from innate instinct. It comes from the singer's sense of the structure of the ornament itself and the ornamental possibilities of a phrase, which may change depending on their mood. It is a unique and completely individual personalization or "flowering" of the vocal line. Although now a style that has been mainly forgotten, at one time singers were comprehensively trained in this tradition and composers expected this style to be "layered" onto their music.

Purists will argue that such modifications of the original vocal line distorts a composer's intention, but that is a view evolved from many decades of (often misunderstood) concepts of what is, or should be, *come scritto* (as written). As a trained singer, I hold the opposite view. This old tradition can (and often does) enhance, rather than detract from, the beauty of a vocal line—if one knows what one is doing. Even so, the gracing of music is a tricky, stylistic shading. It must be stated that, during her prime, few singers were as gifted as Tetrazzini in knowing how and where to ornament a vocal phrase. By the time of her apex, the tradition was already being discarded. Tetrazzini was one of the last to practice it. Some of her additions are so subtle and logical that you often do not realize that she is adding anything; unless you are following her recording closely with a score. It is then that one realizes the degree of her art. Today such improvisational additions would not be tolerated.

As Michael Scott noted in his book, *The Record of Singing, Volume I*, Charles Scribner's Sons, NY, 1977:

> ...she had developed a phenomenal florid technique and acquired a vocal poise that no passing mishap could shake. To this she added an intuitive musicianship, a feeling for the shape of a phrase, where to interpolate a trill, mordent, or high note, so as to make it sound appropriate, spontaneous and inevitable—if the composer did not put it there then he should have!"

Her unshakable vocal poise can be best heard in recordings wherein there is a slight mishap, such as the staccato note that fails to sound in the 1911 Carnival of Venice variations, or in the bell song from *Lakmé*, or the phlegmy chromatic scale in alt. that is near the finish of one of her versions of the Proch Variations. Even with such occurrences, these recordings are stunning renditions that are attributable to Tetrazzini's exhuberant, authoritative delivery. These blemishes make her virtuosic art more human than mechanical.

Not everyone loved Tetrazzini's singing. As Michael Aspinall wrote in his notes for the 1992 EMI release:

> ...Lady de Grey, the social power behind the throne at Covent Garden, said, 'Well I can't bear her. I think she sings like a dwarf in a gramophone.'"

Lady de Grey was the power behind Nellie Melba at Covent Garden so one would not expect her to be a fan of the Italian diva..

Henry Russell, the impresario who hired Tetrazzini for the Boston Opera once said, "I hired Tetrazzini but I don't have to listen to her." Toscanini disliked the virtuosic individuality that Tetrazzini represented and never conducted any of her appearances at the Metropolitan Opera.

Gerald Fitzgerald writes:

> Though beloved by the public, friends and colleagues, she was not more than tolerated by most conductors; for when Tetrazzini stepped onstage she not only sang the tune, she called the tune. What saved her, even when she misrepresented the printed score, was an innate musical sense. (A Path of Roses, *Opera News*, December 12, 1964)

Operatic colleagues, however, were a different matter. Caruso adored her. John McCormack called her his "fairy godmother" (she was primarily responsible for his engagement at the Manhattan Opera in New York). Pol Plançon, the French bass, famous for his own remarkable florid technique and trills, considered Tetrazzini a genius. Victor Maurel, who sang in the world premiere of Verdi's *Falstaff* once commented that it was her singing of an andante that impressed him the most. Adelina Patti was very fond of Tetrazzini, once writing to her and praising the soprano for her sensitivity and the moving pathos in her voice. Frieda Hempel, Tetrazzini's contemporary, and a florid star in her own right, was usually quite critical of her soprano colleagues. She loved and respected Tetrazzini.

Critics not only complained about Tetrazzini's excessive ornamentation, but her refusal to abandon a repertoire that was considered trashy and old fashioned as well. It should be noted that Nellie Melba was considered a modern singer as she sang in new works like Puccini's *La bohème*, while Tetrazzini's repertoire was no longer considered fashionable. Much the same criticism was leveled against Amelita Galli-Curci.

Tetrazzini was one of the first Italian-born sopranos to specialize in coloratura repertoire and it was this decision to specialize that was so criticized.

Tetrazzini replied:

> People blame me sometimes...for confining myself mainly to music of a certain school. But I think I know best as to this and that I am exercising sound judgment in adopting this course. There is music which I admire and love, but I do not always try and sing it. In the same way I may admire frocks which I see on other women, but I do not necessarily try to wear them myself. I have the good sense to recognize that they would not suit me. (*How to Sing*, C. Arthur Pearson, London, 1923)

Luisa Tetrazzini on Stage

Ivor Newton, who played for many of Tetrazzini's recitals gives a fascinating description of her preparation for a recital:

> In the artists' room, before the concert began, she would try out her high D flat. If she found the note immediately and without strain, she would turn happily and say, 'It's there, there's nothing to worry about.'" (*At the Piano*, Hamish Hamilton, London, 1966)

In addition to the glory of her top register and vocal acrobatics, it was this natural, child-like quality of Tetrazzini's personality that audiences found so endearing. Quaintance Eaton describes Tetrazzini's typical interaction with audiences:

> As Vladimir de Pachmann remained almost the sole survivor of a vanishing race of pianists in the grand manner, so Tetrazzini seemed to perpetuate the ancient line of divas who are a law unto themselves. Even Melba had kept within the framework of an opera's story, maintaining her dignity and that of the theatre. Younger coloraturas, like Frieda Hempel and Selma Kurz, chose to follow new ways, but Tetrazzini innocently and honestly hewed to the old ones. Listeners expected her to curtsey and smile, wave her arms in embracing gestures, and kiss her hand to the audience before setting about Lucia's melancholy and mellifluous soliloquy. At a curtain call within memory, she had tossed a flower to the conductor and cried 'Thank you! Thank You!' in an ecstatically childish voice. (*The Boston Opera Company*, Appleton-Century, NY, 1965)

Opera performances with Tetrazzini were usually interrupted by applause so lengthy that an aria had to be repeated. She often had to repeat theme and variation pieces she would insert into the lesson scene of Rossini's *Il barbiere di Sivigila*, the "Caro nome" in *Rigoletto,* and the cadenza in the mad scene from *Lucia di Lammermoor*.

Naturally, there are drawbacks to such willful behavior. For example:

> In the most heartbreaking moment of Traviata, a spectator detected her in an open and flagrant wink at an acquaintance in the wings. (*The Boston Opera Company*, Appleton-Century, NY, 1965)

She was famous for her entrances in concert programs, bouncing, almost running, to the piano, throwing kisses to the audience and then, when she was ready to begin, signaling the accompanist by tossing her long strand of pearls over her shoulder. Understandably, audiences adored the buxom soprano's open friendliness—her obvious joy in being there with them. It was almost as if she was a personal friend.

One chef admired her so much that he created "Chicken Tetrazzini," a chicken dish prepared with mushrooms, pasta, and a white sauce seasoned with sherry, served au gratin, a baked dish still a favorite today. Although its exact origin is not known, it is generally accepted that the dish originated in Tetrazzini's favorite American city, San Francisco.

A 1920 review is particularly colorful in describing Tetrazzini's stage behavior:

> Luisa Tetrazzini, the world's foremost coloratura soprano threw kisses to some 5,000 admirers at the Coliseum last night, when she came upon the platform, sang five stated numbers and three encores and at the close of her performance received an ovation really without precedent.

> It is but fair to say that the diva cast a spell over the throng by a personal pageantry down the center aisle, and during her royal progress kissing her gloved hands right and left, impartially to parquet, balcony and gallery. Retracing her steps at the end of the long lane she imprinted resounding smacks on several of the women and thus wrought a state of ecstacy the like of which is not recallable by seasoned concertgoers. (St. Louis, Missouri, Globe-Democrat, February 7, 1920)

What spared such behavior from becoming merely self-serving or obnoxious was her obviously sincere desire to please. Her behavior, although seeming tacky to us today, was simply a reflection of the joy she felt in doing what she was doing. Tetrazzini loved her work and it was that pure, unreserved, almost childish excitement that shone out upon the audience and drew them to her.

This is supported by Ivor Newton's observation:

> ...(she) would cross herself before making her entrance and then set off for the stage at a brisk run, arriving before the audience breathless and panting. Invariably the audience had overflowed on to the platform, and Tetrazzini, struggling to regain her breath, would walk around the semi-circle they made and greet them warmly, shaking hands with some of them and kissing any very young child who might be there. Her friendliness and warmth—she not only enjoyed but reciprocated the affection of her public—would bring the entire hall to a state of excitement before she had sung a note. There was never any sense of insincerity about these effusive ceremonies; she was behaving with complete naturalness. (*At the Piano*, Hamish Hamilton, London, 1966)

Tetrazzini was an adept entertainer as well as an artist. She loved to show off and knew what to do to elicit the greatest applause from her audiences. For instance, when she sang Violetta at the Manhattan Opera in New York, John Fredrick Cone described the theatrical (and clever) stage business she used to finish the famous "Sempre libera." At the end of the aria she interpolated a traditional, penultimate high E-flat and while:

> ...singing that magnificent note, Tetrazzini bent to gather up the long train of her gown and proceeded to walk off the stage, all the while affecting the utmost insouciance and all the while holding on to that phenomenal E-flat til she had disappeared from view. This tour de force brought the house down. (John F. Cone, *Oscar Hammerstein's Manhattan Opera Company*, University of Oklahoma Press, 1964)

All of this sounds provincially quaint (and quite unprofessional) to us today, but an illuminating glimpse into the core of who Tetrazzini was can be seen in a film clip found in *The Art of Singing* (Golden Voices of the Century), an NVC Arts video. The black and white clip lasts only one minute and was made during Tetrazzini's visit to the HMV shop in Oxford Street, in London, on December 9, 1932. It shows Tetrazzini sitting next to a large Victrola in a fur coat and hat, a black dress, and a long strand of pearls, listening to a 78 rpm recording of Enrico Caruso singing "M'appari" from Flotow's *Martha*. Old and obese, the diva nostalgically listens, then sings, along with the recording, the end of the aria (with its high B-flat) in a voice still solid and imposing. In the next few seconds of the clip she breaks into a spontaneous peal of infectious, charming, and girlish laughter. It is an endearing moment that provides rare insight into the cheerful, giving, and youthful nature so obviously a part of this extraordinary woman and her art.

This is made all the more moving when one recalls that things were not always happy for the Italian soprano:

> ...beside the peaks of glory, her long career contained dark and tragic hours. She was well over thirty before she finally overcame the poverty of her early struggles and poverty returned after the decades of triumph, when she was cheated of their fruits by a young lover—how often, incidentally, this almost pathological trait features in the lives of prima donnas. She attended spiritualist séances as an escape from the bitter reality of her existence. (Kurt Pahlen, *Great Singers from the 17th century to the present day*, translated by Oliver Coburn, Stein and Day, New York, 1974)

The Art of Being Divatic

Like many illustrious predecessors, Tetrazzini was a diva in that she possessed a strikingly individual personality. Hers was an earthy personality governed by a sunny disposition and a seemingly unquenchable belief in her fellow man despite personal disappointments. Frieda Hempel, who spent much time with Tetrazzini in her declining years commented:

> [She] was the most generous person alive and always in a good humor. What was her humor like? Childlike, refreshing, very innocent. She never grew old... She would call me Fridolina. When she wrote to me she would put on the envelope, 'La Mia Cara Amica, Frieda Hempel, New York.' She was heart, heart, nothing but heart. I cried when I heard she was living in poverty... She never gambled, never squandered her money. But she had an open hand for everybody, and of course, people took advantage of her." (Obituary by John Pitts Sanborn, 1940)

Typical of a strong personality, however, Tetrazzini was often led by her own caprice, vocally as well as personally. When she admired someone she made it known. Hempel recalls Tetrazzini enthusing over her predecessor, Adelina Patti:

> I shall never forget her admiration for Patti. She wouldn't rave about Patti's high notes and stunts others did. No. She once told me how she heard Patti sing 'Pur dicesti.' 'You should have heard her trill in the medium range,' she said. 'It was sublime. I fell down on my knees and kissed Patti's hand. It was so perfect and artistic.' (Obituary by John Pitts Sanborn, 1940)

However, when Tetrazzini disliked someone, she could be both unforgiving and brutally outspoken. An anecdote tells of a time during which both Melba and Tetrazzini occupied suites on the same floor of a famous London hotel. Melba complained to the management that Tetrazzini's vocalizing disturbed her rest. Tetrazzini got wind of the complaint and, while walking down the hotel corridor with a member of the staff, she heard Melba vocalizing. Tetrazzini turned to her companion, "and with a mischievous glint in her eyes, said, 'Ah, so you have cats in zee 'otel!'" (Caesari Herbert, *The Alchemy of Voice*, London, 1965)

Melba often aimed private barbs at Tetrazzini. During dinner parties the "tomboy element in the Australian diva's personality led her to get down on all fours and impersonate the unfortunate horse destined to carry the bulky soprano in Les Huguenots." (Michael Aspinall, Liner Notes for EMI Melba album)

Tetrazzini held negative opinions of other singers as well. In the 1920s, when her voice was in its decline, she was fiercely jealous of the then-rising Italian soprano, Toti Dal Monte. When asked about Lily Pons, the then-current favorite at the Metropolitan, she laughed robustly and replied, "picola, picola voce." She detested Melba's vibrato-less voice—"like a horn" she was heard to say.

Tetrazzini was, however, very aware of her own shortcomings. When she sang her first American Philine in *Mignon,* with the Boston Opera Company, the pants role of Frederick was sung by Jeska Swartz. Standing backstage, Tetrazzini giggled at Swartz's Frederick:

> This leetle boy is supposed to be in love with me? Like a peanut next to a mountain. (Quaintance Eaton, *The Boston Opera Company*, Appleton-Century, NY, 1965)

Even at the end of her career, when not always in the best of health or mood, she managed to keep her sense of humor. Fred Gaisberg tells of an incident in London on November 12, 1933, when Tetrazzini was to sing her Sunday afternoon farewell concert in the Albert Hall:

> I was in the Artists' room with Tetrazzini. She was in a terrible state, and although she pulled through the concert, it was pathetic. She attempted to play her old role of Prima Donna but the going was heavy. She managed nevertheless to retain her sense of humour. As she came onto the platform she brushed against one of the orchestra and apologized saying: 'I would have gone sideways—but I have no sideways!' Charles Neilson Gattey, *Luisa Tetrazzini, The Florentine Nightingale*, Amadeus Press, Portland, Oregon, 1995)

No matter her shortcomings, Tetrazzini's timing was just right. During her prime, she reigned supreme over Europe and America. As Vincent Sheean writes:

> Her supremacy in her own field was not challenged...until she retired: Marcella Sembrich made her farewell in the following season (1909) and Melba was far too wise to sing the same repertoire in the same city at the same time as Tetrazzini. Melba outlasted Tetrazzini, as she did everybody else, and there can be little doubt from the critical accounts given of the two that Melba had the lovelier voice and the more exquisite control, but I have a fairly good idea that if I had been able to hear opera in those days I should have admired Melba, but spent my money on Tetrazzini. (*Oscar Hammerstein I*, Simon & Schuster, NY, 1956)

Luisa Tetrazzini and Recording

As has been mentioned elsewhere in this book, to fully appreciate singers from Tetrazzini's era, the listener must accept a few things. The sonics of their recordings are not what one is accustomed to today. It may take a bit of work on the part of the listener to hear through the background noise.

One must remember (and this is important) that many of her recordings were made more than one hundred years ago when stylistic and vocal priorities were different from those we hold today. Many dismiss these early recordings as the worthless vanities of indulgent singers.

78 rpm recordings are equivalent to live performances. They are free of editing and reflect a single take, start to finish, immortalizing all that occurred during that single recording session—to a fault.

In today's era of digital music, one must remember that these early recordings were not intended to be listened to in groups of twenty at a time; they were meant to be enjoyed one at a time. When Tetrazzini made her 1907 Gramophone discs of arias from *Lucia, Lakmé,* and *Dinorah,* it was not expected that selections would be listened to one after another, without a break, for an hour or more. In 1907, when one bought a record, it was usually just one, as their high cost prohibited multiple purchases by the average buyer. Thus, a recording was meant to be savored as its own entity.

Luisa Tetrazzini's recordings demonstrate her voice to have been an unusually large instrument within its upper reaches, a factor not at all common with coloratura sopranos during that era. Unfortunately, as Henderson criticized, the lower reaches did not possess an equivalent fullness, sounding anemic or underdeveloped. Different from many of her florid sisters, Tetrazzini thrust her high notes into the acoustics with rare abandon.

She was one of the first of the recorded coloratura sopranos to incorporate drama into her singing, especially in her approach to high notes. She also used understatement, as in *Dinorah* and *Lucia.* Her range was quite wide, from A below the staff to high E above. Her technical battery was unusually advanced and included an ability to sing a top E-flat pianissimo. She also did such things as a high, double messa-di-voce (a vocal feat not heard today) which became a trademark Tetrazzini effect, as well as perfectly gradated morendi.

Tetrazzini was a prodigious recording artist, recording about one hundred and twenty sides. She often recorded more than one version of an aria. Sometimes this was to replace an older recording, but usually she merely duplicated selections for each of the two branches of Gramophone (America and Europe). For instance:

Delibes: "Bell Song" (*Lakmé*), four versions: 1907, 1911 (twice), 1913
Donizetti: "O luce di quest anima" (*Linda di Chamonix*), 3 versions: 1910, 1911, 1914
Donizetti: "Mad Scene" (*Lucia di Lammermoor*), three versions: 1904, 1907, 1911
Thomas: "Polonaise" (*Mignon*), four versions: 1907, 1908 (unpublished), 1911 (twice)
Rossini: "Una voce poco fa" (*Il barbiere di Siviglia*), three versions: 1904, 1907, 1911
Verdi: "Caro nome" (*Rigoletto*), three versions: 1904, 1907, 1911
Verdi: "Sempre libera" (*La traviata*), three versions: 1907, 1911 (twice)

She also made two versions of many of the arias in her repertoire, including:

Bellini: "Ah non credea" (*La sonnambula*) 1909, 1911
Bellini: "Ah non giunge" (*La sonnambula*) 1904, 1911
Benedict: Carnival of Venice Variations 1909, 1911
Bizet: Micaela's Aria (*Carmen*) 1910, 1914
David: "Charmant Oiseau" (*La perle du Brésil*) 1911 (twice)
Meyerbeer: Shadow Song (*Dinorah*) 1907, 1914
Proch: Theme and Variations 1911 (twice)
Venzano: Waltz 1911 (twice)
Verdi: "Saper voreste" (*Un ballo in maschera*) 1909, 1911

Despite what one might expect, when Tetrazzini re-recorded an aria it is not always the newer version that is to be preferred. It varies. Sometimes it is a tie. For instance, in regard to Lakmé's Bell Song, the first (1907) version out-ranks the other three recordings. In the case of Bellini's "Ah non credea" from *La sonnambula* it is a tie between the two versions. With Rosina's "Una voce poco fa," however, it is the last (1911) USA recording that best exhibits the humor and brilliance she brings to the aria. Philine's polonaise is a tie between the first (1907) disk and the last (1911) recording. All of Tetrazzini's recordings are interesting and do much to explain the kind of artist and person that she was. Her earlier recordings, made in London between 1907 and 1910, show the exceptional brilliance of her voice and attack, while recordings made after that show vocal changes attributable to aging, and vocal mannerisms that she came to rely on (such as the use of a straight, laser-like tone that will be explored later).

Tetrazzini's recording career can be broken into three segments:

Five arias made for the American Zonophone company (Universal Talking Machine Company of New York) (1904)

The London Gramophone series (HMV) (1907–1922)
The American RCA Victor series (1911–1920)

When one reviews the years during which Tetrazzini made recordings, one might wonder at the break in activity between 1914 and 1920. This was due to World War I (1914–1918), that also terminated her stage career. Tetrazzini stopped touring and recording to settle in Italy for the duration. By the time she returned to the studios in 1920, her international career had (understandably) begun to wind down and her recording activities eventually dissolved.

CD Collections

Throughout the LP decades (1950–1980) numerous collections of Luisa Tetrazzini were made. These came not only from mainstream labels such as RCA Victor and EMI (especially an elegantly produced COLH [136] release of selected London recordings), but some of the smaller, independent labels such as Club "99", Scala, Court Opera Classics, Top Artists Platter, Voce, Rococo, Pearl (which issued the first "complete" Tetrazzini collection), ASCO, I.R.C.C., and U.O.R.C., as well.

In 1989, the enterprising firm, Pearl, took a leap and released the first complete set of Tetrazzini recordings in a boxed set of five CDs (9220). (Originally, Pearl released the recordings as an 8-LP boxed set in 1981.) At that time, this was a delightful surprise for collectors. Included in the set were a number of unpublished items. (Recent scholarship has unearthed more unpublished discs.) Pearl's example was followed by EMI, who, in 1992, released a complete set of her London recordings (three CDs – CHS 7638022) that included all sixty-two recordings Tetrazzini made for Gramophone, fifty-three of them between 1907 and 1914, and nine in 1922. Sixteen sides offered on the EMI set had never been issued on 78s and seven sides remained unpublished until the 1992 release, superbly restored by one of the masters, Keith Hardwick.

Nimbus got into the game by offering two volumes (1992, 1998) in their Prima Voce series transcribing original 78s recorded with their digital ambisonic technique (7808, 7891). Finally, in 1997, Romophone released the complete American Victor recordings (1911–1920 on two CDs – 81025).

The EMI three-disc set of her London Recordings continues to be found in some second-hand record shops, such as Academy Records in New York City, and also on line. This is an excellent set and preserves some of the soprano's freshest, dynamic singing. It was also one of EMI's finest issues devoted to an historical singer. Not only are the recordings presented with great sonic elegance, the accompanying booklet contains excellent, erudite articles by Michael Aspinall, and also the texts of the songs. It was a deluxe treatment befitting the singer it was meant to honor.

The Nimbus volumes are available on Amazon.com and the Nimbus website, although Nimbus ceased producing their "Prima Voce" series years ago.

Romophone went out of business in 2003, after sixty-four releases and a decade of providing listeners with some of the most important integral collections of historical singers ever to be produced by a single recording firm.

As to which of the collections one should look for to purchase, that depends on your sonic preferences.

I find the EMI set to be well restored and an easy listen. Most critics seem to agree, including Alan Blyth.

In a review for *Gramophone* in September, 1992, J. B. Steane points out that he feels most listeners will prefer the EMI set.

> The Pearl transfers have their merits, but they are likely to appeal primarily to those who are already well-practiced in listening to 78s....

He continues:

> ...a more impressive and readily enjoyable Tetrazzini is found on EMI and Nimbus. Of course those two have to be differentiated: at the very name of Nimbus heat rises in some quarters, 'top-cut' and added reverberation being well-known subjects of complaint. It is not possible to make direct comparisons, as EMI take the HMV records, Nimbus the Victor, but I have just now (in mid-sentence) played the two versions of "Una voce poco fa" and have greatly enjoyed both. The one in no way contradicts the other as far as perception of the voice is concerned, and though with the EMI I seem to be physically closer to the singer, with the Nimbus I have changed seats, gone (as it were) to another part of the opera house, hearing differently but essentially the same, and I enjoy both."

Depending on my mood, at certain times, I favor the Nimbus Tetrazzini releases over other editions. One reason is that they give an idea (even if this is illusory) of what Tetrazzini's voice might have sounded like in an operatic theatre or concert hall, the voice bouncing off the wood walls. With Tettrazzini, this would be a fascinating aural impression to experience. The Nimbus technique tends to shear off the hard brilliance of Tetrazzini's upper register in some of her 1911 and later recordings. In addition, in such pieces as the virtuosic Proch Variations, one gets a very good idea of the power of her upper register at the conclusion of the Nimbus pressing.

That Intangible Something

A final consideration. When one listens to Tetrazzini's recordings a question may arise about her phenomenal popularity. One can tell from her recordings that she has a splendid coloratura technique and a potent personality, but there are issues in the lower register and other problems that one easily discerns. There must have been something else that appealed.

Indeed, it would appear that there are qualities of this soprano's art that were completely eluded by the recording process of the time.

At the time of her debut as Violetta at Covent Garden (1907), the critic of the Daily Mail wrote:

...(Tetrazzini's singing offered) a human tenderness and a pathos few of us realised (*La traviata*) possessed. She has the magic gift of 'tears in the voice' and is withal a consummate actress...There were actual tears among the audience, too, on Saturday night when she sang 'Dite alla giovane' lifted out of its customary vocal display into a song of renunciation, heart-rending in its emotional intensity. Never in late years have we seen *La Traviata* acted as Tetrazzini played it on Saturday night; rarely, if ever, have we heard Verdi's music so exquisitely sung.

Strongly disagreeing with Henderson (quoted earlier), Henry Krehbiel (*New York Tribune*) felt that Tetrazzini's allure as Violetta was due to "the combination of beautiful singing as such and acting. Not acting in the sense of attitude, motion and facial expression, although these were all admirable, but in the dramatic feeling which imbued the singing—the dramatic color which shifted with kaleidoscopic swiftness from phrase to phrase, filling it with the blood of the play."

In comments for an obituary for Tetrazzini, Frieda Hempel emphasizes a quality that we, today, do not associate with this singer or her recordings, but which must have been present when heard in person:

Tetrazzini always sang in full voice, a luscious voice, full of personality and sensuality. You must have the erotic in your voice. Tetrazzini had it tremendously. (Obituary, by John Pitts Sanborn, 1940)

Singers often sound different in front of an audience than they do in a recording studio. That is easily proven by comparing the commercial and live recordings of Maria Callas. Her studio efforts were remarkable achievements, no matter what standard one wishes to apply. When in front of an audience, however, there was an electricity in her singing that can only be experienced from live recordings. Even such an elemental thing as the rate of vibrato oscillation undergoes drastic alteration. In Tetrazzini's case, it seems the difference between singing live and recording in a studio applies.

Vincent Sheean comments:

Searching for some explanation of the Tetrazzini phenomenon we find in all the newspaper writing, both in London and in New York, an element that we who have not heard her could not possibly expect. She is said to have had an 'extremely emotional voice' in the passages that permitted or called for its use. This we could never have learned from the phonograph records now accessible. From those we are able to perceive a very long breath and a remarkable high coloratura, but no emotion at all. At the actual performances in the opera house there was apparently some almost electrically emotional quality, because it is stressed again and again by quite competent reviewers...

When we see photographs of Mme Tetrazzini now, we find them a trifle ridiculous. Her weight was excessive by our standards, and seems worse because it was so obviously encased in rigid armor. That a woman with such an appearance could have been actress, and could with her acting and her voice reduce an audience to tears is hard for us to believe. And yet the evidence is all there, many columns of it in the New York press of the time, providing a least a psychological basis for the unreasoning mania with which her appearances were attended.

What she did as a coloratura we know—that is fully shown by the public prints—and it was remarkable enough, although we can understand it technically. She had absolute control of runs, trills, staccati, and every other ornament of the coloratura soprano voice in its upper range. This alone might dazzle an audience, but it could never shake them emotionally in the way described by those who heard Tetrazzini. There was another quality, probably apparent only in actual stage performance, which no recording device could capture. (*Oscar Hammerstein I*, Simon & Schuster, NY 1956)

Careful listeners will hear instances of this quality on a few of her recordings. In arias like "Ah non credea" (*La sonnambula*), "Saper voreste" (*Un ballo in maschera*), Annetta's aria (*Crispino e la Comare*), the mad scene (*Hamlet*), and even the bell song from *Lakmé,* there are variations in timbre that show an interpretive mind at work. Tetrazzini's colorations on recordings, however, come through only as pastel shades of the differently brilliant colors that must have appeared to live audiences. If one listens with this awareness, these disks paint quite a different picture of this singer than was previously thought.

It should be remembered that tempi also play into this. A 78 rpm recording lasted approximately four minutes. Most arias had to be cut severely to make them fit that brief period, greatly affecting what a singer was able to do, interpretively. For example, compare Lily Pons' 1930 Victor recording of the bell song (about six minutes) with one of her live performances (more than seven minutes). Obviously, Pons was doing *something* during that additional minute. This, no doubt, applies to Tetrazzini's recordings as well, although we have no live performances against which to match that supposition.

The Recordings

Of the many disks made by this diva, the most impressive are those made between 1907 and 1913. These best demonstrate her incredible abandon and prodigious upper extension, as well as the occasional weakness at the other end of the scale. Rather than try to discuss all of her recordings, I have chosen those that I feel are of merit. These choices are wholly subjective.

J. B. Steane sums up the value of her recordings when he writes:

But Tetrazzini remains. She is another who suggests an ideal and sometimes fulfils it. The suggestion itself is a great contribution to singing. We know, through her, how certain kinds of music can sound, and it is the better part of her voice that we hear singing these when we listen inside our own heads. She is also a tonic. After listening to the more enervating beauties of the German coloraturas and the drooping loveliness of some of our own contemporaries, we feel how refreshing a little simple, forthright liveliness would be; and then it is time to look out a good Tetrazzini." (*The Grand Tradition*, Charles Scribner's Sons, NY, 1974)

Part I: Arias not Considered to be in Tetrazzini's Standard Repertoire

Mozart: "Voi che sapete" (Act II) (*La nozze di Figaro*)—London, 1907
Mozart: "Batti, batti" (Act I) (*Don Giovanni*)—London, 1907, 1911

Tetrazzini made only one recording of "Voi che sapete" but repeated "Batti, batti" in 1911. These were her first Mozart recordings, made early in her association with Gramophone (HMV). Neither opera was in her performing repertoire, so one wonders at her reasons for recording them. (This is especially curious inasmuch she recorded these arias before such pieces as "Saper voreste," "Regnava nel silenzio," and the "Carnival of Venice Variations," all staples of her performing repertoire.) Tetrazzini probably found them appealing because their tessitura was predominately low thereby providing some contrast to her usual repertoire. It becomes apparent, after examining her discography, that there were a number of arias like these, ones that she enjoyed singing even though they would not be considered within her normal repertoire.

It is not likely that either aria will appeal to modern listeners. Her generous use of portamento and odd, grace note descents into the chest register are now considered vulgar. The use of the voce bianca is also somewhat distracting. It is probable that many will cringe at Tetrazzini's emphatic descent into the final (chested) note of "Batti, batti" despite the fine display of legato and the nicely emphatic "si,si,si,si,si,si" that precedes it. What is interesting in these recordings is the sturdiness of her low register and the rich, almost mezzo soprano timbre she produces in the upper middle area.

Michael Aspinall comments: "The speeding up of the middle section of 'Sospiro e gemo' (in Voi che sapete) with the ritard, leading back into the repeat of 'Voi che sapete,' with a very long breath, is the kind of magical touch that such arias demand." (EMI notes, 1992)

Not to be denied is the smooth flow of Tetrazzini's legato and her attempts at characterization through varying textural effects. (Instead of arching through a phrase, she will "point" the top note, or instead of singing a series of notes in pure legato, she will detach one or two.) These touches provide aural contrasts within the music that are supported by excellent tempi. Even so, these recordings remain curiosities of Tetrazzini's discography and their interest is only peripheral.

Verdi: "L'insana parola" (Act I) (*Aïda*)—London, July, 1911

Essentially, this is the second half of Aïda's famous "Ritorna vincitor." Whether or not Tetrazzini actually sang such roles as Aïda in the early part of her career does not change the fact that she obviously relished programming and recording arias from the spinto/dramatic repertoire. One can only imagine the impact this record had on Tetrazzini's original listeners.

The aria is sung with great intensity and a remarkably strong, innate sense of the dramatic style so necessary for this music. Although the tempi are a bit rapid for us today (in order to fit it all onto the single side of a disk) this is a surprisingly satisfying performance full of subtle interpretive effects. Especially nice is her intense emotionalism and the definite coloration of timbre for the line: "I sacri nomi di padre, d'amante ne proferir poss'io, ne ricordar." Her voice has the satisfying, dark lushness of a dramatic soprano in the upper middle area and although a bit pinched, the chest voice is secure and obviously holds no terrors.

Verdi: "Pace, pace mio Dio" (Act IV) (*La forza del destino*) – U.S., May, 1914 (Victor); England, June, 1914

This is hardly an aria one would associate with Luisa Tetrazzini and her often-criticized pallid lower register, but, as Michael Scott notes:

> If her recordings of 'Pace pace mio Dio' and 'Ritorna vincitor' are not among her best, many another soprano would have been well satisfied with them. (*The Record of Singing*, Volume I, Charles Scribner's Sons, NY, 1977)

I prefer the first version of this aria. She recorded it again a month later in London, but, oddly, omitted the initial "Pace, pace" for that session. Both versions are emotional and satisfying renditions. They both show an impressive, surprisingly expressive, lower register.

The tempi in this aria are more rapid that we are accustomed to hearing today, having a definite forward momentum in the piece. This is complimented by the wonderful, natural thrust of Tetrazzini's singing and her smoothly spun legato. Generally, there is little "gracing" of Verdi's melody, just some fine, sturdy singing. She sounds completely comfortable in this music, so much so that she inserts a short cadenza up to high C at the end of the main section of the aria. I find that I enjoy Tetrazzini's personalization of this music and its unabashed individuality, even though this would not be tolerated today.

Most affecting is her entrance in measures 60 and 61 on "Ah! in mezzo a tanto a tanto duol" where the subtle emotionalism serves to disguise a pinched chest register (brought rather high, up to F). The infamous B-flat octave-jump during "invan la pace," so often the bane of other sopranos, is cleanly done and offered as piano, as Verdi wanted it. The interpolated cadenza, although not necessary, is a good touch, and its structure stays within Verdi's harmonics. The conclusion, with its "maledizione," is as successful as one would expect from this soprano. Tetrazzini digs deeply into her chest register with abandon to offer another fine B-flat at the finish. This is an imaginative and individual recording.

Verdi: "Tacea la notte placida" (*Il trovatore*) – U.S., February 1913 (Victor)
Verdi: "D'amor sull' ali rosee" (*Il trovatore*) – U.S, February 1913 (Victor)

Luisa Tetrazzini's 1913 recordings of Leonora's arias are certainly individual. "Tacea la notte placida" contrasts her dramatic soprano-like timbre in the upper middle and top registers with an aggressively used, but pinched, bottom register.

There is an odd, note-by-note handling of Verdi's music that makes this less attractive than some of her other disks. As did Lillian Nordica, Tetrazzini inserts a short cadenza at the end of the first section, finishing on a laser-like A-flat, a favored mannerism of hers by 1911. (This is discussed in greater detail under the Delibes bell song.) Enjoying the challenge of Verdi's closely written fioriture in the cabaletta, Tetrazzini adds energetic triplets to the phrase "ah sì esso morirò," substituting "Ah!" for the text. (This was an embellishment adopted by Maria Callas in various performances of this aria.) In exultation, Tetrazzini interpolates a brilliant penultimate high E-flat.

Tetrazzini's "D'amor sull' ali rosee" was one of the first 78 rpm disks to include the recitative "Timor di me?" which is dramatically interpreted. Despite renown as a florid specialist, Tetrazzini had a natural instinct for dramatic inflection. The aria boasts a lilting tempo and an authoritative delivery. Like other Italian singers of this era, she substitutes an E-flat for Verdi's G at "Ai sogni dell'amor." She also adds improvised grace notes to Verdi's line and uses her chest voice with abandon. The final cadenza is successfully altered and Tetrazzini's singing is sensitively restrained, but the augmented finish is too aggressively constructed to suit Verdi's original, gentle ending.

Part II: The 1904 Zonophone Recordings

Tetrazzini's American-made, Zonophone recordings (on Romophone) are an interesting appendix to her recording career, but are predominately embryonic in their display of her talent. On September 8, 1904 she recorded five arias with careless piano accompaniment by her brother-in-law, Cleofonte Campanini. Overall, they are a fine "experiment" but provide few insights into this singer's art or voice. The diva tried to pretend she never made them.

She recorded arias from *La sonnambula*, *Rigoletto*, *Lucia di Lammermoor*, *Romeo et Juliette*, and *Il barbiere di Siviglia*.

Donizetti: Mad Scene (*Lucia di Lammermoor*)
One Zonophone recording highlights some interesting specifics about this soprano, the mad scene from *Lucia di Lammermoor*. Lucia was Tetrazzini's favorite operatic role, and by the time she made this recording she had already sung the role for twelve years. She first sang it in Buenos Aires in November of 1892; her last stage performance (in Boston) as Lucia was in 1914. A phrase from the mad scene is inscribed on her tombstone: "Alfin son tua." (At last I am yours) Considering her love for Lucia, it is surprising that she made only three versions (of which this Zonophone is the first) and only one version of Lucia's act I scena, "Regnava nel silenzio."

Piano-accompanied, the disk begins with "Alfin son tua" and continues through the voice/flute duet. In this 1904 disk, Tetrazzini's familiarity with the music is made clear by the easy grace with which she caresses some of its lines. The voice is remarkably agile and seems to glory in executing complex ornamental patterns.

The first ornament she introduces is on the fifth note of the recording. This is an improvisational triplet figure on "fin" of "Alfin son tua." This is a perfect example of Tetrazzini spontaneously gracing Donizetti's music.

Luisa Tetrazzini is a master of this type of ornament and uses it often. For lack of a better term, I refer to the method that she (and others) use to execute this feat, a "vocal flip," as that is essentially what it is, a tiny movement of the diaphragm that, when supported by the breath, ripples through the voice. Although primarily used for executing clean triplet figures, it is also an indispensable method (or technique) for accurate florid work. Many singers mastered it, including Lilli Lehmann, Nellie Melba, Miliza Korjus, Maria Callas, Joan Sutherland, Beverly Sills, Edita Gruberova, Luciana Serra, Gianna Rolandi, Ruth Welting, and Beverly Hoch. Others never managed to do so: Lily Pons, Rita Shane, Amelita Galli-Curci and Selma Kurz, for example. To get a better idea of what is being discussed, compare the recordings of Philine's Polonaise (*Mignon*) as sung by Tetrazzini and by Lily Pons. You will immediately recognize the differences in how they negotiate the close intervals, trills, and triplet figures.

Interestingly, Tetrazzini dropped this ornament (on "Alfin") in later recordings, supporting the idea that it had been done on the spur of the moment. Another interesting ornament is an intense trill on "ogni piacer" which is followed by staccati that lead to high B-flat with the lightest of touches. Her upper register has a sweet sheen that will eventually turn hard, even brilliant, within seven years.

Fascinating in this early recording is Tetrazzini's inventive pointing during coloratura flights. The cadenza is sung accapella (absent of the usual flute) and displays her secure sense of pitch. It also highlights her ability to peak each phrase with contrasting rhythmic alterations or marcato effects. The final high E-flat is approached by a connecting swoop, an approach seldom used by this singer as it usually proved to be less successful than a clean-cut attack.

Part III: The Gramophone and Victor Recordings (1907–1922)

It is the Gramophone disks (beginning in 1907) and the Victor records (beginning in 1911) that provide a vivid portrait of Tetrazzini's allure as a singer. It is almost impossible for us to understand the impact Tetrazzini's recordings had when they were first issued because we are now accustomed to the florid recordings of such full-voiced singers as Maria Callas, Joan Sutherland, Montserrat Caballe, and Edita Gruberova. In 1907, however, the Tetrazzini disks were staggering. For simplicity, they are organized alphabetically by composer.

Bellini: "Vien diletto" (*I puritani*)—London, July, 1912

Surprisingly, Tetrazzini never recorded the cavatina of this famous mad scene, only both verses of the cabaletta. Some of the vocalism on this disk is impressive, especially when considering the tempi. The chest register is solid, if a bit pinched, but the top rings out with uncommon clarity. (In at least two spots you can hear the recording apparatus "ring" with the brilliance of her tone.)

The second verse reveals some fascinating ornamentation: descending staccato scales, rubato effects, piano shadings, grace notes, and an elegant series of descending triplet figures. As if that were not enough, she follows this with a complicated figure of repeated, rhythmically accentuated staccati, grace notes, and triplets that leaves the listener breathless. No penultimate high E-flat, just a fine thrust to a B-flat that settles into a tonic A-flat. It is said that Tetrazzini did not like this cabaletta all that much. One certainly cannot tell that from this recording.

J. B. Steane writes about this recording:

> Not once does one feel that the technique is being arrogantly exhibited at the expense of musical sense. Tetrazzini always maintained a clear sense of where the melody and ornamentation were leading, and when we reach the aria's final climax the combination of her urgency and the sheer beauty and accuracy of the voice make for an exhilarating experience. (Voice of a Century, *Opera Now*, April, 1990)

Bellini: "Come per me sereno" (*La sonnambula*)—London, July, 1912

Tetrazzini made just one recording of this aria. In many ways it is surprisingly effective despite the nine-minute scena being squeezed onto a four-minute disc. "Come per me" is sung with robust tone in the upper middle and some surprisingly sturdy descents into the chest register. Tetrazzini graces Bellini's lines with ornamental turns and triplets that lend grace to the vocal line and do not offend. This section of the scena lasts less than two minutes, but the cadenza she interpolates is imaginative and well phrased. The cabaletta has fine florid clarity, although it seems to be thrown at the listener without much thought as to content. Ornamentation abounds, and is sung with such authority that, unless consulting a score, you wouldn't know which figurations are Bellini's and which are Tetrazzini's. Her finish is refreshingly different. There is no penultimate high E-flat, but a run up to a D-flat that gives a wholly different feeling to the cadence harmonics.

Bellini: "Ah non credea" (*La sonnambula*)—London, June, 1909; U.S., March, 1911

Either recording can be recommended. The 1909 disk is five seconds shorter than the four minutes and thirty seconds of the 1911 American record, but both are representative of this singer's interpretive abilities. They are among Tetrazzini's most original and beautiful recordings. Listened to carefully, they demonstrate her ability to color phrases that further her interpretation. Modern purists will gasp in horror at some of her interpolations, including a final cadenza/duet with cello, but her ornamentation is securely within tradition. (Most date back to Pasta, Malibran, and Patti.) Tetrazzini's handling of them is exquisite.

In this, as in many of her recordings, Tetrazzini proves that it is not what you interpolate that is important, but how it is done; the manner in which it is presented. The most traditional ornaments can sound vulgar if not phrased with sensitivity to the ornament itself, and where it fits within the receiving phrase; that instinct was inherent in Tetrazzini.

Of her aria recordings, this one (and, perhaps, the *Hamlet* mad scene) offers the greatest insight into the emotional intensity that Tetrazzini is said to have possessed in tragic stage roles. There are a number of moments in which this occurs. Among the first is during the phrase, "che un giorno solo, ah, sol duro." On the "che" there is a gulp or choking sound (as if Amina were crying) that is instructed by Bellini's score. The next time this phrase occurs, this effect is amplified in an emotional effect that is prompted by the singer's spontaneous reaction to Bellini's music. The embellishments that follow might seem a bit wayward to today's listener, but the aria's text, its harmonics at those moments, and Tetrazzini's authoritative delivery, along with the soft texture of the high notes, make them all fitting ornaments. Indeed, it is the ornamentation, and Tetrazzini's caressing delivery of them, that provides the vocal élan in this recording.

There are other textural touches with which Tetrazzini shades Bellini's music, but most are impossible to describe on paper—they must be experienced. The concluding short cadenza with cello, an expansion on what Bellini wrote, is lovely for its emotional content, and Tetrazzini's superb handling of the long phrases. It features a Tetrazzini specialty: a high A sung first in full voice that is immediately repeated pianissimo without a breath. This particular vocal effect appears on a number of Tetrazzini's recordings, always lending grace to the phrase.

As if this were not enough, on the 1909 disk she offers her famous double-swell on a final, pianissimo high C. Taking this note up an octave (she takes a final high C on both versions) was somewhat of a tradition among Italian coloraturas at that time. Others who used it were Amelita Galli-Curci and Anna-Maria Guglielmetti.

Of all the Tetrazzini disks, this aria best displays her ability to depict tears with the voice ("l'armes dans la voix").

Modern-day listeners often react negatively to Tetrazzini's liberal ornamentation, as they have to the ornamentation of the more-recent Beverly Sills. Both singers are strikingly individual musicians. This controversy often sparks arguments on the relevancy of florid vocal writing.

Tetrazzini defends her repertoire and ornamentation:

> What is the difference in principle, I would ask, between the fioriture passages of the vocalist and those introduced as a matter of course in the most serious instrumental music? Why should a cadenza for the voice be reckoned less worthy than a similar passage for the violin or the 'cello? All the greatest masters have introduced florid passages in plenty in the noblest instrumental music. Yet the view is generally adopted that these are inadmissible, or belong to an inferior phase of the art when the instrument employed happens to be the voice. (*How to Sing*, C. Arthur Pearson, London, 1923)

Bellini: "Ah non giunge" (*La sonnambula*)—America, March, 1911

This record has always been a favorite among record collectors. Bellini's cabaletta brings out the best in Tetrazzini. Her energy while singing this music can easily be felt while few singers can match the exuberance she displays on this recording. It also shows her fondness for straightening out a high note for effect, while it is sustained. The short voice/flute duet at the conclusion is especially fine—the singer dashing up and down scales faster and faster. To finish, she sings a grand turn to high D, attacks a high C incisively, and then settles on a final B-flat. Inventive and brief, this brings the aria to a brilliant close. The version recorded for Zonophone in 1904 is not as exciting as this one.

Many of Tetrazzini's most brilliant effects (such as those on this disk) are attributable to her ability to use her breath to its fullest capacity. In her treatise, *How To Sing,* she spends pages emphasizing to the reader the importance of the correct use of the breath. Here, she describes her own method:

> I breathe low in the diaphragm, not as some do, high up in the upper part of the chest. I always hold some breath in reserve for crescendos, employing only what is absolutely necessary, and I renew the breath wherever it is easiest.

> In breathing I find, as in other matters pertaining to singing, that as one goes on and practices, no matter how long one may have been singing, there are constantly new surprises awaiting one. You may have been accustomed for years to take a note in a certain way, and after a long while you discover that, while it is a very good way, there is a better. (*How to Sing*, C. Arthur Pearson, London, 1923)

Benedict: Carnival of Venice Variations—London, May 1909; America, March 1911

This two-part vocal tour-de-force was originally written for Adelina Patti's sister, Carlotta. Considering the vocal obstacles in this piece, she must certainly have been a proficient technician. Unfortunately, no recordings exist of her voice or its "lark-like" high notes. Tetrazzini was fond of interpolating this concert piece into the lesson scene of Rossini's *Il barbiere di Siviglia*. (Indeed, she would often offer both Benedict's "Carnival of Venice Variations" and Proch's "Theme & Variations" during the same lesson scene)

Tetrazzini recorded this piece twice. Both versions offer spectacular pyrotechnics, each version having its own rewards. In 1909, Tetrazzini's high notes carry a lovely, soft texture, while the 1911 version offers more virtuostic abandon and dramatic thrust. As in her recordings of the "Venzano Waltz" and "Proch Variations," Tetrazzini is having a wonderful time recording this music. One can almost see her smile of delight as she gets ready to dart through some of the more difficult coloratura; this may be one of the most arresting aspects in all her virtuosic recordings—rather than make the music sound impossibly difficult, Tetrazzini seems to be having the time of her life.

The opening section of the 1911 recording finds Tetrazzini's voice round and nicely shaded, the fioriture notable for its elasticity, freedom, and rhythmic propulsion. In the familiar theme of the second section, high staccati are seemingly picked from the air, while rapid chromatic scales, and long, finely-rolled trills are energetically presented by Tetrazzini's easy, nonchalant delivery. The third set of variations is a remarkable study in rapid triplet figures. Near the end of this variation, there is a series of descending triplets of tremendous difficulty, that Tetrazzini flips through with uncanny ease and clarity. This section (on the 1911 recording at least) remains one of the most amazing things this soprano has ever recorded; every note is clearly audible. Beside her Spanish contemporary, Maria Galvany, and yet-to-come Miliza Korjus, this level of virtuosity will not be heard again on recordings until Joan Sutherland in the 1960s.

The extensive final cadenza, with its echo effects, rhythmically-accentuated staccato, and thrusted high notes, is as exciting as it is impressive for its accuracy. (The one high staccato that fails to sound makes no difference whatever on the singer's impact.) A penultimate high E-flat brings both renditions to a brilliant close. This piece, along with the "Venzano Waltz," the "Proch Variations," and the mad scene from *L'étoile du nord* represent the epitome of fine coloratura singing. When one considers that editing was not possible at that time—that these recordings are the equivalent of live performances—the degree of accuracy shown here emphasizes the extent of Tetrazzini's natural gifts.

Bizet: Micaela's Aria (*Carmen*) (sung in Italian)—England, July, 1911; U.S., May, 1914 (Victor)

It is a toss-up as to which version of this aria is better; both have their merits. Sung in Italian, the timing of each recording is within seconds of the other. The listener immediately notices that the aria is sung with sturdy tone, often gentle lyricism, generous portamento, and a vocal style that does not meet current taste as to French music. While perhaps not idiomatic, there is an obvious commitment to Bizet's music. Tetrazzini's tone is full and round in the upper middle regions and her sense of the dramatic underlines the intense middle section.

Both versions of the aria have gotten notorious criticism due to Tetrazzini's interpolation of a final, pianissimo high E-flat that is held through the postlude. Most modern listeners cringe. What is never mentioned is that, although Tetrazzini interpolates an E-flat, she sings it pianissimo. Understanding the context of the aria, she does not scream out a high note, but incorporates it into the dynamic fabric of Bizet's music. Today, this may be considered an unacceptable interpolation, but that doesn't take away from it having been executed with taste.

As to transfers of these recordings, because of the ambient acoustics, for some reason, the Nimbus issue does not emphasize the fact that she sings the E-flat pianissimo. On the Romophone releases (or on the earlier rendition on EMI) this becomes more than obvious.

Bizet: "Siccome un di" (*Pescatori di Perle*)—London, June, 1909
Bizet: "Brahma Gran Dio" (*Pescatori di Perle*)—London, July, 1909

Leila's Cavatina, "Siccome un di," from act II presents rich tone and smooth, lyrical legato, as well as round, soaring top notes of high B and C. Leila is a role that Tetrazzini sang often; her familiarity with the music is obvious. Her authoritative delivery, combined with her fresh vocal state at the time, makes this a quite beautiful recording. That allure is somewhat compromised by her use of the voce bianca, but not enough to detract from the beauty of her legato, or the sheen of her high notes. The improvised Tetrazzini ornaments, including turns and triplets, make their appearance and grace Bizet's vocal line. Especially lovely is her repetition of the main melody. The ending cadenza is delivered close to what Bizet wrote and capped by a perfect messa-di-voce on high C.

If Leila's act II cavatina is impressive, the bravura prayer, "Brahma gran Dio," that closes act I, is even more so. Due to time restrictions, cuts are made, but they are sensible. There are many wonderful touches that Tetrazzini brings to Bizet's music; her rhythmic accentuation is superb. Textural, tonal, and ornamental emphasis abounds in the short aria. High Bs shine like beacons as fioriture is cleanly articulated. Of special note is her pointing of coloratura, especially during the final, extended cadenza. It is there that Tetrazzini adds a passage of high staccati that bounce between high C-sharp, D, and E (four of them) that ping (even in the dry acoustics of the recording studio) with a heady brilliance that one rarely finds on early disks. Because of the ease with which Tetrazzini sings this passage, most listeners do not notice the amount of textural pointing (or leaning into the notes) that Tetrazzini does within this series of high staccati. Most singers would be grateful just to be able to sing the notes. Tetrazzini toys with them!

Chapi: Carceleras (*Las Hijas del Zabedo*)—England, July, 1909; U.S., March, 1911 (Victor)

When Tetrazzini recorded this unusual Zarzuela aria, it was not the repertoire rarity it is today. Having a wordy text, it also has perilous passages of triplets, and other ornamental figures. The difference between this aria and other florid pieces in Tetrazzini's repertoire is that its floridity lies about two octaves beneath where she usually cavorts. It is in these low-lying, rapid figurations that one easily hears the benefits of the vocal-flip technique.

A number of operatic sopranos have recorded this aria, including Maria Galvany, Maria Callas' teacher, Elvira de Hidalgo, and, shortly after, Tetrazzini and Amelita Galli-Curci. It is surprising that Tetrazzini would choose to record this at all, as the tessitura lies low and requires forceful and fluent singing in the lowest extremes. She obviously enjoyed performing this aria as she often programmed it for concerts. As seems to be true with a number of her concert pieces and recordings, Tetrazzini enjoyed the challenge that certain music presented her.

She made two versions of this aria, one for Europe and one for America. The first, recorded in July 1909, shows that her voice has a fullness in the lower region when she allows it to flow naturally (not manipulating it into the "baby-talk" timbre of which she was so fond). The American disk was recorded two years later (in 1911) and finds the lower register even more telling. Both recordings take virtually the same amount of time and both feature an anonymous castanet player. Although both are well done, I prefer the slight difference in the lower register that is evident in the later recording. Both end with an excellent lunge to high A.

David: "Charmant Oiseau" (*La Perle du Brésil*) – U.S., March, 1911; England, July, 1911

This aria is sung by the character Zora, who, after a storm in act III, awakens to the sound of the Mysoli (a Brazillian bird). Recognizing its chirping, she sings this piece in praise of its beauty.

This unusual aria was a favorite of Tetrazzini's, and one she programmed on most concerts through the 1920s. It suited her voice and bravura flair. During her career it was one of the staples of the coloratura soprano repertoire and many of Tetrazzini's colleagues made recordings of this aria. In recent decades, however, it has fallen from favor. In the 1960s the French coloratura, Renee Doria, recorded it, but the next recordings do not appear until 1994; Korean, Sumi Jo, and French, Elisabeth Vidal. In the next year, 1995, Karen Smith Erickson presented her version of the aria on a small independent label, Centaur.

Tetrazzini made two recordings of this exotic aria. It seems to be the only florid aria that she recorded in French. Her American disk far surpasses the London pressing made in the following July. Not only does it contain more of David's atmospheric prelude, but it is a better demonstration of Tetrazzini's aviary art (despite a few awkward lunges down to low D). One verse of the aria is included, with some beautiful trills and phrasing, as well as an extended voice/flute cadenza. In the cadenza, she carefully modulates her voice to blend (beautifully) with the accompanying flute. Tetrazzini enjoyed these exhibitionistic contests with partnering flutes, never more in evidence than here. Volleys of high staccati Bs and Ds abound, as do straight-tone effects. Especially nice is her ascent to a staccato high E through a series of rising trills followed by an emphatic punch on a penultimate high D. This ability to forcefully attack high notes adds a tremendous sense of dramatic urgency to climaxes on her recordings.

The second (London) version is more than a minute shorter (much of the prelude is cut) and finds Tetrazzini in not as good voice as the earlier rendition. Some of the singing is heavy-handed and the phrasing is not as elegant as it was months earlier. The cadenza, although impressive, has very bright, knife-edged staccati that veer toward brittleness. There is a swooped (almost cheating) glancing at the high E. The penultimate high D wants constantly to shift in and out of placement.

Delibes: "Blanche Dourga" (*Lakmé*) (sung in Italian)—London, July, 1911

Tetrazzini never recorded Lakmé's lyrical aria from act I or the beautiful act III Berceuse, but she did make this recording of Lakmé's entrance; her prayer to the Indian god, Dourga. This was a most unusual selection for recording at the time, as few artists chose to record this atmospheric music. Recorded in the same year as her performances of *Lakmé* at Covent Garden, it gives a good idea of the quality of her voice at that time. The last page of the opening prelude is included, but seventy-one measures of Nilankantha's recitative and the chorus are cut. Tetrazzini maintains the eerie atmosphere that is created by the orchestra by using her straight-tone effect, lending an appropriate aura of the exotic to this recording. Her control of vibrato and pitch are excellent, and the subtle ornaments she introduces during the second verse remain within Delibes' musical boundaries. A rag-tag chorus of men from Covent Garden assist the diva, singing and humming (as is written in the score) under her warbling. Some of the notes they sing, however, are *definitely* not in Delibes' score.

Delibes: Bell Song (*Lakmé*) (sung in Italian)—England, December, 1907 and July, 1911; America, March, 1911 and February, 1913

Tetrazzini was one of the great Lakmés even though she did not undertake the role until November, 1904, in Mexico City, after she had been performing for more than a decade. Lakmé was the last "new" role that she was to learn. The bell song remained one of her favorite arias, although she once admitted it was the most difficult in her repertoire. Even so, it is her most often recorded aria, she released four, Italian-sung versions with orchestra during the six years between 1907 and 1913. It was the bell song that Tetrazzini performed in a special concert given at the Royal Albert Hall in London on October 10, 1920, specifically to dispel rumors that she was losing her voice.

Her first bell song was recorded on December 20, 1907. It was the last of three arias recorded during her first session for the London-based Gramophone Company (HMV), the two others being "Caro nome" from *Rigoletto,* and the flashy polonaise from *Mignon*. Although heavily cut, this is a performance that has rarely been equaled in brilliance. Ignore that it is sung in Italian, not its original French, or that it is heavily abridged. This doesn't matter. It ranks as one of the classic recordings of this aria.

Tetrazzini's voice is fresh, limpid and used with great vitality. No vocalise is sung, but from the first, round and full-throated F-sharp, the listener recognizes an individual, authoritative presence. In the central aria she uses white vowels (the voce bianca) and piano effects to emphasize the heroine's youthful innocence and pathetic situation. This is a masterful performance with big, round sound above the staff and excellent pitch-pointing.

One of the more interesting things about this recording is Tetrazzini's decision to use two contrasting tonal colorations as interpretive devices for the two sections of the aria. In the first section she often uses a white, pallid timbre, but in the second section her tone is more robust in character and strikingly individual. Clean, interpolated triplet figures grace Delibes' vocal line, and although only one bell strophe is offered, it has superb trills and pointed, full staccati that are sung within the musical phrase rather than pecked. The only blemish in this recording is some approximated scale work near the coda that is attributable to the impossibly fast tempo. The staccato coda, with its excellent peak on D-sharp, has a wonderful insouciance. This is followed immediately by a rippling high B trill, and an instantaneous leap to a ringing high E that is held almost to the end of the postlude.

By 1911, and her next recording of this aria, there had been significant changes in her voice and her manner of using it. Now forty years old, it is evident that Tetrazzini's upper register has grown and darkened. Because of these natural changes, she has become enamored of a vocal mannerism that plays with the surrounding acoustics, adopting a kind of laser-like effect. It is a controlled, directing of pitch into a column of sound, similar to the way an actor emphasizes words during a speech. It is different, however, from the Germanic straight-tone technique used by Irene Abendroth, Margarethe Siems, or Miliza Korjus in their high register work, or the straight, narrow emissions of Marchesi students, Yaw, Melba, and Calvé. Tetrazzini's usage was as an effect, not a technique, its premise and expected result not the same. This effect lends a laser-beam clarity to high notes, shooting them into the surrounding acoustics, providing the singer with a satisfying sense of power and penetration. Dramatic sopranos often use this mannerism to highlight their music, Emmy Destinn and Dame Gwyneth Jones being examples. It is similar to the mannerism that Slavic sopranos favor in combining their timbre and various resonances with the acoustics of a theatre or concert hall to point various tones within a musical phrase. Used in the opera house, it can be an intriguing coloristic device.

Tetrazzini relied more and more upon this mannerism. By 1911, it had begun to creep into the emission of her high register which, being manipulated, gradually began to lack its former, vibrant freedom. In the opera house, with acoustic distance between herself and the audience, this would have been interpreted aurally by listeners as an additional carrying "edge" to the voice. (Reviews in that time often speak of the "new diamond-like brilliance" of her top register.) In the close, dry, acoustics of a 1911 recording studio, however, it often lent a brittle quality to her upper extension.

Interesting comparisons can be made between the high registers of Luisa Tetrazzini and Dame Joan Sutherland. On early recordings both voices experienced occasional placement shifting during the sustaining of high D and E-flat. As they matured, both artists similarly adopted a preparatory hesitation, a monitor-like control of their high notes, as if to insure their quality. Because of Tetrazzzini's heavy reliance on this controlling mannerism, high notes began to lose their former freedom and become more white-toned.

Her second version (for American distribution) was recorded for Victor in Camden, New Jersey, in March, 1911 (now available on Nimbus CD). For that session the voice seems to sit quite high and is buoyant. Because the voice is so responsive, she is able to color the music with nice shading and executes some wonderful, nonchalant phrases of the aria's staccati. Her continued fondness for bianca vowels, to suggest Lakmé's fragility and youth, still predominate; the high B that ends the central aria is right on pitch. Despite a flawed entrance, the bell strophe is excellent; the staccati are full, clean, and excellently pointed and the penultimate high B trill is propulsive. Although the final E is muscularly controlled, the tone is true, has vibrato, and is admirably held to the end.

Her third version, made in London four months later, finds her having an off day. The voice seems ponderous; is darker, heavier, and less responsive to her demands.

The orchestra plays sloppily as well. There are some unusual problems with pitch in this performance, as if the soprano was having trouble hooking into her support. The voice also tends to catch in staccati passages—where attack must be short and immediate— as if she were not sufficiently warmed up and the voice won't "speak" easily. Her trill on high B is quite good, but the high E sits on the low side of the note and never centers. Not daunted by this, Tetrazzini rigidly sustains the note to the end of the postlude.

February 18, 1913, finds Tetrazzini in Victor's Camden, New Jersey studios for a fourth and final version (to replace the previous Victor). Her voice seems to have regained the freedom it exhibits in the second version. Because of this, she again provides the listener with a most rewarding rendition. The central aria offers delicate, pastel shadings, some surprisingly wistful. The generation of tension between the two segments of the aria is better handled this time. She makes sure that her staccati phonate, and, although the top of the voice is as bright as lightening, she offers a fine top E that she holds triumphantly to the end.

Donizetti: "O luce di quest anima" (*Linda di Chamonix*)—England, November, 1910 and 1911; U.S., 1914

This is a recording often selected for anthologies because of Tetrazzini's robust manner with the music. Although she re-recorded the aria in London a year later, and again in America in 1914 (that includes the preceding recitative), it is the first, the 1910 London version, that best represents her take on this aria. It is joyous singing, that is all the more impressive because it is underscored by Tetrazzini's potent understanding of the rhythmic drive that is inherent in Donizetti's music. This disk sparkles from beginning to end, the staccati, turns, and trills right on the mark. The ending, with Tetrazzini jumping to a penultimate high D and then high C, is especially successful. The 1911 London session finds her voice not speaking as well when seeking high staccato, and 1914 finds her intentionally leaving out (or forgetting to include) some of her usual ornamentation.

Donizetti: "Regnava nel silenzio...Quando rapito in estasi" (*Lucia di Lammermoor*)—London, May, 1909

This is one of the great Tetrazzini records. She recorded this scena onto two 78 rpm sides. The recordings are clean and clear with the singer's voice forward and full of presence. Beyond some pinched notes in the lowest register, both sections of the scena are successful performances that display the soprano's remarkable agility and her firmly supported legato. Interpolations include improvised grace notes, mordents, trills, and additional high staccati passages. One trill, inserted on "fe" of "fra l'aure udir si fe," successfully depicts Lucia's shiver of horror at having seen the ghost. Throughout, Tetrazzini's tone has a golden sheen to it and she shows great intensity when within upper-middle reaches.

During the cabaletta she makes use of the white voice to highlight her concept of Lucia. In the repeat, Tetrazzini dazzles the listener with complicated cascades of staccato; to finish the aria she ascends a staccato scale to high E, which then yields to a beautiful, easy, penultimate high D. It is a remarkable and individual finish. I like the Nimbus transfer. Their transferring process, with its soft, reverberant acoustics, adds a patina of mystery to the qualities of Tetrazzini's voice. It also highlights the heady ping of her high notes.

Donizetti: Mad Scene (*Lucia di Lammermoor*)—England, December, 1907, America, March, 1911

Tetrazzini recorded this aria three times: the 1904 Zonophone (previously discussed), December, 1907 in England, and March, 1911 in America. All are interesting, although the 1907 recording perhaps more so.

It begins with "Splendon le sacre faci," earlier on than in the 1904 Zonophone, and although cuts are made, none are obtrusive to the enjoyment of her rendition or her imaginative ornamentation. One embellishment, thrusting into the chest register with a grace note, may sound odd to modern ears as it is a type of rhythmical ornament that is no longer favored. There is, however, something spontaneous about it that I find has appeal. Various mordents and grace notes make new appearances and a telling tenuto is affectingly done on "del ciel clemente."

The main focus by original listeners would have been on the (expected) cadenza with voice and flute. This, Tetrazzini sings with musicality and good instinct to building toward a climax. Roulades and scales are phrased with élan, and staccati are clean and pointed. Here again is her special effect of reiterating a high note first forte and then piano. The penultimate trill on high B-flat is supple and rolled with obvious relish.

The final high E-flat is more successful than her effort three years earlier for Zonophone. What many critics neglect to point out is that it is offered as an easy mezzo piano. Tetrazzini could have sung the note as forte with a grand thrust, but she chose not to.

In the *New York* Sun, W. J. Henderson describes her technical abilities during the cadenza:

> There were leaps, runs, staccati, double swells from piano to forte, twice repeated, and a finish on the high E flat.

That is exactly what one hears on her 1907 recording. Unfortunately, she never recorded the final cabaletta of the mad scene ("Spargi d'amaro pianto").

Tetrazzini was not infallible. Even as early as 1911, she experienced occasional problems with her high register. In a review of her debut in *Lucia di Lammermoor* at the Metropolitan Opera in December 27, 1911, Richard Aldrich writes:

> The desire to hear Mme. Tetrazzini, who made her first appearance on this occasion in the Metropolitan Opera House, was very great, and the audience was one of the largest of the season— practically as large as the house would hold... Mme. Tetrazzini is not quite the same as when she last sang here in opera. Her voice seems to have gained in fullness and even in power; its lower ranges have improved in quality. They have in a measure lost the infantile character that used to be so striking a defect in

her singing, and some of the constriction that used to make her lower tones sound pinched, she has apparently overcome... She dealt out a good many high notes last evening, but in some cases not without a certain amount of caution— thus, at the close of the Sparzi d'amaro, [sic] after the mad scene, which she sang brilliantly, she very speedily dropped her high E flat and took the octave lower. (*Concert Life in New York, 1902-1923*, G. Putnam's Sons, NY, 1941)

Not everyone found the soprano's art to their taste. W.J. Henderson writes of the same debut performance:

Mme. Tetrazzini has long been popular in the rôle of Lucia. At Mr. Hammerstein's... she always attracted and interested large audiences in this part. Last night the house was sold out...

She has the same scintillating and amazing staccati and she introduces them entirely for their own sweet sake and with a queenly disregard for the rhythm of the melody or the outline of the phrases. To come to the summary of the whole matter, Mme. Tetrazzini is now, as she was when New York first made her acquaintance, a vocal virtuoso who has a small stock of extremely effective artifices. These she uses over and over again without any attempt to hide her purpose which is to focus attention on certain splendid tones of her voice and on her command of the artifices themselves. But one grows weary of reiterated holds which are made in order to introduce long swelling notes, and of other technical tricks when used simply for the passing effect...

Indeed there is so much to enjoy in the beauty of a certain part of Mme. Tetrazzini's unique voice that it is most regrettable that she detracts from her own possibilities by unmusical singing. She gains much applause from those who clearly love to be astonished by skill in the performance of difficult vocal feats but she grieves those to whom high musicianship stands above technical facility. (*New York Sun*, Metropolitan Opera Archives, accessed January, 2015)

Eckert: Swiss Echo Song – U.S., March, 1911

This was a popular parlor song in Tetrazzini's era. It was one of her preferred pieces for concerts well into the 1920s. When Tetrazzini sang this piece in concert, it was always singled out for comment by critics.

It was the 'Echo Song' that stirred the house; for in the rendition the singer made use of all the artifices of her art, or rather fully employed all her marvelous skill in intricate singing. That 'Echo Song', with its haunting reverberations, was superb vocalization." (St Louis, Mo. Globe Democrat, February 7, 1920.)

Tetrazzini's virtuosic Italian arrangement of the piece is one of the better ones and includes both verses. She originally recorded it in London the previous November but it has not survived.

The American-made Victor recording is one of those disks one wants to repeatedly savor. Admittedly, it is light-weight fluff, and of no great importance, but when it is accepted for what it is, there is much to enjoy. As with the Proch "Theme and Variations," and the Benedict "Carnival of Venice Variations," Tetrazzini has full reign to do as she pleases and she does so with spectacular results. The famous

Tetrazzini staccati, improvisational triplets, turns, echo effects, chromatic descending scales, and trills are all sung as if improvised on the spot. Not at all inappropriate in this piece is an occasional yodel-like descent into a sturdy chest register. The concluding cadenza, sung accapella, contains roulades and high staccato echo effects that would terrify other singers. In typical, brilliant Tetrazzini manner, she finishes with a flourish: a series of rapid-fire staccati high As (similar to the finish of the mad scene from Meyerbeer's *L'étoile du nord*), and a rare swoop to a solid high D. This is one of her most delightful recordings.

Gounod: "O legere Hirondelle" (*Mireille*) (sung in Italian)—London, July, 1909

This is one of my favorite Tetrazzini recordings and one that displays her considerable florid technique at its best. Oddly, she was fond of interpolating this aria into the finale of Donizetti's *La fille du regiment.*

There is remarkable delicacy to Tetrazzini's singing in this recording. Especially delightful are her staccati flights that ping through the studio acoustics with great brilliance. She was in remarkable voice during this session, and she sings the aria with the rapidity of a whirlwind. There is a delicious use of tenuto that raises her performance from a mindless display of virtuosity to the level of a lesson in the art of phrasing coloratura. It is obvious that Tetrazzini is having a grand time as she flings intricate passages of grace notes, grupetti, and high stacacati at the listener. The end of the aria has a remarkable effect—a short, chromatic rise from high D to E in a marcato passage that is followed by another sustained, penultimate high D. This lends an unusual air of grace and élan to the disc. During a BBC broadcast in 1959, Dame Joan Sutherland selected this disk as one of her desert island recordings.

Grieg: Solveig's Song (*Peer Gynt*) (sung in Italian)—England, 1910; U.S., May, 1914

Tetrazzini made two versions of this lovely song. The 1910, London-made disk (with piano) is fine, but I feel the better version is the 1914 American disk with orchestra. There is something very special about the way she sings this piece, and there is wonderful vocal pointing in this recording. Tetrazzini's combination of a plaintive tone with a youthful timbre lends an attractive, wistful, aura to the music that haunts one long after the recording is over. Subtle echo effects are used to enhance the humming section. The timing for the 1910 disk is 3:38, while the American-made version is 4:00. Those extra seconds allow Tetrazzini to expand her presentation. Her use of a pure straight tone for the final note (high A) of both verses promotes the haunting quality that lingers.

Lama: "Come le rose"—London, 1922 (unpublished)

This was Tetrazzini's last recording. It was made with orchestra on September 15, 1922. "Come le rose" was a popular Italian song at the time and this recording proves that her voice was unimpaired despite the hiatus of the war years. Although short (not even three minutes long), she covers two octaves. The voice seems larger than ever, especially in her upper middle and top registers, which seem now to have the weight of a lyrico-spinto. The lower is still lighter in texture, but more evenly welded to the middle. Overall, the voice has a more unified timbre. This waltz was an excellent way for the diva to exit the recording studio. As if sensing that this might be the case, the irrepressible Tetrazzini throws in a superb, ringing high D at the finish.

Meyerbeer: Shadow Song (*Dinorah*) (in Italian)—England, December, 1907; U.S., 1913

Dinorah's semi-mad scene, where she dances and speaks to her shadow, was always a favorite with Tetrazzini and her 1907 disk is one of the best available.

Occasionally coy and flirtatious, yet always brilliant, her singing is far superior to the later, 1913 version. Although Amelita Galli-Curci's 1917 recording surpasses Tetrazzini's in vocal velvet, it cannot match hers in playful virtuosity. Typical with recordings made at that time, many cuts occur in order to make the aria fit onto a 78 rpm side. The largest, yet most successful cut, is a huge chunk of 94 measures. It cuts from the echo effects directly into the Allegro con spirito coda. Tetrazzini sings a lovely diminuendo on high A-flat and, as she holds this note, the orchestra re-enters on a tonic D-flat. The echo effects are nicely done (these must have been very difficult to do in the cramped confines of a tiny recording room). Tetrazzini experiences a rare placement problem during "se no ten vai," but all phrasing is well thought-out and, despite the rapid tempi, the accuracy of the coloratura is amazing. This is especially apparent during the coda with its fioriture of close intervals.

The concluding cadenza with flute has superb blending between the two instruments and is one of the most inventive on recordings. There is a charming playfulness between Tetrazzini and the flautist that bears up well to repeated listening. Tetrazzini treats the listener to some of her most beautiful fioriture: well-phrased and articulated scales, dainty staccati, and gentle high notes plucked from nowhere. One phrase, near the end, is particularly striking—a rolling trill on high A-flat, followed by a volley of high staccati that peak at top E-flat. In this phrase one understands the Tetrazzini allure. It is not only that these complicated phrases are attractive for their construction, but also because of the way Tetrazzini phrases and presents them to the listener.

The conclusion of the aria is surprisingly elegant. Tetrazzini offers a finely-rolled trill on high A-flat that ascends to a softly textured high D-flat—all within a single breath.

Her later rendition (U.S., February, 1913) finds the sonic properties of the recording improved, but the vocalism is not quite as scintillating. There is an added fullness in the voice, but with that comes a sense of caution and some odd glottal strokes, suggesting that the diva may have been having an off day. Coloratura is still fleet, but the echo effects are not as successful as in the earlier disk, and the staccati have a cutting edge that is occasionally brittle. A few new ornaments (mordents and grace notes) make their appearance, but, overall, it is inferior to the previous version. The final cadenza with flute is the same as it was in 1907, although now some of the highest staccati sound a bit tight. The final high D-flat is attacked strongly, however, and has quite a punch.

Meyerbeer: "O beau pays" (*Les Huguenots*) sung in Italian—London, July, 1912

It is surprising that Tetrazzini did not re-record this aria as this disk does not represent her art at its best. Marguerite de Valois was one of her famous roles, and the difficult act II scene should have been perfect for her abilities. Unfortunately, things did not go quite as hoped on the day she recorded it. This is a long scena, but for the purposes of recording it onto one side of a 78 rpm disk, it was mercilessly cut to its bare essentials. Even with cuts, time restrictions forced the tempo for the first half to be ridiculously fast, robbing it of any of the dreamy atmosphere the scene calls for. As if sensing the heavy time restraints, Tetrazzini rushes through the entire aria, seemingly with little interest, although some individual ornaments do appear.

The second half, the cabaletta, is interesting only for the type of embellishments Tetrazzini chooses to exploit in the upper regions of her voice. Even these vary in their pitch and accuracy. A short cadenza appears at the conclusion that takes the soprano to high E in a staccato flight. After a successful lunge to high C-sharp, a final D is fearlessly attacked, but slightly under pitch. When the orchestra enters in key, and Tetrazzini realizes her error, she does her best to raise it to match the orchestra. The whole thing sounds frantic and under-rehearsed and one wishes she had had another go at it—or had, at the least, decided to spread it over two sides.

Meyerbeer: Mad Scene (*L'étoile du nord*) (in Italian)—London, September, 1913

This disk presents one of the most impressive pyrotechnical displays that Luisa Tetrazzini left for posterity. Her singing is as breathtaking as it is lovely. This aria's uniqueness is that the voice/flute cadenzas are accompanied by not one, but two flutes. The vocal demands of this music are formidable, but Tetrazzini bursts through them with a smile and some fine vocal characterization during the central section. Oddly, despite this aria's virtuostic appeal and the grace of Meyerbeer's melodies, it has rarely been recorded. Tetrazzini's is one of the earliest recordings of this music, and only a handful of other artists have recorded it, including Ellen Beach Yaw, Selma Kurz, Joan Sutherland, Sumi Jo, and Elisabeth Futral.

The day this was recorded (September 26, 1913) the soprano was in a superb vocal state as she also recorded the famous aria from Ricci's *Crispino e la Comare*; both are classic recordings.

As with the 1907 Dinorah, much of what is attractive here is Tetrazzini's vital rhythmic sense and her loving caress of Meyerbeer's music. Tetrazzini's disk includes most of the aria as she elects not to sing an expected cadenza with flute at the end.

Of special note is the opening cadenza (with one flute) in which her pitch is as sure as the superb technique that she uses to great advantage. The difficult staccati passages boast round, firm tone and have a fine pointing of the peaks of phrases. A short recitative follows in which Tetrazzini indulges in voce bianca. Soon, another flute joins the first as Tetrazzini intricately weaves her way through both flutes employing figurations of arpeggios and trills with nonchalant abandon.

Only then, after two and one half minutes of extended cadenzas, does the orchestra join in. This following section has an appeal that is extremely difficult to define. Tetrazzini's manner of tossing off trills and arpeggiated fioriture is so aurally sumptuous that her caress of the music is almost sensuous. (This manner of singing is perhaps what Frieda Hempel refers to when speaking of Tetrazzini's voice as being erotic.)

The finish is brief, but spectacular. After a volley of ascending triplet figurations, Tetrazzini executes a series of rapid, perfectly pointed, high A staccati that are immediately followed by a rippling trill and a thrust to a sustained high C-sharp, then a final D. (The Pearl edition seems to have the better transfer: clean, clear and startlingly vivid; the EMI sounds "boxy" to me.)

Mozart: "Der Hölle Rache" (*Die Zauberflöte*) (sung in Italian)—England, September, 1908 (unpublished); U.S., 1920 (unpublished)

Tetrazzini tried to release a record of this aria twice;—in 1908 (in the EMI collection) and again in 1920 (on Pearl and Romophone). Neither was considered fit for publication. It is good that we have the opportunity to hear un-released recordings, but, in this case, the reasons that they remained unpublished are not difficult to understand. The aria is sung down a full step from its written pitch on the 1908 disk. Despite what one might think, this aria does not suit Tetrazzini. She makes a good go of it; the staccati are clean and some unusual ornaments appear, but it has none of the dramatic heft or fire that it should, or that one would expect from this intense singer.

Although the 1920 version is sung a half-step higher than the 1908 recording, her voice is on the heavy side with only one volley of high staccati in the first section. Triplets seem curiously labored in this version, and Tetrazzini's singing is too athletically "clean" to be effectively dramatic. Her interpolation of a final high note (an old tradition) does little to rescue the piece. No matter the drawbacks, one is still grateful that these disks were discovered, giving us the opportunity to hear Tetrazzini's take on one of Mozart's most difficult arias.

Proch: Theme and Variations – U.S., March, 1911; England, July, 1911

This pyrotechnical showpiece is a playground of delights for a singer like Tetrazzini who enjoys darting through intricate fioriture. Many of her colleagues recorded the piece: Frieda Hempel, Maria Galvany, Regina Pacini, Maria Barrientos,

Margarethe Siems, Lalla Miranda, and Elvira De Hidalgo. None of them, however, have Tetrazzini's audible smile of delight. Although both versions are excellent, the first, the American disk, shows audacious virtuosity and the clean brilliance of her top register. Both versions have a few smudges, but, overall, her degree of accuracy is astounding. Typical of recordings of this piece at that time, the main theme is presented as quickly as possible, followed by two variations that lead into a coda and final cadenza with flute.

Occasionally, on both versions, there is the feeling that Tetrazzini's voice is experiencing slight difficulty in wrapping itself around the rapid-fire staccati of her arrangement. There are some impossibly difficult patterns: winding scales, wide leaps, intricate grupetti, grace notes, improvisational triplets, and rising staccati passages. The earlier version has the more exciting (and accurate) final cadenza.

The cadenza offers some colorful, yodel-like descents in and out of the chest register contrasted by a remarkable jump to a soft-textured, high E-flat that is struck again and immediately followed by a chromatic scale down and back up to the E-flat. This is followed by a final leap to what sounds like a massive high D-flat with a wonderful ring to it. It has the bright, clean sound of a Bach trumpet that J.B. Steane proclaims in his description of Tetrazzini's voice in *The Grand Tradition*. The Nimbus transfer is preferred for the attractive aura of the added ambience of surrounding acoustics.

The London recording of four months later is slightly marred by a phlegmy chromatic scale during the return ascent to E-flat. Otherwise the pyrotechnics are just as impressive. The finish, however, does not have the (seemingly) huge sound of Tetrazzini's top D-flat heard on the previous version.

Tetrazzini's uusual chromatic flourish has recently been adopted by English-born soprano, Jessica Pratt (1979–) for her own performances of Proch's Variations.

Ricci: "Io non sono piu l'Annetta" (*Crispino e la Comare*)—London, September, 1913

This is one of Luisa Tetrazzini's most infectious recordings, a bravura aria of great brilliance. It was also recorded by the Spanish virtuosa, Maria Galvany, and the German, Frieda Hempel. It was revived by Joan Sutherland during the 1960s and recorded on her two-LP disk set *Command Performance*.

It comes from the second act of the opera when Annetta finds out that she will soon have a great fortune at her disposal. She sings of how she plans to spend it. The humorous content of the aria is perfect for Tetrazzini's comedic side and she is utterly charming. While "Ah non credea" (*La sonnambula*) shows her tone-painting within tragic music, this aria shows her abilities to portray an entirely different type of character. She brings a captivating coyness into play, especially with the line, "A dozzine gli eleganti mi faran da spasamenti" complete with a charming sigh. (That phrase also has additional gracing triplets that Tetrazzini seems to have thrown in for fun.) The roulades of coloratura that frame the humor are tossed off with nonchalant grace and additional sparkling high staccati are brought in to enhance the effect of Annetta laughing with delight.

After a flourish that sweeps over high E, a clear, shining, penultimate high D brings the aria to a brilliant finish.

Rossini: "Una voce poco fa" (*Il barbiere di Siviglia*) – U.S., March, 1911

Although Tetrazzini recorded this aria a number of times, this final American version, made in March 1911, best represents her concepts for and abilities in this music. On no other disk can you find the intricate roulades of this aria sent forth with such ease and humor. There is incredible ornamentation and it appears that much of it is improvisational. (Tetrazzini's ornaments can be found in the Ricci and Liebling books of embellishments.) Tetrazzini sings the aria in its original key of E.

A reviewer for *The Sun* (November 15, 1908) comments on Tetrazzini's performance of Rosina with the Manhattan Opera Company:

> Mme Tetrazzini did not entirely hide the outlines of Rossini's melodies but she decorated them most liberally with all those ornaments with which she is most skillful. She sang all kinds of staccato leaps and progressions, chromatic scales upward and downward, swells on high notes and soaring tones at the ends of airs.
>
> She prattled recitativo secco in her own peculiar infantile manner and sometimes she just talked out and out baby talk... She introduced Proch's air and variations in the lesson scene, and this ancient epitome of vocal 'stunts' won her most enthusiastic applause and the inevitable encores.

On the 1911 disk, Tetrazzini perfectly captures Rosina's tongue-in-cheek humor and her strong, defiant personality. This is accomplished through some unique (if admittedly elaborate) ornamentation: triplets, grace notes, mordents, volleys of sparkling, laughter-like high stacatti, roulades of twisting fioriture and her inimitable presentation of them. It all projects and underscores Rosina's humor and manipulative personality.

The ending to this aria has rarely been done better. After a brief ornamental flourish, Tetrazzini offers a propulsive trill on high B and leaps to a final, sustained high E. This is a recording that is a brilliant testimony to her gifts, not only as a virtuoso, but also as a comedic interpreter.

Rossini: "Bel raggio" (*Semiramide*)—London, November, 1910

Tetrazzini frequently programmed this aria on concerts and, fortunately, she left us this recorded memento. At the time, this was one of this music's first recordings. (Irene Abendroth recorded the aria in Dresden in 1902, and Sembrich recorded it in 1908.) It is an exceptional performance of great virtuosity governed by Tetrazzini's vital rhythmic sense and her seeming ability to improvise ornaments on the spot. There is the occasional juggling of registers, while roulades and ornamental patterns are flung out to the listener as if in a tornado.

Despite a misplaced pitch here and there, this is a delightful disk and one you may be compelled to re-hear a number of times. Especially dynamic are the scales of "il bel momento" in which Tetrazzini rapidly travels in and out of the lower register in runs of great rapidity. What is fascinating during these passages is the smoothness of Tetrazzini's delivery. There are no disfiguring yodels, just cleanly articulated passage work sung at break-neck speed. Tetrazzini does not offer a penultimate high E, but a rather wonderfully dramatic soprano-like thrust to high B followed by a roulade and trill on the G-sharp, leading into a final tonic, high A.

Strauss: Voci di Primavera (Voices of Spring) Waltz—London, September, 1908

A favorite with audiences and record buyers, this waltz provides sopranos with the opportunity to show off their abilities, and, in some cases, their high F. Tetrazzini never recorded a high F and it is doubtful she ever sang that note, even during the first years of her career. She stated herself that her range ascended to high E and she never goes above that note on recordings.

In this piano-accompanied Italian version of the "Fruhlingstimmen Walzer," vocal feats of descending high staccati, rippling trills, and cascading fioriture have an instrumental precision presented with a dramatic soprano's fullness of timbre. Compared to other recordings of this piece, Tetrazzini is rather restrained in her ornamentation. Typical phrase ornaments appear, and the rhythmic accuracy of the coloratura is breathtaking, as is Tetrazzini's ease in delivery. Her final short-cadenza is echoed by the pianist. The cadenza is to the point, and, different from many other versions, maintains the rhythmic tension that has been created during the song. There are no disfuguring rallentandos. Everything leads to the brilliant finish. Especially notable, at the end, is her rise to high C and then E-flat in pointed staccati. The final abandoned thrust to an immediate high B-flat shows typical Tetrazzini flair and brings the piece to a rousing finish.

Tate: "Somewhere a Voice is Calling"—London, June, 1914 (unpublished)

How does one describe the sweet charm of this unpublished recording? Written by the brother of the famous soprano, Maggie Teyte, this is a nostalgic ballad typical of the period and popular with many singers. Tetrazzini had a special affection for the piece and often programmed it on concerts through the 1920s. Her performances were popular with both critics and audiences.

The bittersweet lyrics and Tate's chromatically tinged music must have struck a chord in Tetrazzini's sensitivities as she puts forth a lovely, haunting performance. Although a short song, just over three minutes one may feel compelled to play it over and over to savor Tetrazzini's timbre in the upper middle area and the gentle, almost wistful sweetness of her singing. Her English is charmingly stilted, but the voice is in excellent shape, having the dark, rich power of a dramatic soprano.

Why this record was not published is a mystery as it is quite lovely. This is especially true at the end. The final phrase, "Dearest, my heart is dreaming, dreaming of you" is crowned with a gentle swoop to an exquisite high B that is gradually softened to pianissimo. This note is sustained as a perfectly even straight tone (her laser effect) and is a beautiful ending to a movingly sung performance.

As with other pieces in her repertoire, Tetrazzini did not always sing this song in the same way or in the same key.

Enthusiasm was lifted to its apex, however, when for the last note of Tate's 'Somewhere a Voice Is Calling' the singer without any effort whatsoever reached for, intoned and held for twelve beats an opulent, unforgettable E flat, which caused even the unmusical to gasp, and sent the cognoscenti into fine little frenzies of delight. (Saint Louis, Missosuri *Globe-Democrat*, February 7, 1920)

Thomas: Polonaise (*Mignon*) sung in Italian—England, December, 1907, 1908; U.S., March, 1911; Europe, 1911

The December, 1907 recording of Philine's virtuosic polonaise demonstrates what the Tetrazzini furor is all about. More than one hundred years later, it remains classic.

Ivor Newton, the famous accompanist who played for many of her recitals, once said:

She had a wonderful inborn sense of rhythm. Such artists do not need to count; with them rhythm is an instinct. I remember when she sang 'Je suis Titania,' the rhythmic drive was incredible... (*Gramophone*, December, 1974, Interview with Alan Blyth)

The first thing that is apparent in this recording is Tetrazzini's flair for the dramatic and her immediate, rhythmically based attack. Scale passages and the many triplet figures (so important in this aria) are incredibly accurate despite the rapidity of the tempo—Tetrazzini's energy crackles with electricity. Chromatic scales show an unusual play of color and her subtle use of tenuto is tellingly effective. So, too, is the occasional register break that lends a feeling of abandon to the aria missing in other early recordings.

In this version, during the final solo cadenza, Tetrazzini only touches the top E-flat in an arching scale passage, descending with an amazing chromatic scale in which every tone is audible. Not sitting on the high E-flat allows the aria to maintain its forward impetus so carefully created. The final and crowning touch is the elegant chain of rising trills (she omits the half-tone trill) and her thrust to a final, full-voiced and thrilling high B-flat.

Tetrazzini again recorded the aria during the following year, but it went unpublished until 1992 when it was released as part of a three-disc EMI CD set. It is surprisingly close to the 1907 recording in execution and accuracy. It does, however, show the soprano choosing to sit on the top E-flat in the unaccompanied cadenza. Perhaps because of this, the rhythmic momentum of the aria is lost and never regained. It is fascinating to compare the two versions.

Tetrazzini next recorded the aria in March, 1911 in the U.S., and again, one last time, the following July in London. As in the case of a number of the March (Victor) versus July (Gramophone—HMV) 1911 recordings, when one compares the two it is often the earlier Victor disk that is preferred. Part of this is because Tetrazzini's singing is regularly better on the Victors and part is due to the quality of the recordings.

The Victor disk displays spectacular florid singing and excellent examples of Tetrazzini's use of the vocal-flip during triplet figures and trills. There is a marvelous sense of abandoned thrust throughout, and the new fullness of the lower register provides some striking contrasts to the earlier 1907 recording.

The conclusions differ in that Tetrazzini sustains the top E-flat in the solo cadenza and then treats the listener to a remarkably accurate descending chromatic scale and a series of lovingly rolled trills. The final flourish is now expanded and boasts a thrust to high D followed by an emphatically punched high C which then settles to a final high B-flat.

She duplicates this in London in July, but the finish is not as propulsive as in the U.S. and again, much of the rhythmic tension is lost.

Thomas: Mad Scene (*Hamlet*) (sung in Italian)—London, July, 1911

Interpretively, this is one of Tetrazzini's most fascinating recordings. The mad scene was a concert favorite on her programs through the 1920s. Both Tetrazzini and her nemesis, Nellie Melba, were famous for Ophelia but, artistically, they represented opposite poles of vocalism. Melba's pure, angelic singing has little to do with Tetrazzini's earthy portrait of madness. Tetrazzini took great care in this aria's interpretive presentation as her full-throated, dramatic vocalization is coupled with unique tone-painting.

The disk begins about half way through the mad scene with one verse of the ballad. An interesting change in timbre occurs when she sings (in Italian), "Happy is the wife in the arms of her husband. My soul is jealous of such sweet happiness." For this phrase Tetrazzini uses an emotional, naive shading that is quite affecting (baby-talk). Especially interesting is her decision to ignore the traditional arpeggio flourishes after that phrase. Instead, she offers a surprisingly realistic burst of laughter pitched at F-sharp, then goes immediately to a top C-sharp followed by a brilliant, descending chromatic scale. This is a stunningly effective mood change.

"La, la, la," the next section, finds Tetrazzini making audible changes to the shade of her timbre to suggest Ophelia's madness; at first it is round and firm, then flat and white. It is as if she is attempting to depict Ophelia's wandering mind while she mumbles nonsense. This is immediately contrasted by a forceful thrust into "Ah!" that follows, another brilliant mood change.

The end of the aria boasts triplet and grace note interpolations and reaches its climax with an excellent chromatic scale up to high E. There is a rare placement flip on the final high B. None of the recordings of this aria created by her contemporaries exhibit such audible interpretive powers. Indeed, it would not be until Maria Callas' celebrated 1958 version that one can find Tetrazzini's equal in the dramatic perception of this aria.

Tosti: "Aprile" – London, 1909
Tosti: "Serenata" – London, 1909

These two disks of Tosti's songs have been favorites with listeners since they were released. There is a magic to them that is as attractive as it is almost tangible. Tetrazzini's voice, recorded closely, is generously used and full of subtle coloration and textural effects, framed within a smoothly flowing legato graced by additional turns and gentle mordents. Both songs are addictive.

The most famous of the two is "Aprile" and it is a stunner not only for the lush quality of Tetrazzini's voice in the upper middle register, but also her loving manner of sensuously wrapping her voice around Tosti's vocal lines. One can also hear (track 17, 1:17 on EMI CD) Tetrazzini move slightly away from the recording horn as if swaying with emotion while recording the piece. That second or two gives a brief glimpse of her voice as it bounces off the walls of the room, where otherwise it was concentrated into the recording horn. (Because of Nimbus' added acoustics, this movement away from the recording horn is less noticeable.)

Venzano: Grande Valse – U.S., February, 1913

Tetrazzini first recorded this concert piece in London the year before, but that version does not have the appeal of the 1913 U.S. recording which contains more music. Tetrazzini's voice also has a more appropriate, brilliant edge.

Although a bit of froth, this waltz demands great virtuosity and calls upon most of a coloratura soprano's technical battery. It is a period piece recorded by a number of Tetrazzini's colleagues, including the Spanish soprano, Josefina Huguet (Nedda in the first recording of *Pagliacci*). It was also a concert item regularly singled out by critics in praise of Tetrazzini's bravura handling of the music's demands. It is a perfect piece for Tetrazzini to exhibit her wares: superb rhythmical verve, clean staccati, and finely rolled trills—including one repeated as a soft echo during the bridge between the two verses of the main theme. Tetrazzini did this by almost closing her mouth while still rolling out the trill, a remarkable effect.

The conclusion has a cadential formula Tetrazzini uses in a number of recordings: a thrust up to a high, leading tone that resolves into the upper tonic. She probably found that this pattern helped her place her voice in the upper octave, even though it occasionally resulted in the final high note ending up a bit on the white side. Tetrazzini is having a good time with this music and her excitement during some passages is evident. This is a wonderful recording with a fine, steel-bright high D at its finish.

Veracini: "Meco Varrai su quella" Pastorale (*Rosalinda*)—London, June, 1914

Veracini was an Italian composer and violinist (1690–1768). This aria, known as the "Pastorale" is from his 1744 pastoral opera, *Rosalinda*. Today, most of Veracini's operatic output has been forgotten save for this aria (at one time sung by Richard Tucker).

Both Tetrazzini's published and unpublished versions of this lyrical aria are fine. I am partial to the unpublished version. It is quite a change from the standard coloratura war-horses, its differences being like a breath of fresh air.

It very much sounds the pastoral period piece, graceful in its composition. Tetrazzini sings it with beguiling relaxation. Trills ripple with warmth and purity; her approach to Veracini's music is respectful. The use of voce bianca lends an innocent quality to the lower register. A few of the sustained low Ds sound awkward, but counter-balancing this, the recording displays the many vocal effects that Tetrazzini brings into play to promote Veracini's lovely music. Especially lovely is the conclusion, with its noble sweep to high B and the final, softly sustained (straight-tone) high G.

Verdi: "Saper voreste" (*Un ballo in maschera*)—London, May 1909; America, July 1911

Tetrazzini's recordings of this aria have always been popular with listeners. Like her contemporary Selma Kurz, who reigned supreme at the Vienna Stattsoper, Tetrazzini adds ornaments and cadenzas. This is a practice not favored by today's come scritto musical culture, but it is one that helps underline the witty, flighty character of Oscar.

Listeners tend to prefer the 1911 Victor recording although I find that the bright sonics of that disc, combined with the more open (less covered) diamond-like brilliance of Tetrazzini's top register makes it more difficult for me to enjoy. I prefer the earlier, 1909 recording on which Tetrazzini's high notes have a more alluring, soft texture. As in other comedic music (Rosina's "Una voce poco fa"), this aria brings out the best in Tetrazzini's wit. The first twelve measures are probably some of the most descriptive she ever put onto disk; the listener can practically see her coy smile as she sings "tra la la." Unfortunately, this section has some odd, almost frog-like tones in the low register.

There is wonderful improvisational ornamentation in this aria, as well as an extensive cadenza. Tetrazzini's cadenza, although not as long as Kurz's, includes a series of trills followed by staccato high Ds and a two-octave chromatic descent that must be heard to be believed. As if this is not enough, she interpolates a penultimate high D at the conclusion. During the course of this short aria she sings fourteen high Ds.

When she recorded the aria again in New York in 1911, she added additional improvisational mordents and even more high Ds (to rhythmically accentuate the finish). No matter which version you prefer, the aria suits Tetrazzini to a tee. Comparisons between Tetrazzini and Kurz's ornamentation find Kurz's to be beautiful, but languid; the roulades and trills are not as effective in projecting Oscar's character as is the almost masculine swagger of Tetrazzini's rhythmically driven ornamentation.

In *The Record of Singing, Volume I*, Michael Scott notes:

> There is no other performance on record that so perfectly marries wit to prodigious vocalism. How roguishly she teases – 'Oscar lo sa ma nol dirà'. And then that cadenza with its repeated staccato high Ds! Those who complain that it holds up the action should know that that is what it is supposed to do, for the fermata marked in the score means just that. (Charles Scribner's Sons, New York, 1977)

Verdi: Bolero (*I Vespri Siciliani*)—London, November, 1910; America, 1914

This aria was still something of a rarity when Tetrazzini made her 1910 recording. Because of the outrageously fast tempo, the aria is almost uncut, but surely there is no other version of this aria that sounds so harried and rushed. The only point at which the tempo is allowed to relax is during the phrase "che tutti i sense i nebbrio." Tetrazzini's success in getting through the aria with any amount of clarity (or composure) is a feat of virtuosity in itself. Even so, some of the intricate passages near the finish are only approximated. One thing that is perfectly clear, however, is the striking clarity of her triplet work. After all this frenetic singing, Tetrazzini shocks the listener by interpolating a brilliantly sustained, penultimate high E. This is a virtuosic recording, but not a good representation of the gracefulness of Verdi's composition.

Four years later, in the U.S., Tetrazzini recorded the aria at a more sensible tempo, but it lacks the former disk's brilliance. Some of the coloratura sounds labored and staccati occasionally do not "sound." Although her composure during the intricate coloratura is impressive, the recording lacks the sparkle of energy that marks the earlier effort. There is no high E interpolation in the 1914 version.

Verdi: "Ah fors'e lui...Sempre libera" (*La traviata*)—England, 1907-08; U.S., July, 1911

Violetta was one of Tetrazzini's most famous roles. Today, among our figure-conscious audiences, many would find it hard to believe that the character Tetrazzini is playing is dying of consumption. Even so, audiences of her day were tremendously moved by her portrayal of the doomed courtesan. Some of her more dramatic details upset some patrons:

> One realistic detail horrified the oldsters. The dying Violetta, after a racking cough, inspected her handkerchief with the care of a sanatorium patient. 'Disgusting!' shuddered the dowagers. (Quaintance Eaton, *The Boston Opera Company*, Appleton-Century, NY, 1965)

Critics of the time were divided about Tetrazzini's concept of Violetta. It may be hard for us to imagine today, but at that time, *La traviata* was considered "old fashioned." It was often dumped into the same bin as *Lucia di Lammermoor*, *I puritani* and *La sonnambula* as "trash" by more stodgy critics. Tetrazzini was one of the first artists of the twentieth century to return the role to being one of dramatic import. Many critics bemoaned her use of voce bianca in the opera, while others found the differences between the timbres in her voice emotionally illuminating.

Tetrazzini made three versions of this scena. The first was split between 1907 (Sempre libera) and 1908 (Ah fors'e lui). The complete scena (with huge cuts) was eventually recorded in March, 1911 (in the U.S.) and then again in July, 1911 (in London). Of the three, I call it a tie between the first and the last versions.

Her first recording of "Sempre libera" (1907) is of great importance because it accurately reflects her voice and manner with this music at the time of her famous debut as Violetta at Covent Garden. It also shows the unusually dramatic approach that Tetrazzini brings to this music. In 1907, this must have been riveting.

The disk includes the "Follie, follie" recitative and displays a wonderful thrust on the high B-flat of "gioir." This is followed by a lovely piano top D-flat, with an excellent chromatic scale descent. Time restrictions only allowed for one verse of the cabaletta (because she had included the recitative), but the dramatic thrust and vocal abandon are truly impressive. Unfortunately, this is balanced on the negative side by a frenetic tempo that causes Tetrazzini to grab breaths whenever she can, often in the middle of words. (From what W.J. Henderson wrote [quoted earlier] this poor plotting of breaths may either have been a flaw in her musicianship, or simply personal whim.)

An ornament appears that was later adopted by Joan Sutherland. It comes near the end of the aria when Verdi asks for a number of repeated high Cs. Tetrazzini turns those notes into a string of twelve perfectly-etched staccato high Cs that not only prick the acoustics attractively, but also help to accentuate the rhythmic drive of the music. As Henderson noted, to do this, she merely checks the flow of breath between the notes rather than to attack each note separately, providing a fascinating aural texture. Despite the fast tempo, descending scales are uncanny in their accuracy, and the interpolated penultimate high E-flat is triumphantly approached without pause.

It is on this high E-flat that we notice a slight shifting of placement right before her release. This occurs in a number of her 1911 recordings. For instance, it can be heard on high notes in Benedict's "Carnival of Venice Variations" (New York), Oscar's "Saper voreste" (New York) and the Proch "Theme and Variations" (London). It was probably due to the abrupt manner in which she leaps suddenly to these tones (perhaps without sufficient preparation). This seems only to happen on either high D or E-flat. To her credit, this never phased Tetrazzini. This shifting of placement is probably what Henderson heard when he reports that the high E-flat Tetrazzini takes at the end of Sempre libera "...was a head tone of thin quality and refused to stay on the pitch."

Tetrazzini's second recording of this scena (both parts on one side) was recorded in the U.S. in March, 1911. Because of time restrictions the opening recitative was omitted, as were some ornaments that appear in the other two versions. In this recording, the tempi and high notes are quite brilliant. Although the high C diminuendo at the end of "Ah fors'e lui" has some bumps, the dramatic Tetrazzini thrust is present. Generally, however, the singing is not as clean or impressive as in the other two versions. The cuts made to make the nine-minute aria fit onto a 4:37 disk are greatly disfiguring. At the conclusion of this version the orchestra tacets while Tetrazzini offers her penultimate high E-flat. They re-enter after she resolves to the final A-flat.

It is the third version (two-sided), recorded in London in 1911, that we find a recording that vies with her first effort. Although the "Ah fors'e lui" omits the "E strano, e strano" recitative (and Verdi's rests between "Ah-fors'-e-lui") there are some new examples of "flowering:" grace notes, mordents, and portamenti. The phrase "de suoi colori occulti" has a lovely piano A with a diminuendo. Many phrases show the unique vibrancy of this singer's voice and demonstrates that there is definitely an interpretation at work no matter how subtle this may seem to us today as it carries through the antiquated recording process. Appropriate improvisational ornaments appear on "del l'universo," and the thrust on "croce" is as wonderful as the smooth diminuendo on the interpolated, penultimate high C.

This version of "Sempre libera" has both verses intact and is unusual for its inclusion of the "Follie, follie" bridge between them. There are fabulous thrusts up to high C and D-flat and the descending chromatic scale is offered staccato. Unfortunately, the awkward, bumpy breath spots continue to be present suggesting that this was simply the way she sang those phrases. These blemishes are offset by fabulous descending scales and an almost fanatical intensity on "il pensier" directly before the final coda. Tetrazzini's individual ornament, repeated staccati high Cs, is especially brilliant, as is her leap, without pause, to a penultimate high E-flat. Due to the rapidity of the tempo and Tetrazzini's frenzied singing, there is a sense of the manic in this recording that is not only vocally stunning, but dramatically appropriate.

Alan Jeffreys writes of this recording: "She sounds really triumphant in the 'Sempre libera' and produces a telling echo on the second gioir in a first class demonstration of clean coloratura singing. The orchestra seems to take fire from her as well, for they all play away for dear life in the 'Sempre libera'... It is a stunning record."

Verdi: "Caro nome" (*Rigoletto*)—London, December, 1907

This was probably the aria most often programmed in Tetrazzini's concerts. A favorite with audiences, she was often forced to sing it as an encore. She made three recordings of it during her career (1904, 1907, 1911), but it is the middle, London-made, disk that best sums up her thoughts on this aria. It is unfortunate that she never made a recording of her usual ending to this aria, a spiraling ascent to high E. That would have been interesting to hear.

The 1907 version is the first side she made during the initial Gramophone session in London, on December 20, 1907. There are a number of differences between it and her earlier Zonophone rendition. First of all, there is an orchestra instead of a piano. The recitative that precedes has been discarded to allow for greater phrase expansion during the aria. More startling, however, when both recordings are played side by side, is the difference in her voice. In 1907 it seems fuller, rounder in the middle register, and the top has definitely gained in power. The lower regions continue to sound a bit undernourished, but they gain in power and fullness depending on the vowel she is singing (and whether she is using her baby-talk effect). All in all, the voice seems better equalized than in 1904, and her sensitivity to the style of the music is evident.

There is technical polish and complete mastery of her breath control, allowing her to do practically anything with her voice. Contrasting this, however, are odd musical and artistic alterations. These stem from the "old tradition," but, to us today, they often sound distinctly odd. All of Veri's rests between the syllables of "no-me che il mio cor" have disappeared, replaced with a sturdy legato. In another spot, Tetrazzini uses an odd, almost vulgar, grace note descent to help her dig into her chest register. Unwritten trills and triplet figures appear. Some listeners might consider this merely Tetrazzini's willful disregard for the written page, but it is a perfect example of her personalizing Verdi's music. Furthering this supposition, different from many of her contemporaries, she alters the famous cadenza at the end of the aria, eschewing the traditional top E-flat. This alteration allows her not only to exhibit a few more of her sparkling high staccati, but also to remain closer to what Verdi wrote. The overall effect of the aria, however, is definitely her own.

Ivor Newton writes:

> I played for her farewell tour as much out of affection as for any other reason. The royal suite in the Savoy was beyond her reach, and she had to be content with a small eyrie without a view. There were no baskets of flowers; costume jewelry had taken the place of her many diamonds. What was left was only a memory of the rich warmth her admirers had loved and the vitality and dramatic strength that was part of her nature.

> In Bristol, in the middle of the tour she sang 'Caro nome' with the old effortless precision and brilliance, and to hear her do so was extremely touching. 'Madam!' I said as soon as we reached the side of the stage, 'that was wonderful.' 'It was not wonderful' she murmured, looking surprised and crossing herself devoutly, 'It was a miracle.'" (*At the Piano*, Hamish Hamilton, London, 1966)

How fortunate we are today, that we, and the generations to follow us, have the ability to experience some of Luisa Tetrazzini's miracles. Her protégé, the American-born Lina Pagliughi, sums it up best, saying:

> 'She was the most wonderfully kind, humane person, and everyone who knew her could not help but respect and love her deeply.' (Lanfranco Rasponi, *The Last Prima Donnas*, Victor Gollancz Ltd, 1982).

It is this humane quality that one recognizes time and again throughout Luisa Tetrazzini's discography. It is the very quality that draws one back to her recordings. It is through her unapologetic individuality and joy of singing that Luisa Tetrazzini reminds us that, above all, the act of singing should be a thing of joy and celebration. The reasons are heard on all of her recordings—a strong, vital sense of rhythm, outrageous daring in embellishments, and a top register that pealed forth with great brilliance. Her singing always displays a *joie de vivre* that is so often lost during the journey from the vocal studio to the stage.

(A much-abbreviated version of this article appeared in *The Opera Quarterly*, Volume 20, #4, 2004)

Lightning Source UK Ltd.
Milton Keynes UK
UKHW030718250122
397668UK00006B/299

9 781936 411436